FAITHFUL PERFORMANCES

The metaphor of performance has been applied fruitfully by anthropologists and other social theorists to different aspects of human social existence, and furnishes a potentially helpful model in terms of which to think theologically about Christian life.

After an introductory editorial chapter reflecting on the nature of artistic performance and its relationship to the notions of tradition and identity, Part One of this book attends specifically to the phenomenon of dramatic performance and possible theological applications of it. Part Two considers various aspects of the performance of Christian identity, looking at worship, the interpretation of the Bible, Christian response to elements in the contemporary media, the shape of Christian moral life, and ending with a theological reflection on the shape of personal identity, correlating it with the theatrical metaphors of 'character' and 'performing a part' in a scripted drama. Part Three demonstrates how art forms (including some technically non-performative ones - literature, poetry, painting) may constitute faithful Christian practices in which the tradition is authentically 'performed', producing works which break open its meaning in profound new ways for a constantly shifting context.

Ashgate Studies in Theology, Imagination and the Arts

Series Editors:

Trevor A. Hart, St Mary's College, University of St Andrews, Scotland
Jeremy Begbie, Ridley Hall, UK
Roger Lundin, Wheaton College, USA

What have imagination and the arts to do with theology? For much of the modern era, the answer has been, 'not much.' It is precisely this deficit that this series seeks to redress. For, whatever role they have or have not been granted in the theological disciplines, imagination and the arts are undeniably bound up with how we as human beings think, learn and communicate, engage with and respond to our physical and social environments and, in particular, our awareness and experience of that which transcends our own creatureliness. The arts are playing an increasingly significant role in the way people come to terms with the world; at the same time, artists of many disciplines are showing a willingness to engage with religious or theological themes. A spate of publications and courses in many educational institutions has already established this field as one of fast growing concern. This series taps into a burgeoning intellectual concern on both sides of the Atlantic and beyond.

The peculiar inter-disciplinarity of theology, and the growing interest in imagination and the arts in many different fields of human concern, afford the opportunity for a series which has its roots sunk in varied and diverse intellectual soils, while focused around a coherent theological question: How are imagination and the arts involved in the shaping and reshaping of our humanity as part of the creative and redemptive purposes of God, and what roles do they perform in the theological enterprise?

Many projects within the series have particular links to the work of the Institute for Theology Imagination and the Arts in the University of St Andrews, and to the Theology Through the Arts programme in Cambridge.

Other titles in the series:

The Passion in Art
Richard Harries

Faith and Beauty
A Theological Aesthetic
Edward Farley

Baptized Imagination
The Theology of George MacDonald
Kerry Dearborn

Faithful Performances
Enacting Christian Tradition

Edited by

TREVOR A. HART
St Mary's College, University of St Andrews, UK

STEVEN R. GUTHRIE
School of Religion, Belmont University, Nashville, USA

ASHGATE

© Trevor A. Hart and Steven R. Guthrie 2007

All rights reserved. No part of this publication may be reproduced, stored in a retrieval system or transmitted in any form or by any means, electronic, mechanical, photocopying, recording or otherwise without the prior permission of the publisher.

Trevor A. Hart and Steven R. Guthrie have asserted their moral right under the Copyright, Designs and Patents Act, 1988, to be identified as the editors of this work.

Published by
Ashgate Publishing Limited
Gower House
Croft Road
Aldershot
Hampshire GU11 3HR
England

Ashgate Publishing Company
Suite 420
101 Cherry Street
Burlington, VT 05401-4405
USA

Ashgate website: http://www.ashgate.com

British Library Cataloguing in Publication Data
Faithful Performances: Enacting Christian Tradition.
 – (Ashgate Studies in Theology, Imagination and the Arts)
 1. Identity (Psychology) – Religious aspects – Christianity. 2.Drama in public worship 3. Rites and ceremonies 4.Theater – Religious aspects – Christianity 5.Identification (Religion). 6.Christian drama – History and criticism. I. Hart, Trevor A. II. Guthrie, Steven R.
 246.7'2

Library of Congress Cataloging-in-Publication Data
Faithful performances: Enacting Christian Tradition /
   edited by Trevor A. Hart and Steven R. Guthrie.
       p.   cm. – (Ashgate Studies in Theology, Imagination, and the Arts)
   Includes bibliographical references.
   1. Theater – Religious aspects – Christianity. 2. Performing arts – Religious aspects – Christianity. 3. Identification (Religion). I. Hart, Trevor A., 1961– . II. Guthrie, Steven R., 1967– . III. Series.
PN2049.F35 2007
246'.72–dc22   2006013181

ISBN 978-0-7546-5525-1

Printed on acid-free paper.

Printed and bound in Great Britain by TJ International Ltd, Padstow, Cornwall.

Contents

List of Illustrations	vii
List of Contributors	viii
Introduction *Trevor A. Hart*	1

PART 1: THEOLOGY, FAITH AND THEATRE

1	Real Enactments: The Role of Drama in the Theology of Hans Urs von Balthasar *Ben Quash*	13
2	A Cautionary Note on the Use of Theatre in Theology *Ivan Patricio Khovacs*	33
3	Can an Act be True? – The Possibilities of the Dramatic Metaphor for Theology within a Post-Stanislavskian Theatre *Joshua Edelman*	51

PART 2: DISCIPLESHIP AND THE ENACTMENT OF CHRISTIAN IDENTITY

4	Performing Faiths – Patterns, Pluralities and Problems in the Lives of Religious Traditions *Michael Partridge*	75
5	Temples of the Spirit: Worship as Embodied Performance *Steven R. Guthrie*	91
6	Rhetoric and the Literary Sense: The Sacred Author's Performance in Cajetan's Exegesis of Scripture *Michael O'Connor*	109
7	Seeing Through the Drama: Reframing Violent News *Jolyon Mitchell*	123

8	Improvisation in the Theatre as a Model for Christian Ethics *Samuel Wells*	147
9	The Sense of an Ending: Finitude and the Authentic Performance of Life *Trevor A. Hart*	167

PART 3: ARTISTRY AS CHRISTIAN PRACTICE

10	The Arts of Redemption *Patrick Sherry*	189
11	Our Truest Poetry is Our Most Feigning … Poetry, Playfulness and Truth *Malcolm Guite*	199
12	Seeing the Word: Aspects of the Visual Culture of the Reformation *William Dyrness*	219
13	Created and Uncreated Light: The Transfiguration in Western Art *Rosemary Muir Wright*	241
14	The Ascension and Transfigured Bodies *David Brown*	257

Resonances and Challenges: A Response to the Volume *Jeremy Begbie*	273
Index	*281*

List of Illustrations

Figure 1	Sieger Köder: *Verklärung* (© Sieger Köder)	255
Figure 2	Fra Angelico (1387–1455): *Transfiguration* (© 1990; Photo SCALA, Florence – courtesy of the Ministero Beni e Att. Culturali; Florence, Museo di San Marco)	255
Figure 3	Raphael (1483–1520): *Transfiguration*, (© 1990; Photo SCALA, Florence; Vatican, Pinacoteca)	256
Figure 4	Fra Angelico (1387–1455): *Noli me tangere* (© 1990; Photo SCALA, Florence – courtesy of the Ministero Beni e Att. Culturali; Florence, Museo di San Marco)	256

List of Contributors

Ben Quash is Dean and Fellow of Peterhouse and Lecturer in Divinity, University of Cambridge

Ivan Patricio Khovacs is a PhD student in the Institute for Theology, Imagination and the Arts, University of St Andrews

Joshua Edelman is a PhD student at Trinity College, Dublin

Michael Partridge is Honorary Lecturer in Theology in the University of St Andrews

Steven R. Guthrie is Assistant Professor of Religion, Belmont University, Nashville

Michael O' Connor is Program Administrator and teaches at St Michael's College, University of Toronto

Jolyon Mitchell is Senior Lecturer in Communication, Theology and Ethics and Director of the Media and Theology Project at New College, University of Edinburgh

Samuel Wells is Dean of Chapel at Duke University, Durham, North Carolina

Trevor A. Hart is Professor of Divinity and Director of the Institute for Theology, Imagination and the Arts, University of St Andrews

Patrick Sherry is Professor Emeritus of Philosophical Theology at the University of Lancaster

Malcolm Guite is Chaplain of Girton College, Cambridge

William Dyrness is Professor of Theology and Culture at Fuller Theological Seminary, Pasadena

Rosemary Muir Wright (d.2006) was Senior Lecturer in the History of Art at the University of St Andrews

David Brown is van Mildert Professor of Divinity at Durham University

Jeremy Begbie is Honorary Professor of Theology and Associate Director of the Institute for Theology, Imagination and the Arts, University of St Andrews

Introduction

Art, Performance and the Practice of Christian Faith

Trevor A. Hart

"He that bigan in you a good work, schal performe til into the day of Jhesu Christ"

Engagement between Christian theology and art has a long history. In practical terms, the relationship between Christian faith and artistry stretches back to the earliest decades of Christian history, and the subsequent history of art in the Western tradition is one in which the presence of the Christian church (its beliefs, its practices, its patronage) dominates the horizon for better or worse. Over the centuries, serious intellectual integration of the understanding of faith and of artistic practices and outputs was often occasioned by very concrete concerns about the use and possible abuse of art works within specific religious places and practices. One thinks, for example, of the fierce deliberations which raged over the use of icons in eighth century Byzantium, of medieval discussions about the liturgical mediation of 'spiritual' presence under the 'corporal' forms of painting and statuary (directly concomitant, of course, with the emergence of a 'high' doctrine of the Eucharist), and of the sharp reaction of some of the Reformers to all this, resulting in deep-rooted iconoclastic attitudes from which some strands of Protestantism have never quite recovered.

While such disputes produced highly sophisticated responses and categories, some of which remain helpful in our approach to central questions that are still relevant today, they were nonetheless by nature largely reactive and lop-sided in their attention, and hardly amounted to a carefully considered theology of human artistry. In the modern era, with the consolidation of a particular notion of 'the arts',[1] the attempt has been made to situate the various human practices and products falling under this rubric more positively within a metaphysics of some sort, and, more often than not, one of identifiably Christian provenance or influence. Historians of 'fine art' have, for their part, traced the vital 'iconological' links between artistic styles and outputs and the wider currents of 'religious' sensibility which informed and were duly shaped by them. Philosophers and theologians have, in their turn, sought

---

1   On this see, e.g., Paul Oskar Kristeller, *Renaissance Thought and the Arts* (Princeton NJ: Princeton University Press, 1980), 163-227; also Nicholas Wolterstorff, *Art in Action: Toward a Christian Aesthetic* (Carlisle, Solway, 1997).

to understand artistic creativity as such as a human phenomenon, and to relate it to things believed about God, the world, and what it means to be a creature. From the theological side, too, there has been increasing recognition that critical attention to certain art forms might furnish important intellectual resources for constructive theological work itself. This has been apparent, for example, in the attention afforded to the study of literature, sometimes as a fresh and illuminating way of approaching the Christian tradition's own literary sources in Scripture, and sometimes as a locus of vital concrete engagement with questions and concerns about human existence with which theology itself has to reckon and to which it must respond. More recently, there has been a marked rediscovery of the 'theological' contribution of much western painting across the centuries, not least among biblical scholars, who now regularly engage with examples of a mode of 'visual exegesis' which they perceive in painted depictions of biblical stories and themes. Such attention is being granted now not in order to serve the related interests of art-historians, but those of professional interpreters of the biblical text.

Literature (especially poetry) and the visual and plastic arts have typically enjoyed the most central and exalted places in modern conceptions of 'the fine arts', and it is perhaps to be expected that they should occupy similar privilege and priority in theological engagements with the arts more widely. Thus, even when other artistic forms (music for example, or drama) have occasionally been reckoned with, they have too often been treated as essentially analogous to poetry and painting, being addressed and analysed at the level of their existence as inert 'texts'. But these forms (and others, such as opera and dance) cannot adequately be treated in such a two-dimensional manner. The 'works' proper to them do not properly exist at all apart from some *performance* in which the relevant 'text' is brought to fulfilment or completion through embodied action, and to exclude this dimension is to overlook all that is most distinctive to their art. Performance, in other words, is not secondary to these forms of artistic engagement with the world, but essential to their artistry. It is therefore very welcome that, in recent decades, there has been a growing theological interest in music and drama precisely as performing arts, and in the performative dimensions of them in particular. This has occurred as theology has sought models to help it understand better aspects of Christian faith's own peculiar situation with respect to a text, a text which must be 'brought to completion' through forms of embodied action in which it is 'interpreted' faithfully for a world (and not just a world) which looks on as it does so.

The metaphor of artistic performance (especially its theatrical versions) has seemingly enjoyed some place in the religious modelling of life in God's world since ancient times. Whatever one may make of those anthropological theories which would trace the roots of theatre itself in religious ritual of one sort or another,[2] the existence of links between the two spheres is apparent enough, stretching back identifiably at least as far as classical appeals (in first century Stoicism for instance)

---

2 See on this, e.g., Richard Schechner, *Performance Theory*, 2nd edn. (London: Routledge, 2003), 1-25.

to the image of the 'world-stage', and perhaps much farther than that. The various elements of the model make such a link natural enough, not least for Christian faith and theology, although the history of the Church's relationship to the theatre has rarely been a happy one over the centuries, which may account for the relatively late appropriation and deliberate development of the image by Christian theologians.[3] As well as the relationship between a script/score which must not just be 'read' but rather 'played out' on a stage, before an audience, in ways which may constitute a more or less 'faithful' interpretation of it, there are other equally fruitful metaphorical entailments[4] having to do, for example, with matters of *character*, dramatic *parts* which must be played out, which are both *scripted* (allocated a certain given unity or pattern) by a playwright, and yet must be *performed responsibly* and with a certain skilled *creative spontaneity*, parts which perhaps entail the *assumption* by the actor of a *persona* or set of dispositions other than that which is his or her 'natural' one. There are issues, too, about different *traditions* of performance, about the sort of *training* which a skilled performance may require and how this acquired, about the *communities* within which certain works are habitually played out and the place of those works in shaping and defining those communities as such, about what might constitute an *authentic performance* of a work (or an inauthentic one), about how the actor's own character may be modified or transformed by repeated playing of a particular role, and so on. At the very least, perhaps, the metaphor of artistic performance is suggestive in theological terms because of the fundamental religious conviction that human life is indeed lived (a work 'played out') not just in the sight or hearing of other people, but before a God who (however else he may be held to be involved in things) looks on and listens with great interest, and makes judgments about what he sees and hears. This conviction grants all life lived in terms of it a 'performative' aspect from beginning to end. Our true character, it has been said, is what and who we are when we think that no one is watching! But, strictly speaking, for faith there is no such moment. Life is lived in its completeness under the watchful gaze of God, a fact which may instill either fear or confidence, depending on what 'character' God himself is duly held to have.

It is not theology alone, we should note, that has appropriated artistic performance as a fruitful way of modelling human life. In fact, fifty years or more ago, strands in emergent sociology and social psychology were beginning to appeal directly to elements of dramaturgy in particular, duly borrowing such dramaturgical notions as 'Self', 'Transformation', 'Role Taking' and 'Role Distance' to model human life as a 'social reality'.[5] The 'sociology of knowledge' and other elements among the social

---

3 Some of the wider links between religion and performative aspects of drama and music are explored helpfully in Salim Kemal and Ivan Gaskell (eds), *Performance and authenticity in the arts* (Cambridge: Cambridge University Press, 1999).

4 For the helpful notion of the 'entailments' attaching to the use of particular metaphors within image schemata see Mark Johnson, *The Body in the Mind: The Bodily Basis of Meaning, Imagination and Reason* (Chicago: University of Chicago Press, 1987), 130-137.

5 For a convenient anthology see Dennis Brissett and Charles Edgley (eds), *Life as Theater; a Dramaturgical Sourcebook* (Chicago: Aldine Publishing Company, 1975). The

sciences have since explored the possibilities further, lending to 'performance' and its attendant categories ('tradition', 'script/text', 'communities of interpretation', relevant 'skills' of performance, 'defining practices', etc.) the status of conceptual tools in terms of which one may usefully approach human behaviours of various sorts, so that 'performance' has in effect become, in the words of one recent study, 'a paradigm for the investigation of culture at large'.[6] With the advent of so-called 'post-modernity' all this has been fused with a specific epistemological agenda, the idea of artistic performance (especially 'improvised' performances) as something radically particular, essentially open-ended (there can be no final or definitive performance of a work, as and when a 'work' can be identified at all) and indeterminate (and thus inherently ambiguous, resisting claims to absolute closure), appeals naturally to the more Heraclitean streak in post-modern sensibility. Indeed, at its starkest, the post-modern appropriation of performance as a paradigm for our engagements with 'reality' insists – after the manner (though not necessarily the spirit) of J. L. Austin's linguistic analysis of various sorts of 'performative utterance' in human discourse – that the meaning of and warrant for even 'scientific' knowledge gained through research and experiment, is not to be had by supposing (wrongly) that it produces an accurate or adequate model of the world. Rather, what is sought here, as Fredrick Jameson notes, is "a non- or post-referential epistemology" for which truth is a function of performance itself (putting the 'story' or 'text' into play through continuous fresh action) rather than being measured in terms of the alleged correspondence between some 'text' and a state of affairs lying 'beyond' or 'outside' it.[7] Closure is endlessly deferred. The legitimization of 'knowledge', like the meaning of a performed work, must be realized anew every moment rather than a matter of 'deference' in the face of some absolutely authoritative product of the epistemic past.

With such deliberate broadening of the remit of performance-related talk, it has been suggested, the term has now entered our language as one that shifts easily and quickly between different "areas of meaning". We advertise 'high-performance' vehicles, measure 'performance' in the workplace and mete out 'performance-related' pay, watch the financial pages to see how stocks and shares are currently 'performing', and urge our small children not to 'make a performance' in public when we will not buy or give them exactly what they want.[8] Yet, in so far as this wider set of social uses of the term is indeed identifiable as an appropriation of artistic models, there is an interesting irony to be observed. For the roots of 'performance' as a (relatively modern) artistic concept are themselves sunk deep

---

earliest piece incorporated in this volume was first published in 1949. others were first published between 1955 and 1973.

6   Simon Shepherd and Mick Wallis, *Drama/Theatre/Performance* (London: Routledge, 2004), 1.

7   In his 'Foreword' to Jean-François Lyotard, *The Postmodern Condition: a Report on Knowledge*, translated from the French by Geoff Bennington and Brian Massumi (Manchester: Manchester University Press, 1984), ix. On the link between post-modernity and 'performance' more broadly, see Shepherd and Wallis.

8   So, e.g., Shepherd and Wallace, *Drama/Theatre/Performance,* 1.

in the soils of more ancient, socially diverse uses, *par-* or *perfourmer* ('to carry through in due form'?) being linked to the etymologically prior *parfournir* ('to accomplish entirely, achieve, complete'). Thus at the end of the fourteenth century Wyclif (1382) translates Philippians 1:6 as "He that bigan in you a good work, schal performe til into the day of Jhesu Christ"; while Chaucer (1386) marks the mundane passage of time with the poetic "Parfourned hath the sonne his Ark diurne".⁹ So, while they did not have to cope with needlessly powerful four-wheel-drive vehicles on their roads or share the preoccupation of our age with constant monitoring and measuring of whatever in life can be monitored and measured, earlier generations certainly already knew 'performance' as a socially mobile term, applicable to God's redemptive activity, to the movements of the sun around the earth, and, of course, much else besides. The particular development of 'performance' talk within the discourses of the arts has, through the mechanisms and strategies of re-appropriation referred to above, duly *returned* it to society with interest added. The accrual has by now been significant, and the past several decades have witnessed the sedimentation of a discrete academic discipline and associated literature, 'performance studies', dedicated specifically to exploring the performative dimensions of music and drama, and their relationship to wider patterns of human practice.¹⁰ The language itself has, we might say, 'performed' well in semantic terms!

Specifically theological borrowing of 'performance' talk from the arts is also largely a phenomenon of the past twenty years or so. The metaphor was proposed first by writers concerned with the nature of biblical interpretation, a discipline that had become somewhat hide-bound by the dominance of historical-critical models which, by their emphasis on the antiquity and essential 'strangeness' of the biblical text, tended to exalt (or relegate) it to the status of a valuable artefact, but thereby easily lost sight of its role as a living Word to the Church. Interestingly, it was not New Testament scholars proper who first advocated the model, but systematic theologians and patristic scholars, whose own work was necessarily concerned with Scripture as possessed of contemporary as well as historical significance, and with the ways in which, over the centuries, it has been 'played out' variously within the living traditions of the Church.¹¹ The metaphor of Scripture as 'script' or 'score' has, though, duly been taken up by practitioners within New Testament studies

---

9   Both cited in *The Oxford English Dictionary*, second edn., prepared by J. A. Simpson and E. S. C. Weiner, Vol. XI (Oxford: Clarendon Press, 1989), art. 'Perform', 543. The *New Revised Standard Version* renders the relevant portion of Phil. 1:6 as: "the one who began a good work among you will *bring it to completion* by the day of Jesus Christ" (my italics).

10   See, e.g, John Rink, *The Practice of Performance: Studies in Musical Interpretation* (Cambridge: Cambridge University Press, 1995). Cf Richard Schechner *Performance Theory* (London: Routledge, 2003). *Text and Performance Quarterly*. (London: Routledge).

11   See, for example, Nicholas Lash's essay 'Performing the Scriptures' in Lash, *Theology on the Way to Emmaus* (London: SCM Press Ltd., 1986), Frances Young, *The Art of Performance: Towards a Theology of Holy Scripture* (London: Darton, Longman and Todd, 1990).

itself as a fruitful corrective and counterbalance to other mainstream approaches.[12] Its metaphorical entailments re-establish a close link between the reading (or 'interpretation') of the biblical texts and wider patterns of action within the life of the Christian community. These are texts, it insists, whose meaning may only be had as something is done with them and on the basis of them, and that something involves much more than what we typically do in libraries and lecture theatres. They are texts which, like dramatic scripts or musical scores, must be interpreted through forms of public performance, played out in the life of Church and society, and in ways which are concerned not simply with faithfulness to the shape of some 'original' or 'authentic' mode of performance (where that is capable of recovery), but also with the particularities of the ever-changing circumstances within which performance must be attempted. What constitutes a 'faithful' performance will, therefore, be judged in accordance with a more complex set of criteria, drawing on the accumulated wisdom of earlier generations of performers and the examples furnished by particular 'classic' performances ('tradition'[13]), as well as relying upon the spontaneous creativity of the moment in which through the actors' 'skill', and in engagement with the particular audience, the scripted word once again 'takes flesh' ('inspiration').

Where the Church's approach to the Bible as Scripture is concerned, it is not just forms of human action that are under consideration, of course, but God's action too. The God whose character is narrated in the biblical texts is precisely a God who acts and who is known in – and not apart from – his acts. Furthermore, the appeal to Scripture itself as a living Word of God to us is predicated not just on a past activity of God lying on the far side of some supposed 'big ugly ditch' of history. It rests on the conviction that the same God whose activity is depicted supremely in the Old and New Testaments nonetheless continues to be active, a player together with us, as it were, in the ever fresh performance of this same text; or, if we prefer to take our theatrical image in a slightly different direction, the one together with whom we are now engaged in improvising the final 'lost' act of a drama whose first several acts (and hence the key characters and as yet incomplete plot) are thoroughly familiar to us.[14]

---

12 A helpful engagement with Lash and Young, and other early examples among New Testament scholars is provided by Stephen C. Barton, 'New Testament Interpretation as Performance', *Scottish Journal of Theology*, 52/2 (1999), 179-208.

13 The term 'tradition' in this context, it should be noted, pertains to a broad set of human phenomena and practices through which the Gospel is transmitted and actualized in the church. Understood thus, as Richard Bauckham notes, "Tradition .. consists not only of creeds, council decrees and the teaching of bishops, but of liturgy, hymns, popular spirituality, art, poetry, stories, preaching, forms of pastoral and missionary activity, academic and popular theology, charitable and educational institutions and so on" (Bauckham, 'Tradition in relation to Scripture and Reason' in Benjamin Drewery and Richard Bauckham (eds), *Scripture, Tradition and Reason : A Study in the Criteria of Christian Doctrine*, Edinburgh: T & T Clark Ltd, 1988), 131.

14 This image is developed suggestively by N. T. Wright in *The New Testament and the People of God* (London: SPCK, 1992), 140ff.

Of course it is equally important for certain purposes to insist upon the otherness of God, and his transcendence of history and creatureliness as such, and to this end we may prefer to picture him as one 'offstage', in whose presence or before whom we are called to perform our part in the drama. But unless we would lapse into a wholly unbiblical form of deism, we cannot limit God to the front row of the balcony, even if, in doing so we dignify him with the role of playwright in the house. Even the image of God as Director of the performance, while fruitful in many ways, must not be allowed to compromise this other claim, that God is also a character in the drama we are called to perform or to improvise. In the incarnation, of course, he takes flesh and becomes an actor on the stage together with us; but while his involvement in the action is certainly concentrated here it is not limited to this particular part. More widely, the perception of Christian faith is, as one recent study has it, that "If Christian faith is from start to finish a performance" it is so precisely because "our God is a performing God who has invited us to join in the performance that is God's life".[15] Such theological emphases have seen theatrical metaphor taken up and explored deliberately within the mainstream of systematic theology and ethics, thereby holding 'doctrine' closely together both with its Scriptural source (the text to be performed) and its practical outworking (the performance). So, for example, Kevin Vanhoozer's recent work *The Drama of Doctrine* proceeds on the working assumption that "an *analogia dramatis* illumines both the nature and function of theology".[16] The theologian, he suggests (in the midst of a thorough and wide-ranging exploration of the theme) is best associated with the figure of the dramaturge, the one who advises on how best to understand and perform the script.[17]

Work such as Vanhoozer's builds consciously on the insights of what remains the most sustained and programmatic treatment of an *analogia dramatis* in theology, Hans Urs von Balthasar's multi-volume *Theo-drama*[18]; but it sees that, despite the magnitude of von Balthasar's agenda-setting contribution, there is plenty on the agenda to which due attention has not yet been granted. While recognising

---

15 Stanley Hauerwas (with James Fodor) in Hauerwas, *Performing the Faith: Bonhoeffer and the Practice of Nonviolence* (London: SPCK, 2004), 77.

16 Kevin J. Vanhoozer, *The Drama of Doctrine: A Canonical Linguistic Approach to Christian Theology* (Louisville, Kentucky: Westminster John Knox, 2005), 243. This book offers a large scale development of germinal ideas contained in the essay 'The Voice and the Actor: A Dramatic Proposal about the Ministry and Minstrelsy of Theology' in John G. Stackhouse (ed.), *Evangelical Futures: A Conversation on Theological Method* (Grand Rapids: Baker Books, 2000), 61-106. It should be noted that *The Drama of Doctrine* was published when the essays in the present collection were already at an advanced stage of editing. Initial engagement with Vanhoozer in the volume was thus directed wholly to the aforementioned essay. At the suggestion of the editors, though, Joshua Edelman kindly reworked his critical response to Vanhoozer's work late in the day in order to accommodate its more developed presentation.

17 Vanhoozer, *The Drama of Doctrine*, 32.

18 Hans Urs von Balthasar, *Theo-drama: Theological Dramatic Theory*, in 5 Volumes (San Francisco: Ignatius Press, 1988-98).

that theology as a whole is "full of dramatic tension, both in form and content"[19], von Balthasar's primary focus is on the dramatic nature of the gospel itself, as an account of human existence concerned with the interplay of divine and human action in the world.[20] Vanhoozer's contribution, meanwhile, is to the field of biblical hermeneutics and theological method. Others have appropriated dramatic metaphor as an exploratory tool in Christian ethics.[21]

Metaphors of performance (artistic and other sorts) remain laden with theological possibilities which, if not endless, nonetheless extend far beyond the horizons of exploration and development to date. The present volume, which gathers together papers delivered at research colloquia or in the research seminar of the Institute for Theology, Imagination and the Arts in the University of St Andrews during the period March 2001 – March 2004, is intended as a step in the direction of such exploration and development. It does not seek to offer a systematic or comprehensive analysis of the metaphor and its entailments for theology, but to point to some of the different directions (among others) in which such an analysis might duly proceed. To pick up Jeremy Begbie's fruitful image in the postscript, the book sounds forth some (by no means all) of the theological resonances set in motion by the metaphor of performance. Part One attends very directly to some deliberate engagements between Christian theology and theatre, and enquires in particular about the importance and implications of theatre's essentially embodied and performative nature as not just 'word', but 'word in action'. Part Two takes the metaphor of performance in a broader sense, applying it to the 'action' of lives lived faithfully within religious traditions, and considering aspects of the Christian tradition in particular (worship, the interpretation of Scripture, the pursuit of goodness, and critical response to elements of contemporary culture) where such faithful performances might be sought and found. Finally, Part Three turns to the arts (including what are generally understood as 'non-performative' ones), and invites reflection on ways in which (since art is, as Wolterstorff reminds us, precisely a form of human *action*[22]) artistry may provide its own distinctive and important instances of the performance of the Christian tradition. The volume closes with a theological response by Jeremy Begbie, which both draws us back to some of the key threads that are woven through and hold it together, and points ahead to the challenges which remain for further careful work in the ongoing dialogue between theology and the arts.

I am grateful to all those whose contributions appear here, and to others who participated in the colloquia and research seminars from which the substance of this book is chiefly drawn. I am especially grateful to my former colleague, Steven

---

19 Von Balthasar, *Theo-drama*, Vol. 1 (San Francisco: Ignatius Press, 1988), 125.

20 Drama is fundamentally all about action (from the Greek *drao*, 'to act'). The gospel, too, is about action; specifically " the history of an initiative on God's part for his world, the history of a struggle between God and the creature over the latter's meaning and salvation" (von Balthasar, *Theo-drama*, Vol.1, 125).

21 See, e.g., Hauerwas, *Performing the Faith*, and Samuel Wells, *Improvisation: The Drama of Christian Ethics* (Grand Rapids: Brazos, 2004).

22 See Wolterstorff, *Art in Action, x, 3, et passim*.

Guthrie, for his invaluable assistance in the preparation and editing of this volume. Thanks are also due to Cambridge University Press for permission to publish some material in the chapters by Jolyon Mitchell and William Dyrness, and to Scala and Sieger Köder for permission to use the images included in Part Three. It is with sadness that I must note the death of Rosemary Muir Wright while this volume was in preparation. It is a privilege to be able to include her essay in it, a fitting tribute to a colleague and friend whose own daily work and life was, as all those who knew her will attest, identifiably a performance of the Christian gospel on so many different levels.

Trevor Hart

PART 1
Theology, Faith and Theatre

The first part of this book attends specifically to the phenomenon of dramatic performance and possible theological applications of it, including critical reflection on and response to seminal initiatives in the field by von Balthasar and Vanhoozer. Ben Quash's opening essay engages with two key theological commitments which drive and inform von Balthasar's agenda-setting 'turn to drama': first, the essential 'linearity' of history and the radical particularity, irreversibility and 'momentousness' of events and actions occurring within it; and second, the '*diversified* and *communal* character of Christian life before God', a 'polyphonic, unfinalizable and dialogical' encounter with truth which resists too rapid or easy a move towards any fixed, monological perspective, and thereby conscripts us as participants in a continuing conversation, rather than passive recipients of an omniscient narration. Ivan Khovacs urges that von Balthasar's project, while tantalizing and full of promise, demands to be pushed much further yet if the deeper veins of promise are ever to be tapped. Specifically, there must be a genuine *exchange* of insights between theology and theatre, rather than a mere quarrying of drama 'to enrich the language of theology'. Theologians must take fully seriously and learn to respect the peculiar artistry of the theatre, engaging with it, for example, as a 'three-dimensional, performative event', rather than an alternative body of literature, something which Balthasar shows some reluctance to do. Khovacs directs us to the work of Kevin Vanhoozer and Shannon Craigo-Snell for helpful examples of a theological exchange with 'theatre' in this more full-blooded sense, taking rehearsal and performance respectively as paradigms for the interpretation and embodiment of a text. Joshua Edelman, writing from the side of theatre, continues the line of enquiry, offering a sharp critical reaction to Vanhoozer's work which, he argues, while breaking important and fruitful inter-disciplinary ground, does not yet go as far as it might in quarrying the available resources, and leaves itself vulnerable to criticism by its focus on a particular strand of dramatic theory and practice. In particular, further engagement with some key figures in post-Stanislavskian dramaturgy – Brecht and Mamet are the examples treated here – would, Edelman suggests, raise rather different questions and thereby furnish a more adequate set of resources with which to pursue the dialogue further.

Chapter 1

Real Enactment: The Role of Drama in the Theology of Hans Urs von Balthasar

Ben Quash

No one can appreciate the full truth of the Christian revelation unless he or she is a player within its distinctive dynamics – participating in the drama of God's self-communication to the world and living out its implications in committed action. This is why von Balthasar does not write the part of his trilogy that deals with *knowing the true* until he has written the parts that deal with *seeing the glorious* and with *doing the good*. There ought not to be any presumption to having an analytical distance from God's action in and for the world, in whose middle human beings are situated. How could anyone possibly hope to be able to step out of this drama – a drama that so fundamentally determines creaturely existence? How could anyone look at it from 'outside' or 'above'? Such a viewing platform is not available. As von Balthasar himself puts it:

> The life common to Christ and the Church is ... actual life poised between perdition and redemption, sinfulness and sanctity. The existence of sin within the field of force of grace, the impact, here and now, between despairing obduracy and crucified love, these, and not a colourless and static world of philosophy, are the matter of theology. This is why it cannot be expressed *solely* in the sleek and passionless form of the treatise, but demands movement, sharp debate ..., the virile language of deep and powerful emotion ...[1]

Theology is done not outside or above the drama of Christian living, it is itself part of the drama: and von Balthasar's writings try to express this. He is 'concerned with expounding the word of God, which is as much a word of life as a word of truth'.[2] And his theological heroes are those great teachers of the Church who managed never to be the victims of such a false separation between knowledge and life.

In this chapter, I want to isolate two of the central theological commitments that drive von Balthasar's thought and which his turn to drama is designed to carry forward. They can be summarised at this stage as (first) a concern to take the linearity of history seriously, and therefore the uniqueness and 'once only' character of actions in the world. This is the context for what might be called the 'tragic sensibility' in his theology, which although it is often undermined by his synthesising and

---

1   Hans Urs von Balthasar, *Explorations in Theology I: The Word Made Flesh* (San Francisco: Ignatius, 1989), pp. 204–5.
2   Ibid., p. 183.

idealist instincts (as I have argued elsewhere),[3] nevertheless exists, and is perhaps the principal reason for Donald MacKinnon's admiration of his thought. We will approach this first Balthasarian commitment via a more general set of reflections on tragedy that will help to sharpen an appreciation of the importance of what von Balthasar is suggesting in his description of human lives as being situated in a real drama.

The second central commitment is that to the social and 'many-voiced' character of the Christian witness to truth in the world – a witness made up of many perspectives, and enacted in many 'missions'. This social and many-voiced quality is manifest in the scriptures themselves and by their role in Christian life and thought. It is also displayed in the character of the *Church*. We will come at this second area of investigation by seeing why neither lyric poetry nor (for the purposes of this essay) the *novel* quite meet von Balthasar's theological requirements – why drama is the only really satisfactory artistic embodiment of the social (and what von Balthasar believes to be its consummate form, the ecclesial). This will involve a comparison with some of the Russian theorist Mikhail Bakhtin's discussions of genre.

We begin then with a look at tragedy, and its quintessential embodiment of something that von Balthasar takes to be true of *all* drama, and that adds to drama's attraction for him as a field of ideas: its linearity.

1. Tragedy

Two Versions of a Genre

Even a brief tour through the historical application of this most famous of all genre terms will reveal a vast and internally contradictory set of understandings. For Aristotle, tragedy dealt with 'spudean' matters – that is to say the actions and passions of the noble, people of high character, the good, the superior and the heroic. Some later medieval interpreters supposed on the contrary that it dealt with the filth and foul deeds of the degenerate; things base, low and fetid; supposedly goat-like things (the word tragedy itself, literally interpreted, seeming to mean 'goat song'). In actual fact, all of the many medieval interpreters of tragedy were largely in the dark as to its ancient forms and origins, and made more or less random guesses on the basis of one reference in Boethius' sixth-century *Consolation of Philosophy*, some biased Christian material like that bequeathed by Isidore of Seville, and a little later in the fourteenth century some bits and pieces of Seneca that turned up in Padua. Thus, some think tragedy to be about the vile and unspeakable deeds of kings – primarily *crimes* – and others think it to be about any kind of lamentable misfortune – *sad things*. Its style is thought by some to be loud and bombastic, but by others mournful and song-like. And while some presumed tragedy to have a dramatic (or at least narrative) form, others (including Dante) were content to look on lyric poems

---

3   Ben Quash, 'Drama and the ends of modernity', in L. Gardner, D. Moss, B. Quash and G. Ward, *Balthasar at the End of Modernity* (Edinburgh: T&T Clark, 1999).

as tragedies too. There was no unitary understanding of tragedy in the Middle Ages. It did not have to include a disaster factor (though neither did it in fifth-century BC Athens); there was little sense of it as a special genre of literature; and in most of medieval Europe there was a general lack of awareness and a puzzlement concerning the term *tragedia*.[4]

Despite this range of conflicting or ambiguous usages of the term, it seems worthwhile to try to narrow the tradition down, and to highlight *two* main applications. Boethius' influential reference in the sixth century is vital to this. Its appearance in Boethius' writing ties the idea of tragedy to the concept of Fortune. Fortune is repeatedly personified in medieval writing after Boethius as the mistress or goddess of good and bad luck, spinning her wheel. As H.A. Kelly says, it is an 'easy and overworked poetic ploy', and the Lady Fortune becomes so devoid of personality, and so little regards the persons over whom she rules, that 'Boredom must have been [her] frequent companion'.[5] Chaucer's host in his comments after the Monk's Tale makes his feelings on this matter abundantly clear. If medieval concepts of tragedy come to settle around this particular trope of Fortune and her wheel, then what we have in tragedy at the time of Chaucer is little more than a 'soporific' (to use H. A. Kelly's word)[6] – a predictable and characterless lamentation over misfortune. So this is the first possibility of a tragic 'form' – a 'soporific' on the vicissitudes of life.

But Chaucer, and thanks to him eventually Shakespeare, reconstituted the form he inherited in a way that has retained its vitality to the present day. Chaucer responded to those ideas that limited tragedy to the downward movement from prosperity to adversity. The complete cycle of Fortune's wheel was interrupted by Chaucer; his interest was in only a *part* of that trajectory in human affairs represented by the trope of the wheel. He concentrated on the decline into wretchedness. And the effect of this concentration was to renew the dramatic force of a linear progression of events rather than a cyclical one; a progression of events which could lead more compellingly to definite, final endings, and endings all the more terrible for their finality. This revitalized the genre, and it proceeded with time to leave the idea of Fortune behind. Here, then, we see a second possible 'tragic form' which we are more likely to recognize – and which is more the one that lies behind our metaphorical extension of it in modern usage: tragedy as the irreversible encounter with overmastering, destructive and estranging forces that press a terrible definiteness and constraint on what Donald MacKinnon might call our 'purposings'.[7]

Incidentally, by a combination of luck and imagination, Chaucer and Shakespeare returned to tragedy a lot of the qualities that gave it its force and momentum in ancient

---

4   The best survey of the understanding of tragedy in this period (and I have drawn heavily on it in this section) is H. A. Kelly, *Ideas and Forms of Tragedy: from Aristotle to the Middle Ages* (Cambridge: Cambridge University Press, 1993). On tragedy as 'goat song', see 104, 143.

5   Kelly, *op. cit.*, p. 221.

6   Ibid.

7   D. M. MacKinnon, *Explorations in Theology 5* (London: SCM, 1979), p. 105.

Greece. The subsequent rediscovery of the fifth-century tragedians – of Aeschylus, Sophocles and Euripides – in many ways confirmed the emphases that Chaucer and Shakespeare chose to give to tragedy.

So, we have two contrasting 'tragic forms' in rough outline to take with us into a consideration of the possible attraction of drama for a theologian like von Balthasar:

i) a cyclical one reflecting the perpetual vicissitudes of the world and the human's place in it; and
ii) a more linear one hinting at possibilities of ultimate and inescapable disintegration in individual human lives and perhaps, by extension, in the history of the world itself.

John Beer considered the word 'vicissitude' in his 1993 inaugural lecture in the English Faculty at Cambridge (entitled *Against Finality*)[8] and saw its latent potential as a term of consolation. Although Newton's demonstrations seemed to subvert the metaphysical securities of earlier ages, Beer pointed out, the new universe Newton offered was at least one in which while everything fell nothing fell forever. All fallings were eventually caught up in that cyclical round of the planets which in turn allows us to *enjoy* the changes it creates. This sense of an 'ultimate mercy'[9] in the Newtonian universe persists, and is traceable (to take one example) in the poetry of Wordsworth – here in the last stanza of an epitaph:

> No motion has she now, no force
> She neither hears nor sees,
> Roll'd round in earth's diurnal course
> With rocks, and stones, and trees![10]

In the solar system things end 'neither in an endless falling nor in a fixed stasis but in a reversion to the cycling processes of ordinary nature'.[11] It is not that the epitaph presents a *joyous* vision; it is certainly sombre. But utter desolation is avoided by the fact that the last image is of trees and not of the deadness of rocks: a 'marginal consolation'.[12] Though pre-Copernican, and pre-Newtonian, the shade of a Boethian attitude to human life and death lurks in the background, having found new and unexpected applications in a world re-envisioned by Newtonian physics. The epithet 'tragic' as Boethius used it might lend itself here to a vision of the world as a place

---

8   John Beer, *Against Finality* (Cambridge: Cambridge University Press, 1993).
9   Ibid., 31.
10   'Song' in William Wordsworth, *Lyrical Ballads with Other Poems in Two Volumes by W. Wordsworth*, 2nd edn., Vol. 2 (London: T. N. Longman and O. Rees, 1800). The poem is quoted by Coleridge in E.L. Griggs (ed.) *Coleridge: Collected Letters* (Oxford: Clarendon Press, 1956–71), vol. I, p. 479, and cited in *ibid.*, p. 30. As Beer notes, 'when Wordsworth included the poem, untitled, in the 1800 *Lyrical Ballads* he changed "mov'd" to "rolled"' (Ibid., 45, note 53).
11   Beer, *Against Finality*, 31.
12   Ibid.

of vicissitudes and the marginal consolations they afford. Fortune's wheel might somehow have found the means to a new significance recast in the light of the insights of science and technology and the Newtonian revolution.

Theodramatic Implications: Why Christianity Cannot Be Soporific

But theologically (and this is the sort of question von Balthasar is inclined to pose) what are we to make of the idea of 'ultimate mercy' and a universe in which, to quote again, 'while everything falls nothing falls for ever'? Does it seem to conform to what is revealed in Jesus Christ? Or does the rival outline of tragic form as a progress through irreversible and absolutely destructive events come closer to being an adequate field of metaphor (though it too will need correction)?

There are a number of different metaphysical approaches which we might choose to associate with the 'vicissitude' model. Its influence on idealism and idealism's vision of the tragic could be explored here. As MacKinnon puts it:

> in a certain sort of idealist theological tradition, the category of the decisively significant is ... replaced by the vague concept of a developing spiritual tradition which somehow plays down the heights and depths of human existence, mutes the cry of Jesus in Gethsemane, turning his agony into a kind of charade ... We have ... to resist the drift into a state of mind which regards all that passes before it as a kind of play ... empty in itself of deep and drastic significance.[13]

He goes on to characterize 'the most profound spiritual error of transcendent metaphysics' as *any* 'relegation of evil, whether physical or moral, to the category of *sterēsis*'.[14]

The danger, as von Balthasar argues throughout his theodramatics, is clearly that of 'drawing the teeth' not only of human suffering, but also of the once-for-all character of the person and work of Christ. God's affirmation of his world – demonstrated in the death and resurrection of Jesus – seems to require humanity not to get enmeshed in doctrines of 'eternal recurrence', or a smooth evolution propelled simply by resources internal to the creation itself. God's pledge in Jesus Christ is a free, personal commitment to the finite. As von Balthasar points out on numerous occasions, it cannot be recast as some kind of impersonally valid natural law. Moreover, this free personal commitment – this unreserved self-giving which is an absolute yes to humanity, requires with absolute acuteness a response. The absoluteness of the 'word' addressed by God to humanity suggests that the reply – if we believe that humanity is given space and freedom to reply – will have an absoluteness about it too.

One of the areas in which von Balthasar and MacKinnon are most at one is in their conviction that there are real and not simply illusory outcomes at stake in the harsh necessity that makes the cross a central part of God's coming to us. This is not

---

13 MacKinnon, *Explorations in Theology 5*, 58–59.
14 Ibid., 103.

make-believe, or the 'ballet dance of ideas'.[15] Judas having one moment slipped out into the night slips all the way into the oblivion of a bloody death. Jerusalem finds its daughters warned to weep for themselves, suggesting a freedom that has resulted in an *actually* 'irretrievable disaster';[16] that the city's refusal to accept what Jesus represents will have actually irretrievable consequences.

Christians cannot deny the personal, particular, concrete quality of God's action on the creation's behalf – its fleshiness and its bloodiness. Only a view strangely detached from this can see Calvary as a mere vicissitude. If this is the fierce way that God sues for our love (to echo the poet Geoffrey Hill[17]), then we have little cause to take soporific consolation in it. MacKinnon excels in driving home the implications of this: our approach to the mysteries of that deed requires that we 'evacuate our understanding and imagination of the illusion that we shall find here a metaphysically assimilable solution of the problems set by the world's existence'.[18] Instead, we are 'alerted to refuse the solution of a humanly tidy dismissal of life's roughest edges'.[19]

Moreover, as David Ford has pointed out in an essay on 'Tragedy and atonement',[20] the tragic is not negated by Christ, but taken into a transformation that sharpens it (though the category of the tragic is also revealed not to be adequate by itself). Those who preach Christ can, as 2 Corinthians indicates, be to some 'a fragrance from death to death'. In fact the whole urgency of the Gospel seems really to spring from the possibility of tragic disobedience. Ford is in the company of a long line of Christian thinkers, from at least Irenaeus' time, who insist that humanity retains freedom to decide for or against grace: a person can refuse it, in which case he or she freely chooses separation from God (that is, death). Thus, with the advent of the grace of Christ, there is a heightening of the danger implied in freedom. On this account, what is at stake is an eternal Yes or No. And as a thoroughly Balthasarian perspective would have it, only after Christ does there arise the concentration of satanic and anti-Christian powers in world history. Thus the eschatological saving events do not overtake and supersede the drama of existence, they actually raise it to its real stature. Christ's work is, to quote MacKinnon again, 'no wilful wresting of an unambiguous triumph over circumstance that will, by its seeming transparency, satisfy our own conceit'.[21] On the contrary, the path God must take for our sakes requires us to shun any facile teleology. It renews our sense of the deeply intractable in human life.

---

15   Ibid., 68.

16   Ibid., 194.

17   Geoffrey Hill, 'Lachrimae Amantis', in 'Lachrimae: or seven tears figured in seven passionate Pavans', *Collected Poems* (Harmondsworth: Penguin, 1985), 151.

18   MacKinnon, 68.

19   Ibid.

20   David Ford, 'Tragedy and Atonement', in Kenneth Surin (ed.), *Christ, Ethics and Tragedy: Essays in Honour of Donald MacKinnon* (Cambridge: Cambridge University Press, 1989), 117–30.

21   MacKinnon, *Explorations in Theology 5*, 137.

The Dramatic Character of Time

It will have become clear by now that I consider the second of the two tragic forms outlined above – the linear path through irretrievable affliction – to be the more appropriate to the shape of human existence defined by the revelation in Christ. It is of course the tragic form with which we are more familiar anyway. The metaphorical extension of the genre term tragedy to the 'quick, broken movement'[22] of Jesus' short life is appropriate in ways that it would take a long time to analyze exhaustively – and in some ways the metaphor is inappropriate too. Yet if we believe that Jesus Christ in some way defines the human situation, and reveals its real dimensions, then part of what he defines is its harshly constraining realities. This harshness is never for a moment denied by Christ.

That said, tragedy is not despair, and for von Balthasar most certainly, the emphasis on the momentousness and irreversibility of historical action in the theo-drama (both Christ's and ours) should certainly *not* issue in resignation, nor in a negative evaluation of our finitude. On the contrary, it should positively enhance our sense of the significance of each moment of time, and of the action of human agents in time. The dramatic sensibility given its acutest expression in tragedy is 'very different from the mood of tired impatience which finds nothing new under the sun'.[23]

A contrast might be drawn here with what is arguably the characteristic theatrical genre of the twentieth century, this being neither comedy nor tragedy, but tragi-comedy: that undecided, undecidable alternation between laughter and tears (*never* conclusive) which is given especially concentrated form in the Theatre of the Absurd – funny, and yet 'desolate', 'terminal' and 'obsessional'.[24] The Theatre of the Absurd depicts the world as having a 'fundamentally mysterious and indecipherable nature', and characters afflicted with feelings of 'loss, purposelessness, and bewilderment'. It leaves the observer 'baffled in the face of disjointed, meaningless or repetitive dialogues, incomprehensible behaviour, and plots which deny all notion of logical or "realistic" development'.[25] The Theatre of the Absurd gives us a powerful portrayal of the human condition as 'one of ignorance, delusion, paralysis', mixed up with tantalizing 'flashes of human sympathy, hope, and wit'.[26]

Waiting for Godot (first staged in English in Cambridge in 1955) is one of the most influential plays of the post-war period. The two tramps in the wilderness are in thrall to the arbitrary. Alternately frenzied and directionless, they obey an injunction they don't understand, for reasons they don't understand: to wait for Godot. Each act

---

22   Ibid., 79.
23   Ibid., 6.
24   Descriptions of Beckett's work in particular; see 'Samuel Barclay Beckett', in Margaret Drabble (ed.), *The Oxford Companion to English Literature*, 5th edn. (Oxford: Oxford University Press, 1985), 78.
25   'Theatre of the Absurd', in ibid., 3.
26   '*Waiting for Godot*', in ibid., 1038.

ends with the same exchange between the two tramps, 'Well, shall we go?' 'Yes, let's go', and the stage direction, 'They do not move.'

And all Beckett's plays show us characters like this – *Endgame*, 'a one-act drama of frustration, irascibility, and senility',[27] features a blind man called Hamm and his attendant Clov, and Hamm's 'accursed progenitors' – his parents – whom he keeps in two rubbish bins on stage; *Krapp's Last Tape* is a monologue in which an elderly and down-at-heel man called Krapp tries to recall the intensity of earlier days by playing himself recordings of his own younger self; *Happy Days* portrays Winnie buried in a mound, up to her waist in the first act, and up to her neck in the second, but still 'attached to the carefully itemized contents of her handbag'[28] – toothpaste, hairbrush, spectacles, hat.

If we look at the Greek tragedies or the tragedies of Shakespeare, we find worlds in which time is super-charged. The characters stand and face decisions of momentous significance; decisions which press upon them on which lives and loves hang; decisions on which they will be judged. There is a fierce fullness to be reckoned with in these tragic universes – a fullness of meaning and irresistible demand, in which death can be made sense of and greatness is possible. If we look at the drama of the nineteenth century we will see a change underway. In Chekhov's plays, and Ibsen's, people yawn, are bored, are afraid of their own dullness and obscurity, fear most of all that they are non-entities. Mundanity takes the place of the extremity of the plays of earlier ages. Entrapment takes the place of great falls. Their world is stale. Look at the Theatre of the Absurd, and the change is complete. Time is purposeless, meandering, flat. It is undifferentiated. 'What time is it?' asks Hamm in *Endgame*; 'The same as usual', replies Clov. In *Waiting for Godot*, the tramps make what is clearly a hopeless attempt to conjure a destiny for themselves (we are not alone, waiting for the night; waiting instead for Godot); in *Endgame*, all Hamm waits for is his next painkiller.

One of the things von Balthasar is most concerned to demonstrate by his orientation to drama is that this flatness and staleness of time – this movement which leads nowhere in particular, but is just a sort of drifting towards death – cannot ever be Christian time, even if it may overwhelmingly seem to be time as felt by a certain modern sensibility. To take up discipleship of Christ – to agree to be led by God – is to have time recharged with intense significance again, to know oneself summoned to a sort of destiny, though not a solitary and self-aggrandising one but rather a social one in which people and cities and the creation are made new. It is to see one's time as given for the purpose of witness and transformation. It is to be called to performance. The time of the Christian is therefore more nearly like the time of fierce plenitude – that fullness of meaning – to which Shakespeare and the tragedians testify; at its heart there stands the urgency of the divine call which addresses the whole of a person – everything he or she is – and asks that person to make something of his or her life.

---

27   'Samuel Barclay Beckett', in ibid., 78.
28   Ibid.

> [The] point of contact between God and the world in Christ is the eschatological turning-point of the ages. The Cross is the final point within the old aeon, and the Resurrection is the beginning of the new aeon. It is for this reason that the Cross is not merely the image of the principle inherent within the created world – as if this were but a vale of tears with suffering as its embodiment. Rather, the Cross lifts up on itself the whole inadequacy of the world, in order to bear the sin to Hell and to set man free for God. This raises the question of the meaning of human *existence at the turning-point of the ages*.[29]

To be sure, drama in von Balthasar's vision inhibits ambitious metaphysical constructions in a necessary way. But in order to avoid the kind of trivialisation that would empty of significance the complexity, the pain, the weight of decision-making, and the call to responsible 'performance' that are intrinsic to human existence (reducing them all to the facile rotations of a Boethian wheel, perhaps), drama, and especially the super-drama taken up and transformed in Christ, also constrains us to acknowledge the fact that finitude and non-repeatable particularity can genuinely mediate the divine purpose. Finite people and possibilities can be the bearers of glory. This means that the path to holiness - to sainthood - is not principally one of withdrawal from all the contingent aspects of personhood, according to von Balthasar, but doing things that are uniquely one's own to do. Von Balthasar's use of drama thus shows the same concern with the concrete as can be seen in his theological aesthetics (*The Glory of the Lord*). As in the aesthetics, so in the theo-drama, what is aimed at is a more full entry into specifics, into *particularity*. Becoming holy as an actor in the theo-drama means becoming more distinctively *oneself* (though always for the sake of Church and world).

> For each Christian God has an Idea which fixes his place within the membership of the Church; this Idea is unique and personal, embodying for each his appropriate sanctity.[30]

And again:

> No-one is so much himself as the saint, who disposes himself to God's plan ...[31]

Above all, it is Christ who represents this capacity of the finite and the once-only to be the vehicle of the fullness of the divine presence and purpose. And here is where a thoroughly Christian view of the world will see more than can be seen by the sort of dramatic theory I have been outlining above. Here is where the analogies between tragedy and a Christian understanding reach their limits. For drama (and tragedy most intensively of all) teaches us about the inescapability of the linear and historical, the inescapability too of the limitations of physical, creaturely space, and this is of great

---

29 Hans Urs von Balthasar, *The Glory of the Lord: A Theological Aesthetics V: The Realm of Metaphysics in the Modern Age*, Joseph Fessio and John Riches (eds), (Edinburgh: T&T Clark, 1991), 517.
30 Hans Urs von Balthasar, *Thérèse of Lisieux: The Story of a Mission* (London and New York: Sheed & Ward, 1953), xii.
31 Ibid., xiii.

importance. But *Christ*, meanwhile, teaches us that these 'tragic' limits of concrete human existence need not prevent the expression of the divine life itself. Yes, our finitude imposes (MacKinnon's words again) an 'obstinate, ineluctable truncation' on human effort that even belongs to 'the very substance of Jesus' defeat'.[32] But at the same time, Jesus Christ's acceptance of the human situation, as an act of obedience to the Father, expresses an eternal response to the Father in the unity of the Holy Spirit. As von Balthasar insists in his theodramatics, God's ways are displayed in this work of engagement with the extremities of the world's plight, in this endurance and agony and this defeat and destruction. This is so even though the engagement with extremity seems to jeopardise the very constitution of the godhead:

> Jesus is the authentic and unsurpassable interpretation of God. In the apparently finite medium of his deeds, sufferings, and attitudes the ever-greater of the infinite God is made known.[33]

At this point, I want to move to a consideration of another of the key theological gains von Balthasar makes by his turn to drama – a gain in terms of what it enables him to say about the *diversified* and *communal* character of Christian life before God. Our way of approach to this theme will be through a brief reflection on genre.

2. Poetry, Novels and Drama

The Possibilities and Limits of Poetry

I quote below a passage from a book by J. Neville Ward on prayer, called *The Following Plough*. It is very striking for the way in which what it seeks to say about poetry, as against prose, is very much the sort of thing von Balthasar would say about drama:

> T. S. Eliot once said that prose is the language of ideals, while poetry is the language of reality. It is an idea that surprises people and makes them think at first that it is the wrong way round, that surely prose deals with reality, poetry with ideals. However, if you stay with it you see the kind of truth it has. Prose, using logical procedures as traditionally understood, is the appropriate vehicle for coming to a conclusion, making a practical recommendation, finding a solution to a problem. Poetry is the kind of language in which a whole situation is presented and its feeling communicated, so that you know what it means to see a certain segment of reality with your whole feeling self, to contemplate a person or an object sympathetically enough for it to exercise its full force upon you. Pages of prose could be written to set out what Blake's poem 'The Sick Rose' is about, but, however full such treatment might be, something, indeed the all-important thing, eludes

---

32 D. M. MacKinnon, *Themes in Theology: The Threefold Cord* (Edinburgh: T&T Clark, 1987), 163.
33 Von Balthasar in Medard Kehl and Werner Löser (eds), *The Von Balthasar Reader* (Edinburgh: T&T Clark, 1982), 341.

that procedure. You can find the poem real, and presumably share something at any rate of the experience of the poet, only by living encounter. You have simply to read the poem and you will come face to face with it.[34]

Drama, for von Balthasar, is not going to lend itself easily to the tidy business of 'coming to a conclusion, making a practical recommendation, or finding a solution to a problem'. Whereas the monological character of much prose may make it a thoroughly useful vehicle for presenting a series of events as a *fait accompli*, and for suggesting a finished product from which all the intermediate disagreements and conflicts have been ironed out – thus a genre good for instrumentalised uses – drama is the kind of genre in which 'a whole situation is presented and its feeling communicated'.

What, for Ward, seems to characterize poetry most certainly characterizes drama for von Balthasar. It finds its realization through calling its audience to a 'living encounter'. Something *authentic* is opened up by this encounter (Ward calls it the 'all-important thing'); something that we reach when (for example) *sympathy* is allowed a role in our knowing activity, thus enabling a new quality of knowledge – perhaps even, in some cases, a special kind of knowledge not attainable in any other way.

For von Balthasar, though, the theological value of poetry is limited. This is something I have shown at greater length elsewhere.[35] It would not surprise him that its commendation here, by Ward, is in the context of a book of devotional writing. Poetry of the sort Ward is referring to works with the perspective of immediate feeling and individual association. It is what von Balthasar (borrowing categories from Hegel) would call 'lyric' in its generic character: it works by the individual's integration of metaphors, images and associations, and this can have the consequence that the shared, public world of experience and action is either assimilated or excluded from consideration. Von Balthasar says that this 'lyricism' results in 'a romanticism remote from reality' and in the Church produces a pious but largely 'affective' theology.[36] Drama's appropriateness to the expression of Christian theology, meanwhile, is demonstrated in the interaction of individual (lyric) persons with one another, and with the collectively-held content of Christian faith. The 'truth' of this revelation is a truth that discloses itself not only in terms of life and decision, but also incorporation in a community.

The Possibilities of The Novel: MIikahil Bakhtin

Might there be other genres that *are* a match for drama in this regard? It is at this point that I want to give room to the claims of Mikhail Bakhtin for the *novel*. I want

---

34   J. Neville Ward, *The Following Plough* (Cambridge MA: Cowley Publications, 1984), 111; I am grateful to Anna Williams of Cambridge for pointing me to this book.
35   Cf. Quash, 'Drama and the ends of modernity', 145–59.
36   Von Balthasar, *Explorations I*, 208.

to give room to Bakhtin partly because his arguments for the merits of the novel (rather like Ward's for poetry) lend themselves very readily to adaptation to von Balthasar's case for the value of drama. He generates useful categories which help one appreciate all the more fully why theodramatics is such a good idea. But partly too I want to give room to Bakhtin so as to be able to suggest a crucial contrast between Bakhtin's preference for the novel, on the one hand, and von Balthasar's for drama, on the other.

Bakhtin thought there had been a widespread failure of literary criticism to do justice to the novel in its own right. Poetry seemed to him to receive extensive treatment as a form of literary 'art', while the novel was treated as debased and hybrid, haphazard in its use of the purer forms of the language of 'poetics', heavily diluted with 'non-' or 'extra-artistic' discourse. Bakhtin, by contrast, called the novel the 'genre of genres', and attempted to redress the injustice done to it.

He did this first by celebrating the very thing the literary critical establishment (in his view) disparaged: the novel's affirmation of the aesthetic value of the ordinary – its use of everyday speech. Vigour and creativity, both social and individual, are sustained and renewed precisely in and through such everyday speech, he argued. This in fact is where I imagine his defence of the 'prosaic'[37] quality of the novel would lie if J. Neville Ward's critique of prose were put to him (the critique of prose as using 'logical procedures', for instance). Bakhtin frequently attacks the sort of 'monologism' that would frame the superabundance and indeterminacy of novelistic facts in the terms of a unifying explanatory theory. The multiple meanings generated in the movement and interpenetration of people's everyday communicative activity (meanings that the novel so sensitively registers) cannot be exhaustively mapped. No all-encompassing pattern is exhibited by them. They represent a myriad 'tiny and unsystematic alterations', all of which contribute to the continued making of language and culture, and they do so, often, in wholly unpredictable ways.

Second, Bakhtin celebrates the novel's unfinalizability. Again, a contrast with Ward's criticism of prose emerges here. Again, there is a marked similarity with von Balthasar's interest in the 'linearity' of drama. Unfinalizability is for Bakhtin that which most nearly shares the character of 'real historicity'.[38] It is a concept that reflects his commitment to ethical responsibility and his belief in the manifold possibilities present to us in every moment in our real lives in time (a reality which the novel can honour and reflect). Unfinalizability safeguards the reality of individual and social creativity and freedom in the midst of unfolding processes and events in time. Every reality 'is only one of many possible realities; it is not inevitable, not arbitrary, it bears within itself other possibilities'.[39] There is room here for human

---

37 See Gary Morson and Caryl Emerson, *Mikhail Bakhtin: Creation of a Prosaics* (Palo Alto: Stanford University Press, 1990), 27ff.

38 Ibid., 47.

39 'Epic and Novel', in *The Dialogic Imagination: Four Essays by M. M. Bakhtin*, ed. Michael Holquist, trans. Caryl Emerson and Michael Holquist (Austin: University of Texas Press, 1981), 37.

agency and choice, in shaping what comes to pass in the ongoing development of the world's story.

And finally, dialogue, which for Bakhtin reflects the 'nonself-sufficiency' of the self.[40] 'Life by its very nature is dialogic', Bakhtin writes. 'To live means to participate in dialogue: to ask questions, to heed, to respond, to agree, and so forth. In this dialogue a person participates wholly and throughout his whole life: with ... eyes, lips, hands, soul, spirit, with his entire self in discourse, and this discourse enters into the dialogic fabric of human life, into the world symposium.'[41]

In the view of Gary Morson and Caryl Emerson, real dialogism as Bakhtin advocates it will 'incarnate a world whose unity is essentially one of multiple voices, whose conversations never reach finality and cannot be transcribed in monologic form'. The unity of the world will then appear as it really is: 'polyphonic'.[42] The world is depicted enthusiastically by Bakhtin as like a great and chaotic medieval fair or Rabelaisian carnival, in which the merging and hybridization of languages is the healthy and creative norm. Images of perpetual surplus abound here. All the participants supplement each other, each having the richness of a unique field of vision, but each profiting from the bounty of the vision of those around her, which is necessarily additional to her own, and helps to fulfil (though never to finalize) her own sense of herself.

This, it seems to me, is pre-eminently a dramatic vision, and it is defined over against the epic one, just as von Balthasar's dramatic vision is. It is a dramatic vision, even when talking about the novel, because it is concerned with the assimilation and encounter and interpenetration of discourses; it is concerned to register the many ways that the discourses of ordinary life are continually being re-accentuated. A dramatic approach to the characterisation of reality can combine many styles. It, like the novel, can be a 'style of styles, an orchestration of the diverse languages of everyday life into a heterogeneous sort of whole'.[43] And if its characterizations are good, it does not finalize the lives and thoughts of its characters and the events they undergo, but evokes the 'endlessly forward momentum'[44] which, for Bakhtin, also characterizes historicity.

In drama, as in the novel, we encounter *polyphony*. To be frank, polyphony as Bakhtin describes it (and he does not describe it in relation to drama) is to be found only in novels by Dostoevsky (and in only *some* of *them*!). But the possibilities that are opened up by this glimpse take on a great significance for Bakhtin. What Dostoevsky so uniquely offers us is a dialogical alternative to any systematic conception of truth, because of the integrity he allows to his characters, and the creativity they are

---

40   'Towards a Reworking of the Dostoevsky Book', Appendix 2 in *Problems in Dostoevsky's Poetics*, ed. and trans. Caryl Emerson (Minneapolis: University of Minnesota Press, 1984), 287.
41   Ibid., 293.
42   Morson and Emerson, *Mikhail Bakhtin*, 61.
43   Ibid., 17.
44   Ibid., 184.

permitted to exercise, even over himself as authorial emcee. He allows himself to be *surprised* by his characters. Bakhtin argues that it is possible for an author like Dostoevsky to be affected by his various 'voice-ideas' as he engages and develops them. These 'voice-ideas' can come to represent particular persons and their integral points of view on the world: 'When two such voice-ideas come to interact, they may produce a dialogue changing both of them and giving rise to new insights and new dialogues.'[45] Dostoevsky understood this, according to Bakhtin, because 'to speak paradoxically – [he] thought not in thoughts but in points of view, consciousnesses, voices'.[46] Thus it is that, in his hands, characters can come to be *'not only objects of authorial discourse but also subjects of their own directly signifying discourse'*.[47] The characters' 'truths' are not merely partial, not merely relative to the author's overarching 'truth'. The author renounces, on one level, his 'essential surplus of *meaning'*,[48] so enabling his characters to be relatively free and independent.[49]

Of course, in order to be able to create a novel at all, the author has to be able to hang on to a second kind of surplus, which Bakhtin calls 'that indispensable minimum of pragmatic, purely *information-bearing* "surplus" necessary to carry forward the story'.[50] He puts his characters in situations with each other, makes opportunities for their mutual engagement. But in a really polyphonic encounter, what happens after that should be well and truly unfinalizable. One image to illustrate this unfinalizability premised on the relative independence of the voice-ideas might be that of 'character zones': the field of those tendencies, habits, concerns which congregate around any one figure. In a literary work, these characters participate in an overall scheme that must be sufficiently extended to cope with the expansions and contractions in their inner relation; to allow them, as Francesca Murphy puts it, to 'create a mobile "space"' as they 'pull away from one another in their various directions'.[51] And, to draw (with Murphy) on Jacques Maritain's thought in this regard, the space can then be 'filled with significative meanings ... tensions and pressures (silences, voids ... blanks reserved for the unexpressed)'.[52] These may well not all have been anticipated by the author herself.

It is worth emphasizing that Bakhtin was aware of the difference between this kind of diversified polyphony, and mere *cacophony*. He did not suppose that a lot

---

45 Ibid., 237.
46 Emerson (ed.), *Problems*, 93.
47 Ibid., 7.
48 Ibid., 73.
49 In his notes 'Towards a Reworking of the Dostoevsky Book', Bakhtin explicitly draws an analogy between this and the Christian idea that God created morally free people (285). 'God may argue with people, as he argues with Job, but Job retains the power to agree or disagree, if only silently' (240).
50 Emerson (ed.), *Problems*, 73.
51 Francesca Murphy, *Christ the Form of Beauty: A Study in Theology and Literature* (Edinburgh: T&T Clark, 1995), 49.
52 Jacques Maritain, *Creative Intuition in Art and Poetry* (New Jersey: Princeton University Press, 1953), 365.

of random, unconnected voices all speaking at once was to be celebrated as a blow against monological form. He sought literary theory capable of appreciating the immeasurably important reality of voices that genuinely *interact* in time – and he did allow the language of unity (*always provided* it presupposed diversity, rather than seeking to deny or suppress it) to have a place in this regard. He attributed deep importance to experiences of 'dialogic' concordance (for example, 'the unified "feel" of a conversation'), and he indicated his belief that when we meet such unity and appreciate it properly, we are nearer to understanding the 'unity of "truth"'. Really interesting unity is 'not the unity of a single proposition, however complex';[53] it is what might be called 'unity of ... event'.[54]

Admittedly, he leaves such ideas rather vague, but they are of great importance. They have something to do with the way that '[i]n conversations with independent participants arguing intensely about matters of great concern to them, the whole may have a unifying spirit, regardless of the divergence among positions'.[55] We may lack an easy vocabulary for that kind of unity, and that may be one reason why we lapse quickly into scepticism about its possibility). Where static unities are concerned, we can always give them the name *structure*, and we discriminate between kinds of structure. But there is value in searching out appropriate terms and metaphors for 'the unity of event, and for the different kinds of "eventness" we have experienced'.[56]

Tantalizingly, for a theological reader, Bakhtin saw the provisional possibility of the Church representing a kind of polyphonic unity, as 'a community of unmerged souls, where sinners and righteous men come together'. He also made a comparison with Dante's world, 'where multi-levelledness is extended into eternity'.[57] But it was precisely because of his distrust of an intruding unity of structure, rather than one of event, that he afterwards rejected the comparisons. He concluded the Church is 'too static, too closed ... and too easy to conflate into an ideological and monologic unity'.[58]

Here is where what has seemed to be a remarkable similarity between Bakhtin and von Balthasar in terms of their intellectual instincts (and targets) breaks down somewhat. Von Balthasar shares with Bakhtin a concern with polyphony, historicity and dialogue. Indeed, it is Bakhtin's emphasis on dialogue that above all resonates with what is at the core of von Balthasar's theological project: his desire to open up the inner structure of God's self-disclosure to the world, and to show that this structure has the character of address, response, and counter-response, in an ongoing, ramifying series of articulations of truth, goodness and beauty, all born out of the mutual interaction of God and his free creatures. But von Balthasar holds out – where Bakhtin (after a brief dalliance) does not – for the possibility of there being

---

53 Morson and Emerson, *Mikhail Bakhtin*, 237.
54 Emerson (ed.), *Problems*, p. 21.
55 Morson and Emerson, *Mikhail Bakhtin*, 256.
56 Ibid.
57 Emerson (ed.), *Problems*, 26–27.
58 Morson and Emerson, *Mikhail Bakhtin*, 255.

a genuinely Christian embodiment of that polyphonic, unfinalizable and dialogical ideal in the form of the Church. It is this key concern of von Balthasar's with the Church that I want to highlight before closing.

To do so, though, means also highlighting the way von Balthasar handles a topic to which the doctrine of the Church is fundamentally linked: namely, Scripture.

Von Balthasar's Dramatic Theology of Scripture and the Church

All contributors to the practice and worship of the Church – and preachers and theologians in special ways – become the inheritors of the 'many-voiced' legacy of traditional genres and their residues of accumulated wisdom. It is their task to create a 'unity of event' out of this diversity (while allowing it to remain unfinalizable and dialogical). As von Balthasar has pointed out, working with the generic plurality of the Bible itself, as it has been given to us by the Church, is at the heart of this task. None of its plurality must be suppressed. He writes,

> what seems on the surface to be a book is inwardly 'spirit and life' ... '*Biblia*' is a collection of writings of every possible literary genre, including occasional writings (the apostolic letters), poems, prayers, proverbs, laws, chronicles, oracles, secret revelations, laments, sober instruction for the Christian life ... This apparent confusion is criss-crossed by threads, open and hidden, linking everything with everything else; thus a kind of vast net is created ... within which the attested and generative word of God can traverse unhindered. The net embraces the contents, and yet it does not hold them fast: it is so loose and broad that, in principle, it loses nothing of the contents, but it does not claim to be itself the whole content.[59]

All of these genres are valuable. Each has its own surplus of meaning to contribute to the others. Each genre will have particular strengths at opening up and exploring particular aspects of reality. Each will have a particular range and depth of penetration. Thus the theologian who has the ability to command a wide set of genres will find his or her capacity to conceptualize, to interpret, and to participate in the life of the Christian community and the wider world, enriched in consequence. Kevin Vanhoozer puts it as follows:

> [T]he task of systematic theology is to 'knit together' the diverse genres of the Bible into the tensile unity of a dialogue. Interpretation may require the service of concepts, but the end result is not a static system so much as a dynamic equilibrium. To the extent that we learn to prolong canonical practices in our own contexts, Scripture becomes efficacious in 'educating' our feelings and in shaping our 'settled instincts'. If there is something that absorbs us, it is not merely narratives or stories, but the whole intratextual dialogue. What we have in the Bible is an absorbing theological conversation.[60]

---

59 Hans Urs von Balthasar, *Theo-Drama: Theological Dramatic Theory II: Dramatis Personae: Man in God* (San Francisco: Ignatius Press, 1990), 108–9.

60 Kevin Vanhoozer, 'Taking Every Thought Captive? "Greek" Orthodoxy, Practical Reason and the Ethics of Biblical Interpretation' (Paper delivered at King's College London,

Theology in its turn can try to encourage the 'dialogization, and conflictual interaction of genres', not only in relation to the biblical genres, but in relation to contemporary voices inside and outside the Church, the voices of other theologians, and so on. Its images can activate and develop some of the latent potential of the 'heteroglossia' it inherits, the wisdom such languages could impart in the right situation. The theologian, like the novelist and the playwright, can draw 'dotted lines'[61] between languages that in everyday life have not yet entered into a profound dialogue. He can stage dialogues between the results of these dialogues as well. It is something like this, I think, that von Balthasar both advocates and achieves in his own theology when it is working well. This is not only because of its quite extraordinary (for a Roman Catholic theology of its time) attention to scriptural sources and imagery – much of which it shares with Barth's approach (indeed, it may well be that it is precisely to Barth that von Balthasar owes this concern to create a pervasively biblical theology). It is also because of von Balthasar's hugely ambitious experimentation with the concepts and characteristic forms of expression he finds in Christian tradition, literary thought, ancient and modern philosophy, and so on – an experimentation that marked his theology from its earliest days, when he aligned himself with the *aggiornamento* in Catholic theology, and remained a feature of it until his death. At his best, he genuinely wishes to 'stage dialogues' between these concepts and forms of expression – to inhabit the worlds of discourse to which they belong, to enquire after what they make thinkable, and to see what sparks they will strike off each other. He is happy to acknowledge that in many cases such language and concepts will have to remain in suspended tension - unreconciled within the Christian thinker's current capacities to understand and interpret them. But he can accommodate this possibility because truth, for him, is dramatic; the interpretative key to all the trajectories of thought there are in the world is given in and with the creative, redeeming and sanctifying activity of God in relation to his creatures: this is the world's dramatic heart. Dramatic tension between a plurality of perspectives is not always, in other words, a sign of failure in the human appropriation of truth, it may be the disclosure of a deeper level of truthful reality than our rational minds are accustomed to allow us to appreciate.

The pluriform (or 'plurivox') character of Scripture is corresponded to perfectly in von Balthasar's theology by the 'constellation' of forms that he sees as constitutive of the Church in its irreducible sociality. The ecclesial analogy here to the diversity of genres in Scripture is the diversity of saints – each of them a unique and distinctive transposition of some aspect of the Christ-form (the *Gestalt Christi*). In his doctrine of the Church, as in his account of Scripture, there is a governing concern with articulating the dramatic heart of reality by which Scripture and Church alike are animated. Inasmuch as both Scripture and Church are participations in (and mediations of) the Christ-form, both must share the Christ-form's dramatic structure. To look at the Church rightly, von Balthasar thinks, you need to have seen that it is a

---

April 1997), 19.
    61   Morson and Emerson, *Mikhail Bakhtin*, 247.

dazzling firmament of people in interrelationship – many of them highly diverse, but none of them dispensable in making legible the full riches of Christ. The point is not to see some one thing that really makes them all the same. The Church is embodied in them because of and not despite their collective character. Their individuality in each case finds consummation in the loving gift of the others. The fullness of the Church is a fullness that establishes the integrity of the individual form even as it emphasises dependence upon (indeed, definition by) others, in a set of dramatic relations. And their unity is therefore something more like a 'dialogic concordance' than it is a monological statement of identity; it is more a unity of event than a unity of structure. It is polyphonic.

The Limits of the Novels

This vision is full of Bakhtinian affinities, to be sure. Von Balthasar's theodramatics, like Bakhtin's theory of the novel, delivers a decisive blow to the epic genre. The monologically narrated, universalizing world of the epic stands condemned: 'There is no place in the epic world for openendedness, indecision, indeterminacy. There are no loopholes in it through which we glimpse the future; it suffices unto itself, neither supposing any continuation nor requiring it.'[62] There is also no room for the plurality of perspectives that both arises from and facilitates this 'openendedness'.

But von Balthasar is in my view right to privilege drama over the novel in realising this end. Bakhtin cannot quite make the novel do all he wants it to.

My reservation about Bakhtin's theory is not a reservation about what it ends up endorsing. It is a reservation about whether the novel is quite up to it – and I regard the difficulty he has in identifying novels that *actually* exemplify what he is talking about to be evidence for this. In staged drama there actually *are* many voices; interacting interpretations. There actually *are* spaces which can be 'filled with significative meanings' (as Khovacs illustrates excellently elsewhere in this book with his account of Kevin Klines' performance of Hamlet). There actually *are* 'blanks reserved for the unexpressed'. One might want to add the proviso here that improvised drama will realise this possibility even better than scripted (authored plays being that bit nearer to novels), but there is still an excess of possibility that drama has over the novel. Maybe Bakhtin neglected drama because of the dreariness of the examples that were to hand. What is clear, though, is that von Balthasar's option for drama is able to achieve all that Bakhtin looked for in the novel and probably more.

3. Conclusion

The two parts of this chapter have read von Balthasar's work in a spirit of affirmation – and they have in particular affirmed his choice of a dramatic field of metaphor for

---

62 'Epic and Novel', p. 16.

two things that it makes it possible for his theology to prioritise. The first has been the linearity of time, and the sense that there is genuinely something at stake in how we live in time. The second has been the polyphonic character of Christian life, witnessed to both in the Scriptures and in the Church.

The affirmative treatment of von Balthasar's work offered here should not obscure the case I have argued in other contexts than this,[63] that despite the inherent advantages his genre of preference has over (say) Bakhtin's, he can hardly be said to have made the most of its possibilities in every instance – as is increasingly remarked upon by students of his theo-drama who come with theatrical interests and expect to find more consideration given to forms of drama such as improvisation than there is. Moreover, despite its best intentions, his theodramatics sometimes fails to be as much of a 'style of styles, an orchestration of ... diverse languages' as it might like to be.[64] To be such a thing, its business (unlike the 'centripetal' forces of poetics, which Bakhtin so resisted) needed to have been even more bound up than it was with the 'competition, dialogization, and conflictual interaction of genres'. Its form needed to have been more in tune than it was with its content. It needed to have been a theology more genuinely open to the future; one which exercised a more stringent critical reservation about its own structures and the wider ecclesial structures within which it was brought to birth. Although his theology contains a strong endorsement of the idea of performance, it also contains the seeds of an undramatic reliance on a standardized model of Christian obedience to which the variety of saintly missions is asked to conform, and which it is expected to display.

Nonetheless, where von Balthasar's theology is at its strongest is in the way that, with a powerful conviction, it aims to recall Christian life from the lyricism which too often passes itself off as 'spirituality', and from the dry-as-dust scholastic text-books which he found so infuriating, to a corporate, and whole-hearted common task: the live performance in solidarity with others of witnessing to and sharing in Christ's all-encompassing mission to the world. As he puts it, a 'too-individualistic idea of contemplation', wherever it is found, will not be fruitful for the Church. Holiness, to be Christian, must 'radiate out' into the active apostolate.[65] And it is in the context of this active apostolicity that we can see most clearly how the linearity we looked at in the first part of this chapter, and the sociality we looked at in the second, are linked. To hear Christ's word is to encounter a call to performance in which the salvation of our souls is worked out. To perform Christ's will is necessarily to find oneself in the company, as well as in the service, of others.

Von Balthasar thinks that what he titles the theo-drama is a real set of events – the *most* real events in history; the events on which history hangs. He thinks that in the Cross, which is the heart of this theo-drama, is a *real work*. It is not just an illustration of God's judgement and love; it is not fully described if described only

---

63 Above all in my book *Theology and the Drama of History* (Cambridge: Cambridge University Press, 2005).
64 Morson and Emerson, *Mikhail Bakhtin*, 17.
65 Von Balthasar, *Explorations I*, 238.

as 'revelation' (though it is that). Something momentous is achieved by it, and by the resurrection that follows it. It changes things. And it faces us with an unavoidable call to response, in company with others, that is the most important act we will ever undertake.

Chapter 2

A Cautionary Note on the Use of Theatre for Theology

Ivan Patricio Khovacs[1]

1. The Theological Drama

As a convert to theology with formal training in the dramatic arts, professional experience in theatrical production, and who occasionally 'walks the boards', I find myself committed to the premise behind Hans Urs von Balthasar's use of drama as analogue for describing God's incarnate action in the world.[2] Equally, however, I am increasingly persuaded that his *theological dramatic theory* is but an early stage in an emerging exchange between theology and the theatre. From this initial vantage point, questions relating the theatre's own metaphysical strands[3] and Christian thinking are fascinating indeed. For the moment, however, the note of caution I wish to add to this discussion is that merely exploiting the drama to enrich the language of theology frustrates what could otherwise be a real commitment to a theological-theatrical exchange. Furthermore, that the commitment would be real to the extent that the theologian learns and respects the artistry of the theatre. In the end, I will have done no more than insist that theological engagements with, in or through the theatre, whatever their origins and motivations, treat the theatre as a three-dimensional, performative event. To that end, I shall begin by following von Balthasar's theological-dramatics, pointing out along the way his reluctance to take on the liveness of the theatrical act (preferring instead to abstract from the wealth of dramatic literature formal categories for his theological project). Then, after sampling current theological interest in theatre, I will conclude with the general proposal that a theological interaction with theatre should account for the rich particularities of performance interpretation.

---

1 For John Harrop, Robert Egan, and Bert O. States: mentors and *dramatis personae*.

2 Hans Urs Von Balthasar, *Theo-drama: theological dramatic theory* (San Francisco: Ignatius Press, 1988–98), vol. II, 77–89.

3 Occasionally one finds allies in the likes of Robert Potter's 'The Holy Spectacles of Hildegard of Bingen', in Sydney Higgins and Fiorell Paino (eds), *European Medieval Drama: Papers From the Third International Conference on Aspects of European Medieval Drama* (Camerino: Centro Linguistico di Ateneo, 1999).

Epic, Lyric and Dramatic

Hans Urs von Balthasar, for whom theology is an event (originating from and attending to God's activity in the world), adopts dramatic art in so far as it angles the human perspective in the direction of the divine event. His *Theo-Drama* is partly motivated by a desire to thwart two extremes present in contemporary theologies, both of which obviate the dramatic aspect of theology. On the one hand, von Balthasar opposes scholastic approaches that do not require the theologian's involvement in his or her subject to hand (namely, God). He rejects, on the other hand, Procrustean theologies that define God a priori and tie him down to the contingencies of the world. He proposes the theological-dramatic stance as an alternative to either 'epic'[4] distance from the divine subject or a 'lyricism' that so identifies God with the theological inquirer that the distinction between the two becomes blurred. His quest for the more dramatic angles in the divine act begins then with the theologian's relative stance toward the event, or in the case of Scripture, an event put to story. We can illustrate this with a story drawn from a study in the 'theatrics' of terrorist activity; a story that exhibits what in Balthasarian terms would be called an epic narrator, a lyric participant, and a dramatic actor.[5]

> The Munich Olympics [of 1972] were designed to mark the reacceptance of the German people by the rest of the world ... Instead, what the world saw was a paroxysm of violence, the slaughter by eleven members of the Israeli Olympic team by eight young [Palestinians], five of whom also died. ...The young Arabs, operational members of the Black September Organisation, had a more specific objective in mind. They were determined to use the Olympics to shock the world into acknowledging the Palestinian cause. *The dramatic implications of this tragic event were immediately recognised on the streets of Palestine.* An old Arab sipping coffee from a tiny cup while watching the sun go down behind [the hills of] Amman, patted the head of his grand-daughter and said: 'We recognise that sport is the modern religion of the Western World. We knew that the people of England and America would switch their television sets from any programme about the plight of the Palestinians if there was a sporting event on another channel. So we decided to use the Olympics, the most sacred ceremony of this religion, to make the world pay attention to us. We offered up human sacrifices to your gods of sport and television. And they answered our prayers. From Munich onwards nobody could ignore the Palestinians [and our] cause.' Brian Jenkins, Research Analyst in Terrorism and adviser to the U.S. State Department on political conspiracy and violence puts it more tersely but comes to the same conclusion. 'Terrorism,' he says, 'is aimed at the people watching, not at the actual victims. Terrorism is theatre.'[6]

---

   4   The typology is uniquely applied by von Balthasar but is very helpfully traced through Hegelian dramatics in J. B. Quash, whose lead I follow in this section. J. B. Quash, '"Between the Brutally Given, and the Brutally, Banally Free": von Balthasar's Theology of Drama in Dialogue with Hegel', *Modern Theology*, 13:3, July 1997, 293–318.
   5   Cf. TDII, 53–62.
   6   Adapted from Christopher Dobson and Ronald Payne, *The Carlos Complex: a study in terror* (London: Hodder & Stoughton Ltd., 1977), 2–3; my italics.

Epic Narrator

Structurally, our retrospective look at the events in Munich is guided by a third-person narrator, one who has either observed the occurrence firsthand or collected the relevant facts in order to render a vivid yet objectively detached account of the event. In so doing, the narrator evaluates the role of every participant involved as well as the importance of the story's components (setting, chronology, historical backdrop, and so forth). In retelling the events, then, he arranges them in such a way that the strung narrative communicates something of the dramatic act experienced by the original participants. Yet, for all his investigative work and fidelity to the original drama, the narrator's involvement in the event remains indirect (and is, in essence, inconsequential to the story's origins, development or outcome). The epic narrator's un-stated premise is that any personal investment in the recounted events would prejudice his ability to report without bias: it would spoil the objectivity of the third-person narrative essential to the storyteller. And while we value the narrator's ability to translate the live event into a compelling story, we are equally appreciative of the appropriately distanced perspective, one we might associate with the reportage of historical account. For von Balthasar, this evaluative distance is characteristic of the epic perspective and is evident in the objectification of the Divine subject, when theology effects one-sided propositions *about* God.

Lyric Participant

Narrators, however, are not always unaffected by the stories they tell and may in fact be in the position to account more fully for an event by considering their personal involvement. The expert analyst in our story, given his professional understanding of the drive behind terrorism, generates *a self-involved narrative* told with greater personal investment than was possible by the epic narrator. This is the lyric posture: placing himself within the reach of the events, the lyric participant resists the detached objectivity of the third-person narrative without actually surrendering to the contingencies of the event. Terrorism, he avers, is aimed at those who witness the event, and this would include the expert-witness himself. Far from being a curious bystander, the expert's 'insider' perspective renders him a 'player', if not in the immediate proceedings, then in the storied re-enactments of the event. His self-involved stance, furthermore, guides us through the comprehensive scope of this event whose consequences are hardly confined to its immediate surroundings. It is the lyric stance, in fact, straddling both the inner workings of the event and its intended audience, which enables us to raise the question of location of *dramatic action*. Is an event dramatic in and of itself or does it become dramatic, and therefore theatrical, insofar as it reaches its target audience? The lyric narrator's subjective participation effectively negotiates the tension between these poles so that the event's 'inner drama' might be communicated ad extra.

Von Balthasar illustrates the subjectivity of the lyrical posture through the practice of Ignatian exercises: "'Lyrical' here means the internal motion of the devout subject, his emotion and submission, the creative outpouring of himself in the face of the vivid re-presentation, in its pristine originality, of what is a past event.'[7] In other words, the divine act is dramatic in that it re-*presents* itself through personal expression of faith. The emphasis on the event's self-presentation broadens the field of the dramatic from what happens within the event itself to include the experience of the self-involved lyrical witnesses. Representation of an event, therefore (through anamnesis, in story, or in a drama), is as much a part of what makes the event dramatic as the event itself. Nevertheless, given the distance between the event and its retelling (or representation) we might still suspect that our lyric participant, while abandoning any pretence to removed objectivity has not entirely relinquished the option of personally disengaging from the events if need be. We suspect, moreover, that the lyric's investment only goes as far as he is able personally to comprehend the event.

Dramatic Actor

But there is a third perspective from which the events in the Olympic stadium are retold; we see it in the narrative of the old man and his appropriation of this life-changing drama. Although not a causal agent, considering the event from a coffee-shop in Amman, the man rightly recognises that the world will perceive him and the Palestinian people in light of the carnage at Munich. The appearance of coffee-sipping aloofness is easily betrayed when he casts himself in the story estimating the event to have taken place at least partially on his behalf. He does not so much 'take ownership' of the event as is dramatically owned up by it – a fact to which he responds, for good or ill, by entering into the story and its consequences with the self-inclusive language of the first person plural: 'we decided', he says, '...we offered up human sacrifices...', 'our prayers' were answered, 'our' cause cannot be ignored. The enrapturing vitality in the man's personal identification with the drama has something of von Balthasar's theo-dramatic perspective in which the theologian, apprehended by the Christ event, becomes a personified retelling of the event: a living echo of the living Word.

Analysing Balthasarian terminology, Ben Quash[8] defines the epic perspective as that which relates past events as events past and accomplished: 'Its concerns', writes Quash, 'are often with the careful appropriation of the historical and textual traditions *about* God's action, and their redescription in terms of some kind of abiding "universal significance"'.[9] The epic perspective requires a reporter's removed objectivity in order to make sense of the 'brute facts' of the event. Much of theology, von Balthasar fears, is seduced by the search for brute objectivity. An epic theology, however 'is usually too 'distanced' from the events to be helpful as an

---

7   TDII, 55.
8   Cf. footnote 4.
9   Ibid., 296. Italics added.

exclusive guide' through the events.¹⁰ The epic stance, moreover, with its totalising perspective, resists the contingency of 'the transitory world on its pilgrim path' and the individuation of particular persons and events.¹¹ In this regard, the Catholic Balthasar remains unconvinced by the imposition of 'narrative theology' and its gravitation towards the (Lutheran) *sola scriptura* principle '... [w]here the norm is no longer *revealed action* but [rather] its mirroring in Scripture' (recognising, however, that the two are ultimately inseparable).¹² The danger, he says, is that 'epic-narrative theology – accredited by the distanced attitude of the reporter – will quite logically assume the role of judge over the events and their actualization'.¹³ Yet the divine drama which comes to a climax in Jesus Christ, if it is to draw 'all truth and objectivity into itself',¹⁴ and if it is to become 'the norm of every real and possible drama',¹⁵ runs contrary to theological constructs 'from which we could observe and portray events as if we were uninvolved narrators of an epic'.¹⁶

But if the epic mode leads to a detached form of discourse *about* God (in which God is a third person He) then the lyric mode generates dialogue *with* God; God becomes the Thou to the self-involved believer; it is a posture that requires a personal and affective involvement not seen in the movement of the epic. To go back to our story, the expert commentator is drawn into the lyricism of narrative when he participates not just as an interested witness but as one who, given his particular training, has a special 'vocation' for retelling that story.

Lyric modes of theology, nevertheless, bring the seeker into personal involvement with the divine subject. To follow von Balthasar's illustration, Ignatian awakening of the past event, bringing it 'alive to such a degree that the "will" can draw consequences from it ... just as if the event itself were here and now',¹⁷ goes someway to invigorate the spiritual imagination.¹⁸ With this imaged perspective, '[t]he objective circumstances of the past event are filtered and appropriated by the subjective consciousness ... as an opportunity for giving expression to [it]self.'¹⁹ This stance betrays, however, an 'exaggerated self-importance, on the part of creaturely freedom':²⁰ lyrical theologies, for von Balthasar, are credible insofar as God is contingent on the world structures, sharing, therefore, more in common with Greek mythology than with the God of the Incarnation.²¹ Clearly, while the affective

---

10 Aidan Nichols OP, *No Bloodless Myth: A guide through Balthasar's dramatics* (Washington, DC: Catholic University of America Press, 2000), 50.
11 Ibid., 50.
12 TDII, 58.
13 Nichols, 50.
14 TDII, 58.
15 Nichols, 55.
16 Ibid.
17 Ibid., 51. Cf. also TDII, 55.
18 Ibid.
19 Quash, 298.
20 TDIV, 327.
21 Cf. TDIV, 319–32.

investment of the lyrical moment is essential for the experience of the dramatic, it is not the lyric perspective 'alone and undifferentiated'[22] that accounts for the whole of the dramatic event. The very question driving the Balthasarian approach is whether theology can do justice to God's dramatic action in the Incarnation, death and resurrection of Christ, as well as to its retelling through the biblical Script.[23] Clearly, neither the subjective self-involvement of the lyric nor the dispassionate objectivity of the epic will do. Neither the insights of the lyric that intuit in the direction of the devotional inscape,[24] nor the epic's systematizing of the theological landscape are able to bear the drama of *Immanu-El*, the God who is with us. In von Balthasar's cosmology, the dramatic nature of the Christ-event presses for an equally dramatic theologizing of that event.

> For God does not play the world drama all on his own; he makes room for man to join in the acting. In other words: when God, acting in Jesus Christ, utters, expresses himself, his language must... *become* intelligible through the divine Spirit, who teaches men's hearts to listen and to speak so that they can utter a word in reply. [...] And only through the Spirit of God in man, who explodes his narrow, anthropocentric horizon of interpretation and causes him to adopt God's standpoint, can man understand this language; only thus can there be an 'adequate response' to God's self-disclosure, a response which, because it is adequate, is in turn the 'express word of the event of God'.[25]

2. Theology and Performance Interpretation

Von Balthasar's vision for a theological exchange with drama in the Germanic (and Catholic) world of the latter half of the twentieth century may not seem particularly remarkable given Europe's general state of revision, reconstruction, and reinvention. Nevertheless, even if von Balthasar himself underestimates the value of the dramatic dialogue with theology, one cannot overestimate the hermeneutic value that this represents. The present concern that theology *and, with or through drama* be done with some fluency and commitment to the art of the theatre, therefore, leads me to two theologians who have attempted their own theo-dramatic interpretations.

Kevin Vanhoozer and Shannon Craigo-Snell, both of whom see in theatre a metaphor for the Christian's embodied interpretation of the biblical script, come into our discussion for their receptivity to the live-action phenomenon that presents human action in the medium of human action.[26] Von Balthasar's use of theatrical analogues, by contrast, tends to foreground a dramatic structure in theology at the expense of the performance act inherent to the theatre. One may well suspect that

---

22   Quash, 295.
23   TDI, 25; then at length in pp. 26–50.
24   To use Hopkins' coinage.
25   TDII, 91.
26   To paraphrase Bert O. States, *Great Reckonings in Little Rooms: on the phenomenology of theatre* (Los Angeles: University of California Press, 1985), 49.

the *Theo-Drama* suppresses the dramatic possibilities in theology from the onset, though not necessarily when it speaks of the 'study [of] the phenomenon of the theatre – as a metaphor that is closely bound up with life's reality – in order to gather materials (including both form and content) yielding categories and modes of expression for our central venture'. Yet when putting a finer point on his attraction to the stage, von Balthasar concedes that dramatic theory and its phenomenological realization as theatre 'will be of use only if we realize that, in employing them, we need to complement them and go beyond them'.[27] This is just the sort of seemingly marginal aside that, in fact, reinforces the critique that von Balthasar's theatre is merely an occasion for rendering a more interesting dogmatics: adopting a dramatic style and form but not its content. Or perhaps it is the form he misses in dealing with the theatre. For Balthasar accepts the essence of what makes the dramatic (i.e., the obstacle of freedom and conflict of will)[28] yet pays scant attention to *performance* as the form in which theatre mediates the dramatic. This is something that, at minimum, tends to undermine the value of the theatrical for theology. Von Balthasar's Damoclean 'question mark over even the most interesting dramatic categories, a question mark that must apply, ultimately, to every attempt to present this unique reality [i.e., theology] in the forms of speech',[29] questions, in turn, his own commitment to the theatre as a theological player (so that in the end one is not sure whether to speak of a theological drama, a dramatic theology, or neither).

This overly simplified presentation of the *Theo-Drama* notwithstanding, Vanhoozer and Craigo-Snell's sensitivity for the peculiarity of embedding a text into human action, or rather interpreting text through an embodied performance, (whether speaking of a playscript or of Scripture) will show, I hope, some implications of von Balthasar's theological dramatic theory. Their awareness that '[w]hat the text loses in significative power in the theatre it gains in corporeal presence',[30] as one might describe the arc between text and performance, means that they can help us take theo-dramatics closer to a phenomenological presence on stage, effectively applying von Balthasar's theological principles in ways anticipated but never realized in his own work. Theirs is a welcome contribution to the self-aware *novum*[31] emerging in von Balthasar's text.

Kevin Vanhoozer, explicitly taking his cues from Balthasar's *Theo-Drama*, sees an obvious parallel between dramatic interpretation and the biblical emphasis on hearing *and* doing the Word.[32] In suggesting that Scripture requires interpretation

---

27 TDI, 11. My italics.
28 TDII, 38; 62–3. 'The confrontation between divine and human freedom has reached a unique intensity; the contest between the two has moved into the centre – the really dramatic centre stage – of the problem of existence.' TDI, 50.
29 TDII, 17.
30 States, 29.
31 Nichols, 49. '... though, like any well-founded development in the act of faith's reflection on itself ... by no means a wholly unheralded one.'
32 Kevin Vanhoozer, 'The Voice and the Actor: A Dramatic Proposal about the Ministry and Minstrelsy of Theology', in John G. Stackhouse (ed.), *Evangelical Futures: A*

through performance, Vanhoozer is appealing to the theatrical (and seemingly self-evident) principle that plays (with rare exceptions) are written for performance. Equally, Scripture in the life of the believer can only be meaningful when it animates the person to perform his or her life with 'creative fidelity'[33] to the text. 'The word of God,' says Vanhoozer, 'is something to be spoken, something to be *done*.'[34] The performative aspect of the Christian faith may not be particularly new to theology and has been taken up from various angles. Vanhoozer, however, very helpfully identifies communicative action as the epistemic basis for pairing dramatic performance and theological interpretation.

For Vanhoozer, theology has to do 'with God in self-communicative action (incarnation) and with Scripture as God's self-communicative act (inspiration).'[35] Relying on d'Aubignac's dictum that "*Parler c'est agir*" ('To speak is to act'),[36] Vanhoozer understands Scripture not as a text unto which meaning is ascribed by the reader or from which meaning may be abstracted by unscrupulous interpreters. Insofar as Scripture is taken to be Word of God, it must necessarily be seen as an act of the Divine, an event longing to be given form in time and space. It is not the case that the Bible merely recounts God's actions in the world but that it is one of God's communicative acts in the world.[37] In this, Vanhoozer concords with von Balthasar for whom

> ...Scripture mirrors the drama [of salvation] and can only be understood in reference to it; it is part of the drama. It does not stand at some observation post outside revelation. And insofar as it is part of a greater whole, it points beyond itself to its content, and its content is *pneuma*, which is always more than the *gramma*, the letter.[38]

In this light, Vanhoozer sees Scripture not only as relating divine action but as one of its very forms[39] – in Scripture, he sees God's action in the world transmitted through a story, one that invites the reader to become a participant in its cosmic plot. Revelation, in this view, is entirely God's communicative initiative to which we 'can only respond, and hence "understand", through action on [*our*] part'.[40] Although Vanhoozer's language regarding 'Divine communicative action *embedded* in the canonical texts' somewhat obscures his point that it is in *doing* the word that we find and realise its meaning,[41] he nevertheless points to the text as the source for our

---

Conversation on Theological Method (Grand Rapids: Baker Books, 2000), 90.
33   Vanhoozer, 69.
34   Ibid., 91.
35   Vanhoozer, 74.
36   Abbé d'Aubignac, *La Pratique du theatre* (Paris, 1657), quoted in Vanhoozer, 73.
37   Vanhoozer, 72.
38   TDII, 58. Moreover, says von Balthasar, 'The great unwritten acts of God and Jesus are also part of the drama of world salvation.'
39   Vanhoozer, 76.
40   Vanhoozer, 73; TDI, 15.
41   As 'embedding' hardly implies the need for verbal realisation *ad extra*.

interpretation through performance, or, in his words, as 'the final criterion for the church's communicative action'.[42]

Vanhoozer uses a particularly theatrical metaphor to say that knowledge of the word comes by doing the word. He speaks of the need for believers to take up 'an apprenticeship to the biblical texts'.[43] Biblical readers, theologians and laity alike, have to be willing to '*live* as well as to look "along the text," according to the Scriptures ... [as] [t]he biblical interpreter is not an autonomous knower but an apprentice to biblical literature.'[44] Similarly, in theatre, learning in apprenticeship to a text is the structural basis for performance interpretation. On the Jacobean stage, for instance,

> Shakespeare and his peers created their wonders in the sole expectation that they would appear on stage, not on the printed page, and we owe it to them to try and identify as closely as we can just what such creators expected their written texts to be turned into on the stages of their time.45

In the translation of text from the page to the stage, actors, directors and designers read along the text not only for what the text means (i.e., the word) but also for how one might arrive at an authentic performance of such meaning on stage (i.e., the word *in action*). For the dramatist, the playscript as a communicative act fraught with meaning goes without saying, as does the fact that not only the text but also the actions implied 'between the lines' *mean*. So it is not merely that playwrights have something to say (that plays 'mean') but that they want to say it in a certain way – that plays mean through performance. Performance, moreover, happens as an interpretive process when playwrights put ink to paper, directors elicit truthful emotions, as designers manipulate space, light and sound in service of dramatic action. The actor, for her part, takes up the playscript and commits body and voice to performance under the conviction that the author's communicative act demands an incarnate equal. Actors apprentice themselves to the text, paying attention to 'the way the words go ... to the *circumstantia litteratum*' to use Vanhoozer's guideline for the theologian. And while in theological interpretation God's communicative agency is authored by Trinitarian self-communicative action,[46] the creaturely-authored stage play is no less able to bear the vestiges of meaning, and indeed to gather its participants into a matrix of meaningful relations.

Communicative action theory, nonetheless, can only get us so far in explaining how dramatic performance illuminates the theological path. In locating us within the reach of the divine action of the text, the speech-act concept is good at telling us that speech (and, implicitly, text) communicates. That, however, still leaves the

---

42   Vanhoozer, 85.
43   Ibid., 82.
44   Ibid., 85.
45   Andrew Gurr, 'Door at The Globe: the gulf between page and stage' in *Theatre Notebook*, vol. 55, no. 2, 2001, 59. My emphasis.
46   Vanhoozer, 74.

mediation of the action unexplained. Speech-act, in other words, is good at telling us that a clock tells time, but it is not so good at showing us the relationship between the mechanism and temporality. But what, then, does a play performance communicate? It cannot be the *text* of the play (anymore than the clock dial communicates twelve numbered segments),[47] if that were the case, it would not be obvious why plays should be *performed* at all: 'anyone can read the text at home'.[48] The fact that we read as well as *act out* plays, however, says that the stage production is more than mere repetition of the text, albeit illustrated in costume, props and choreographed with movement. Neither should we think, however, that there is a one-to-one correspondence between playscripts and the performances they generate on stage. In theatrical performance, as we have suggested, much may be said in the spaces between the lines to denote the non-verbal characterisation of role and action. To give an example cited in a discussion on performance interpretation:

> During a production of *Hamlet* ... Hamlet, played by Kevin Kline, sits against a column with a book on his lap while Polonius stands besides him. Polonius has tried to engage Hamlet in a discussion, and Hamlet has brushed him off. Polonius bids Hamlet 'Fare you well, my Lord,' and exits behind the column. Hamlet mutters bitterly to himself, 'These tedious old fools!' Instantly, Polonius's head pops back around the column. Hamlet looks up, gives a forced smile, and points to an open page in his book, as if to say, 'I was just reading the book aloud to myself.' Polonius smiles and disappears again.[49]

Note that none of this action is actually indicated in the text but that the choice works given this production's interpretation of the play as well as Kline's characterisation and embodiment of Hamlet.[50] This 'between the lines' quality of performance interpretation drives the action at least as much as the text itself. The point is eloquently made by Peter Brook when he says that, 'There is one possibility that belongs uniquely to the theatre, and that is the possibility of entering into the arena that lies in between the words, in the tiny spaces between the words.'[51] If communicative action is to do with the words, then dramatic action is to do with what happens in the spaces between words.[52] In submitting the performance phenomenon primarily to the scrutiny of a speech-act theory, therefore, we run the risk of obfuscating the action latent in these empty spaces. We risk, moreover, construing the dramatic performance as the playwright's mouthpiece, as an instrument for saying, thereby

---

47   Although clearly it does that too.
48   Vanhoozer, 95; quoting Stanislavski.
49   David Saltz, 'What Theatrical Performance Is (Not)', in *The Journal of Aesthetics and Art Criticism*, 59:3, Summer 2001, 301, 302. Kindly brought to my attention by my colleague Michelle Stearns.
50   '... the business plays up to Kevin Kline's strength as a comedian'. Ibid., 302.
51   Sharon Bailin, 'In the Spaces Between the Words: play production as an interpretive enterprise', in *Journal of Aesthetic Education*, 35:2, Summer 2001, 69.
52   Accounting for unscripted 'improvisations' called for in the performance of the Christian faith.

missing the 'thing itself' which involves players and their audiences in the life of the drama.

Worst of all, however, an undue emphasis on the communicative action of the play makes it all too tempting to transcend the performance in order to get at what the author *really* wants to say *by way of* the play – to go behind the performance and tease out some meaning which can then be submitted to public evaluation. Again, it is not a question of whether the performance bears meaning. Nevertheless, the stress on meaning as the hallmark of the drama risks devaluing the performance as the occasion for presenting a certain message that might be communicated just as easily through other means: a sermon that, like a *Deus ex machina*, ushers in the 'real' message behind a dramatic presentation in the worship service, for example. Presumably, however, there is more to the drama than a message that can be distilled in propositional fashion (i.e., in words). It is in fact the drama's pull on the complete faculties of actors and audiences alike that gives it its particular eloquence. (In saying this we come close to following McLuhan's well-worn aphorism that 'the medium is the message', but part of my argument is precisely that form, in the dramatic presentation, has theological purchase that has not been sufficiently understood.) The question arises, therefore, whether the communicative act theory espoused by Vanhoozer relies too heavily on a privileged role of cognition as the locus where, at the end of the day, when the curtain is drawn and costumes are hung, one has to decipher and 'make sense' of what has been communicated in the performance. Vanhoozer speaks of what remains with an audience following the performance as 'the play's central image or idea, *the essence of what it had to say...*'.[53] But surely, though it is true that a play will communicate some central meaning, and that its imprint is made on the imagination largely through textual utterance and reception,[54] we cannot ignore that this is interpreted for an audience in the aesthetics of live-action. Whether we understand performance interpretation as happening primarily through identification (as in Chekhov, Ibsen), semiotics (Eco, Pavis), political effect (Piscator, Boal), or the Brechtian *Gestus*,[55] to name just a few possibilities, live-action is at least a phenomenon of *in*communication that makes audience and

---

53 Vanhoozer, 102; my emphasis.

54 Although in saying this, we have already compromised the 'purity' of text, so to speak, by putting it through the rigours of audition: auditors are hearers not readers of the word.

55 'A useful term in the analysis of Brecht's plays [...] is *Gestus* (untranslatable: attitude as shown in the signs we use in communicating with others). At its widest this means the basic attitude which informs any particular transaction between people. The transaction can be a whole work of art presented to a public, a conversation, a single speech considered as an independent component of a conversation. Gestus concentrates on interactions between people. [...] Theatre aims to communicate from stage to audience a demonstration of social facts, so the basic gestus of theatre is demonstration.' Alfred D. White, *Bertolt Brecht's Great Plays* (New York: Barnes & Noble, 1978), 41.

actors alike player participants in the drama.⁵⁶ And whether one believes suspension of disbelief to be an operative precedent to the reception of performance (*contra* Brecht), clearly, cognitive faculties do not cease to be engaged in the appreciation of the dramatic moment. Nonetheless, the body and its senses are invested in a dramatic performance not only so that it may communicate *to* us but precisely because we expect the performance to communicate through sensorial participation, as an incommunication of acting persons and not just as cognitive transmission of a central message or core idea. It would be a mistake, therefore, to understand the affective aspects of the drama as merely a back door entry into the sobriety of cognition.⁵⁷ If there is anything to Shakespeare's maxim that 'the play is the thing', the pull toward propositional renderings of what that thing is should be tempered by a more sophisticated statement of the drama's incommunicative power.⁵⁸

Yet a speech-act theory is attractive to the theologian who pays attention to 'the way the words go', that is, text and its meaning. Nevertheless, the speech-act leaves us wanting when interpreting the live act and, consequently, in using performance as a paradigm of faithfulness to the Gospel. Furthermore, speech-act theory (i.e., 'to speak is *to act*') locates the interpretive moment on the performance generated by the text. In fact, at what point 'interpretation' occurs in the theatrical process is an open debate in the philosophy of drama.⁵⁹ For our purposes, the fallout of the argument seems to be that a performance cannot be properly considered an interpretation of a play but is rather a 'token' of a more encompassing 'type' called 'the play production'. To equate the performance with interpretation per se leaves us to contend with a multiplicity of interpretations of the same script when a play is given more than one performance.⁶⁰ It is far more useful, then, to see the interpretive

---

56 Here, I do not denote the extent to which the audience is a participant in the drama, nor how much of the drama depends on its meaningful reception. My point is, nonetheless, that audiences *are* actors and have their role to play in the performance so that while the actor does not die on stage, Hamlet always does, and so does the audience's hope for Christian reconciliation.

57 Although this may well be the case in propaganda or theatre that is propagandist in tenor.

58 When deploying this term, I have in mind something like what takes place at communion where the text is scant ('This is the body ... this is the blood ... given and shed for you. Take and eat.') yet demands physical, psychological and affective participation on the part of its 'actors', and in doing so brings us into relationship with the actualised presence of God in Christ as well as to the surrounding community of believers, the 'cloud of witnesses', past and present, who partake in this holy drama.

59 Very helpfully taken up by David Saltz, *op. cit.* and Noël Carrol, 'Interpretation, Theatrical Performance and Ontology' in *The Journal of Aesthetics and Art Criticism* 59, No 3 (Summer 2001), 313–16..

60 This, at least is the view which Saltz defends and which I find compelling from the standpoint of phenomenology. 'Hence, the proposal that "performances interpret plays" cannot explain what *constitutes* the relationship between a play and its performances, since it *presupposes* that relationship'. Ibid., 301. The discrepancy (or 'hiatus', to use Balthasar's word, TDI, 112) between page and stage is bridged by the interpretive phenomenon of the

act as happening throughout the process of the play production. Set and lighting design, what costume is given to Hamlet and how he delivers his lines, for example, are all decisions that fall under the interpretation of *who* Hamlet is and *how* he is given life on stage. In keeping with my cautionary note that if we are to avoid a facile use of the theatrical metaphor we would do well to pay close attention to these particulars of performance and play interpretation, let us now turn to Shannon Craigo-Snell who alights on the rehearsal as the theatrical event where we can best situate our performative-theological conceptions.[61]

3. The Theo-dramatic Rehearsal

In her essay 'Command Performance: Rethinking Performance Interpretation in the Context of *Divine Discourse*', Shannon Craigo-Snell tackles Nicholas Wolterstorff's authorial-discourse preference for interpreting the God who speaks, touching along the way on Hans Frei's narrative theological focus and the structure of story as the place where meaning is to be located. Craigo-Snell argues for a performance interpretative model which, like Vanhoozer's, begins with the explanatory speech-act theory[62] but overcomes its weaknesses with a richer articulation of theatrical phenomenology. Picking up Wolterstorff's point (derived from musical interpretation) that 'Interpretation occurs in the space between a score's specifications and its realisations',[63] Craigo-Snell focuses her theological energies on the play's rehearsal process as her analogue for interpreting the biblical text in action. Her concern is to confront Wolterstorff's apprehension and subsequent dismissal of performance interpretation as unable to make truth claims about the authorial intent behind a text (i.e., 'The performance interpreter doesn't claim to have *found out* what the author said.')[64] Craigo-Snell observes that Wolterstorff's position would have 'The end results of a performance interpretation […] judged as correct if they abide by the specifications of the score or text.' Furthermore, that 'The criterion of correctness encompasses a great number of interpretations, which are deemed good or bad on the basis of value for the community rather than on the basis of making accurate truth

---

production and its corresponding rehearsal. In the process of interpretation, therefore, one may make performance choices which are not specifically called for in the text but nevertheless remain faithful and nourishing to the script.

61   Although she does not make direct reference to Balthasar's work, as we shall see, her able handling of a theo-dramatic hermeneutic would nevertheless seem to bear the marks of his influence.

62   Shannon Craigo-Snell, '"Command Performance": rethinking performance interpretation in the context of *Divine Discourse*', in *Modern Theology*, 16:4, October 2000, 475–94.

63   Craigo-Snell, 476; quoting Wolterstorff.

64   Ibid., 478.

claims about what the discourser said.'⁶⁵ To revisit our example from Kevin Kline's performance of Hamlet, Kline would not claim to have found a more authentic interpretation of the scene with Polonius (than has been achieved heretofore), nor to have discovered Shakespeare's original intent for playing the 'beat' generated in the line, 'These tedious old fools!' His is simply a character moment, Wolterstorff might say, which works well for that community of theatrical interpreters. Craigo-Snell, however, traces Wolterstorff's early dismissal of performance interpretation to a narrow understanding of the relationship between performance and text, or to keep to his original analogy, musical performance and score. The musical score, says Wolterstorff, is 'a set of guidelines for producing a musical performance' and notes that 'no matter how detailed, however, scores always come far short of specifying the resolution of all the issues that must be faced if the score is to be "realised"'.⁶⁶ Not far beneath this hermeneutic is the problematic suggestion that the score (or script) is somehow incomplete and requires further 'resolution' of its issues in performance. Craigo-Snell, to her credit, avoids this implication by placing the biblical text and the playscript side by side to show that although both are complete works, they nevertheless call for an in-the-flesh realisation that can faithfully stand alongside the text.⁶⁷ Moreover, she conceives of this enfleshed realisation as taking place not only at the moment of performance but largely through personal commitment to the rehearsal process. Wolterstorff, for his part, rightly observes that the interpretation process occupies the space between page and stage. What Craigo-Snell is able to appreciate more fully is the space occupied by the rehearsal in this interpretive act. Interpretation is therefore not left up to the performance but happens rather in a process of research and discovery, of guesses where one has not arrived at a final understanding, of learning to make choices in keeping with ones role.

In the end, the city of God may indeed be given and not arrived at in pilgrimage, as John Dixon would have it.⁶⁸ For the pilgrim, however, the journey is as important as the destination. Equally, one's role in Christ, as much as it is given, nonetheless

---

65   'For Wolterstorff, who is not merely observing but prescribing, this is fundamentally why performance interpretation "is not relevant" to his purposes in *Divine Discourse*'. Ibid.

66   Ibid, 481.

67   Ibid. On this point, it may also help to touch on Nelson Goodman's distinction between autographic and *allographic* works of art, the latter referring to those which require performance interpretation. Bailin explains it thus: 'Autographic works are identified with physical artefacts, paintings, or sculptures for example. Allographic works, on the other hand, cannot be identified with any particular physical object. They have to be re-created in performance. A play is an allographic work. It must be completed through performance [sic]. A playscript is necessarily open in that the way the play is to be performed cannot in principle be completely specified. [T]the act of bringing to life a playscript involves, at its centre, the activity of interpretation ... Thus performing a play, for both director and actor, involves a kind of co-authorship with the playwright.' Bailin, 68–9.

68   John Dixon, *The physiology of faith: a theory of theological relativity* (San Francisco: Harper & Row, 1979), 299.

requires apprenticeship for learning to 'put on Christ',[69] a lifetime's rehearsal that will determine the quality of the end performance. This theology in rehearsal is what Craigo-Snell comes upon in her keen exploration of the dramatic analogy. For her, the activities that make up the rehearsal process are 'not merely the results of an understanding that comes from interpretation'. In the rehearsal, it is not simply that I move on stage this way and that because I have understood Hamlet to be such and thus *a priori*. Rather, Hamlet takes shape and becomes animate on stage by physically 'working out' the text in rehearsal. Consequently, the way we know Hamlet in performance is to do with the way we come to know him in the rehearsal (where physicalization, vocalisation and characterisation make up the process of interpretation).[70] Likewise, we learn theology in the very form and process of 'fleshing out' our faith; or as Craigo-Snell would say, 'We teach our children to sing "Jesus Loves Me" not as an affirmation of something they know, but as a way for them to know it'.[71] Rehearsals are characterised by their faltering performances where lines are dropped and actors fail to stay in character or loose the plot, only to be brought back into scene by the prompt of the director. This is all part of the process, however, and faithful to the concern for rendering truthful interpretations of the text. Adding to this the 'guidelines of a tradition', a cast and crew engage in performance interpretation as a way of rendering an embodiment of the text.[72]

Taking the performance rehearsal for our metaphor sheds some light on the temporal location of the Christian between Scripture and the eschatological performance yet to come. To say that our Christian situation is an ongoing rehearsal that anticipates a performance at the resurrection has nothing to do with the attitude that 'this world is not my home, I'm only passing through' as the revival hymn goes: it has everything to do with recognition that what we do here and now defines the shape of eschatological performance. It is also highly valuing of time and space as our cosmic stage, as well as of the incarnate means we are given to act in it. Finally, the embodied performance interpretation called for by the biblical play, far from involving us in abstractions of meaning from the story, 'leads to and is continued in an embodied performance: the event of worship and of life'.[73] Wolterstorff's reticence is appropriate for pointing out that putting the text through rehearsal and performance may not result in 'verbal truth claims about what the discourser says'.[74] Nevertheless

---

69   'For as many of you as were baptized into Christ have put on Christ' (Gal. 3.27); 'Let us walk properly ... put on the Lord Jesus Christ...' (Romans 13.13, 14).

70   Craigo-Snell, 481.

71   Ibid, 482.

72   The primacy of the body (and its senses) as agent of performance interpretation is explored in actor Diane Borsato's essentially text-less theatrical pieces 'staged' *in situ* on the streets of Montreal. In *Touching 1,000 People* and *Describing/Recognizing the Taste of Love* (October 1999) Borsato casts herself as artistic *amateur*, as actor and lover, not unlike what von Balthasar has in mind for the theologian's continual self-giving to God in the theological task.

73   Craigo-Snell, 482.

74   Ibid, 489.

if 'the fullness of meaning is located at the point where the narrative of the script and the life of the community become the same story in the event of performance', then a theo-dramatic hermeneutic can show something of the telic sense of the Gospel through our faithful rehearsal of Christian praxis in the world.[75] The theological-dramatic framework of interpretation therefore assumes Wolterstorff's preference for authorial-discourse and retains 'an appreciation for both authorial-discourse interpretation and performance interpretation by identifying discourse interpretation as one aspect within the larger performative process'.[76]

4. Theology and Theatricality

In our search for an interpretive structure that is faithful both to theology and to its theatrical analogue we have focused on rehearsal and performance as paradigms for embodiment of a text. Prompted by von Balthasar's development of the theo-dramatic solution to the epic theological approach and its disinterested objectification of God, as well as to the subjectivity of the lyrical encounter with Scripture, we looked for a hermeneutic internal to God's performance in the world and to man's consequent answerability. To that end, Kevin Vanhoozer and Shannon Craigo-Snell deploy their own theological-dramatic methods. Vanhoozer identifies the theo-drama namely with the linguistic epistemology that to speak is to act and considers how the speech-text of Scripture comes to life in performance interpretation. His move, however, was seen to bypass the articulations of dramatic interpretation in favour of performance as the telic element in the play-act; it was also shown to be overly reliant on the cognition of meaning inherent to speech theory. Craigo-Snell, for her part, proved to be a more attentive apprentice of the theo-drama by locating performance interpretation in the plurality of actions that make up the theatrical process. Her theological drama makes itself at home in the 'already/not yet' quality of a performance in rehearsal, subject to faltering, correction, and reinterpretation, all the while edging towards an authentic, eschatological debut. Both Vanhoozer's adoption of performance interpretation and Craigo-Snell's internal approach to the theatre, however, have gone some way in testing the dramatic method and its validity for theological interpretation.

We might, at this point, begin to anticipate a more vigorous theological interaction with theatre than has been possible thus far. Despite the theatre's well-established history, much of it in contention with the church,[77] it is, relatively speaking, a new

---

75 Ibid, 489.
76 Ibid, 490.
77 Not entirely without reason: 'By the time Christianity arrived, there was little left [of the Greek theatre] but a noisy, popular entertainment; it was principally coarse and lewd and often cruel, so that even the pagans themselves turned away from it. All the same, at the time of Tertullian there was not only the vulgar, unchaste *mimus* but also the more humane comedy; tragedy still dealt with the ancient myths. [...] But whether the passions were stirred up by nobler or more crude spectacles, whether it was artificial or real blood that flowed,

and developing phenomenon. In point of fact, the theatre to which Vanhoozer and Craigo-Snell refer, and much of what von Balthasar has in mind, is principally the stage of the last hundred or so years. This theatre, defined, above all, by the appearance of the theatrical director towards the end of the nineteenth century, the rise of 'total design' aesthetics and the idea of 'performance interpretation' in service of the overall composition, at least in our contemporary understanding, do not apply to the classical incarnations of the theatre (or to Shakespeare's stage for that matter).[78] More to the point, however, there is little evidence that this recently evolved theatre has been given theological account as one of God's gifts for mankind's creative enjoyment and knowledge of God. This is not to say that Christians have not written for, performed in and enjoyed the stage but to point out that the church, owing partly to Augustinian heritage (see below)[79] has seldom valued the theatre beyond its utilitarian role: for portraying clearly definable biblical themes, for example. Von Balthasar's own verdict on the matter goes much further:

> Looking back as a theologian at the thousands of attempts made since medieval times to present the dramatic content of Christian revelation on the stage [...] it can be said without exaggeration that none of this has had a fruitful influence on systematic theology. No theological textbook has found it worthwhile to refer to the names of Shakespeare or Calderon.[80]

Seen in this light, von Balthasar's work represents a major shift in the theological perspective on theatre and warrants continuing revisions of the kind. One such 'theo-dramatic' revision is at work in James K.A. Smith's[81] reworking the Augustinian critique of the theatre *through* Augustine's own 'affirmations concerning the goodness of creation and the centrality of the Incarnation'.[82] Citing Augustine's intent in the *Confessions* to 'move the reader' towards the love of God, Smith sees an opening for a theological dramatics within Augustinian doctrine.[83] For, however much Augustine may have opposed theatrical representations and the images they

---

the lower nature was unleashed. [...] Thus, in campaigning for a natural ethical dimension – inner peace of mind and spiritual discipline – the Christian writers are in fact continuing the expressions of protest voiced by pagans.' TDI, 89–90.

78   Carlson, Marvin, *Theories of the theatre: a historical and critical survey, from the Greeks to the present* (Ithaca & London: Cornell University Press, 1993), 302–77. On the rise of the director, cf. David Bradby and David Williams, *Directors' theatre* (Basingstoke: Macmillan, 1988), 1–23.

79   On that score, we might also speak of Tertullian's pervading influence: see Marie Turcan, *Les Spectacles: Tertullien* (Paris: Les Editions du Cerf, 1986).

80   TDI, 125.

81   James K. A. Smith, 'Revisioning Augustine's Critique of Theatre', in *Literature & Theology*, 15:2, June 2001, 123–39.

82   Ibid, 124.

83   'That the *Confessions* are intended to affectively 'move' the reader at all [sic.] indicates that what is at stake is not being passionate *per se*, but rather *what* passions are stimulated and to what *end*. But this intended *telos* will be precisely the grounds for

project,[84] to say nothing of the emotive pull they have for the proselyte writer, he nonetheless affectively engages his readers through a thoroughly dramatic and vividly imaged account of his struggles in the faith. In principle, for Augustine, theatrical images and the emotions they incite in the viewer are but mimetic tokens of reality and therefore fraudulent.[85] Smith, however, makes a case for appreciating the *Confessions*' own emphasis on *intentio*, Augustine's 'iconographic' writing being justified in that it has love and knowledge of God as its chief end.[86]

> In this sense, Augustine's own life is a drama which engages the 'audience' in a way that follows the ordo amoris: the staging of [sic] his story in the Confessions is not intended to be enjoyed as an end in itself but rather a means by which the reader's heart is affectively moved to seek God.[87]

Clearly, it makes a difference whether theatre turns intentionally outward towards God or whether it is allowed to fold in on itself (i.e., art for art). And although Smith somewhat misses the mark in urging a Christian understanding of dramatic performance as 'animated iconography' (the idea of moving icons being more ontologically suited to film than to the stage), he rightly observes that theatre communicates *through* image and does not (necessarily) *intend* imagery as an end in itself. The theatrical production, therefore, 'can have an iconic function which points the audience beyond the production to God'.[88] He then raises the obvious question: 'if the literary work of the *Confessions* can be redeemed by arousing passion to an alternative end (*fruitio Dei*), could we not see the same possibility for theatre?' Is it possible, in other words, to conceive of a theatre whose images direct us towards knowledge and enjoyment of God?[89] The question, I would conclude, can only be raised inasmuch as the theologian takes a serious interest in theatre. Certainly, it urges a far more eloquent and insightful dialogue than even my articulation would make evident. Its leading brings us out of that 'unbroken, but also unreflected and uncritically accepted, tradition' of theological suspicion towards the theatre.[90] It presses the theological amateur of the stage toward an exchange between church and theatre which, far from being provisional, helpfully advances the intent in von Balthasar's own theological-dramatics. For to do otherwise would be to betray the dramatic elements in theology as well as the theological possibilities for theatre implied therein.

---

deconstructing Augustine's critique of theatre in the name of a more consistently Augustinian account.' Ibid, 134.

84   'In *De civitae dei*, Augustine points to theatre as a 'Greek corruption' which infiltrated Rome.' Ibid, 135.

85   Ibid, 126.
86   Ibid., 124–25.
87   Ibid, 132.
88   Smith, 132–33.
89   Ibid, 133.
90   TDI, 104.

Chapter 3

Can an Act be True? The Possibilities of the Dramatic Metaphor for Theology within a Post-Stanislavskian Theatre

Joshua Edelman

How can Christian theologians best make use of the theatre as a tool for understanding? There are differing views. In his effort to build a Bible-based, 'postconservative' Christian theology, Kevin Vanhoozer takes up speech-act theory to understand the nature of divine communicative action in Scripture, and sees theatrical performance as a promising and helpful metaphor for the theologian's task.[1] (He began this task in an essay in 2000 and significantly developed it in his 2005 book, *The Drama of Doctrine*.[2]) From a very different place on the theological spectrum, Max Harris offers that we will be better able to understand Jesus's earthly life if we see it to be 'through and through theatrical, and that the theatre, at its most joyous, occupies common ground with the Incarnation.'[3] I am in no position to comment on either Vanhoozer's or Harris's theology as such, but I do share their interest in the theatrical metaphor for the religious life. However, the metaphor has not yet not been fully developed. Vanhoozer, despite the magnitude of his project, appeals to a very specific conception of the nature of theatre and performance more generally, and I will argue that this unduly restricts the relevance of the metaphor for his theology. This chapter's project, therefore, is to explore the metaphorical reflection in the theologian's work that results from some of the major currents in theatrical thought of the second half of the twentieth century.

Without such updating, theologians' use of the theatrical metaphor will, I suggest, both fail to realize its full potential and remain vulnerable to strong criticisms from the theatre itself. As an example, take Vanhoozer's use of *The Empty Space,* a well-

---

1 Kevin Vanhoozer, 'The Voice and the Actor,' in *Evangelical Futures: A Conversation on Theological Method,* ed. J.G. Stackhouse (Grand Rapids: Baker, 2000), cited hereafter as 'Voice.'

2 Kevin Vanhoozer, *The Drama of Doctrine: A Canonical Linguistic Approach to Christian Theology* (Louisville, Ky.: Westminster John Knox Press, 2005), cited hereafter as *Drama.*

3 Max Harris, *Theatre and Incarnation* (London: Macmillian, 1990), x.

chosen and extremely important contribution to the contemporary Anglo-American understanding of the theatre by Sir Peter Brook.[4] 'Brook's discussion reveals an uncanny resemblance between different types of theatre and their theological counterparts,' writes Vanhoozer, who then describes and draws the theological analogy to each of Brook's 'types,' deadly, holy, and vital (or 'immediate') theatre, concluding that his project, 'evangelical theology[,] serves the church by assisting it to become a holy and vital theatre once again.'[5]

Vanhoozer's language implies that Brook's aim is a 'holy and vital' theatre proper.[6] That, however, is not what Brook wrote. His book spends a chapter each on *four* types of theatre, not three. Though he has a good deal of admiration for the holy theatre, he rejects it as unfeasible; his goal is the immediate theatre alone.[7] The only other type which nearly approaches it is not the holy but the *rough* theatre: an amateurish, bawdy catch-all of 'back rooms, upstairs rooms, barns; the one-night stands, the torn sheet pinned up across the hall.'[8] Neither Vanhoozer's initial article nor his subsequent book make any mention of the thirty pages Brook spends on the rough theatre. If, though, he were to acknowledge the esteem Brook has for the rough theatre, he would likely have a much more difficult time maintaining his analogy. Vanhoozer's problem is more than just the lewd, amoral tendencies of popular theatre that have earned it the ire of churchmen since Collier.[9] Rather, he invests his analogy in a certain phenomenological view of the theatre which is incapable of seeing the rough: a form of wisdom-in-action ('phronesis') which comes from a disciplined, thoughtful, and above all *deferential* interpretation of a given Text. Thus he consciously contrasts his 'receptive' or 'canonical' view of correct interpretation

---

4   Sir Peter Brook, *The Empty Space* (New York: Touchtone, 1968).

5   Vanhoozer, 'Voice,' 101-103.

6   In *Drama,* Vanhoozer modifies this point a bit, writing that 'Brook's own preference is for 'vital' or 'immediate' theater,' but connecting that preference two seconds later to Richard Schechner's attempts at 'recovering the ritual roots of theater common to all cultures' – a project that Brook could not but connect to Grotowski and the holy theatre. Vanhoozer, *Drama,* 406.

7   See Brook, 60ff. He notes that the holy theatre is not just unpopular but unwatchable by nature. It makes no space for the audience. The three Holy Theatre artists he most admires, Merce Cunningham, Jerry Grotowski, and Samuel Beckett, 'almost as a condition, [create] theatres for an *élite* ... Grotowski plays for thirty spectators – as a deliberate choice. He is convinced that the problems facing himself and the actor as so great that to consider a larger audience could only lead to a dilution of the work.' (60) Vanhoozer is correct to cite Brook's lament that 'we do not know how to celebrate,' (Brook 47, Vanhoozer, 'Voice,' 102) but he seems to miss the fact that it is in the rough theatre, not the holy, where a solution to this problem can be found. 'It is always the popular theatre that saves the day,' writes Brook in opening his chapter on the rough theatre (65).

8   Brook, 65.

9   Jeremy Collier, *A Short View of the Immorality and Prophaneness of the English Stage* (London: S. Kelbe, R. Sare and H. Hindmarsh, 1698; see the modern version edited by Benjamin Hellinger, New York: Garland, 1987). Of course, there are countless others who make a similar claim right up to the present day.

('be[ing] obedient to the text,'[10]) with the 'Performance II' interpretation which, he charges, gives too much authority to traditions of reception, 'casting asunder ... authors and their authority.'[11] That Authoritative Author's text, in turn, is a single drama wholly organized by and in service to one great and unitary Divine Plot. Brook's rough theatre, in contrast, is 'freed of unity of style' – it does whatever it must to get the job done.[12] This muck and muddle, though, is not an imperfection; it is its nature. 'If we find that dung is a good fertilizer, it is no use being squeamish,' writes Brook. 'If the theatre seems to need a certain crude element, this must be accepted as part of its natural soil.' Without that acceptance, surely, the theatrical analogy will not hold up long for theologians' use.

Harris does better, in a way, finding the theatre-to-theology analogy not in the structural unity of the dramatic form (which is oft-violated and Aristotelian, anyway), but in the performative nature of the theatrical medium. So theatre's 'licentious' way with time and space has theological ramifications, the difficulty of pure abstraction onstage and the constructive role of the audience can help us with our Christology, and so on. He does a good job of identifying genuine theatrical structures that can be found in almost all theatre out there and are a constitutive part of what theatre actually is – that is, he does not distort – but one may fairly bring up the argument against any all-embracing theoretical structure here. Individual performances sometimes find themselves sacrificed on the altar of the theatrical Platonic Form. Harris does use a good number of clear analogies to specific performance texts, and, still more helpfully, a number of counteranalogies to plays that propose un-Christian metaphors (the work of Anton Artaud, mostly, and T.S. Eliot's *The Cocktail Party),* but because there is still cultural resistance to the use of theatre as a metaphorical way of doing theology, he needs to establish the relevance of the medium of theatre as a whole before he can analyze particular statements within that metaphorical medium.[13]

Harris's ongoing work seems fruitful to me because he is willing to separate out tendencies inherent to the practice of theatre-making from the stylistic tendencies imposed on the theatre of a particular time and place by tradition. He is careful to keep his analogy focused on the former, not the latter. Vanhoozer's approach, by comparison, does not always draw this distinction clearly, and thus builds analogies on relatively unsure cultural ground. It would obviously be quite unfair to expect him to be familiar with such recent theatrical theory as Hans-Theis

---

10 Vanhoozer, *Drama,* 448.
11 Vanhoozer, *Drama,* 176.
12 Brook, 67.
13 Harris's second book, *The Dialogial Theatre* (New York: St Martin's Press, 1993), does start to take up specific examples and case studies and with fascinating results, particularly in regards to post-Conquest drama in Mexico and post-Inquisition drama back in Spain. But his concern in this latter book is still a theatrical genre: so-called 'dialogical' plays. This is important work and this genre as a whole does have important theological contributions to make, but the work is still preparatory for a study of individual performed texts as statements of their own.

Lehmann's *Postdramatic Theatre*,[14] but in practice he pays too little attention to some considerable currents in the last half-century of theatrical development (the rise of the *auteur*-director at the expense of the playwright, for instance). When the only productions *The Drama of Doctrine* mentions from the past fifty years are a pair he cites as 'cautionary examples of performances that were so intent on being relevant that they ran roughshod over the playwright's intent,'[15] one cannot help concluding that Vanhoozer's analogy is not so much to theatre-as-such as to a particular *understanding* of how to perform plays, one every bit as dependent on culture and traditions of use as the Lindbeckian 'cultural linguistic' theology he himself is debating. To be fair, to a certain degree Vanhoozer is quite explicit about this: in *The Drama of Doctrine,* he offers a (rather brief) critical assessment of the theatrical proposals of Augusto Boal, Antonin Artaud, and Jerzy Grotowski, explaining what is 'theologically correct' about them and the ways in which each ultimately 'falls short.'[16] But these are brief digressions that never really rise to an acknowledgement of, much less engagement with, modern theatre's internal debate over what it is and what it does. By and large, in other words, Vanhoozer takes a certain *view* of the theatre to *be* the theatre without, perhaps, acknowledging the full impact of the fact that he is doing so.

Vanhoozer sees a specific link between Christian sanctification and the 'System' of actor training developed by Constantin Stanislavski.[17] At one level, this makes a good deal of sense: Stanislavski is indeed the major theorist of the theatrical model Vanhoozer has in mind. At another level, though, the link is quite startling, as Vanhoozer's analogy is thus not to the great *works* of the Stanislavskian theatre (the Chekhovian canon, in particular) but to a dramatic *pedagogy*. In fact, for his project's own purposes, this is an extremely apt decision on Vanhoozer's part: the sole dramatic text (he would say 'script') with which Vanhoozer is concerned is the Bible. The Biblical canon serves as a theological given, the starting point from which the Christian lives her life. Vanhoozer's insight is to describe that living in performative terms: doctrine as 'direction,' the church as a 'company,' and so on.[18] Theatre scholars would ascribe this analogy as being not to drama (a play's script or

---

14 See Hans-Theis Lehmann, *Postdramatic Theatre,* trans. Karen Jürs-Munby (New York: Routledge, 2006).

15 Vanhoozer, *Drama,* 259. Quite a number modern playwrights do not see themselves as having an intent over which a director *could* run roughshod. 2004 Nobel Prize winner Elfriede Jelinek, for instance, famously gave the director her script *Bambiland* to the director Christoph Schlingensief for its premiere with the comment, 'Machen Sie damit, was Sie wollen' – just do with it whatever you want.

16 Vanhoozer, *Drama,* 404-406. Interestingly, he never actually points out what is wrong with Boal's Theatre of the Oppressed, though he keeps it at a good arm's length from an embrace.

17 Vanhoozer, 'Voice,' 96. and *Drama,* 369. To his credit, he does not overstate his claim, writing only that the System 'bears more than a passing resemblance' ('Voice') or 'is surprisingly relevant' (*Drama*) to sanctification.

18 Vanhoozer, *Drama,* xii and 102.

narrative) but to theatre (the total event) or even performance (what the actor does onstage), though they might notice that in his string of analogues (Bible as script, God as Playwright, Christian as performer, doctrine as direction, and so on), the audience is notably absent. One could imagine the non-Christian world, perhaps, as the audience for the Church's performance, but when he calls for 'audience participation,'[19] this is presumably not what Vanhoozer has in mind. We will return to this question.

The term 'dramatic,' then, is used variously in *The Drama of Doctrine*. Sometimes it simply means 'exciting,' not 'dull.'[20] At other times, it refers to the kind of language that gives rise to performance and, by analogy, Christian living: 'a matter of signs and speeches ...involving speech and action ... [and] overcom[ing] the theory/praxis dichotomy.'[21] This use harks back to the term 'performative' from J.L. Austin's speech act theory, but unlike Austin, who considered theatrical speech illegitimate because of the fictional nature of dramatic role-playing, Vanhoozer has no qualms about using the performance metaphor to describe 'the way of living truthfully.'[22] This is because there is nothing fictional or duplicitous about the particular drama he has in mind: the Bible. That dramatic Text is not really the object of his analysis, largely because he believes that in a critical sense the Bible *ought not be* subject to such human judgments: rather than relying upon our own interpretive practices and traditions, we need to read 'Scripture as used by God.'[23] Again, we are not called to *figure out* what Scripture means; our task is rather to opt for the 'divine author's' meaning *over against* 'the church's.'[24] Vanhoozer puts it very clearly: 'Whose play is it? God's. Why does it matter? Because there is no other gospel; one is either in God's play or in a drama of one's own making.'[25] Vanhoozer's question is therefore at a different level: how ought this text to be *performed,* after it has been received? This is the move that inspires his metaphorical engagement with Stanislavski's acting theory. The content of that theory will in turn have its ramifications for his theology.

1. Stanislavskian and Post-Stanislavskian Theatre

Constantin Stanislavski (1863-1938) remains the sole systematic theorist of the art of modern theatrical acting. While his techniques are rarely used today without some

---

19   Vanhoozer, *Drama,* 16.

20   'The gospel... is intrinsically dramatic. Why is it, then, that Christian doctrine so often appears strikingly dull...?' Vanhoozer, *Drama,* xi.

21   Vanhoozer, *Drama,* 17, 15, and 16. Part of the problem with this double sense is that it can be hard to understand what Vanhoozer means when he condemns certain ways of reading the Bible (as a list of propositions, for example) as 'undramatic.' Vanhoozer, *Drama,* 20.

22   Vanhoozer, *Drama,* 15.

23   Vanhoozer, *Drama,* 17.

24   Vanhoozer, *Drama,* 184.

25   Vanhoozer, *Drama,* 183.

refinement, no alternative systematic pedagogy of acting has yet been developed. His influence has always been greatest in his native Russia and the English-speaking world, despite the serious linguistic and legal problems surrounding the translation of his work.[26] Through a system of exercises making use of the body's physical and emotional abilities and memories and the given circumstances of the script, Stanislavski's System is a means by which an actor can use the rehearsal process to build a character that is both as *true to life* and as *beautiful* as possible. Stanislavski is explicit: 'The fundamental aim of our art is the creation of this inner life of a human spirit, and its expression in an artistic form.'[27] Though the System itself makes much use of circumstances given by an individual script, it is intended as a universal process; a Systematic actor ought to go through the same basic steps for any role she performs, and the goal of actor training should be the cultivation of a set of skills which can be applied in *any* theatrical setting.

Two common misunderstandings need to be avoided here. First, the System does not simply attempt the re-creation of a 'real' human being who just happens to live on a stage. That, Stanislavski says, is both impossible and unnecessary. 'When you reach the point of playing Hamlet' and get to the point of killing Claudius, he asks rhetorically, 'will it be important to you to have a life-size sword in your hand? If you lack one, will you be unable to finish the performance?'[28] Often, those who would characterize the System as pure psychological naturalism neglect the intense and far from natural physical exercises (about breathing and muscle tension, for example) that Stanislavski enjoins on his students. The 'sense of truth' which is so important for the System is not so much a means as an end.

This relates to the second misunderstanding, which conflates Stanislavski's System and the techniques developed by his student Lee Strassberg at the Actors' Studio in New York, known as the 'Method.'[29] Roughly speaking, the Method seizes on Stanislavski's concept of emotional memory to claim that no emotions can be authentically portrayed onstage unless the actor herself can recall them from her own life. One cannot play a jilted lover, then, unless one has actually been romantically jilted at some point in one's own life. To most Systematics, this is a step too far, and it leads to a deeply unhealthy model of the actor's way of life. While Stanislavski certainly advocates using one's personal life (his term is 'emotion memory') in order to make a character truer-to-life, he does not conflate the actor and character, as the Method seems to; instead, he wants the character to be a fully-realized human being *on the model of* the actor herself, a phrase that remains ambiguous in Stanislavski's writings. He talks about the complex interrelationship between physical gesture and

---

26 For more, see Jean Benedetti, 'A History of Stanislavski in Translation,' *New Theatre Quarterly* 6:266 (August 1990).

27 Constantin Stanislavski, *An Actor Prepares* , trans. from the Russian by Elizabeth Reynolds Hapgood (London: Geoffrey Bles, 1937), 14.

28 Stanislavski, 43.

29 See, in particular, Lee Strassberg, *A Dream of Passion: The Development of the Method* (Boston: Little, Brown, 1987).

psychological intention, each with the ability to provoke the other. The goal is always honesty of emotion, but in order to achieve this – and particularly to replicate it, performance after performance – the actor must 'have hold of something substantial' or she will fall into 'the temptation of mechanical acting.'[30] That something is concrete, pre-planned physical gesture. 'Come to the tragic part ... gradually, and logically, by carrying out correctly your sequence of external physical actions, and by believing them,' advises Stanislavski.[31] It is a catalogable series of physical actions, and yet it is to be *believed*. It is this element of faith, basic to the System, which the Method is picking up on: the recognition that the only way an actor can build an authentically human character is to use her real self as a model.

This is perhaps the most problematic point in Stanislavski's work. The System does not simply aim actors towards performances that *seem* authentically human, noetically. It asks, rather, that these performances *be* authentic, ontologically (without, of course, a philosophically sophisticated explanation of what performative truth is or how it is possible). The spokesperson for the 'mechanical' style of acting in *An Actor Prepares* is Grisha, the technically gifted student who acts with no inner feeling. Stanislavski sums up his criticism of Grisha's acting, which he acknowledges is very beautiful:

> Your make-believe truth helps you represent images and passions. My kind of truth helps to create the images themselves and to stir real passions. The difference between your art and mine is the same as between the two words *seem* and *be*. I must have real truth. You are satisfied with its *appearance*.[32]

Here is the paradox on which Systematic acting rests: the artificially given circumstances found in the script and in the process of character development can lead to 'real truth,' by means of what Stanislavski calls the 'magic *if.*' With this 'if,' and with an important but unstated fundamental self-recognition the actor finds in the character, performances that are at best an iconic signifier impressed on the body of the actor can become, for that same actor, true. Truth is an emotional, functional, but not a logical category here – Stanislavski is an educator, not a metaphysician – but the paradox is still very real. The actor is *consciously aware* of the unreality of the magic *if* and that she is not who she is pretending to be, and yet 'what is going on inside [her]' truly can and must be what is going on inside the character. This is the paradox that Strassberg could not accept, and so the Method denies that there can be any real distinction between character and actor. Systematics endeavor to maintain the distinction despite this fundamental self-recognition, but they must do so paradoxically.[33]

---

30 Stanislavski, 150.
31 Stanislavski, 150.
32 Stanislavski, 157.
33 The complication is that Method-ists see themselves as the true heirs to the Stanislavskian mantle, and thus claim that the master himself believed in the fundamental identification of actor and character. They do this largely by citing Chapter 9 of *An Actor*

Vanhoozer, too, rejects this paradox. 'Like good actors, we have to learn not simply how to play-act a role but rather *to become the role we play,*' he writes in a strong echo of Strassberg.[34] Vanhoozer's exclusive use of the drama of canonical scripture, though, gives him a rather different way of replacing the magic *if:*

> Christians should think in terms of an eschatological '*is*': not '*if* all the world were the stage for the coming kingdom of God' but rather '*since* the world is already/not yet the stage for the coming of God's kingdom…'[35]

Perhaps further development of this fascinating eschatological allusion (already/not yet) might go some way to opening up genuinely *different* possibilities for Christian performance; it would also dovetail nicely with recent trends in theatre that focus on the performance's incompleteness. As it is, his understanding of Christian faithful performance of a canonical Script requires Vanhoozer to conclude, citing Galatians 3:28, that all Christians are called on to play essentially the same role.[36]

Properly understood, then, the System is a formal, psychological, but fundamentally pragmatic system of pedagogy for the actor. It was not intended to be a phenomenology of the theatre. But the means by which actors are trained cannot be independent of the theater they are being trained for. So even if Stanislavski did not acknowledge that he had a phenomenology of the theatre, we can legitimately see one in his work. This is far from surprising: like all literary creations, Stanislavski's System was, in large part, a product of its environment: the aesthetic and literary world of pre-revolutionary Russia. Were he a novelist, Stanislavski would be called a high modern: he has a very exalted view of the individual creative mind and its role in the theatrical enterprise. As a theatricalist, this attitude led Stanislavski to focus his work on the actor's private psychology and to take for granted the availability

---

Prepares, called 'Emotion Memory,' where Stanislavski discusses the idea that the seed of all emotions an actor portrays onstage must be emotions he has actually experienced in his own life. The actor's task, then, is to develop his ability to (a) store and remember emotions and (b) recall them in the proper sequence and time. One can only recall one's *own* feelings, and in that sense, one must '*always act in your own person, as an artist .... Always and for ever, when you are on the stage, you must play yourself.*' (Stanislavski, 177, italics in source.) But this notion is nuanced considerably, first, by the importance of given circumstances which will determine what you extract from the experiences '*which have been smelted in the furnace of your emotional memory*' (177, italics in source), and second, by the imagination's ability to transform the sympathetic emotional response of the spectator into the active emotion of the participant, which occurs '*spontaneously.*' This is, then, far from the reproduction of lived emotions in a dramatic context; it is, however, an acknowledgement that the fundamental building-blocks of emotional experience must come firsthand, even if them must be smelted together and transformed before they are ready to be used onstage.

34 Vanhoozer, *Drama,* 366. The italics are Vanhoozer's. His misidentification of this view as Stanislavskian comes a few pages later: 'It is not enough to parrot our lines; we have to *live our parts.* This is precisely what Stanislavski teaches.' (*Drama,* 370).
35 Vanhoozer, *Drama,* 374. The italics are Vanhoozer's.
36 Vanhoozer, *Drama,* 368, especially the note on that page.

of certain rather pricey theatrical accouterments – sets, properties, lighting, makeup, costume, a beautiful auditorium, and so on – that are rarely available to young theatre students today. When Tortsov (Stanislavski's literary alias), wants to get to know his students, he has them perform a few scenes of their own choosing in the main theatre, with full set, lighting, costume, and makeup that seem to simply appear for the occasion. Kostya, the student-narrator of *An Actor Prepares,* thinks nothing of having a make-up man show up on cue to darken his face for Othello. Most exercises are done on the stage and with full set, even with the curtain closed to better simulate a 'real' room. These scenic elements are rarely discussed, and then only when they are *less* than fully realized: when imaginary matches must be used to light a fire in a paper-mache fireplace, for example.[37] They are tangential but essential to the art of acting as the ability of ink to flow onto paper is to the art of novel-writing. A set is necessary to 'help [the actor] to feel her part.'[38]

This is not, as Sartre would have it, simply a matter of the bourgeois economic and political control over the theatre of Stanislavski's day, though certainly without such control such a theatre would have been impossible.[39] This is exactly what one would expect if the point of actor training was to build the casts for Chekhovian naturalism. Naturalism is not the normal state of the theatrical enterprise but a particular development. It required a view of human psychology – and a level of theatrical technology – unavailable before the late nineteenth century. It is also a unique aesthetic taste. Chekhov is most famous for his complex psychological characters; contemporary audiences can find Chekhov hard to watch because his plots revolve around so many mental events and so few physical ones. Historically, the theatre has used both 'rounded' characters and 'flat' ones; rounding everyone was a Chekhovian innovation. It is not coincidental that the main legacy Russian modernism has given to the theatrical world, aside from the plays themselves, is a pedagogical system of characterization.

The effect of this is to put the creation of character at the center of the theatrical enterprise, and to elevate the twin criteria of *beauty* and *truth to life* as the standards by which such creation is to be judged. Many theatricalists have questioned this move on Stanislavski's part, arguing that a different dramaturgical center would make for a more effective and interesting theatre. Critics generally pick a primary weakness of the Stanislavskian approach and build their critiques from there. They remain critics

---

37 Stanislavski, 43.

38 Stanislavski, 180. This is the only explicit discussion of scenic elements in *An Actor Prepares;* it comes in the context of Stanislavski's criticism of scenic designs which, while beautiful, do not 'fit the inner needs of a play' and thus 'lead actors in the wrong direction.' A set needs depth, Stanislavski argues, even if that depth is not visible to the audience, so that the actors have a space in which they 'can move, live, and act.' (182). Note how the design process, like everything else in the theatre, is meant to serve the actor's work.

39 Jean-Paul Sartre, 'Beyond Bourgeois Theatre,' translated by Rima Drell Reck, in *Brecht Sourcebook,* ed. Carol Martin and Henry Bial (London: Routledge, 2000), 50ff. This essay comes from a lecture Sartre gave at the Sorbonne in 1960; the collection will be hereafter cited as *Sourcebook.*

of the System and not builders of systems of their own. I will examine two major examples of post-Stanislavskian theatre: the 'epic theatre' of Bertolt Brecht and the 'anti-Method' of David Mamet and the Atlantic Theatre Company.[40]

One of the most interesting consequences of the System's focus on character-building is the role in which it places its audience. The performance is prepared, and then it is exhibited, but the fact of its exhibition is rarely linked to the means of preparation. In discussing character objectives, a student asks Tortsov if a purely physical objective will be interesting to the audience. Tortsov's advice is, as always, Stanislavski's own: 'Forget about the public. Think about yourself. If you are interested, the public will follow you.'[41] The implication here is that the audience is to *assume the characters' perspective.* Systematics often talk about the audience's 'empathy' for the characters; Stanislavski himself refers to the 'faith' the audience ought to place in the characters; that is, that if the actors are doing their jobs well, individual audience members will discover a commonality between themselves and the characters and will be drawn to follow along with the emotional logic of the performances. Ideally, the audience is emotionally doing the same thing as the characters are; they are mental participants even if physical spectators. But this participation is subservient to the actor's; 'it is necessary that the spectators feel his [the actor's] inner relationship to what he is saying. They must follow *his* own creative will and desires.'[42]

The System requires the audience to fill this role, and the acting process is seriously impaired if they are seen to be doing anything else. In a revealing passage, the young and untrained Kostya shows what can befall an actor who thinks of the audience as *observers:*

> The general appearance of the stage, now that it was lighted, was pleasant, and I felt at home in this room that had been prepared for Othello. By a great stretch of the imagination I could recognize a similarity to my own room. But the minute the curtain rose, and the auditorium appeared before me, I again felt myself possessed by its power .... My fears led me to feel an obligation to interest the audience. This feeling of obligation interfered with my throwing myself into what I was doing. I began to feel hurried, both in speech and in action. My favourite places flashed by like telegraph poles seen from a train. The slightest hesitation and a catastrophe would have been inevitable.[43]

Most performers, of course, freely acknowledge their 'obligation to interest the audience.' Comedians and vaudevillians, in particular, are nourished by the belief

---

40 As a pedagogy, the Mamet system probably has more prominence in the U.S. today than any other school, thanks largely to the Atlantic Theatre Company itself, and Atlantic's ever-popular studio at New York University's Tisch School of the Arts, one of the premier American drama schools. The Brechtian view has fallen out of favor in the States; it still is influential at the Yale Drama School, but far less than it was in decades past. It still enjoys much currency in Continental Europe, though.
41 Stanislavski, 120.
42 Stanislavski, 249, italics removed.
43 Stanislavski, 7-8.

that entertaining the audience is, in fact, their job. Dario Fo finds that the *commedia del'arte* and folk storytelling traditions of his native Italy, particularly the character of the *guillare,* require a very different relationship with the audience. The *guillare,* a kind of traveling satirist-musician, would play characters that the audience was supposed to find ridiculous and absurd: a caricature of the local bishop, say, or a drunkard who mis-hears Jesus's message as one of pure hedonism. Often, there was a social critique embedded in the *guillare*'s performance; he would make fun of things which caused the audience real pain. In *Mistero Boffo,* Fo responds to a lawyer who complains that his jokes about unpleasant current events are more upsetting than funny with the explanation that this was exactly his aim; it was precisely the comedy's bitter aftertaste that enabled it to be socially effective.[44] Fo is explicit that he sees the *guillare* as a pre-Guttenbergian form of the newspaper; a means by which the public can be informed, educated, and persuaded about the events of the day. Of course, the *guillare*'s social satire is neither dryly intellectual or politically neutral; he wants to make his point emotionally and intellectually vivid in the minds of his audience, and he uses all the dramatic resources at his disposal to do so. The audience is expected to be just as emotionally involved as in Systematic drama, but their emotional path is a *reaction to,* or even *against,* that of the character, rather than a *reflection of* it. The success of a performance, then, is not measured by its beauty and truth to life but by the effect it has on its audience.

Fo was an exemplar of this style of theatre, but its great theorist was his colleague, the German Bertolt Brecht (1898-1956). Brecht was a committed Marxist, like Fo, and saw the theatre as a means to serve the ends of social consciousness-raising and education. Though the stage can 'instruct,' according to Brecht, it need not therefore be dull or preachy. 'There *is* thrilling learning, joyous and militant learning. If learning could not be delightful, then the theatre, by its very nature, would not be in a position to instruct …. if it is good theatre, it will entertain.'[45]

By writing 'plays for learning' (*Lehrstück),* Brecht was not abandoning the traditional concepts of plot, character, setting, and certainly not humor, though he did stretch them farther than would have been possible in Stanislavksi's day. Instead, he was asking that the *goal* of theatre be moved to the other side of footlights: from a state of transcendence achieved by the actor to an effect of (self-) transcendence achieved by the audience. Some of his plays are very explicit about the effect that is intended, such as the *Baden Learning-Play of Agreement.*[46] In his better work, however, the audience is not so much spoon-fed a particular moral or political message as it is confronted with a situation and characters over which it is asked to pass judgment. Brecht tried to draw as sharp distinction between his project, which

---

44 Dario Fo, *Mistero Buffo,* translated from the Italian by Ed Emery (London: Metheuen, 1988), 7

45 Bertolt Brecht, 'Theatre for Learning,' translated by Edith Anderson, in *Sourcebook*, 27.

46 *Das Badener Lehrstück vom Einverständnis,* translated by Lee Baxandall, in *Sourcebook,* 89ff.

he called 'epic' or 'didactic theatre,' and the conventional, Chekhovian performance which he called 'dramatic theatre.'[47] In the dramatic theatre, the audience was inclined to 'lose itself in simple empathy, uncritically (and practically without any consequences) in the experiences of the characters onstage.'[48] In contrast, Brecht wanted his epic audiences to respond not as the characters, but as their own selves. In the ideal dramatic theatre, writes Brecht, the audience will respond:

> Yes, I have felt that too. – That's how I am – That is only natural. – That will always be so. – This person's suffering shocks me because he has no way out. – This is great art: everything is self-evident. – I weep with the weeping, I laugh with the laughing.

In contrast, the ideal epic audience will respond like this:

> I wouldn't have thought that. – People shouldn't do things like that. – That's extremely odd, almost unbelievable. – This has to stop. – This person's suffering shocks me, because there might be a way out for him. – This is great art: nothing is self-evident. – I laugh over the weeping, I weep over the laughing.[49]

Directors and theatre critics have often seen Brecht's epic theatre attitude as requiring more work on the audience's part than Stanislavski's naturalistic one. This may or may not be the case. Epic theatre may have all the subtlety of a politician's stump speech, making the audience's intended reaction blatantly obvious. In Brecht's *Galileo,* the scientist is obviously the good guy and we have little choice but to feel the indignity of his persecution. But at its best, epic theatre confronts with a situation which *calls out* for our response, yet we find ourselves unsure of how to do so appropriately. *In the Jungle of Cities* is, in my opinion, one of the finest examples of such a play, though it was written long before Brecht developed his theoretical framework. Both Garga and Schlink are repulsive characters and neither wins our sympathy over the other, but there is something so savage and manifestly *wrong* about their fight that we feel compelled to respond. The simple response of condemnation does not work – there is no obvious villain – and so the audience is led into exactly the kind discussion Brecht wants to encourage: is there something in the *system* of which these two men are a part that deserves our condemnation? As opposed to the response expected to traditional drama, this reaction is intellectual as well as emotional, and it has obvious 'consequences' for the audience in their own real lives.

This is an authentically post-Stanislavskian kind of theatre. I disagree with Eric Bentley, then, that there is no inherent incommensurability between the theatres of Brecht and Stanislavski.[50] Bentley argues that the difference is merely one of emphasis. Brecht was a playwright, and wrote about the construction of scripts, while

---

47 Brecht, 'Theatre for Learning.' This is an acknowledged echo of the Aristotelian distinction between the epic and dramatic forms.
48 Brecht, 'Theatre for Learning,' 24-25.
49 Brecht, 'Theatre for Learning,' 26.
50 Eric Bentley, 'Are Brecht and Stanislavsky Commensurable?,' in *Sourcebook,* 37ff.

Stanislavski was an actor and wrote about character building. The two systems are not incompatible – a Stanislavskian-trained actor could play Brecht, perhaps even well[51] – but both Brecht and Stanislavski have performative phenomenologies on which their writings depend. These phenomenologies are no less firm or important for being implicit or related to the two men's different places in the theatrical process.

Rather than as a radical innovation, Brecht saw his work as a return to the ancient narrative art of performance from which Stanislavskian naturalism was a departure. As befits a good Marxist, he saw the epic theatre as a repudiation of the forms of a bourgeois elite (remember all of Stanislavski's props) and a return to the forms of the people. Dario Fo saw a precursor to his work in the medieval morality play and folk traditions like the *dell' arte*. Brecht used morality plays, as well, especially in the *Lehrstück,* and was also very excited by the American popular westerns and the work of Charlie Chaplin.[52] But intellectually, the development of his theories of epic and didactic theatre owes most to the performance traditions of the Far East, particularly China.[53] It was in discussion of the Chinese theatre that he most fully developed a central property of epic theatre acting; the necessary distancing of spectator from character which he called the *Verfremdungseffekt* – literally, the effect of making foreign, usually translated into English as 'alienation.'[54] Richard Schechner describes the *Verfremdungseffekt* as a 'kind of acting ... where the transformation of consciousness is not only intentionally incomplete but also revealed as such to the spectators, who delight in the unresolved dialectic.'[55] The actor does not exhibit real emotions in his performance; rather, he demonstrates them, performing a set of culturally-established gestures and signs with striking grace which refer to emotion and character iconographically. So the character is much more nearly an artistic *text* we are to read than an ordinary human being with whom we are to empathize. The actor's performance is a language, meant to convey meaning through a cultural sign system.

A concept analogous to alienation, but at the level of the performance as a whole, is 'theatricality,' where instead of (or in addition to) trying to mimetically represent a coherent world, a performance sets its own staged nature out for the audience to understand, acknowledge and respond to. No one ever confused Homer's performed narratives for the events they were portraying, and Brecht is trying to return to a tradition that old when he insists that the meaning of theatre ought not be dependent

---

51 This is the reason for Brecht's list of 'Some of the things which can be learnt from Stanislavski' (reprinted in Bentley, 41-42). Of course there are points of connection: Brecht never developed a systematic theory of acting as Stanislavski did. But I agree with Bentley that this list is a somewhat confusing attempt to paper over the very real differences which do exist.

52 Carl Weber, '*Gestus* and the American Performance Tradition,' in *Sourcebook,* 44.

53 Brecht was also influenced, as many Western theatricalists have been before and since, by the *kabuki* and *noh* theatres of Japan and the *gameln* puppet performances of Java.

54 Bertolt Brecht, 'On Chinese Acting,' in *Sourcebook,* 9ff.

55 Richard Schechner, *Between Theatre and Anthropology* (Philadelphia: University of Pennsylvania Press, 1995), 9.

on their apparent reality. This can be seen clearly in Brecht's approach to setting, recorded in his *Modellbücher* series. Take, for example, his 1948 adaptation of Sophocles' *Antigone*.[56] There is no effort to recreate anything resembling a 'real' place. The stage is bare except for a few chairs, poles, and benches to seat the actors not involved in the current scene. He uses paper masks on wooden sticks and costuming that would have been anachronistic in any time period. There is no sense in which the audience can relate to this space as 'home;' instead, it is a vehicle for the transmission of emotional and intellectual meaning. Stanislavski's audience comes to the theatre to lose itself in the truth and beauty of the characters and situation. Brecht's audience comes to the theatre instead to *find* itself, on the principle that a self-consciously unreal show or demonstration can, by analogy and not identity, help its watchers better understand the truth about their own, very real, lives.

It could be argued that, as Stanislavski wrote about the rehearsal and not performance, the true Stanislavskian 'audience' is an omniscient house of one: the Director. This leads to the second major criticism of the System, that of David Mamet.[57] If, as Vanhoozer alleges, sanctification is something like the System, then Stanislavski is something like God. (Indeed, *The Drama of Doctrine* identifies the director of the Christian drama as the person of the Holy Spirit.) The System requires at its head not just a Director but a Guru, one who understands the nature of the theatrical process and can guide the actor into a performance more authentic, true, and beautiful. The System does not happen spontaneously; it is a creation built for the (artistic) betterment of those to whom it is given. The process is, in a sense, collaborative: the Guru can only create true and beautiful performances through the minds, bodies, and hearts of his actor-disciples. But there is no confusion between master and student. The Director is always present, always aware of what is honest and what is a lie, and what needs to be done to move from pretense to truth. Such an attitude can still be found among prominent directors like Charles Marowitz, who proudly declares that 'the director is a self-obsessed colonizer who wishes to materialize power through harnessing and shaping the power of others.'[58] This extraordinary majesty granted to the director is what Mamet attacks as absurd and unhealthy. Directors are not omniscient, he argues, and they do not know any more about what is going on inside an actor's head than what they can see. He is an ardent phenomenologist, denying the relevance of actors' inner emotions and refusing to consider anything onstage except that which can be seen and heard. Acting need not be anywhere near as difficult as Stanislavski wants it to be, says Mamet. Be loud,

---

56 Bertolt Brecht, *Antingonemodell 1948,* photos by Ruth Berlau, Modelbücher des Berliner Ensemble series, vol. 1 (Berlin: Henschelverlag Kunst und Gesellschaft, 1955).

57 The main source text is David Mamet, *True and False: Heresy and Common Sense for the Actor* (New York: Pantheon, 1997), but this dramaturgy is so anti-System that it eschews the very idea of a systematic treatise on acting. I will call this dramaturgy 'Mametian,' but others call it 'the Atlantic school' or simply 'Atlantic' in recognition that it was developed collaboratively at Mamet's Atlantic Theatre Company in New York.

58 Charles Marowitz, *Prospero's Staff: Acting and Directing in the Contemporary Theatre* (Bloomington: Indiana University Press, 1986), xvi.

clear, and in your light, and the plot will take you along for the ride. All the intricate rehearsal technique of the System is just a way for actors to feel that the job they are doing is actually work and not what it ought to be: play. Actors do not need to understand what they are doing, per Stanislavski, or even understand the effect it will have on the audience, per Brecht: they just need to *do* it. Mametian actors (and directors) have nothing particularly interesting to say about *why* they do what they do onstage: there are neither compelling inner needs to be filled or pointed external meanings to articulate. Instead, there is the story. Actors are there to tell the story as clearly as possible, and not to talk about or make sense of it.

Humility, then, is an essential trait for the Mametian theatricalist. To tell the story, the director need not be a god, and the actor need not be an emotional genius. Aside from this placement of the whole work of theatre in service of the plot, Mamet's theory is more a refutation of those who have come before it than a new pedagogy of acting. It is the closet dramaturgy gets to deconstructionist literary criticism: it asks us to remove the intellectual constructs actors and directors have built up about their craft, and return to the phenomenological fact of enactment as the only real onstage truth. Mamet is more of a heckler than a radical. He treats the Stanislavskian concept of objective (what a character wants to accomplish in a scene), for example, as just as basic to action onstage as the lines themselves, but he has a serious objection to the Stanislavskian notion of superobjective – the single overriding concern that pulls the character through the play. And, in fact, Bella Merlin rightly chides him from his unacknowledged (and likely unintentional) cribbing from Stanislavski's Method of Physical Actions, the technique developed by the Russian master at the end of his career.[59] What Mamet wants is to move the notion of character from the province of the actor's mind to a purely instinctive one over which neither the actor nor the director should attempt informed control.

For a system which sounds so reductionistic, the Mametian approach has been tremendously successful. Even Stanislavski realized that most audiences *want* to see rounded characters, and if the actor does not provide that in his performance, the audience will fill it in on its own.[60] Mamet's own plays and films are emotionally vivid, blunt, powerful, smart, and extremely popular. His work is the opposite of dryly empirical. Eric Bentley's differentiation between Stanislavski and Brecht may also be relevant here: scriptwriting, not acting, has always been the 'clay' with which Mamet works most comfortably. But he still has an inherent phenomenology of the theatre with theological implications. Mametian characters, like Brechtian ones, are not ready recipients of our empathy and do not seem fully real, but Mametian actors do not acknowledge or attempt to manipulate the audience in the way Brecht's so often do. Instead, they place all their focus on what they are doing to each other. For

---

59 See Bella Merlin, 'Mamet's Heresy and Common Sense: What's True and False in '"True and False,"' *New Theatre Quarterly* 16:3 (Aug 2000), 249-254.

60 Stanislavsky, 113: 'They are not carping .... an audience wishes, above all, to believe everything that happen on the stage.'

those of us watching, that action is strikingly compelling, even if unreal and without much in the way of consequences for our own lives.

2. Theological Implications of the Audience and Story

Of course, most theologians are more philosophically sophisticated than to endorse either Brecht's overt Marxism or Mamet's reductionist empiricism fully. But we cannot brush them off as materialists and be done with it. Nor can we simply return to a Stanislavskian dramaturgy. It would not be accepted by today's audiences. We are far better attuned to the ways that the apparently real can be manipulated and filtered than Russian audiences were a century ago. A contemporary theatre which acknowledged the stage's artifice as little as Stanislavski's would strike us as jejune, naive, and irrelevant. Theatres must acknowledge their theatricality, and Brecht has been the main proponent of that in the modern era. Rarely anymore do we either confuse the actor with the character or even attempt to. But in that case, if the dramatic metaphor for theology is to have force today, how should it be conceived?

Vanhoozer's view that there is a *singular* and monovocal tradition of theatrical performance (with only a few eccentrics to disassociate from) makes it much harder for him to answer this question. When he discusses Brechtian alienation, for instance (calling it the 'A-Effect'), he misconstrues it not as an acting technique but as a plot device: not a distance between actor and character but between the action one would expect and a surprising plot twist. This unexpected action is seen as a kind of freedom, and Vanhoozer links it to the Protestant spirit and Shakespearian fools. (So: 'Nothing is more conducive to achieving Brecht's alienation effect than forgiving one's enemies.'[61] True Brechtian alienation would have either the actor or the character forgive, but not the other.) But there is nothing revolutionary about theatrical plot twists; they have been a staple of drama from melodrama to Tennessee Williams. In this view, there is no incompatibility between Brecht and Stanislavski, or, for that matter, Brook. That is, unfortunately, not how theatre has been practiced in the last half century.

The first question to be addressed is that of audience. As noted above, Vanhoozer never specifies precisely for whom his theatrical performance is staged, but in analogy with Stanislavski, the work of Christian living is practiced for the eyes of the Director – in Vanhoozer's analogy, the Holy Spirit. Thus the Christian life is both led by the guidance of God and is performed to the glory of God. The analogy suggests that there is a single capital-M Means – a divinely-revealed superobjective – in accordance with which each of our performances can (in principle if not in practice) be most beautiful and true in the eyes of the Divine Director. Our job is not to discover that means on our own, but to follow God's leadership (particularly as set down in Scripture) and enabling in order more closely to approximate to a perfection that Jesus alone – in the Incarnation – has achieved and can achieve.

---

61 Vanhoozer, *Drama*, 436.

We both perform for a unitary Audience, for whom there can be nothing effective or essentially new in anything we say (after all, it's His text) and we perform a unitary script – the 'theological drama' which is the Bible[62] – in a way that tries to be as faithful as possible to the Playwright's meaning and intention.[63] I don't think this is an inherently unimaginative or uncreative theatre – that there is only one Conclusion to come to certainly does not mean that it takes no creativity to get there – but it is arguably one that does not really serve as a form of communication between people. In the language of the speech-act theory on which Vanhoozer's analogy rests, a System-style performance is a communication which is intended for a particular Audience. In effect, it is a form of prayer. We humans can overhear the prayers of others (or our own) and may learn from them, but they are directed past us, not to us. In that they communicate a meaning, it is one that cannot be received by anyone but God.

Vanhoozer's theatre is so centered on the divine *Tatwort* that is Scripture, though, that it does not seem to leave much space for the imperfections or particularity of the human being – what Brook would call the 'rough.' That is probably a consequence of Vanhoozer's insistence that the Christian drama is a singular great divine communicative act, and not several (it would be hard indeed to maintain that the Christian drama was singular but *im*perfect), and Vanhoozer is certainly right to see a similarity between it and Brook's Holy Theatre. The analogy, though, it might be argued, leads to bad theology for the same reason a Holy production plays gladly to houses of a dozen: it matters not at all to such a theatre if anyone (human) is listening. But what Christians are actually called on to do, surely, is something more complex: the imperative to spread the Gospel *to* imperfect human beings assumes that the audience's presence and activity is of central importance.[64] The preacher's theatre, then, must finally be a Brechtian one: it is a communication *between people*

---

62 Vanhoozer, 64. The full quote is: 'The Bible is not a theological dictionary but a theological drama, and should be used as such.' This point is well developed in *Drama,* where he proposes the model of Scripture as dramatic text as a corrective to the insufficient ideas of Scripture as either the all-propositional 'Hegelian epic' or the too-subjective Schleiermachian 'lyric' views: "Drama combines the inner subjectivity of lyric with the external objectivity of epic .... Drama thus offers an integrative perspective within which to relate propositions, experience, and narrative' (Vanhoozer, *Drama,* 100-101).

63 How we unearth what that intention is (how we can know 'God's use of language', as Vanhoozer puts it [*Drama,* 99]), is a topic he does not address in *Drama.* From his 'canonical-linguistic' approach, one would imagine he would take a Childsean approach, seeing in the Bible's canonical shape a way into the Divine intent. I see this as insufficient, but the topic cannot be addressed here.

64 It will not do to say that Vanhoozer makes a clear distinction between theological reflection, on the one had, and evangelism, on the other. His concept of theology is so bound up with practical, lived wisdom that evangelism would be nonsense if it did not come under the rubric of Vanhoozer's theology. The stated goal 'of canonical-linguistic theology is nothing less than the missing link between right belief (orthodoxy) and wise praxis (orthopraxis): *right judgement* (orthokrisis)' Vanhoozer, *Drama,* 30.

and must be evaluated as such. It should have an effect on his audience, and it must (have the potential to) communicate a novel idea or piece of information to them.[65] And it is not just in formal sermons, of course, that one 'hears' the Christian message: the whole life of a Christian community can be an epic theatrical performance in this sense.

This is nothing new. Whether or not Christians intend the way they live their lives to be taken as a performance in the Brechtian sense, the non-Christian world has always taken them as such. Non-Christians watch the way Christians live, and pass judgments on Christianity as a system on the basis of those actions. Self-proclaimed Christians who appear to act immorally or irresponsibly make the Christian message much harder to accept. It would only make sense, then, for Christians to be aware of this and to cultivate their personal 'performances' in such a way as to make them express the meaning they actually want them to.

What the specific analogy with Brecht can do, though, is to propose a more complex way of conveying Christian meaning than the audience's identification with the characters' deep psychology that was Stanislavski's goal. A preacher does not need us to know every detail of her emotional life to convince us of the truth of what she is saying; her meaning can be *demonstrated* by appeal to the congregation's critical senses, both emotionally and logically. We do not need to identify ourselves with Jesus or the Prophets in order to learn from what they had to say and to change our lives accordingly. Brecht would go farther, arguing that such identification is in fact impossible if what we are to learn from it has anything to bear on our own lives. Christians may disagree here, arguing that the Holy Spirit can, in fact, enable such identification, but that does no harm to the basic point that a convincing performance of Christian ethics can engage audiences as they are, with full critical faculties intact. A Brechtian preacher need not ask her flock to stop being who they are in order to lead them to be someone they are (yet) not.[66]

The most important implication of this – and likely the most controversial one in theological terms – is that if Christian theology is akin to theatre, as Vanhoozer suggests, then Brecht implies that the theologian's personal belief is not directly relevant to her theology. A Brechtian theology judges itself apologetically. That is its *raison d'etre*. It is audience-centered, and cares little what it does for the person creating it. Of course, a person unconvinced by the Christian message would have little reason to spend their time and effort constructing a way for others to be convinced by it. Brecht himself believed his Marxism. But if he had his doubts – and how could he not? – those doubts would not have interfered with his ability to create a meaningful theatre. Because the actor and character are not identified, and

---

65 To say that the Holy Spirit needs to accompany preaching in order for it to be effective is not to fundamentally change this line of argument. Both the Spirit and a Brechtian approach may be necessary conditions without either being sufficient.

66 Ethically, another way of phrasing this distinction is that between 'what would Jesus do' – Jesus replaces the self – and 'what would Jesus have me do' – Jesus informs the self and guides it, even in its own transformation.

because the goal is to affect the audience, not the actor, doubt is not an obstacle for a true Brechtian performance. And as there is always a sense in which a performer watches her own performance, she can become better convinced herself by a performance meant to convince an audience. The understanding comes out of the act of performing, not vice versa.[67]

It was Stanislavski who first claimed that an actor has to live in the emotional world of a character herself before she can perform it truly. The first (of two) postmodern critiques of this view is that performances, like other texts, create meanings at least as much as they express them. So an act can be true: the iconic reference of a performance which could not be conceived of without the iconicity of the theatrical medium can yet be true if the message it has to teach is a valid one. If theology wants to entertain the analogy with theatre in any way, it must accommodate this move. We know the difference between an act and reality, and yet acts can still carry meaning. We can *do* without *belief*; all we need is what is usually referred as, in a truly odd phrase, 'suspension of *dis*belief.' When we watch a play, we do not for a time believe that what we are watching is an actual event. Like Kierkegaard's teleological suspension of the ethical, our disbelief does not disappear; rather, it becomes inoperative for a while as we enter the logical and emotional world of the play. The Brechtian theatre, like all forms of argument or learning, requires no more than that temporary space. This is patently necessary, for most audiences are not willing to give it more until our critical reason and emotional logic are satisfied. A passion play actor who tries to convince us that he *really is* Jesus of Nazareth will inspire nothing but winces. And yet a passion play can still be true; if it could not, the ability to tell the Christian story would have ended with the Twelve.

But that 'suspension of disbelief' might have another function. The second postmodern critique of the Stanislavskian system – one to which the epic theatre is far from immune – is that we do an injustice to the performative nature of actions like theatre when we treat them as pseudo-linguistic communication. Catherine Bell, building on the work of Pierre Bourdieu, has developed this line of argument most clearly in the context of ritual, arguing that the nature of a performative act is that it *does* something before it *means* something.[68] Perhaps the reason disbelief is suspended is that 'belief' is not the operative category. Bell does specifically distinguish her notion of ritualization as a self-differentiated strategy of action from the sort of self-consciously creative expression that the arts have classically seen themselves to be, but it is certainly interesting that she settles on a notion of ritualization as a strategic

---

67 Jewish commentary has made much of the Israelites' response to the first reading of the Covenant at Sinai as an affirmation of action first and understanding second. Upon hearing the law, the people responded 'All that God has spoken, we will do and we will hear' (Exodus 24:7) – doing (*na'aseh*) precedes hearing (*nishma*), not vice versa. The action of covenant comes first, and from that, an understanding of Torah will come. This is one of the reasons for the rabbis' greater interest in *halacha* than what Christians would call systematic theology. On this, see the Talmud, *Shabbos* 88a.

68 Catherine Bell, *Ritual Theory, Ritual Practice* (New York: Oxford University Press, 1992).

practice for the mediation of political or cultural power – not far at all from the Brechtian ideal of revolutionary social change through performance.

Still, the overt manipulations of power in this model may seem to hearken back to the worst excesses of the medieval missionaries. The sovereignty of God might be held to require that a Christian theologian be more humble (faithful to the text, in Vanhoozer's phrase) in her preaching and writing than the Brechtian model seems to permit. Here is where Mamet's anti-Method can provide, if not an alternative to Brecht's approach, at least a corrective to it. Vanhoozer is deeply committed to the truth that 'the Gospel of Jesus Christ [is] normative for faith and life.'[69] Perhaps he would be willing to echo Mamet in saying that it is that Gospel that does the work in the theological enterprise, not the subtle arguments theologians make to appeal to a skeptical audience. The Mametian theologian needs to get out of the way and allow the story to be told. The potency of the Mametian's theatre comes from the immediate, spontaneous, and unpredictable interaction between that story and those who hear it. People will identify with the story even in the absence of any kind of studied emotional reconstruction or planned argumentative strategy. David Brown demonstrates as much in the cases of Catherine of Alexandria and Margaret of Antioch; these two women have relatively sparse emotional detail in their stories and may not actually have lived at all, but their simply-told stories were still focal points for a great deal of medieval piety.[70] In particular, their stories were ways for medieval Christians to relate to Jesus without abrogating their own very different set of, in Stanislavski's terms, 'given circumstances.'[71]

I doubt that this approach can do the difficult work of generating a response to specific theological questions; that might be too heavy a logical task for the Mametian framework to support. And theological conservatives might not be entirely comfortable with the outcome of this way of thinking about the Gospel: historically, Christians have found a bewildering variety of ethical and devotional ideas in the Gospel story as a whole (as, again, the example of the saints in their wide variety makes clear). But if theologians such as Vanhoozer are looking for a dramatic analogy to help describe the place that the Gospels hold in the lives of devout, committed Christians who do not hesitate to talk about their faith, they would be hard-pressed to find a better one than Mamet's dramaturgy, with its iron-clad insistence that the story itself is far, far more important than the person telling it.[72]

---

69 Vanhoozer, *Drama*, note 21, p. 8.

70 David Brown, 'Pattern and particular: Saint and novel,' from *Discipleship and Imagination: Christian Tradition and Truth* (Oxford: Oxford Univ. Press, 2000).

71 Brown, 82: 'The legends grew – at least in some cases – precisely because they were a way of working out what Christ-like sanctity might be like in what had hitherto been uncharted waters, under conditions of life quite different from Jesus' own.'

72 Nor does this move require what to Vanhoozer is an unacceptable move towards Lindbeckian culturalism that ignores the principle that *'neither tradition nor practice can be the supreme norm for Christian theology, because each is susceptible to error'* (Vanhoozer, *Drama*, 22, his italics). If the Gospel itself can have a use and meaning independent of human

Vanhoozer's analogy does hold, but in a much more limited way than he seems to suppose. The Stanislavskian process of character-building is akin to the sanctificatory process of, well, character-building. Vanhoozer suggests that Stanislavski builds his characters out of the text of the script in the way that the virtue-minded Christian builds her character out of the text of the Bible. That may indeed be a helpful analogy in thinking about sanctification, but Vanhoozer hasn't shown us why *this* analogy is a particularly good one, as opposed to, say, the character-formation taking place in a novel-reader's mind.[73] Though he does talk about theology as a phronetic or sapiential task, because Vanhoozer's analogy is not finally to theatrical performance but to the way a performance is *prepared*, the link between live, living theatre and doctrine is unclear.

That leaves an opening for further work to be done. I would argue that a powerful analogy can be made to theology precisely by attending to the performative nature of theatre, rather than turning the stage into an a-temporal, a-physical eternal Ideal (even if a lived, and not a propositional, one). As Max Harris argues, an accurate and helpful theological analogy of theatre must be an *incarnational* one. It needs to rest on those gritty, earthy things that make a script into a play and the Word into flesh: time, space, body, audience, humor, and the creation of meaningful action not despite but through our physical, performed existence in this world.

Bibliography

Catherine Bell, *Ritual Theory, Ritual Practice* (New York: Oxford University Press, 1992).

Jean Benedetti, 'A History of Stanislavsky in Translation,' *New Theatre Quarterly* 6:266 (August 1990).

Eric Bently, 'Are Stanislavsky and Brecht Commensurable?' from *The Brecht Sourcebook,* originally published in *Tulane Drama Review* 9 (1964) 69-76.

Bertolt Brecht, 'On Chinese Acting,' translated by Eric Bentley, and 'Theatre for Learning,' translated by Edith Anderson, both from *The Brecht Sourcebook,* ed. Carol Martin and Henry Bial (London: Routledge, 2000).

———, *Antingonemodell 1948,* photos by Ruth Berlau, Modelbücher des Berliner Ensemble series, vol. 1 (Berlin: Henschelverlag Kunst und Gesellschaft, 1955).

Peter Brook, *The Empty Space* (New York: Touchstone, 1968).

---

tradition and practice – as Vanhoozer asserts it can – there is no reason we have to trace the variety of insights found in Scripture to different traditions or practices of scripture-reading and not, say, to the multiplicity of insights actually present in the canonical text.

73 In fact, Vanhoozer sometimes uses the term 'reader' where his analogy would suggest he use 'actor' or 'performer.' For instance: 'The Fourth Gospel is structures so that by the end the reader, to, is drawn into the trial that has been implicit all along' (Vanhoozer, *Drama,* 24). If the analogy to performance is really that different to the analogy to reading, this ought not be possible.

David Brown, 'Pattern and particular: Saint and novel,' from *Discipleship and Imagination: Christian Tradition and Truth* (Oxford: Oxford Univ. Press, 2000).

Jeremy Collier, *A Short View of the Immorality and Prophaneness of the English Stage,* ed. Benjamin Hellinger (New York: Garland, 1987). Originally published London: 1698.

Dario Fo, *Mistero Buffo,* translated from the Italian by Ed Emery (London: Metheuen, 1988).

Hans-Theis Lehmann, *Postdramatic Theatre,* trans. Karen Jürs-Munby (New York: Routledge, 2006).

Max Harris, *Theatre and Incarnation* (London: Macmillan, 1990).

——, *The Dialogical Theatre: Dramatizations of the Conquest of Mexico and the Question of the Other* (New York: St Martin's Press, 1993).

David Mamet, *True and False: Heresy and Common Sense for the Actor* (New York: Pantheon, 1997).

Charles Marowitz, *Prospero's Staff: Acting and Directing in the Contemporary Theatre* (Bloomington: Indiana University Press, 1986).

Bella Merlin, 'Mamet's Heresy and Common Sense: What's True and False in 'True and False,'' *New Theatre Quarterly* 16:3 (Aug 2000), 249-254.

Eli Rozik, *The Roots of Theatre: Rethinking Ritual & Other Theories of Origin* (Iowa City: University of Iowa Press, 2002).

Richard Schechner, *Between Theatre and Anthropology* (Philadelphia: University of Pennsylvania Press, 1995).

Constantin Stanislavsky, *An Actor Prepares*, trans. from the Russian by Elizabeth Reynolds Hapgood (London: Geoffrey Bles, 1937).

Lee Strassberg, *A Dream of Passion: The Development of the Method* (Boston: Little, Brown, 1987).

Meg Twycross, 'Books for the unlearned,' in *Studies in Drama 5* (Cambridge: CUP, 1983).

Kevin Vanhoozer, 'The Voice and the Actor,' in *Evangelical Futures: A Conversation on Theological Method,* ed. J.G. Stackhouse (Grand Rapids: Baker, 2000).

——, *The Drama of Doctrine: A Canonical Linguistic Approach to Christian Theology* (Louisville, Ky.: Westminster John Knox Press, 2005).

Carl Weber, '*Gestus* and the American Performance Tradition,' from *The Brecht Sourcebook.*

PART 2
Discipleship and the Enactment of Christian Identity

We have already seen that the metaphor of performance brings with it a whole set of suggestive images situating questions about texts (or 'works') and their interpretation within wider patterns of human action: the lives of communities; traditions of thought and practice; the inculcation of appropriate character through forms of training and practice; criteria for measuring the satisfactory completion of some task or set of responsibilities; the identification, realization and transformation of a particular role or identity; and so on. Accordingly, this volume now shifts its focus from the ongoing conversation between theology and theatre as such to consider some concrete instances of how, within the community of the Church, Christian identity or tradition may be thought of as 'performed' more widely in practice; in worship, in the interpretation of Scripture and various practical aspects of discipleship, and in the shaping of a Christian life as a whole. The opening essay by Michael Partridge draws our attention deliberately to the wider picture, reminding us that where religious traditions are concerned, performing, en-acting, is something which goes on unceasingly in everyday life, as well as in consciously staged special 'performances' of one sort or another. By teasing out some of the threads that connect faith, identity, tradition, and responsible activity in a world that is religiously (and in many other ways) plural, and by posing theological questions about how in all this we may be concerned not just with patterns of human action, but also with the creating, revealing and guiding action of God, Partridge offers a broader 'phenomenological' account of religious performance in terms of which the more precisely focused studies that follow it might helpfully be understood. Echoing the recognition that performance (dramatic, musical) is never a matter of facilitating our mere engagement with texts, but has its own distinctive semantic surplus bound up with its bodily manifestations in time and space, Steven Guthrie explores the significance of physical and kinetic dimensions of Christian worship. Bowing down, kneeling, standing, lifting up eyes and hands, clapping, singing, shouting, dancing – these, he suggests, are not incidental to our approach to God in worship, let alone mere metaphors for an essentially 'spiritual' engagement. Rather, such gestures and movements are a vital part of the way in which, as embodied beings, we organize meaning or make sense of what is happening, and, being inseparable from the cognitive dimensions of liturgical meaning-making, are central to the Spirit-directed transformation of our humanity through praise. Reading biblical texts is, of course, central to the performance of Christian faith in every age. The reading – as indeed the writing (since even the inspired biblical author "is not a passive instrument") – of these texts entails the exercise of both skill and responsibility, whether by the novice or the accomplished master. Michael O' Connor's essay introduces us to a *virtuoso* in his account of Cardinal Cajetan's exegesis of Scripture within the context of renaissance humanism, attending in particular to Cajetan's faithful elucidation of the text's essentially literary features – metaphor, narrative, rhetoric – amidst an approach which nonetheless insisted upon and granted priority to its 'literal' sense. From a 'classic' historical performance, Jolyon Mitchell brings us back to the present with a jolt, inviting us to consider what an authentically Christian response to one peculiarly modern phenomenon – the depiction of violence by our news media – might look like. Taking instances from the New Testament as his guide, Mitchell argues that violent news can and should be deliberately 'reframed' in the light of Jesus' death and resurrection, enabling those who identify themselves as Christians to see "our bruised world" differently, and in consequence to act differently in it. Sam Wells also takes ethics as his theme, and directs us again to the world of theatre, taking dramatic improvisation as a way of modelling what a faithful performance of Christian character in the 'unscripted' particularities of individual lives and divergent sets of circumstances might entail. Part Two ends with an exploration by Trevor Hart of the shape of personal identity understood in eschatological terms, correlating it with the theatrical metaphors of the world stage, 'character' and performing a particular 'part' in a scripted drama. Engaging with the thought of Barth, Hick and Moltmann on the nature of eschatological identity, the essay enquires how it might be that, "in our post-mortem existence with God, the broken, distorted and incomplete patterns of particular lives may yet, in God's hands, come to satisfying closure and be rendered fit for our eternal enjoyment, and God's".

Chapter 4

Performing Faiths – Patterns, Pluralities and Problems in the Lives of Religious Traditions

Michael Partridge

If someone speaks of *performances* of a religious faith, we are liable to think of 'dramatic' and perhaps 'artistic' performances: of liturgies, songs and music, painting and architecture. We forget that people are always doing, acting; and we do not observe that it is mostly in everyday life that religious faith is enacted, or performed. That thought can be disturbing! But if we follow it up, persistently and curiously, we can build up a picture of the living of faith in which we recognise the unceasing performances of everyday life – and also such special performances as the making of doctrines, the forming of church institutions, and the excluding of individuals and groups from 'churches' and from communion. In this picture there also come into view parts of the patterns and weave of a faith *tradition*. The myriad performances are made within a tradition, being formed by it and forming it. Two features of this scene are given particular attention here: a. the *diversities* of any faith tradition; and b. the *responsibilities* of a tradition.

1. Encountering and Performing Faith

1. We *encounter* many different faiths, in the world. We encounter them in and through people of those faiths, people who live their faiths and whose lives are permeated and shaped by them. We find faiths in the lives and forms of life of those people; in what they are like as people; in their relationships and communities; and the ways and the histories of the communities.

We *respond* personally to those encounters. Our responses may be superficial: our relationships and dealings with people of faith may be very slight – 'business' or 'tourism', perhaps – and the people and their faith may make little impression on us. Or we may visit (say) temples, mosques, synagogues, churches; we may see services or processions. In that way we may gather some very lively impressions. Lively but not deep – unless our meetings begin to take us into the lives of people, and open up to us what they are, as people. To 'take in' much of a faith, to grasp and find it, to come to know it, we have to live with its people, to share something of their lives. The more we share, the closer and deeper we can get to people of faith, their communities – and their faiths.

The sharing is of course relational. On one side we have: encountering, responding, taking in. On the other side: *enacting* the faith, showing it forth in life, *performing* it. The people we live amongst, and in whose lives we encounter their faiths, are performing those faiths. And we, too perform our faiths; whilst others, sharing a bit of life with us, take in our faiths We can say: every person enacts, performs a faith – their own. And others can and do encounter that faith in the life of the person; they can make something of it; can be affected by it. We may not often be aware of this performance. Mostly, it is tacitly involved in our living – but it is involved.

2. Faith and Tradition(s)

1. So far, our picture takes in individual people – people *of* many faiths. But what *are* these *'faiths'*? Why do we talk about them in this *general* way? This turns out to be a far more puzzling and complex question than is often supposed. From our initial perspective, we might be tempted to ask: why don't we just take it that each person has their *individual faith*, as particular to them as their individual life, and their 'identity' as a person? There is something deeply important about the idea of the individual faith: there is individuality, particularity, in faiths as in people. But the individual faith cannot exist in isolation.

People live in communities. There is more to this than simply living in various particular relationships (though that is part of it). People do things together, and the things they do have common patterns: the patterns of buying and selling; taking meals together; praying; ... So there are common forms in their lives: practices, ways of life, habits, and so on. Life in a community is very intentionally patterned in these many ways; there is a vast network of shared living pursued in shared ways.

The weave of these shared 'ways' and practices is dense, multiply threaded and layered, intricate. Within the ways and weaves of life which we fall 'faiths' we can draw out such bundles of practices as these:

(i) liturgies where distinctive kinds of performances bear special meanings (and provide space for a wide range of experiences);
(ii) festivals and special days, with accompanying practices;
(iii) private and public prayer and/or meditation;
(iv) telling and using stories in distinctive ways;
(v) ways of forming personal lives; 'ethical' ways; and
(vi) patterns for relationships; for social groups, institutions, practices; for political groups, institutions, practices;
(vii) beliefs, and patterns for seeing and understanding things – people, lives, the natural world, and so on.

All this is part of 'a faith'. And in the nature of it, these forms cannot be followed simply by individuals (though individuals do follow them); they are forms of activity of the community.

2. We can speak here of 'traditions'. Religious *faiths* are (amongst other things) religious *traditions*. But the 'tradition' which is (say) a religious faith is a broad shape, covering complexity. There is a kind of historical 'cluster' of a vast (indefinite) number of varied sub-traditions; and of branchings of traditions; and local traditions – right on down to (for instance) family traditions; and to the individual ways of individual people. And this same sort of pattern is to be seen in each of the 'elements' listed earlier. There are, for instance, many different liturgical traditions; local festivals; varying traditions for the practice of prayer/meditation; and so on.

Traditions – including religious traditions – live, and are livingly encountered, in myriad particular people and particular lives. Each person lives their own 'particularised version' of the tradition. In turn, each affects and helps to shape the tradition (though to hugely varying degrees). And the traditions do much to form particular people; and continue, throughout their lives, to provide the forms in which they can live particular lives and be particular people. Traditions, lives, persons: each essentially linked with the others.

These links are all cultivated, and passed on, in the lives of traditions. Innumerable vital patterns for living – and for being a person – are formed (though not completely determined) by imitation and example; by doing as others do, doing 'what is done'; by following customs and practices; and more deliberately and explicitly, by training, teaching, apprenticeship, as higher, more skilled levels are reached. (*Note* that *skills* are multiply involved in all this.) These are the sorts of ways in which traditions are passed on from person to person, and from generation to generation. Faiths are rich, complex traditions, potentially affecting all areas of life; and their patterns are cultivated (explicitly and implicitly) in every area.

3. Let us explore a bit further the complexities of a particular faith tradition: *Christian* tradition. 'Christian tradition' is itself a broad cluster of tradition(s); there is huge internal diversity here. The performance of Christian faith varies from group to group and person to person. Performance of the faith seems incessantly to throw up variations, some of which become branchings and divisions; these may be relatively short-lived, or persist and develop. There is constant yeasting in the tradition, and a growth which tends to be fissiparous and branching, though there are also various kinds of coming together – and various kinds of 'unity'. There are, then, in history, many traditions (or 'sub-traditions') under this broad head of 'Christian', with complex links to one another in time and space. So perhaps we should speak of Christianit*ies*, not Christianity? [And similarly: Judaisms, Islams, Buddhisms, Hinduisms, and so forth] There would be a point to that. But there is also is also use for speaking, at times, simply of Christianity.

Suppose, then, that a person comes to the Christian cluster of traditions and wishes to enter in (for a bit), explore, try out. He or she may well be faced with a multitude of choices – even locally, several Christianities may be available. For there are many possible ways of being a Christian. But how did this variety come about? Why is it there? Some indications have already been given. This is the way people are, and this is the way traditions are.

We can trace the variety-making and hence fissiparousness of Christian traditions back through their histories. What happens when we go further and further back? If the pattern of development begins to look at least partly like a multiple branching from earlier traditions, can't we trace it back to a 'trunk' and even 'roots'? Or (rather differently) to a 'source'?

Christianity is one of the faith-traditions for which this can indeed be done. For it is deeply characteristic of Christian traditions that they all 'refer back' in a distinctive way to certain historical events (and persons), which they treat as 'sources'. And their 'scriptures' are largely concerned with just these events and persons, with the living interpretation of them, with their significance, with their roles in the living of these traditions, and so on. Let us here distinguish three broad 'sections' in the Christian scriptures:

(a) There is the large section which is also the 'founding scripture' for the Jewish people. It is very diverse, but includes some of Jewish history up to roughly the first century before the Common Era.
(b) Then there comes something different (even though it is also strongly continuous with the Jewish tradition that precedes it). The most central, the most dominant, events in forming Christian traditions are those surrounding Jesus of Nazareth: his life, his work, his death by crucifixion, his resurrection and ascension.
(c) Finally, a record of a selection of events for a short period following Jesus' time is included, along with letters and so forth The recorded events are of course continuous with later events – the historical development of Christian tradition(s), of 'Church' and churches, and so forth, up to our time. In Christian (sub)traditions various selections of these later events are given more or less importance, too, as 'formative', and as events to 'hark back' to'. But they do not have the same standing and importance as those selected early events of the 'early Church/churches'; nor do their leading people have the same status.

These are not just 'sources': they are also 'living roots' for a living plant – kept living '*by* tradition'. They play a huge part in forming Christianities. 'Harking back' to them is part of everyday Christian living: the 'scriptural' texts concerning them are read publicly and privately, and intensely studied, used as guides, and so forth; they are used in making public liturgies; they are used to guide private ethics, and social and political forms. And they can be used *normatively*: those who seek to be 'more faithful', 'true to the tradition', and so forth will very often 'hark back' in this norm-seeking way. Fundamental changes are often justified thus.

4. What are we to make of the variety and fissiparousness of Christian traditions? The question, what to make of this phenomenon, turns out *not* to be simply answered by tracing back to sources. We see the same variational and 'fissiparous' tendencies there from the start. The records of the earliest tradition – and, once again, tradition*s*! – even devote quite a lot of space to this. There are four different accounts and interpretations of Jesus' life and work. They share many things, so that readers can (for instance) 'see the same people' in and through them; but they are diverse. In the

book of Acts we read of the beginnings of many sorts of variations and dividings; problems they raised; attempts to solve them. Large parts of Paul's letters are concerned with them.

Significantly, but perhaps unsurprisingly, a good many of the differences arise out of differing interpretations of the character of the sources themselves – and not least, of the central person, Jesus of Nazareth. And there are different ways of using, in faith-life, these sources. So, diversity appears also in the performance of *these* particular tasks of interpretation and use.

We are still left asking: what are we to make of the variations and plurality in Christian (and other religious) traditions? How are they to be viewed, understood, reacted to, coped with, handled, in life situations? And especially, by people who are trying to live well and faithfully in a Christian tradition?

3. Performance and Responsibilities

1. In this weave, we have seen links between religious *traditions* and the *performances* of faith. Let us look more closely.

   (a) We have already seen that performances are not culturally isolated: they take place within traditions, and draw on and are formed by traditions. A priest performs a liturgy in accordance with a liturgical tradition. A kind and generous act (an 'act of charity') is also traditional.

But:

   (b) Tradition does not determine performance. Performances are those of unique people, and they take place in circumstances which are always unique. Within a traditional pattern, there are variations just from one performance to another: flowing from varying circumstances – but also from personal interpretations, improvisations, variations in imagination. Performance is not just traditional, contextual and personal; it is also essentially creative. It is easier to make it so in some areas than it is in others; but the potential is always there. So performance is unlimitedly variable within (and sometimes breaking out of) tradition. Any tradition or sub-tradition has to allow space for that; and here, too, are some of the roots of diversity and plurality.

   (c) Performance is *shaped* and *trained* in the life of tradition. We have already noted the presence and the vital roles of imitation, upbringing, training, apprenticeship, and so forth They build on common human capacities and tendencies. But s*kill* is also deeply involved: the skills of the 'trainee' are being developed and honed. This requires skill on the part of the trainer. There is a lively traffic in skills. For instance: people are shown, helped, taught, guided to pray – with skill; the trainee priest learns to perform the liturgy skilfully.

   (d) Connectedly: performances can be, and are, assessed, appraised, evaluated, criticised, and so on. 'Good' and 'bad' are very general words for this: but large vocabularies of specific evaluative words have built up around each specific area of skill. To take a different field: scientific experiments are well or less well conducted – and assessed for this by 'peers' (trained journeymen of the science). And in faith's field, each strand that we noted has its skills and assessments: we learn to conduct a service properly/

well/movingly – and we may make it dull/boring; we preach or teach well/sensitively/ineffectively; and so on.

(e) So too, performances are *responsible* – and in a number of ways. I want to single out three in particular:

  (i) We are responsible *to* our faith traditions. We talk of 'being faithful to a tradition' or 'true to a tradition'. We cannot perform a faith as we please; cannot improvise freely; cannot just do what seems good to us apart from the traditions of the faith. Faiths are not made by one person; they cannot be lived as if they were.

  (ii) We are also responsible *for* the faith tradition – and here the emphasis falls on the 'tradition' rather than the performance. Is the tradition itself – or more specifically, is this or that (sometimes quite small) part or feature of the tradition – faithful or 'true'? (Many other assessments are also made). To this responsibility we attend explicitly only now and then (though some have more regular concern with it); but it is implicitly there at all times.

  (iii) Differently, we are responsible, in our performance, to the people around us, who are affected in all sorts of ways by us and by our performances. We are responsible to the 'influenced others', whether they be 'neighbours' or 'strangers'. (Here is yet another 'root' of diversity/plurality, as we shall see.)

2. Religious faiths show concern for each of these. With the third, for example, we find showing and teaching which spread the network of responsibilities wider for us ('love your neighbour' – who may be a Samaritan); and breaking down differentials ('love the stranger', care for the oppressed and despised). No one person can carry too much of such time-and-effort-involving responsibility. But these responsibilities are very relevant to performance – and to traditions. They are also 'built into' (woven into) religious practices and life-ways; also into upbringing and training and apprenticeships. And there is yet more to see. We will begin with the responsibilities *to* and *for* Christian traditions, focusing attention particularly on questions relating to the *diversity* and *plurality* of these traditions.

Christian traditions (like other traditions) have sought to limit, and to control, variation of their tradition(s), in explicit and deliberate ways. More or less from the start, the 'new Christians' were faced with variants which seemed 'too far out'; variants too much influenced by other traditions (or influenced in the wrong way); interpretations too much formed by personal idiosyncrasies, or by selfish motives; and so on. In the history which followed, some traditions tried to limit themselves quite narrowly, and to control more strongly. There were diverse motivations for all this; but a major, and common, one was and is the simple-seeming desire to be faithful ('responsibilities to and for'). It turns out to be anything but simple. For a start, that ubiquitous human characteristic, diversification, affected also these attempts to limit and control diversity! One person's or one group's ideas as to how to be faithful – and as to what we are to be faithful to – differ from those of others. It is a kind of irony, that the quest for faithfulness should itself have led in its turn to more diversity, division – and conflict.

So, different Christian traditions have developed various sorts of 'disciplines' (including control-practices) to try to limit and control variation and branching. One result is, a plurality of 'orthopraxes' and 'orthodoxes'. And institutions, liturgies, ethics and politics, belief, have all been systematically ordered and controlled. The methods and institutions of discipline and control were and are various. The Roman Catholic Church (and its predecessors, especially in the West) developed bit by bit an elaborate institution for order and discipline; one distinctive feature is a hierarchy centralised around the Pope and the Vatican. In Eastern Christianities, different systems evolved. Various Protestant 'denominations' have not simply followed Roman Catholic ways, but have worked out (sometimes as part of their 'foundational acts') their own systems of 'faith and order' – though taking over not a few characteristics of the 'older orders'.

Here, too, then, there have been 'performances of faith', and by them Christian traditions have been (partially) formed, reformed, and made what they are – in pursuit of responsibility to and for the faith. We might call them performances of limiting, disciplining and controlling. And we can not only try to trace out these performances and give an account of them, but also to evaluate them: that is, to evaluate (responsibly) the past and present performances of those seeking to set up, and those seeking to apply, limits and disciplines – to devise and exercise controls. It is also one of our responsibilities to do that; it forms part of our responsibility to and for faith traditions (even if the 'performers' are sometimes 'great councils'). In every such case, it is always possible to question, and to re-evaluate the appropriateness, the effectiveness, and in particular, the faithfulness, of the means and methods by which discipline and control have been exercised. In *these* performances: how well did the performers discharge their responsibilities to and for the tradition? These re-evaluations can go back even to the beginnings: they are never 'over and done with', they can never be put in the archives!

'Limiting and disciplining performances' can be tested and assessed in all sorts of ways. Quite centrally, we can look back to the 'sources', and to the ways in which they have been used to justify institutions and disciplines of control. At times in Christian history (not least, the 'Reformation and Counter-Reformation', and the nineteenth and twentieth centuries) this sort of questioning, testing and assessing of older traditional 'ways of discipline' has been pursued very actively – often with quite profound effects on the various traditions and the whole Christian cluster of traditions.

4. In many traditions ('churches') 'official responsibility' *for* tradition is placed in the hands of a selected group ('church hierarchy', clergy); the others ('laity') supposedly share mainly in the responsibility *to* tradition. But all responsibilities for a faith-tradition can be seen as belonging to all those who hold and live the faith in that tradition. Indeed: if one comes to trust not simply a specific tradition, but with that, its ways of limiting and controlling its tradition, then one is tacitly, implicitly, taking responsibility for *all* of that – including the institutions, decisions, and performances by which limits and controls came into being and are maintained. These, too, are

accepted 'in faith'. Compare this with the manner in which scientists put responsible trust in the ways in which responsible training and testing and evaluation (personal and institutional) give discipline to their traditions. It is certainly possible to question such things, and (as the histories show) to seek and get better alternatives.

This involves beliefs and doctrine, too. In effect, each Christian embraces a necessary but largely tacit part of an overall 'creed' or 'confession'. We could call it 'the control-creed' ('discipline-creed'). The control-creed of (for instance) the Roman Catholic Church is long; and much of it is spelled out in full in Catechisms and other texts. It needs to include clauses about, for example, the function of a central Papacy and Curia, their powers and the exercise of those powers (through a long history), the ways of enforcing disciplines, and so on. The histories of discipline will also cover quite a variety of things, for example church order (including, say, the exclusion of women from the priesthood – and so from the 'disciplinary elect'), ethics (such as, for example, the ethics of contraception), doctrine, and so forth.

4. God's Involvements – in Diversity

1. Thus far, we have drawn out of the weave threads which may seem to be largely concerned with 'human things': with human performances, human traditions, human assessments, human attempts to control, human responsibilities, and so on. Aren't there other, vital threads, of a different kind and a deeper colour, which we should also be seeing? Where is God, in all this?

God is at the heart of Christian traditions. Not just as a kind of centre for beliefs, but as an incessantly and variously creative wellspring, and an underlying 'voice', in all performances of the faith. This, or something more or less like it, is the case for a good many faith traditions – for instance, Jewish and Muslim ones. What makes Christianity distinctive is a centring also on Jesus of Nazareth as somehow intimately linked with God (no easy generalisation: diverse traditions!); and on the Holy Spirit which is God's spirit, Jesus' spirit (again diversities), and so on (for most – with diversities – a Trinitarian picture, with Trinitarian patterns pervading the 'weave'). Jesus/Christ and the Spirit play vital roles in God's involvements.

God *has* already appeared in our weave through Jesus of Nazareth. And since there the weave is fully human, but not 'merely human', that helps to raise the possibility that much else in the weave – even all, or nearly all – may be more than 'merely human'. Apart from our references to the central role of the God in Christ, we could have seen – from this different angle – the God in the events of Jewish history, in the early church, and so on. And what of the (possibility of) God in other faiths, too? God in 'others'? God in 'the stranger'? Our weave may be full of the 'Spirit'... and so, of God.

When we first traced back to Jesus of Nazareth, we were looking for 'sources' and 'roots'. This was partly to understand some essential things about the way Christian faiths 'function' and are lived. But there was also the idea that here, 'at the roots', Christian diversity and plurality might somehow be 'resolved'. There was a third relevance: this 'reference back to sources' plays (in various ways) a central role in fulfilling Christian responsibilities. And a fourth: there is the same ultimate 'reference back' in many attempts to discipline and control Christian traditions.

So isn't God the ultimate 'root' and 'source' – and by God's own initiatives; by God's grace? Cannot all questions and problems – and divisions and variations – be referred back to God and thus resolved? Can't Christian responsibilities be seen simply as responsibilities to God; and God be the ultimate determiner of any 'controls'? It is easy – and in many ways profoundly right – to say all this. And there would be very widespread agreement amongst Christians about it. But it does not lead to the answering of all questions, the solution of all problems, the 'resolution' of divisions and variations. It does not seem to take controls out of human hands and beyond variation and division. Nor, I believe, does it take from us huge responsibilities for the Christian faith and its life. Instead, one can come to think, it looks as though God has chosen to give these responsibilities to us. (Though not without God's involvements.)

We have already pointed to the basic 'problem'. But is it *just* a *problem*?. As far back as we can trace the living of Christian faith, we find disagreements, variations and fissiparousness. And that applies equally to the historical attempts to 'refer all back to God'. When we look at the history, God is not seen to 'take responsibility' in such a way as to 'settle everything once and for all' – nor in such a way as to settle all or at least most differences, and enable us in that simple sense to make 'one faith'. So we are driven back to consider *our* responsibilities ('under God' and 'with God') in the ways traced earlier. What kinds of performances will honour and fulfil our responsibilities to God? The pattern repeats itself. Difference and divergence – even on such fundamental questions about roots and sources as these:

When, where, and how, has 'God's voice' entered lives and traditions? And how has the 'voice' been transmuted into human traditions and performances? How well and how deeply have they been permeated and transformed? What, in them, is then 'of God' and what is 'human'? (Or is that perhaps a 'bad question', leading us in some wrong directions?)

So many answers have been given, so many different pictures drawn. For a start, many different events and experiences have seemed to people to involve God, in one way or another. [And if the performance of faith is as wide as we pictured, surely that is to be expected?] As we noted, there are, for Christian traditions, especially those events and experiences involving and surrounding Jesus of Nazareth at a certain time in history. But there are also innumerable others, not just in the earlier history of the Jews, but also in 'Church history' (in the histories of traditions), and in all sorts of devotional, liturgical, 'mystical', and social events.

One source of difficulty and divergence is then simply – and so tellingly – this. All these events and experiences (and not least those surrounding Jesus of Nazareth) seem to point to, and somehow 'involve', things so deep and full of 'mystery' that people have found it difficult, daunting, to 'render' them in any human performances (including human words). And those who sought to render them differed in their renderings. That, too, makes it seem inevitable that people should have found it difficult, not only to live from and draw from these mysteries, in and for the making and developing of definite traditions, but also to settle questions and differences that arose. God is creative source and guide. But how are we to find – and justify – the confidence and responsibility to render (in words – liturgies, stories, creeds, even philosophically-framed texts; and in other forms of living) the 'deep essentials' of 'sourcing and guiding' events and experiences.

We may note, too, the extensiveness, variety, and complexity of (actual or claimed) 'divine involvement and guiding' in the formation of traditions. We have already remarked on *some* elements in this. It is not least in the work of disciplining and controlling that guidance is often claimed. It is part of most Christian traditions that God (most often in the person of the Spirit) guides people and especially church institutions – and in particular, in these crucial performances. Yet here too the historical outcome has been highly pluralistic. In this very work people divide – and their 'control-creeds' come to differ. So we are left again with puzzles about the involvement of God. And what, then, are our responsibilities?

5. Christian Reactions to Diversity

1. Christian reactions to the ever-present variation and plurality in Christian traditions have varied greatly, too.

> (a) We have seen already how people have sought to limit the variation. But nearly always they have accepted, realistically, that there is and will be some variation. Sometimes variety is even welcomed – a great and influential Christian writer like Augustine does so (in, for example, *Civitas Dei*). But within disciplined limits. How could it be otherwise? we might ask. How can a faith tradition retain any identity at all, if it allows for unlimited variation? And how can it claim to be faithful (and generally responsible) to its roots? The early Christian Church had to face radical questions about how it was to vary, spreading to the whole 'gentile' world, as well as to Jews. They had to react to 'Gnostic' and other 'wild' interpretations. What were they to do? Surely these can't all be included as Christian ways?
>
> Even if we don't try to set strong or sharp limits to what can be taken to be a branching from Christian roots, must we not at least *distinguish* different 'families' and branchings? And that, of course, is in part what we have come to do. But it still leaves us with deep questions about how and where, if at all, 'outer limits' are to be set; how major (and minor) branchings are to be distinguished; what disciplines each will have; what relations are to be like between them; and so on. And can there still be *some* sort of *unity*, some way of 'being one', amidst all this diversity?
>
> (b) One sort of reaction to Christian divergence and plurality takes a much darker turn. Many differences were (and often are) seen as anything but 'normal and expectable developments'; still less as good, and creative. They were not to be accepted, let alone desired and fostered. On the contrary, people of faith – and their church institutions – often responded to them with many accusations, of (for instance) false faith, betrayal of faithfulness, heresy; and with exclusions, bans and excommunications. To this they often added violence; they attempted to force 'others' into line – their line. There were hostilities of many kinds; torture and executions; dreadful wars. All these between

different groups and different traditions, who all called themselves Christian; and often believed that they were the followers and upholders of 'the true faith'. They were prepared to die for their own 'variant' of the traditions – and to kill for it.
(c) Do these kinds of reactions, actions, and attitudes seem faithful to the roots of Christian traditions (for they often aimed to be so)? Not all Christians have thought so. And oppositely, from those same roots have grown branchings which fostered beliefs in, and practices of, *non*-violence (in various forms). And many Christian traditions would today reject at least physical violence. Torture, executions, and war look evil to many. Some have come to look with dismay at these past chapters of Christian history; some have – both formally and informally – expressed repentance, and apologised for past sins (including attitudes, claims, and so on) against 'others'. Yet bans, exclusions, excommunications, do continue.
(d) Looking over this history – and the questions it raises – with much bewilderment and not a little pain, my own thoughts have been increasingly impelled in directions which are less familiar, less explored (though they *have* been explored).

Do we need to picture God in God's creating, revealing, guiding, in ways rather different to what has been common in the traditions? We go back again to this: people and their world (or 'worlds') seem not only to be diverse but also to continue always to change, diversify. Individuality, particularity of context, change, all seem to lead this way. And this seems to spring 'naturally' and inevitably from the very 'nature' of people, communities, traditions. In particular, it seems to spring up within religious traditions. And so, too, faithful and responsible performance of faith often leads to creative and life-bringing diversities. Is this then just part of God's ways with things?

That seems to be saying that God's creating – here especially of people and their communities – is plural in design and intent; even at times in major (and, often, surprising and unexpected) ways. It would then be not at all surprising if God's guiding of people and traditions (through the Spirit who blows where it lists) followed this same pattern and direction: guiding, fostering, and enabling diversities of many kinds, which are both creative and faithful. Perhaps God is a 'pluralist'? Are God's presence, God's guiding and shaping, perhaps far more variable and diverse than we are accustomed to suppose?

If this 'theological picturing' (and reading of scripture and history) is going in something like the right sort of direction, then our performances and understandings of faith will have to try to take that in, thoroughly and deeply – and then to be faithful and responsible to it in our performances. But what would that mean, in detail? That is a deeply difficult question, and surely not one to be answered quickly. (And: there will inevitably be a plurality of answers!) Nothing in the picture so far need suggest, still less imply, that *all* diversities and branchings are 'equally faithful' or 'of equal value'. For a start, we want to work out and put behind us (for example) the oppressive, cruel, and often violent (sub)traditions of the too-dark past. Again: 'apartheid is sin'. We would still have to make distinctions and choices; to test and assess performances, especially those liable to modify traditions.

6. Responsibility for 'the Other' – Inculturations

1. We come, finally, to the third kind of responsibility we noted (briefly) above: the performer's responsibility to the people around, who take things in, who are affected, who are involved. Of course we are responsible, as we perform, not just to 'the past' and the tradition(s) in which we live, but also to 'the present', and especially to the living people in the midst of whom we perform our faith.

We perform our faith amongst 'others', and sometimes 'strangers' (roughly, people whose differences we feel more deeply different). Some people try to restrict the variety of people around them; others spread their lives widely amongst different people. But most faiths enjoin, encourage, nurture, the 'going out amongst others and strangers'. In Christianity and Judaism (amongst others) there is a deep and central imperative to be aware of, to have respect for, to have compassion and care for, to reach out to, those around you. 'Love your neighbour as yourself'; and add, too, 'love the stranger.' This is even put alongside the imperative to love God; and there is a strong link between these imperatives. So – included in this but by no means exhausting it ('love' is much richer) – Christians (and Jews) are made responsible to their neighbours, and to the strangers in their midst.

Faiths can be interpreted and performed in other directions. Some, for instance, seek faithful 'exclusivity': preserving and nurturing a select group, (members of which do take care and responsibility for their fellow-members); excluding others. They want, perhaps, to protect themselves from a world which is 'unfaithful', 'unholy', 'impure', 'evil', in order to strive for the faithfulness, purity, and so forth of the select group. Yet other groups and traditions practice a different, supposedly 'inclusive', kind of 'differentiation': they do take 'others' into their world, but not in the same way as they accept 'their own'; instead, they may (for instance) try to 'convert' them.

2. Our responsibilities to the others around us are profoundly affected by the diversity of these people. To take account of others, let alone to take on responsibilities towards them, we have to take on who they are; and where they are, in their lives and 'worlds'. To perform effectively amongst them, we have to 'reach' them, and to 'reach them where they are' – hoping that they, from their place, will be 'reaching out to us'. This is no small requirement. Just for a start: if the performance involves (as so often) language, then the performer must speak a language known to the 'receiver'. That may go right down to 'dialect' and 'idiolect'. And in any case (both when language is and when it is not involved), we have to 'reach' people in their cultures and traditions. We do not have to belong to the same culture, but we have to reach them in their culture. That begins with sharing some deep-seated human traits, capacities, concerns, and so forth But it has to go beyond that: into 'otherness', and even 'strangeness' (for each person involved).

For the most part, in familiar surroundings and amongst largely familiar people, we do all this naturally, and without having to direct too much of our attention to it, or to take too much thought. But the demands stand out more fully and starkly when we look at performances amongst 'strangers'; and still more, in 'strange lands'. Those who carry their religious traditions into 'other' cultures, and perform their faiths there, become aware of the need to adapt the tradition they live to the culture: to *'inculturate'* (as the jargon has it). Some are not deliberately, or at least not mainly, 'bringing their faith to others': they have just settled amongst others, for whatever reasons – but they have inevitably brought their faith, too. For other people this is a task, a 'mission', springing directly from their faith.

Not a few have recorded their experiences. One example: in Vincent Donovan's *Christianity Rediscovered* he recounts his work bringing Christian traditions to the Masai people of East Africa.[1] Christian 'foreign missions' had been there for many decades, but with rather little effect: they had not really reached the people to whom they came. Donovan's sense of responsibility *to these people* is very clear and penetrating. It led him to adapt his tradition quite radically, to innovate and experiment, to be creative in both performance and tradition. But he is also trying to be faithful *to the tradition:* after all, his aim is to bring *Christianity* to these people, and to bring them into a Christian tradition. In doing that, this version of the 'tradition' is adapted and varies from others; diversity increases.

This is a particularly lucid (and well-recorded) instance. But this sort of mutual adaptation of faith-traditions and cultures is going on all the time. Those who have experienced living in 'other cultures', and who have seen Christian faith-traditions in various forms there, will be aware of the phenomenon – and of the questions and difficulties presented to both parties. It affects both the 'in-coming' faith-tradition and those amongst whom it is lived. So, amongst Christians concerned with 'missions to strangers', there is and has long been a great deal of imaginative work, of soul-and-mind-searching, of controversy and divergence: concerning how, how far, and in what ways, to adapt to cultural *differences*; about what things can be changed and what not.

3. Adaptation and even 'inculturation' extend way beyond the somewhat special sphere of interaction with 'other peoples' in 'other countries'. Let us bring it 'nearer home'. Cultural diversities and variations are everywhere, not just 'abroad', or between broadly brushed 'culture-families' ('Western European', 'African'...). There are sub-cultures (traditions) and sub-sub-cultures, all the way down to the individuals and their idio-cultures. Around us and amongst us, in our own 'country' and 'place', there are these variations and diversities. In particular, they are found also amongst and within Christian traditions and those who live in them. Even 'at home', people have to vary and adapt the performance of their faith to the people amongst whom they perform: they have to reach them where they are.

It is familiar that our societies already are, and increasingly become, pluralist. The people amongst whom we live are mixed, diverse; and so are their cultural traditions and faith-traditions. This is not an entirely new situation for Christians:

---

1   Vincent Donovan, *Christianity Rediscovered: An Epistle from the Masai* (London: SCM Press Ltd, 1982).

indeed, their traditions were formed in such a situation, in the Mediterranean and Middle-Eastern 'worlds' of the first century C.E. But some things are different. With people around from so many different cultural traditions, we pick up bits and strands from others – though often in 'garbled' ways. Some pick and choose pieces in an almost consumerist fashion. And where faiths, in particular, are concerned, there are both the presence of many major families of faith-traditions, and great variations within them – not least, now, in Christian traditions.

Anyone seeking to 'inculturate' Christian traditions in such a society will be faced with the question: to *which* culture(s) do I adapt? For it looks as though attempts to inculturate will have to be as diverse as the people around. Is there even some way to inculturate pluralistically? These may be difficult thoughts. But they have profound implications for faith performances. If a performer (any and all of us) wants to meet people where they are, she or he is going to have to be willing and able to 'journey' to a great variety of different 'cultural places', adapting and improvising as he/she goes. Performance will have to reach down to a very fine cultural grain – and in the end, down to individuals. It has really always been somewhat like that – but in our present plurality, it places many more, and stronger, practical demands on us. Faith-performances need to be open, sensitive, adaptive, creative, perhaps as never before.

4. We can turn again to Christian sources. Diversity (as we have seen) breaks out from the start; and with it, 'inculturation problems'.

> i. In the early church – as seen, say, in Acts and the letters of Paul – the occurrence of, and problems of, 'inculturations' are only too evident. The move to make this new tradition open to the Gentiles – with adaptations – was an enormous spring for many Jews; too radical for some. And it opened the way to varied Gentile cultures – and to the need to 'reach' them, culturally. Paul is aware of the problems this causes. So: we see clearly here how responsibility to and for the tradition, the faith, itself seems to require *variation by inculturation.* It appears from the start as an unavoidable accompaniment of the way of the faith.
> ii. Looking to something that is in a sense more ultimate and more authoritative, we see how Jesus of Nazareth performs amongst a great diversity of people. (Sometimes to the puzzlement, dismay, even hostility of some of those around him, who fail to understand his ways. Here is one root of the desire to 'get him out of the way'.) He 'takes on' and reaches people of any kind: fishermen, traders, Roman-employed tax collectors, educated and wealthy city people, peasants on the land, Roman soldiers, prostitutes, highly-trained scribes, people with all sorts of diseases and handicaps, learned rabbis, Samaritans… It is remarkable that he even involves himself with so many of these 'others' and 'strangers'. But see too how he does it: for each person he has a distinctive approach, a distinctive way, a distinctive kind of performance. From this, over a slightly longer period of time, branchings and diversities will flow. But there is no doubt about the 'identity' of the faith he is presenting and performing!

5. These observations and reflections bring us to ask once again about *God's* part in all this. We might think: God wants, and we want, for God to enter into our lives and lifeways, and so, necessarily, into our varied cultures – shaping and transforming all of these. We would want that to be part of the development of our faith-tradition; and that must include the places where it meets 'others', where they are.

Can't God somehow permeate our religious language and culture, and transform them? Perhaps God can, perhaps God does: many of us believe so. But perhaps God does so more diversely than many have supposed: some of us believe that, too. And perhaps God helps create, and permeates, many cultures – and leaves us with (guided and shared) responsibility for living faithfully with the resulting diversity.

We may then also come (as I suggested earlier) to see these very phenomena of cultural diversity and inculturation in religious (including 'theological') terms. We may come not only to feel – and to think we can see and experience – great ('cultural') variety in God's presences and activities. We may also come to see, and feel, God as appearing to us 'in the stranger' – just as we hope that those who see us as strangers may at times see something of God 'in us'. There are things to prompt us in this direction: experience of close relationships with 'strange people'; experience of performing faith amongst others; experience of sensing God in strange places and strange people; Christian (and other) scriptures.

Questions press in all around: about where and when and how God is; about God's ways of being present, active, transformative, creative. How does God permeate the world? How does God permeate cultures? And: how can people performing their faith find God's ways (transformative and creative) in their diverse performances amongst diverse others?

Chapter 5

Temples of the Spirit: Worship as Embodied Performance

Steven R. Guthrie

> One of their poets, Coleridge, has recorded that he did not pray 'with moving lips and bended knees' but merely 'composed his spirit to love' and indulged 'a sense of supplication'. That is exactly the sort of prayer we want ... At the very least they can be persuaded that the bodily position makes no difference to their prayers; for they constantly forget, what you must always remember, that they are animals and that whatever their bodies do affects their souls.
>
> – Screwtape, to Wormwood[1]

1. Learning the Body

Here are just a few of the things I have going on right now: as I sit at my desk typing this chapter, not only am I manipulating the keys of the computer keyboard; not only am I glancing back and forth over several earlier drafts; not only am I recalling what I have written to this point and considering what I might write next. In addition to all of these activities, I am at the same time balancing myself upright upon my chair –tipping neither to the right nor the left. That might not seem like much of an accomplishment, but in fact, it is not something I have always been able to do. It is a *skill*; one I have had to *learn*.

I know this now, because I have two little boys at home, and over the past three years, I have watched each of them slowly (and sometimes painfully!) learn to balance himself. Among his baby photos there is a picture of my youngest son, Noah, perched tenuously upon the living room sofa. Pillows are piled around him as supports. His eyes are wide with concentration and effort, arms stretched out to either side like a circus performer on a tight rope. One fist clutches desperately to Mother's little finger – and despite these aids, he is still beginning to tip.

You will be happy to know that both of my sons are now well able to balance themselves. (Indeed, to my horror, I often enter the room to find one or the other of them balanced atop a bookshelf, a window sill or the dining room table.) In the same way, each day most of us enjoy a level and range of activity that is made possible by

---

[1] C. S. Lewis, *The Screwtape Letters* (Glasgow: Collins, 1942), 25.

this ability. Maintaining balance means that we can stand, sit, walk, run, roller-skate or climb onto the china cabinet. Again, for most of us, the ability to balance has become more or less transparent; it doesn't occupy much of our conscious attention. But we should not lose sight of the importance and developmental priority of this sort of basic bodily competency. In our conscious engagement with the external world, one of the first things we must learn (if not the first), is our own body – its way of being and moving and interacting with the environment.

The Body and Learning

The psychologist Jean Piaget proposed that these sorts of bodily competencies allow us considerably more than freedom of movement. He contended that our very reasoning has its roots in the kind of physical experience of the world we have been describing. According to Piaget, the development of cognition in children begins with a period of sensori-motor engagement with their environment.[2] Children are not the passive objects of stimulus and input – they actively and creatively explore their surroundings.[3] Through movement, touch, observation, and hearing, the infant interacts with the physical world. This physical, bodily engagement with the world gives rise to what Piaget called schemes – abstract internal representations of patterns of movement or activity.[4] These schemes, in turn, form the basis for higher levels of cognition and abstract thought. They become, as it were, the building blocks of reasoning; the categories around which we continue to organize our thoughts and experiences.

Over the last fifty years, much of Piaget's account of development has been challenged, and in many ways, superceded. There are, however, at least two concepts central to this theory which continue to find widespread acceptance.

First, the concept of internalized representations or schemes (often called *schemata*) continues to play an important role, particularly in cognitive psychology.[5] Schemata, once again, are generalized patterns or sequences abstracted from our

---

2   See Jean Piaget, *The Origin of Intelligence in the Child*, trans. Margaret Cook (London: Routledge & Kegan Paul, 1953), esp. 357–59; 407–19. I have also drawn upon the summary in Usha Goswami, *Cognition in Children* (Hove: Psychology Press, 1998), 259–79.

3   'Piaget's theory ... places action and self-directed problem-solving at the heart of learning and development. ... In human beings, learning how to act on the world and discovering the consequences of action form the bedrock of thinking itself.' David Wood, *How Children Think and Learn: The Social Contexts of Cognitive Development*, 2nd edn (Oxford: Blackwell, 1998), 5.

4   'A scheme is the structure or organization of actions as they are transferred or generalized by repetition in similar or analogous circumstances.' J. Piaget and B. Inhelder, 'The Sensori-Motor Level', in John Oates and Sue Sheldon (eds), *Cognitive Development in Infancy* (Hove, East Sussex: Lawrence Erlbaum Associates, 1987), 52, n. 2.

5   See, for instance, Michael W. Eysenck and Mark T. Keane, *Cognitive Psychology: A Student's Handbook* (Hove and London: Lawrence Erlbaum Associates, 1990), 275–94.

embodied experience. Second, there is considerable agreement that our active, corporeal engagement with the world is fundamental to cognitive development.[6]

Not only psychologists, but also a number of twentieth-century philosophers have proposed this sort intimate connection between embodiment and rational thought.[7] Michael Polanyi sought to 'throw light on the bodily roots of all thought, including man's highest creative powers'.[8] Even more famous is the work of Marcel Merleau-Ponty, who argued that 'the *perceived world* is the always presupposed foundation of all rationality, all value and all existence'.[9] I would like to give particular attention however, to the work of the contemporary American philosopher Mark Johnson.[10] Johnson, much like Polanyi and Merleau-Ponty, maintains that the very roots of our rational engagement with the world are to be found in patterns of gesture, motion and embodied experience. In language strongly reminiscent of Piaget, he suggests that abstract representations of these recurring patterns are internalized as 'image schemata'. These image schemata become the dynamic structures around which meaning is organized, as they are metaphorically extended from the realm of the physical to the conceptual.[11] Johnson explores dozens of image schemata in his

---

6 Goswami, 266, 278.

7 It should be noted that affirming bodily participation in understanding does not commit one to a particular anthropology. While such an account may tend toward holism or physicalism, it certainly does not exclude some variety of unitive dualism (that is, an anthropology in which body and mind, while separate entities, exist in close relationship and continuing dialogue). The case for 'non-reductive physicalism' is given an attractive presentation in Warren S. Brown, Nancey Murphy and H. Newton Malony (eds) *Whatever Happened to the Soul? Scientific and Theological Portraits of Human Nature* (Minneapolis: Fortress, 1998). A careful critique of physicalism and an argument for 'integrative dualism' can be found in Charles Taliaferro, *Mind and the Consciousness of God* (Cambridge: Cambridge University Press, 1994).

8 Michael Polanyi, *The Tacit Dimension* (London: Routledge & Kegan Paul, 1966), 15.

9 M. Merleau-Ponty, 'The Primacy of Perception and Its Philosophical Consequences', trans. James M. Edie, in John O'Neil (ed.), *Phenomenology, Language and Sociology: Selected essays of Maurice Merleau-Ponty* (London: Heinemann, 1974), 197. My emphasis.

10 Mark Johnson, *The Body in the Mind: The Bodily Basis of Meaning, Imagination, and Reason* (Chicago: University of Chicago Press, 1987). Johnson's work is profoundly influenced by the interdisciplinary field of cognitive science. While there are considerable differences between modern cognitive science and the developmental psychology of Piaget, there are also some striking resemblances, including the two concepts noted in the body of the text, above. These common ideas have been recognized by a number of cognitivists; for example: 'The most commonly used construct to account for complex knowledge organisation is the schema ... In a developmental context, Piaget (1967; 1970) had also made use of the concept of a schema to understand the changes that occur in children's cognition.' Michael W. Eysenck and Mark T. Keane, *Cognitive Psychology: A Student's Handbook* (Hove and London: Lawrence Erlbaum Associates, 1990), 275.

11 Johnson, xix, xx.

work, but to illustrate this concept, I will take as an example the physical skill we mentioned a moment ago, that of balance.[12]

2. Maintaining – and Extending – Balance

Whether we speak of balancing ourselves, keeping other objects balanced, or observing one or more objects balancing – all of these involve a complex and dynamic interplay of physical forces. At a very early age, we develop an experiential knowledge of what is involved in maintaining balance. This internalized awareness of the dynamic structure of balance is one instance of a schema. Crucially, Johnson argues that these schemata are not amorphous, but rather, possess a clearly defined internal structure. We will not explore the structural descriptions of these schemata in any detail, but briefly, Johnson suggests that the internal structure of the BALANCE schema comprises three properties: symmetry; transitivity and reflexivity.[13] Because our experience of BALANCE possesses this definite structure, we may apply this schema – metaphorically, but *meaningfully* – to other experiences and processes which are similarly structured. So when we say for instance, that a tragic event has *set us reeling*, we are not arbitrarily lighting upon this physical metaphor of loss of balance. Rather, in such an instance our *bodily* experience of BALANCE enables us to articulate – through metaphorical extension – the structure and dynamic quality of our *emotional* experience. The dynamic structure of this schema becomes a means of organizing and making sense of other dynamic structures in our experience.

So, we may speak of psychological health in terms of balance and imbalance:[14] indeed, we aim to be people who are *balanced*, *stable*, and maintain some sort of *emotional equilibrium*. While all of us *carry baggage*, and *bear the burdens* of everyday life (metaphors suggesting a physical pressure that may create imbalance), we for the most part manage to remain on *an even keel*. In demanding situations, we may find ourselves *shaken*, but hope to remain *even-tempered*. However, when *loaded down* and *under pressure*, even the most *poised* and *steady* among us may feel him- or herself *tipping over the edge*.

Similarly, we may speak of legal or moral balance:[15] a judge *weighs the facts* of a case, and is expected to remain *even-handed*. *Crooked* lawyers seek to *skew* the truth, and put their own *slant* on everything, hoping to *sway* opinions and *tip the balance* in their favour. At the same time, the legal system seeks to ensure that there is *an even playing field* for all parties involved. As arguments are *piled up*, a jury may begin to *lean* toward *one side or the other*. Meanwhile, the fate of the poor defendant *hangs in the balance*.

---

12   I am drawing on the extensive treatment of the 'Balance' schema in Johnson, 74–100.
13   Ibid., 97.
14   Ibid., 88. Many of the following examples of metaphorically extended 'balance' terms are Johnson's; others I have added.
15   Ibid., 90.

You get the idea. We may speak of ecological balance.[16] We may speak of aesthetic or formal balance in describing a painting, a film or a piece of music. We also regularly speak of the dynamics of rational argument[17] in terms of this schema. Summarizing this phenomenon, Johnson writes,

> We do not find a large number of unrelated concepts . . . that all just happen to make use of the same word 'balance' and related terms. Rather, we use the same word for all of these domains for the reason that they are structurally related by the same set of underlying schemata, metaphorically elaborated.[18]

What is easily overlooked in all of this is the mundane fact that 'balancing is an *activity we learn with our bodies*'.[19] We cannot articulate propositionally what it means to feel balanced. 'As Michael Polanyi has argued, you cannot tell another what steps to take to achieve the balanced riding of a bicycle.'[20] Such knowledge has its roots in embodied experience. 'The *meaning* of balance', Johnson writes, 'begins to emerge through our *acts* of balancing and through our *experience* of systemic processes and states within our bodies.'[21] And this physical understanding of BALANCE, its properties and dynamic structure, provides us with resources for organizing our experience in many different spheres. Through the dynamic structures arising from our bodily experience of the world, we are able to experience and make sense of other complex dynamic structures – such as those we encounter in art, logic, social interaction, and moral deliberation. Even in these realms of advanced and highly abstract reasoning we may still discern (to use Johnson's title) the body in the mind.

3. The Body at Worship

I have argued that we may discern the role of the body even in those 'higher' human pursuits such as logic or moral deliberation.[22] What then may we say about the role of the body in that activity which might be characterized as 'highest' of all – that of worship? Of course, on one level, the body is necessarily ubiquitous in worship, inasmuch as the Christian is to offer up her whole life as worship to God – 'whether you eat or drink or whatever you do, do it all for the glory of God'.[23] However, I would like to give special attention to the contribution of the body in liturgical or

---

16 Ibid., 88.
17 Ibid., 89.
18 Ibid., 95–6.
19 Ibid., 74; emphasis in original.
20 Ibid.
21 Ibid., 75; emphasis in original.
22 And even as we speak of 'higher' pursuits, we are doing so by means of a metaphor grounded in our physical experience!
23 1 Corinthians 10:31. All biblical citations are from the *New International Version* unless otherwise indicated.

cultic worship (that is, the more formal, corporate worship of the people of God, or the kind of activity that takes place when Christians gather together for 'a worship service').

We must first of all note that when it comes to this kind of worship, the language of the Christian scriptures is undeniably corporeal. The extent to which the Old and New Testaments associate corporate, cultic worship with bodily actions is striking, perhaps even surprising. Even limiting our Old Testament search to the Psalms, we find more than a dozen physical acts closely linked to worship. The parallelisms of the Psalms highlight just how strongly these gestures and movements were connected with worship.

> We are exhorted in Psalm 95:6:
>> Come let us *bow down* in worship,
>> let us *kneel* before the LORD our maker.[24]
>
> Psalm 141:2 reads,
>> May my prayer be set before you like incense;
>> May the *lifting of my hands* be like the evening sacrifice.
>
> Psalm 47:1:
>> *Clap your hands*, all you nations;
>> *shout* to God with cries of joy.
>
> Psalm 22:29:
>> All the rich of the earth will *feast* and worship
>
> Psalm 123:1:
>> I *lift up my eyes* to you,
>> to you whose throne is in heaven.
>
> Psalm 149:3a:
>> Let them praise his name *with dancing*
>
> Psalm 149:3b:
>>
>> and *make music* to him *with tambourine and harp*.
>
> Psalm 118:27a:
>> With *boughs in hand*,
>
> Psalm 118:27b:
>> join in the *festal procession*

---

24 My emphasis added, here and in the verses that follow.

Psalm 84:5:
>Blessed are those whose strength is in you,
>who have set their hearts on *pilgrimage*.

Psalm 51:19:
>Then there will be righteous *sacrifices*,
>whole burnt offerings to delight you;
>then bulls will be *offered* on your altar.

And over and again we find references to singing – the pre-eminent embodied act of worship in the Psalms.

Psalm 33:1:
>*Sing* joyfully to the LORD, you righteous;
>it is fitting for the upright to praise him.

The worship of the Old Testament is worship in motion. It is vital, active, and richly sensual. And many of these same activities appear in the worship of the New Testament. Singing (Acts 16:25), raising hands (1 Timothy 2:8), kneeling (Ephesians 3:14), fasting (Acts 13:2), the sharing of wine and bread (Acts 2:46-7) – all of these are closely associated with the worshipping church. The Apostle Paul even describes the universal affirmation of Christ's lordship in strikingly embodied language: 'at the name of Jesus, *every knee should bow* ... and *every tongue confess* that Jesus Christ is Lord' (Philippians 2:10–11). John's vision of heaven is likewise rich with incense, the playing of instruments, singing, shouts of praise, and 24 elders who *fall down* to worship, *casting* their crowns before the One on the throne.

As we look more closely, we discover that even the generic biblical terms for worship have a distinctly corporeal dimension. An Old Testament scholar writes that 'one of the most general expressions for the act of worship in the Old Testament is the verb "to bow down" or "to prostrate"'.[25] In its Old Testament usage *hishtachaweh* may denote both the physical act of prostration, and, when directed toward a deity, an act of worship and devotion. Genesis 23, for instance, relates the story of negotiations between Abraham and the Hittites over a plot of land. The New International Version translation of verse 7 reads:

'Then Abraham rose and bowed down [*weyishtachu*] before the people of the land.'

We find the same word in Genesis 24. Here Abraham's servant praises God for guiding him on his journey. Verse 26 reads:

'Then the man bowed down[26] and *worshipped* [*wayishtachu*] the LORD.'

---

25 Yoshiaki Hattori, 'Theology of Worship in the Old Testament', in D. A. Carson (ed.), *Worship: Adoration and Action* (Grand Rapids: Baker; Carlisle: Paternoster, 1993), 23; cf. David Peterson, 'Worship in the New Testament', ibid., 53.

26 *wayyiqqod*

Interestingly, in the New Testament there is a similar equivalence between the physical act of bowing down and the act of worship. One New Testament scholar writes,

> By far the most common word translated 'to worship' in the New Testament is the verb *proskynein*. From earliest times this term expressed the widespread oriental custom of bowing down or casting oneself on the ground, kissing the feet, hem of a garment or the ground, as a total bodily gesture of respect before a great one.[27]

As in the Old Testament example of *hishtachaweh*, the term continues to indicate both physical prostration, and by extension, an inward attitude of worship[28]. So in Matthew 8:2, we read of a leper who came to Jesus

> and knelt [*prosekynei*] before him and said, 'Lord if you are willing, you can make me clean.'

While in John 12:20, we read that

> There were some Greeks among those who went up to worship [*proskyneisosin*] at the Feast.

Of course, none of this means that every biblical mention of 'worship' refers to an actual physical act of prostration. In fact, the word often denotes an attitude or way or regarding another, described in terms of a bodily act – not at all unlike the way in which we may describe an emotionally healthy person as 'stable' or 'balanced'. The words *hishtachaweh* and *proskynein* refer to a physical gesture; a physical gesture which the biblical writers often metaphorically extend to represent more than the physical gesture itself.

What we may say then is, first, in the Bible, worship is often linked with some sort of bodily activity or gesture – kneeling, singing, raising of hands, and so on. Many theologians and clergy have recognized this embodied character of worship.[29] Second, and perhaps more important for our discussion, the attitude of worship, or the idea of worship, are often described in terms of bodily actions and gestures (even when these movements are not being literally enacted).

---

27   Peterson, 'Worship in the New Testament', 52. See also H. Schönweiss and C. Brown, '*proskyneo*' in Colin Brown (ed.) *New International Dictionary of New Testament Theology*, vol. 2, rev. edn (Carlisle: Paternoster, 1986), 875–79.

28   'In addition to the external act of prostrating oneself in worship, *proskyneo* can denote the corresponding inward attitude of reverence and humility.' Schönweiss and Brown, '*proskyneo*', 876.

29   Cf, for example, J-J von Allmen, *Worship, its Theology and Practice*, trans. Harold Knight and W. Fletcher Fleet (London: Lutterworth Press, 1965), esp. 87–95; Marianne H. Micks, *The Future Present: the Phenomenon of Christian Worship* (New York: Seabury Press, 1970); Evelyn Underhill, *Worship* (London: Collins, 1936), esp. 29–50.

These observations are true of contemporary Christian worship as well. Christian worship continues to be a deeply corporeal activity. It is perhaps less common in our culture for worship services to feature all of the activities mentioned in the Psalms – dancing, the raising of hands or festal processions.[30] Nevertheless, most Christian worship does include singing and the playing of instruments, standing and sitting at fixed times, and the sharing of bread and wine. Kneeling, and the clapping of hands are also common embodied elements of Christian worship.[31] And like the biblical writers, we often use the language of embodiment to speak of the 'inward' attitude of worship, or the idea of worship. So, for instance, we speak of 'lifting up our hearts', 'directing the gaze of the soul', 'turning our eyes upon Jesus', or 'laying our lives before the Lord.'

4. Body versus Spirit: *'Lay Thy Hand and Hold Them Down'*

We began by suggesting that there is a profound connection between embodiment and rationality. Our knowledge begins with learning our own way of physically being in the world. Moreover, the gestures and patterns of movement we acquire profoundly shape and enrich our thought. We then went on to observe the intimate association of worship and gesture in the Christian scriptures. Action and gesture are not only the ordinary mode of worship, they also provide the vocabulary and concepts by which we speak and think about worship.[32]

---

30   However, this is changing, and will likely continue to change, if charismatic and pentecostal Christianity continue to grow at their present phenomenal rate.

31   When this material was presented at the ITIA Spring 2001 Conference, philosopher Leslie Stevenson wondered about those occasions when Christians worship in motionless silence – such as in some Quaker meetings, when participants silently 'wait on the Lord.' As Stevenson went on to observe, however, even motionless silence is a bodily activity. In fact, it is an activity in which one may be very keenly aware of the body, as one undertakes the deliberate discipline of bodily stillness.

32   Of course, bodily actions and movements do not of themselves *constitute* worship. Amos chapter 5 relates God's stinging rejection of Israel's cultic worship: 'I hate, I despise your religious feasts; I cannot stand your assemblies. Even though you bring me burnt offering and grain offerings I will not accept them. ... Away with the noise of your songs! I will not listen to the music of your harps' (Amos 5:21–23). The people Amos addressed were certainly performing the actions of worship, but their hearts were far from God. They were literally, just 'going through the motions'. It is interesting to note however, the reasons given for this strong condemnation. The prophecy does not fault the people for lacking the proper 'inward attitude'. The problem is that their *actions of worship* stand in such contrast and radical opposition *to all their other actions*: 'you trample on the poor and force him to give you grain' (5:11); 'you oppress the righteous and take bribes and deprive the poor of justice in the courts' (5:12), and so on. It is, in other words, an embodied and enacted hypocrisy. The remedy and way of repentance is also expressed in active and outward terms: 'Let justice roll on like a river, righteousness like a never-failing stream' (5:24). At no point does the prophet urge the people to abandon their outward worship in favour of a silent and inward disposition.

If we hold these first two points together, then it may lead us to re-evaluate what is taking place in our corporate worship. Throughout much of the Christian tradition the body has been considered an obstacle to worship and spiritual enlightenment. Spiritual writers have laid an emphasis upon *theoria* or contemplation as the highest form of adoration. Plato's ancient suspicion has haunted the Church down the ages:

> The soul is most like that which is divine, immortal, intelligible, uniform, indissoluble, and ever self-consistent and invariable, whereas the body is most like that which is human, mortal, multiform, unintelligible, dissoluble, and never self consistent.[33]

The soul that is too deeply bound up with the passions, movements and sensations of the body, warns Plato, will take on the mortal, inconsistent and unintelligible character of the body. So for centuries, pious individuals have sought to grow toward God by turning away from the flesh, the senses and the external world, and instead turning inward, to silence, stillness and contemplation. Consider the classic Christian hymn, 'Veni Creator Spiritus', attributed to Charlemagne[34] and translated by the English poet John Dryden.[35] In it, the poet sets out a series of oppositions. On the one side we have our 'earthy parts', which are identified with the 'senses', as well as (by implication) our frailties and vices. On the other side of the divide are our 'hearts' and 'souls'. The earthy, sensual part of our being is depicted as warring against the spiritual part. The senses rise up and rebel, and it is the duty of the heart, the soul, the intellect, to 'hold them down'. Heart, soul and mind are on the same side as the Holy Spirit, all doing battle against the insubordinate flesh. It is certainly more than simply the rhyme scheme which leads Charlemagne/Dryden to invite the Spirit to 'visit every pious mind'. The Spirit is not invited to the pious body, or the pious senses, but to the mind. Aquinas, citing Aristotle, suggests a similar set of oppositions:

> Contemplation is the activity of the best in man, namely his mind, occupied with its proper object, namely pure truth, whereas action is about external business.[36]

The spiritual life is not a matter of 'action' or 'external business', but of the 'mind' (in light of our earlier discussion, note especially the separation of cognition from action). If worship involves offering our best to God, then the principal site of worship within the human person will be the mind, not the body (and on this account the two are kept well apart). The 1908 edition of the *Catholic Encyclopedia*, in the entry on 'Contemplative Life' asserts:

---

33   Plato, *Phaedo*, 80B–81C, trans. Hugh Tredennick (London: Penguin, 1954), 132.

34   Another well-known version is attributed to Rabanus Maurus.

35   *Hymns of the Christian Church*, Vol. XLV, Part 2. The Harvard Classics (New York: P.F. Collier & Son, 1909–14; Bartleby.com, 2001); accessed on-line at http://www.bartleby.com/45/2/113.html. on 29 November 2006.

36   Aquinas, *Summa Theologica*, 2a–2ae. clxxxii. I, in *St Thomas Aquinas: Theological Texts*, selected and trans. Thomas Gilby (London: Oxford University Press, 1955), 264.

> The act of contemplation, imperfect as it needs be, is of all human acts one of the most sublime, ... [a]ccording to St. Bernard (*De Consider.*, lib. I, c. vii), it is the highest form of human worship...

This pattern of worship is presented as a deliberate program of subduing the body, so as to free the soul for the worship of God. The entry continues:

> '... the rules of contemplative orders especially are admirably framed so as to thwart and mortify every selfish instinct; vigils, fasts, austerity in food, clothing, etc., and often manual labour tame the flesh, and thus help the soul to keep in subjection its worst enemy. Contemplatives, in short, forego many transient pleasures ... but they gain in return a liberty for the soul which enables it to rise without hindrance to the thought and love of God. ... '[37]

According to this entry, the flesh (and here 'flesh' seems to be roughly equivalent to 'body') is the soul's 'worst enemy' – that which hinders the soul from rising toward God. The proper role of the body is to perform acts (vigils, fasts, etc) which will allow one to move *beyond* the body, and toward incorporeal contemplation.[38]

To summarize, in the Western tradition, embodied, physical acts of worship have often been regarded as, at best, a means of moving beyond the bodily. They have also been clearly distinguished from the *mind* – that is, the rational and cognitive – at worship.

A Continuing Concern

Those involved in the music ministries of a local church may recognize that these concerns about the body persist – whether or not their roots can be traced to any of the sources just cited. Physical acts of worship may be embraced or treated with suspicion, but in either case, they are often regarded as the non-rational component of a worship service.

Some view active worship with suspicion, precisely because of its appeal to the body and (therefore, it is felt) its neglect of the mind. And so a service marked by enthusiastic music, loud singing, clapping and raising of hands may be characterized

---

[37] Edmund Gurdon, 'Contemplative Life', transcribed by Suzanne Plaisted, in *The Catholic Encyclopedia, Volume IV* (Robert Appleton Company, 1908), accessed on-line at http://www.newadvent.org/cathen/04329a.htm on 29 November 2006.

[38] A seventh-century Syriac text on prayer advises such a programme. One begins by worshipping in '[an] exterior manner-employing continual fasting, using the voice for psalmody, with repeated periods on his knees ... along with a careful watch over the senses ... when someone can do all this, and achieve it in himself, he will arrive at singing to God in the psalmody that spiritual beings use to praise him. For God is silence, and in silence is he sung and glorified.' Abraham of Nathpar, 'On prayer: how it is necessary for someone who prays to be eager and vigilant in himself', in *The Syriac Fathers on Prayer and the Spiritual Life*, trans. Sebastian Brock (Kalamazoo, Michigan: Cistercian, 1987), 192–93, cited in Victoria Sirotta, 'An Exploration of Music as Theology' *Theological Education* 31, 1 (1994): 165–73, 172.

as 'nothing but emotionalism', 'irrational', 'emotional manipulation' or just getting people 'all worked up.' Others may acknowledge the importance of our bodily participation in worship, while still carefully distinguishing the body's contribution from the realm of reason. Bodily worship on such an account amounts to precisely one half of worship. We sing and kneel that we may worship God with our bodies; we meditate and listen to teaching that we may worship God with our minds. Both are important; both should be included, that we might worship God with our whole selves. But gesture, movement and sensation are perceived to be the non-rational supplement to the rational content of the service.

5. The Incarnating Spirit

The tradition we have surveyed contends that the *mind* is the site of Christian transformation ('come visit every pious mind'), while the *body* is an impediment (or at the very least, incidental) to that regeneration ('submit the senses to the soul'). On the other hand, the account of cognition I sketched at the beginning of this paper maintains that our *embodied experience* is fundamental to our cognitive development. Is it then, the body or the mind which transforms?

When it comes to Christian transformation, of course, the answer is that neither mind nor body is the primary agent of transformation, but the Holy Spirit. 'We, who with unveiled faces all reflect the Lord's glory, are being transformed (*metamorphoumetha*) into his likeness with ever-increasing glory, which comes from the Lord, who is the Spirit' (2 Corinthians 3:18). Having said this, the biblical tradition does not limit or even focus the activity of the Holy Spirit on 'every pious mind'. Neither is the business of the Spirit to 'submit the senses to the soul' or to 'hold them down'. Rather, the Holy Spirit of God is revealed as the incarnating Spirit – One who works in and through bodies.[39]

The angel Gabriel announces to the virgin Mary, 'The *Holy Spirit* will come upon you, and the power of the Most High will overshadow you. So the holy one to be born will be called the Son of God' (Luke 1:35). The Holy Spirit is the divine agent by whom the Word is made flesh. Moreover, it is the Spirit who empowers Jesus to get his hands dirty, as it were, with the very physical and bodily needs of men and women – physical illnesses, poverty, oppression: 'The *Spirit of the Lord* is on me because he has anointed me *to preach* good news to the poor. He has sent me *to proclaim freedom* for the prisoners and *recovery of sight* for the blind, *to release the oppressed*, to proclaim the year of the Lord's favour' (Luke 4:18–19).

The theology of Paul draws out further connections between the Holy Spirit and the physical body. In particular, the Spirit is the guarantor of bodily resurrection; the

---

[39] Cf. Thomas A. Smail, *Reflected Glory: The Spirit in Christ and Christians* (London: Hodder and Stoughton, 1975), esp. 119-33; Jürgen Moltmann, *The Spirit of Life: A Universal Affirmation*, tr. Margaret Kohl (Minneapolis: Fortress Press, 1992), esp. 83-98; Jürgen Moltmann, *The Source of Life: The Holy Spirit and the Theology of Life*, tr. Margaret Kohl (Minneapolis: Fortress Press, 1997), esp. 70-88.

one who reproduces the living Christ in the mortal body of the Christian: 'And if the Spirit of him who raised Jesus from the dead is living in you, he who raised Christ from the dead will also give life to your mortal bodies through his Spirit who lives in you.' (Romans 8:11).

The Spirit does not deliver Jesus from a body, but rather brings new life to and through his physical body. Likewise in the Christian, the Spirit's work is not to eliminate bodies, but to perfect, complete and restore them. Ezekiel provides us with a powerful image of this Spirit at work. The Spirit brings Ezekiel into a valley of dry and decaying bones. There the Lord declares:

> 'I will make *ruach*[40] enter you and you will come to life. I will attach tendons to you and make flesh come upon you and cover you with skin; I will put *ruach* in you, and you will come to life. Then you will know that I am the LORD.' (Ezekiel 37:5–6)

Here is the Spirit of YHWH at work; not destroying and mortifying bodies, but bringing new life to bodies that are broken and decayed. Here is the Spirit at work; not tearing the soul free of the body, but attaching tendons and flesh and skin to dry, brittle and lifeless bones.

The body is not an obstacle to the Spirit's transforming work, but a significant site of that transformation. This biblical affirmation seems all the more plausible if thought and action, conceptual understanding and physical movement, are as tightly bound together as I have suggested. The 'offering of our bodies' becomes one important means by which the Spirit transforms minds (cf. Rom. 12:1–2).

6. The Christened Temple

Let us return to the account of embodiment and cognition with which we began, and consider how this Spirit-directed transformation might work itself out in practice.

First of all, in singing, in raising our hands, in kneeling and standing together in worship, we are offering to God the very building blocks of our rational engagement with the world. We place before him, for the purpose of his adoration, those gestures and movements which are the dynamic structures around which we organize meaning.

One of the grandest and most remarkable products of Roman architecture is the Pantheon. This massive structure stands in Rome's old central quarter, and was originally dedicated to the seven pagan planetary deities. In 609 AD, however, the Pantheon was re-consecrated – literally christened – as the Church of St Mary of the Martyrs. This extraordinary monument, which stood at the centre of the community, and in many ways established its geography and character, was dedicated to the glory of God, and thereby took on a new meaning. By its very presence, it continued to shape the local environment. It continued to fix the identity, coordinates and terrain of its neighbourhood – but it now came to represent something different.

---

40   NIV, 'breath'.

The structure standing at the centre of the landscape had been given over to the worship of God.

Something similar happens when we worship God with hand and voice and limb. Our thinking and reasoning is profoundly shaped by our physical interaction with the world. As we stand, sit, move and reach out we develop the structures of thought. In worship we take those same building blocks of thought and say, *by this gesture, by this movement, by this sensory experience of the world, I worship my God and Saviour.* In this way, worship becomes part of the meaning of these meaning-making movements. These structures which define the character of our cognitive geography are, as it were, christened the temple of the Holy Spirit (1 Corinthians 6:19).

There is a second level at which our embodied worship contributes to Christian transfiguration. If one's thought is shaped by one's bodily experience, then as a group of Christians – the Body of Christ – move *their bodies* together in the worship of God, they develop a shared and distinctive conceptual vocabulary; a common gestural lexicon around which they may organize meaning. Together they engage in an embodied experience of the world, and from that experience they reap new conceptual resources, new embodied metaphors, by which they make sense of things.

How does a Christian community come to understand what it means to worship God? Or what it means to approach God reverently and humbly? Or what it means to adore him? We can and should offer theological definitions, but more often, we articulate one ineffable experience in terms of another. We say, 'I can't write a definition of worship – but it feels something like this. It has *this* sort of movement and sound and gesture to it. I can't articulate adoration, but it has the same sort of shape as when we sing *this* song, or raise our hands *this* way.' The *content* of concepts like worship, adoration, devotion, reverence, arise in large part from our embodied *experience* of worship, adoration, devotion and reverence. And just as we metaphorically extend schemata such as BALANCE to organize a whole range of concepts, so we metaphorically extend the dynamic structures arising from our experience of worship. If this is correct, then the bodily way I express my love for God may well shape the way I think about loving my neighbour. The gestures by which I delight in my Saviour may inform the way I delight in my wife and my children.

7. A Case Study: Motion and Meaning in Musical Worship

Here is an example of how worship, in particular, musical worship, might generate a distinctive conceptual vocabulary.[41] Music, whether we mean singing, playing of instruments, or simply listening, is a form of worship we experience in the body. It is worthy of our consideration, first of all, because most Christian churches

---

41   See also Steven R. Guthrie, 'Singing, in the Body and in the Spirit', *Journal of the Evangelical Theological Society*, 46:4 (December 2003), 633–46.

throughout history have included music in their corporate worship. Second, music is one form of embodied worship which is still culturally available to most of us – something which may not be true of (say) dancing, the raising of hands, or shouting aloud.

While music has at times been characterized as the least physical of the arts,[42] several recent studies have explored its dynamics in terms of gesture and movement. Roger Scruton in *The Aesthetics of Music*, characterizes music as movement in phenomenal space.[43] That is, we hear sounds *as* music when we perceive them as metaphorical movement, gesture and dance. We fail to hear a series of tones as a *melody*, if we only perceive them as a series of discrete, unrelated acoustical events: 'A'; ' F'; 'E'; 'C'; 'B' – like a succession of car horns blaring out at different pitches. Rather, hearing a *melody* means hearing gesture: *A* stretching up to *F*, gently settling back on to *E*, before falling through *C* and *B*, finally coming to rest on *A*. Scruton argues that hearing this sort of gesture and movement *just is* what it means to hear *sounds* as *music*.

So, according to Scruton, we hear music in terms of bodily movement. Part of the extraordinary power of music is that – because it is movement in *phenomenal space* – it allows types of movement and gesture which are completely distinctive. Scruton suggests that in music we enter into a 'dance of sympathy,' moving in responsive identification with the 'human life imagined in the sounds'.[44] The dance of *musical* tone and gesture however, is of a special sort. Among a group of dancers in 3-dimensional space

> each dancer occupies his own space: the harmony [of motion] between the dancers does not cancel their separation. In music, however, movements coalesce and flow together in a single stream. The phenomenal space of music contains no places that are 'occupied', or from which competing gestures are excluded. Moreover, the aural world is transparent: nothing that occurs in it is blocked from view, and all that flows through it is revealed to the ear as flowing.[45]

The musicologist Victor Zuckerkandl maintained that in music we enter a realm of unity without the blurring of distinctions;[46] of coincidence in space without exclusion;[47] of dynamic forces acting through rather than upon bodies;[48] of individual parts which carry within themselves the knowledge of their place within

---

42   See Jeremy Begbie's discussion of this tendency in 'The Ambivalent Rainbow: Forsyth, Art and Creation', in Trevor A. Hart (ed.) *Justice the True and Only Mercy: Essays on the Life and Theology of Peter Taylor Forsyth* (Edinburgh: T & T Clark, 1995), 197–219.
43   Roger Scruton, *The Aesthetics of Music* (Oxford: Clarendon, 1993), 73–7.
44   Ibid., 355.
45   Ibid., 338.
46   Victor Zuckerkandl, *Sound and Symbol: Music and the External World*, trans. Willard R. Trask (Princeton, N.J. : Princeton University Press, 1956), 301–2.
47   Ibid., 297.
48   Ibid., 365.

the whole.⁴⁹ The point is that while we hear music in terms of bodily motion and gesture, music, as movement in phenomenal space allows types of movement and gesture which are entirely distinctive. We hear kinds of movement in music that we encounter nowhere else. Music opens to us a whole world of movement. It expands and reshapes the categories under which we may conceive of force, cooperation and connection.

There is, therefore, a reciprocal relationship between bodily movement and musical perception. The two inform one another. In the first instance, we understand music by metaphorically extending schemata of bodily gesture and movement. In the second instance, these schemata are taken up and transformed in the music. The music has its own way of moving, and its characteristic shapes and movements add to and extend our conceptual repertoire. Music makes us aware of gestures to which we would have no other access. By expanding our gestural schemata in this way, music provides us with fresh and completely distinctive conceptual resources.⁵⁰

8. The Dancing Temple

Other societies kneel, sing and dance together more regularly than we do in the West of the 21st century. For many of us, the only regular occasions when we sing aloud or listen to live music is in a worship service. More than ever, then, these embodied experiences of corporate worship represent an invaluable opportunity. In singing together we broaden our ways of making sense of the world. Moreover, since in worship we all sing together, we together develop a common lexicon of movement and gesture. The music and movement of worship become, not an obstacle , nor a supplement to Christian transformation, but a means and resource for that transforming work. They are not the emotional complement to the rational content of worship, but do themselves fund our conceptual vocabulary. As we sing and worship together, Plato's ancient fear is realized:

> [the soul] will, I imagine, be permeated by the corporeal, which fellowship and intercourse with the body will have ingrained its very nature through constant association and long practice.⁵¹

The old philosopher had it right. Just as mind and imagination may transfigure the flesh, so through long and constant association the body does indeed shape and transfigure the soul. But the image into which we are transformed it is not merely that of our own bodies. Rather, as we offer our bodies in worship (musical and

---

49   Ibid., 205.
50   For a more complete development of this argument see Steven R Guthrie, 'Carmen Universitatis: A Theological Study of Music and Measure', unpublished PhD Thesis (St Andrews, UK, 2000), esp. Chapter 4.
51   Plato, *Phaedo*, 133.

of other sorts) we lay hold of resources the Holy Spirit may use to transform us into the image of Christ. These frail and mortal bodies become singing, dancing, kneeling temples; their very gestures and patterns of bodily experience tracing out the dimensions of a space in which the Holy Spirit may live and work.

Chapter 6

Rhetoric and the Literary Sense: The Sacred Author's Performance in Cajetan's Exegesis of Scripture

Michael O' Connor

1. Introduction

At the age of 55 diminutive Italian Dominican Cardinal Tommaso de Vio, known as Cajetan after his birthplace of Gaeta near Naples, decided to become a biblical scholar. He started to learn Greek and Hebrew, hired expert linguists to assist him – Jewish as well as Christian – and spent most of the final decade of his life commenting on nearly all of the New Testament and a good deal of the Old Testament. His purpose was not, as is widely assumed, a polemical one, fighting the Protestant threat to Catholicism with its chosen weapon of the Bible. Rather his aim was pastoral: to contribute to the reform of the Church through a humanistically inspired 'return to the sources' of faith and discipleship. He was much more comfortable as a reformer than as a counter-reformer. To be sure, his commentaries contain elements of polemical engagement with Protestantism, but they also tilt at Scotists and Arians, cabalists and lazy prelates. Much more frequently, and painstakingly, they search the scriptures for truth for the mind, fire for the soul, and medicine for an ailing Church. To do this, Cajetan drew on the patristic and medieval tradition with which he was familiar, especially the commentaries of Aquinas. But he also made free and frequent use of the work of contemporary scholars, chief among them Erasmus.[1]

In the process, Cajetan elaborated his exegetical principles and methods. He is respectful of the translator's task, wanting to achieve a Latin text that is accurate yet transparent to the ambiguities and fluidity of the original languages. He is attentive to the historical context of words and expressions. And he regards positively the tools of the writer's trade as he finds them used by the biblical writers. It is this last feature that I will concentrate on in this paper: Cajetan's attention to literary style and genre, and in particular metaphor, narrative and rhetoric. His remarks about these elements of writing (or speaking), and the way in which they should be read (or listened to),

---

1   See my 'A Neglected Facet of Cardinal Cajetan: Biblical Reform in High Renaissance Rome', in Richard Griffiths (ed.), *The Bible in the Renaissance: Essays on Biblical Commentary and Translation in the Fifteenth and Sixteenth Centuries* (Aldershot: Ashgate, 2001), 71–94, and 'Exegesis, doctrine and reform in the biblical commentaries of Cardinal Cajetan, 1469–1534', unpublished doctoral thesis (Oxford University, 1997).

demonstrate a striking literary and dramatic sensitivity typical of 'humanist' culture but perhaps unexpected from one most frequently characterised as 'scholastic'.

The remarkable interweaving of so-called medieval and renaissance styles calls for some account of Cajetan's historical and geographical context: the Rome of Michelangelo and Raphael, and popes called Borgia and Medici.

2. Renaissance Rome as an Intellectual Centre

Theology in renaissance Rome reflected the unique character of the city.[2] The Roman ruling class was clerical and the head of state was a bishop. Important civic occasions were liturgical celebrations and the predominant expression of oratory was the sermon. Humanists who came to Rome in search of a career adapted themselves to the demands of Roman society, including the formal acceptance of celibacy. They addressed serious issues in theology and turned their attention to the Christian as well as the pagan past of the City. In Rome, the humanist fascination for ancient texts acquired a biblical and patristic orientation.

Meanwhile, members of supposedly typical scholastic professions, religious friars, contributed to the establishment of Ciceronian Latin as the norm for public oratory. One result of this adaptation was a tendency to play down the potential contrasts between scholasticism and humanism. The methods and styles of both find expression within single works.

What of the resulting theological style? In the past, it has been customary for scholars to characterise Roman theology as an eclectic cocktail of Platonist, cabalistic and Christian ingredients, with a mystical or speculative caste of mind and a preference for allegorical interpretation. There were certainly those who did theology of this sort; for example, Michelangelo's alternating portraits of prophets and sibyls in the Sistine Chapel (1508–12) surprised few of his contemporaries.[3] But recent scholarship has questioned the monopoly of this style; it is certainly not Cajetan's. Two further factors need to be taken into account.

The first is Roman preaching. The humanists were inspired by the classical connection of virtue and good literature; the pursuit of eloquence was a moral

---

[2] For this section on renaissance Roman theology, see John F. D'Amico, *Renaissance Humanism in Papal Rome* (Baltimore: John Hopkins, 1983); John W. O'Malley, *Praise and Blame in Renaissance Rome: Rhetoric, Doctrine, and Reform in the Sacred Orators of the Papal Court, ca. 1450–1521* (Durham NC: Duke, 1979); ibid., 'Grammar and Rhetoric in the *pietas* of Erasmus', *Journal of Medieval and Renaissance Studies* 18 (1988), 81–98; Charles Stinger, *The Renaissance In Rome* (Bloomington: University of Indiana Press, 1985), 140–55. See also Charles Trinkaus, *In Our Image and Likeness: Humanity and Divinity in Italian Renaissance Thought*, 2 vols (London: Constable, 1970).

[3] See, for example, Heinrich Pfeiffer, 'Gemalte Theologie in der Sixtinischen Kapelle. I: Die Szenen des Alten und Neuen Testamentes ausgeführt unter Sixtus IV', *AHP* 28 (1990), 99–160; 'Teil II: Die Fresken des Michelangelo Buonarotti ausgeführt unter Julius II', *AHP* 31 (1993), 69–107; 'Teil III: Die Sibyllen und Propheten', *AHP* 33 (1995), 91–116.

pursuit. Most notably, this brought about a radical reorientation of sermon style. The preachers at the papal court in Rome embraced classical rhetoric as a much desired alternative to scholastic preaching. Dialectic, the driving discipline of scholasticism, generated questions, distinctions, refinement of argument and proof. The humanists' rhetorical style, on the other hand, was content to rest with a few foundational truths, elaborating on these in a manner that sought to affect sentiment and behaviour. The themes chosen were the comprehensive themes of the creed: creation (especially the human part of it), incarnation, redemption. The social virtues of generosity and hospitality were stressed. The incarnation was envisaged as the image of human potential; the resurrection and ascension the image of human fulfilment. Rhetoric exploited the power of narrative, of concrete vocabulary and historical example to persuade and to move the emotions. A joyful panegyric style became the means whereby the deeds of God could not only be explained, but celebrated. This 'rhetorical theology' is the freshest and most original of the features of renaissance Roman theology and constitutes its most public face.

Cajetan was required to preach at the solemn papal mass from time to time. Five of these sermons are conserved and although he was no Ciceronian, there is in these sermons a real, if rather self-conscious, attempt to meet the stylistic requirements of the genre.[4] The influence of this rhetorical theology on scriptural exegesis will be fairly obvious: it will show itself in a keen attention to narrative, a sense of the visual and dramatic, and a preference for the literal–historical sense over the allegorical. There is a parallel here with music. On the one hand, there are those who are concerned with music in so far as, through its measures and proportions, music reveals something of the order and mystery of the universe (Pythagoras, Augustine). Then there are those for whom the power of music is determined by its expressive, rhetorical power (the Italian renaissance theorists). In the first case, music is a science closely related to mathematics, in the latter, it is much more like poetry.

The second major characteristic of renaissance Roman theology instances the enduring presence of scholasticism and, in particular, Aquinas. Research undertaken in the last couple of decades has shown the extent to which Aquinas was not only prominent but was the single strongest theological influence in and around the papal court.[5] Both in the manner of the celebration of his feast day and in the assiduous study of his writings, no other non-biblical saint or scholar was held in comparable esteem. The Vatican library possessed more volumes of Aquinas than any other author; in the pope's private chapel, Aquinas is depicted alongside the Greek and Latin doctors

---

4   *Opuscula*, 133r–139r. Discussed in Wicks, 'Thomism between Renaissance and Reformation: the Case of Cajetan', *ARG* 68 (1977), 9–33. See also O'Malley, *Praise and Blame*, 108–10.

5   In addition to the items mentioned in n. 2 above, see Paul Oskar Kristeller, *Medieval Aspects of Renaissance Learning*, trans. Edward Mahoney (New York: Columbia University Press, 1974, re-issued with new preface, 1992). Originally published, with appended texts, as *Le Thomisme et la pensée italienne de la Renaissance* (Montreal: Inst. d'Études Médiévales, 1967); John Monfasani, 'Aristotelians, Platonists, and the Missing Ockhamists: Philosophical Liberty in Pre-Reformation Italy', *Renaissance Quarterly* 46 (1993), 247–76.

of the early Church in frescoes painted by the Dominican Fra Angelico. On his feast day, the papal entourage attended the solemn liturgy in unprecedented ceremony at the Dominican church of Santa Maria sopra Minerva. During the mass, the singing of the creed indicated an honour reserved at that time to doctors of the Church.

Cajetan's call to Rome in 1501 was no accident; it was an element in a deliberate policy on the part of his superiors to promote the study of Aquinas and extend his influence. This aim is reflected in Cajetan's commentary on the *Summa theologiae*, but it is far from absent in his other enormous theological undertaking, the biblical commentaries.

3. The Literal Sense

In the course of his commentaries, Cajetan repeatedly asserts that the literal sense is his *only* concern. In the dedicatory letter to his commentary on the Psalms (addressed to Clement VII) he complains that the commentaries that have so far been produced have only given the mystical sense; a clear exposition according to the literal sense is required, in order better to serve those who read and sing the Psalter daily.[6] Cajetan was well-aware that Aquinas had established the literal sense both as the means to determine doctrine and as the foundation of the allegorical sense. Evidently, Cajetan considers that, without the firm foundation of the literal sense, the mystical sense is less than helpful in opening up the meaning of scripture. When he alludes to the mystical sense, it is usually as something to be passed over. The literal sense determines faith; the mystical sense is for the edification of those who already believe. In general, there is a reluctant tone is Cajetan's use of mystical interpretation, as if it were a last resort, to be used when all else fails.[7] On one occasion only does Cajetan refer to allegory, and that only when he is led to do so because Paul uses the word first (Gal 4.23–24), and even then, his comments are remarkable only for being so brief.

There is one exception to his reluctance towards the mystical sense. When New Testament writers appear to have misunderstood the literal sense of an Old Testament text, Cajetan readily employs the mystical sense as an ally: the explanation of an apparent misappropriation of the Old Testament is attributed to the apostolic use of it *according to the mystical sense*. Cajetan uses this method repeatedly, both excusing the apostles (such usage is quite deliberate)[8] and apologising for them (we would not have expected this lack of precision from them).

---

6   *Psalmi Davidici ad Hebraicam veritatem castigati et iuxta sensum quem literalem dicunt ennarati* (Venice: Giunta, 1530), Dedication, fol. vii.v

7   On Prov 30.16, III, 593a. Cajetan's commentaries on scripture are cited according to the complete edition in 5 volumes, edited by the Dominicans of Alcalà: *Opera Omnia quotquot in sacrae scripturae expositionem reperiuntur* (Lyons: Iacob. et Petr. Prost., 1639). References are given to scripture verse, volume, page and column.

8   For example, on Ps 19, Intro, III, 69a.

Cajetan gives no detailed exposition of his methods for determining the literal sense of a text. The principles by which he works have to be extrapolated from his practice with no more than occasional support from casual remarks about methodology.

In justifying his exegesis, Cajetan asks the reader to envisage what, in a given context, is most reasonable, most plausible (a criterion of verisimilitude);[9] he seeks the interpretation that best accords with reason, context and other texts of scripture;[10] he suggests that the kind of certainty that obtains in exegesis (as distinct from the certainty of, say, mathematics) arises from the inter-relation of different parts of the text;[11] he chides those who, in addition to examining the context of a passage, also consult apocryphal, that is, non-authoritative, sources;[12] and he asks his reader to be a tolerant judge of his commentaries insofar as the interpretations they contain, however novel, do not contradict the truth of the Christian faith or the teaching and practice of the Church (*even* if they depart from the patristic tradition).[13] In short, the literal sense is the author's intention.

4. Metaphor and Narrative in Genesis 1–3

For Cajetan, the literal meaning of a phrase or verse depends not only on the history and the dictionary definitions of the words used, but also on the *manner* in which they are used by the author.[14] In particular, the commentator will have to judge from the context when a word is being used 'properly', and when metaphorically, or with irony and exaggeration (even by God).[15] Such 'non-literal' devices belong to the literal sense of a text. For example, when Paul says that he had eaten nothing for 14 days, he is surely exaggerating; were this exactly true, Paul and his companions would have died.[16]

Amongst those figures of speech which the sacred authors use and which the commentator must discern, Cajetan makes specific mention of metaphor, parable and similitude.[17] Cajetan underlines that these figures of speech are not departures

---

9 On 1 Kings 10.8, II, 92a.
10 On Gen 2.21, I, 22b.
11 On Pss, Prooemium, III, 3a–3b.
12 On 2 Kings 4.2, II, 136b.
13 'Et si quando occurrerit novus sensus textui consonus, nec a sacra scriptura, nec ab ecclesia doctrina dissonus, quamvis a torrente doctorum sacrorum dissonus, aequos se praebent censores.' On Pentateuch, Preface, I, facing 1.
14 On Pss, Prooemium, III, 3a.
15 On Gen 3.22, I, 31a; on Ex 32.7, I, 251b; on 3 Kings 21.7, II, 222a; on Job 38.3, II, 532b; I Cor 4.8, V, 98a; on 1 Thess 3.8, V, 279a.
16 On Acts 27.33, IV, 482b.
17 E.g. 'Similitudines': on Deut 8.2, I, 451a; 'Metaphoricus est sermo': on Gen 6.6, I, 41b; also on Lev 19.19, I, 317b; on Deut 25.4, I, 482b; on I Thess 4.15, V, 281b; on II Cor 12.7, V, 196a.

from the literal sense; they are part of the variety of the literal sense.[18] Echoing Aquinas, he argues that the literal sense of a metaphorical text is not the metaphor itself, but the meaning that the metaphor intends to convey.[19] Many uses of metaphor are straightforward enough and clearly intended by the author (the 'last trumpet', for example).[20] The difference between a literal-metaphorical interpretation and a mystical interpretation is that, in the former case, the metaphor is an irreducible part of the author's intention. The writer uses metaphors which can only be read as metaphors; if taken 'literally', they would be absurd. The mystical sense, on the other hand, is additional to the literal sense, presupposing it and able to co-exist with it, and an interpretation of what the Holy Spirit has concealed, or even encoded, within the text.

In his exegesis of the opening chapters of Genesis, Cajetan goes to considerable lengths to present a correct and reasonable interpretation. He is concerned that a simplistic reading of some parts of the narrative might appear ridiculous to anyone with any learning and would discredit Christian theology and teaching. In order to avoid this, he insists that the reader be attentive to the use of metaphors.

He prepares the ground for the forthcoming novelty by the use of a thoroughly traditional non-literalism in his comments on Genesis 1. Following Augustine, he accepts that the 'six days' are to be seen as a literary device, a figure designed to express the order and harmony of the created universe. The six days are not, however, a fiction; the narrative description is a fitting and helpful accommodation. The six days express six grades according to which the orderly perfection of the created world is distributed. There exists a relation of proportionality between the work of creation and the days of the week.[21]

Having in this way assured his reader that the text of Genesis makes legitimate and recognised use of such literary devices, Cajetan introduces into his commentary less familiar elements of parable or metaphor. The first element to be approached in this way is the creation of Eve from Adam's rib. For Cajetan, this account is to be taken as a parable.[22] The first reason he gives for this is an anatomical one: either Adam had a rib to spare or he had to live the rest of his life with one rib too few. Adam is therefore either a monster, or incomplete. Both solutions are manifestly absurd.[23]

Cajetan examines the context surrounding this verse: in an earlier passage, Moses (the supposed author of Genesis) tells us that God brings the wild beasts and the birds of heaven to Adam, to provide for him a helpmate. For Cajetan, it is plainly ridiculous to suppose that God actually thought he might find a suitable helpmate for

---

18   On Prov 2.18, III, 512a.
19   On Ps 45.4-5, III, 164a.
20   On 1 Cor 15.52, V, 148a.
21   On Gen 1.5, I, 6a.
22   'Cogor ex ipso textu et contentu intelligere hanc mulieris productionem non ut sonat litera, sed secundum mysterium non allegoriae sed parabolae.' On Gen 2.21, I, 22a.
23   On Gen 2.21, I, 22a.

Adam among the birds. Moses does not intend this to be understood as a description of an actual event. And since this passage *introduces* the account of the creation of the woman, it is reasonable to suppose that both are to be taken metaphorically.[24] A further argument is adduced from a comparison of the two accounts of creation. Since, according to the first account, the man and the woman are said to have been created together on the sixth day, the second account, involving the formation of the woman from the man's rib, is evidently a metaphorical supplement to the first account, saying something about the relationship between the man and the woman, and not a new account of the creation of the woman.[25] A final argument follows from the fact that the woman, after having been fashioned from Adam's rib, is 'brought to him'. Here Moses once more hints that his text is to be taken metaphorically: had the woman actually been made from Adam's rib, she would already have been next to him, having no need to be brought to him.[26]

Cajetan holds that his interpretation accords with reason, with the context and with other texts of scripture.[27] He is not perturbed by the fact that scripture gives this account in the *form* of a historical narrative: the same is said of the six days of creation and of the questioning of the animals for a helpmate for Adam; likewise the talking serpent, punished by having to crawl on its belly. If it is reasonable to interpret such texts metaphorically, then there should be no objections to his interpretation of the rib.[28] These texts not only invite a metaphorical interpretation, they require it. Otherwise, the sense is childish.[29]

Cajetan argues that this approach to these texts is not only reasonable and balanced, but also useful for the witness of the Christian faith amongst the 'wise of this world'. His gain has not been at the level of theological content; there is little difference between his literal-metaphorical explanation of the creation of Eve and the non-literal, mystical explanation of the same text by Aquinas.[30] Rather, his concern has been a pastoral one: he is worried lest the mysteries of faith be dismissed as fables and that those who might otherwise take the Christian faith seriously would be discouraged by exegesis that is puerile, ridiculous and absurd. The commentator has to show that the whole passage is a *metaphorical narrative*, not a properly literal one.[31] In this way, the identification of metaphors takes on a critical importance for

---

24   On Gen 2.21, I, 22a–b.

25   On Gen 2.21, I, 22b. Cajetan is not entirely consistent here: the context also includes the narrative of the formation of Adam from the dust of the earth (Gen 2.7) which Cajetan appears to interpret in a proper-literal sense.

26   On Gen 2.22, I, 23a.

27   On Gen 2.21, I, 22b.

28   On Gen 2.21, I, 22b.

29   '[…] textus ipse ad metaphoricum sensum non solum invitat sed cogit.' On Gen 3.15, I, 29b.

30   Compare Aquinas, *Summa theologiae* I, 92, 3 and Cajetan on Gen 2.21, I, 23a.

31   'Sunt autem sensus isti metaphorici non solum sobrii secundum sacram scripturam, sed non parum utiles Christianae fidei professioni, praecipue coram sapientibus huius mundi; percipientes enim quod haec non ut litera sonat sed metaphorice dicta intelligimus ac credimus,

preachers and teachers: their own performance will be more persuasive if they are alert to the performance methods of the biblical authors they are expounding. While others had expressed concern that poor Christian exegesis of the Old Testament aroused the mockery of the Jews, Cajetan is concerned to keep the 'wise of this world' on board.[32]

5. Moses, the Evangelists and the Rhetoric of Narrative

Metaphor is one rhetorical device amongst many used by story-tellers, one that relates the biblical author to the poet. At other times, the biblical author is more akin to the historian or chronicler, and this raises, for Cajetan, issues of narrative structure: how does a writer first select and then arrange the chosen material? By addressing this question, Cajetan is hoping to initiate the reader into a mature reading of biblical texts.

An illuminating preface to Cajetan's description of the artfulness of the sacred writers is his understanding of the artfulness of God.[33] Cajetan enjoys finding patterns in divine revelation and these he attributes to the deliberate intention of God. Such a pattern is evident, for example, in the manifestation to Samuel of God's choice of David as king. First of all, Samuel is told that the kingdom is to be taken from Saul and given to another; then he is told that the new king is one of the sons of Jesse; then, finally, he is shown which of those sons it is to be.[34] Samuel is led, step by step, to the specific identification of David. Although Cajetan does not state this explicitly, such a method clearly adds to the dramatic effectiveness of the narrative.

Jesus shows a fondness for the same method, likewise in circumstances of mounting expectation. Cajetan discerns this pattern in the prophecies of betrayal, gathered together from the different gospels. The first prophecies speak only of his being rejected (*initially* in unqualified terms, *then* 'in fulfilment of the scriptures').[35] The idea of betrayal is introduced, but not the identity of the betrayer. At the Last Supper, Jesus declares that he is to be betrayed by one of his own disciples; this reduces the catchment to twelve. Next, Jesus reveals that the betrayer is one who has dipped his hand in the same dish as Jesus. This reduces the number of suspects to between six and four, since, according to Cajetan, this is the number of persons who customarily share a dish of food in this way.[36] (This is exactly as depicted in

---

non horrent haec de costa Adam, et serpente tanquam fabellas, sed venerantur mysteria et facilius ea quae sunt fidei complectuntur.' On Gen 3.1, I, 25a.

32   See Centi, 'L'attività letteraria di Santi Pagnini (1470–1536) nel campo delle scienze bibliche', *AFP* (1945)5–51, at 7–8. For Aquinas, Centi refers to ST I, 68, 1.

33   Cortesi argued that, since God himself uses rhetorical techniques in scripture, it is entirely fitting that his creatures should. D'Amico, *Renaissance Humanism in Papal Rome*, 153.

34   On 1 Kings 16.9, II, 104b.
35   On Mk 9.12, IV, 152a.
36   On Mt 26.23, IV, 118a.

Leonardo da Vinci's 'Last Supper', completed in 1497 in the refectory of Santa Maria delle Grazie in Milan, a house to which Cajetan was assigned between 1499 and 1501.) Finally, when Jesus finally identifies his betrayer, he does so only to John, leaning on his breast. Thus, by taking the data from all of the Gospels, Cajetan charts how Jesus' disclosure of his betrayer becomes more specific as the moment of betrayal draws closer, adding to and reflecting the tension of the moment.[37]

So much for God, what of human authors? Cajetan does not attribute to Moses or the evangelists an unreflective cataloguing of events. For example, the order in which things are told is not always the same as the order in which they happened.[38] Sometimes Moses summarises and selects,[39] often giving a general description of a whole episode before going back to account for particular details.[40] If a discourse is to be repeated (for example, God speaks to Moses and then Moses relays God's words to the people) he does not necessarily give all the words both times, for the ease of the reader.[41] At other times, taking up again a narrative thread, he will repeat something already described.[42] And when he has more weighty matters to narrate, he rushes through other material.[43] For Cajetan, the performance of Moses, story-teller and teacher of the law, respects both his message and his audience.

Similar techniques are evident in the work of the evangelists, even more clearly, since they are telling one four-fold story. No single Gospel gives all that Jesus said and did. One adds what another omits.[44] Each evangelist selects and edits in order to improve the narrative, to avoid repetition or tedium, or to point up some facet of the gospel message. For example, according to Cajetan, Matthew has relocated the narrative of the anointing at Bethany (Mt 26.6–13) in order to bring it closer to the narrative of Judas' betrayal, which follows immediately (Mt 26.14–16). He has done this in order to show the close link between the two events: it was because Judas was so incensed that the expensive ointment was not sold to contribute to the purse (from which he would then have stolen), that he decided to 'sell' Jesus to compensate himself.[45]

Amongst the four gospels, Cajetan ascribes to John the greatest degree of historicity. Having read the other gospels himself, John assumes the same knowledge on the part of his readers.[46] Where Matthew and Mark recall certain words of Jesus,

---

37 On Jn 13.26, IV, 385a.
38 For example, on Gen 37.2, I, 128a.
39 For example, on Gen 48.22, I, 147a.
40 And not only Moses. See on Judg 6.24, II, 47a; on Judg 10.17, II, 55a; on 1 Kings 1.23, II, 77a; on 1 Kings, 2.30, II, 80b; 1 Kings 24.5, II, 118a (where an event is 'recalled' which had never hitherto been mentioned); on Mt 27.52–53, IV, 126b.
41 '[...] ne repetitio fastidio esset lectoribus.' On Ex 12.24, I, 181a.
42 On Ex 6.30, I, 167b.
43 'Festinat siquidem Moses ad Abraham.' On Gen 9.29, I, 55a.
44 On Mk 10.11, IV, 155a. Cajetan's assumptions are those of Aquinas, see Smalley, *The Gospels in the Schools* (London: Hambledon, 1985), 269–71.
45 On Mt 26.6, IV, 116b. Mark does likewise, on Mk 14.3, IV, 162b–163a.
46 On Jn 11.2, IV, 366a.

John tells us when and where they were uttered.⁴⁷ Most often, it is John who provides what the other evangelists have omitted; at other times compressing or omitting what the others have included.⁴⁸ For example, in answering the charge of sabbath-breaking, the synoptics report Jesus' words of reproach to the Pharisees; John, however, recounts the words of Jesus that just as his Father goes on working, so he goes on working; this is because John wishes to disclose most clearly the divinity of Jesus.⁴⁹ Cajetan underlines that John's attention to detail reflects his *theological* purpose. Because John is dealing with such challenging and unheard of doctrinal matters (namely, the divinity of the messiah), he describes the circumstances of Jesus' teaching and signs with the greatest detail, that they may be more convincing. Cajetan recalls that Plato passed off some of his own doctrines as the teachings of Socrates and Parmenides. John does not wish to be accused of the same tactic.⁵⁰

Having said this, Cajetan seems to attribute to the evangelist no less a degree of creativity than he has already noted in Moses. He is seen to re-arrange material for reasons of clarity.⁵¹ And John chooses carefully the name or title he will use for Jesus. When John tells us that, before feeding the multitude, 'the *Lord* gave thanks', attention to vocabulary leads to a theological conclusion: the (divine) Lord, gave thanks (in his human nature); John testifies to the mystery of the incarnation revealed in this miracle.⁵²

Cajetan's reflections on scripture, recognising the artfulness of the sacred authors, also assume a responsiveness on the part of the reader. For example, the evangelists do not tell us everything; they leave some scope for the reader's imagination. So Cajetan comments not only on what is in the text, but also on what is absent. He supplements the gospel narrative, filling in background detail, providing missing dialogue, suggesting what people were doing 'offstage' before or after a scene, even trying to visualise posture and attitude.⁵³ Commenting on the conversation between Jesus and the man born blind, Cajetan suggests that John has clearly compressed the dialogue. He speculates on what one of the disciples might have said to the man to encourage him to respond to Jesus' questions; he even offers some additional sample dialogue. The scene, he concludes, would have been rather odd without some such dialogue; the description given by the evangelist is not meant to be exhaustive.⁵⁴ Similarly, when Judas goes to the chief priests and asks, 'What will you give me if I deliver him to you?' (Mt 26.15), Cajetan suggests that these words summarise

---

47   On Jn 13.36, IV, 386a.
48   On Jn 2.23, IV, 299b; on Jn 3.3, IV, 300b; on Jn 11.2, IV, 366b; on Jn 12.3, IV, 372a–b; on Jn 20.30, IV, 425b.
49   On Jn 5.17, IV, 317b.
50   On Jn, Intro, IV, 279a.
51   On Jn 10.27, IV, 363a.
52   On Jn 6.23, IV, 327b.
53   For example, on Jn 4.6, IV, 310b.
54   '*Bono animo esto, permitte luto quod facit seu fecit Iesus ungi oculos tuos.* [...] A ratione humana alienum est quod res sic nude gesta sit, cum solis verbis Evangelistae.' On Jn 9.11, IV, 355b.

a much fuller speech. We know that Judas is a liar; Cajetan suggests that the event which was the *occasion* of the betrayal (the anointing at Bethany) may also have presented Judas with an *excuse* for his betrayal. He supposes that Judas would have justified himself in the light of Jesus' behaviour in these or similar words: 'I used to think that Jesus was a spiritual man but now I have changed my opinion of him; I am scandalised by his sensual behaviour, by the way he allowed himself to be anointed at this woman's hands.' Even though the gospels give no clearer evidence elsewhere, for Cajetan this lie is implicit in the accounts. It is just the kind of camouflage people employ when they want to draw attention away from their own wickedness.[55]

Cajetan's experience of hearing excuses informs his pursuit of realism in explaining the scene. The reader is assumed to be curious and imaginative, able to relate personal knowledge and experience to the scriptural narrative, able to enter into the minds and hearts of the characters, and ready to be moved to imitate the example of the good, and to avoid the example of the wicked.

6. Paul and the Rhetoric of Preaching

The sacred chroniclers have been in possession of a certain kind of literary technique (that of narrative), which Cajetan points up and commends. When he comes to Paul, he adds the element of style (that of rhetoric). For Cajetan, Paul excels as a philosopher and orator. Time and again, Paul's style is acknowledged to be artful and astute:[56] he uses a rhetorical question rather than expressly blame the Corinthians ('Shall I commend you in this?', 1 Cor 11.22);[57] he combines arguments from custom with those of reason, in order to make his case more persuasive;[58] he shrewdly praises the Corinthians for their obedience to previous commands, before giving them new commands;[59] he even admits to using praise of others and envy to motivate generosity.[60] In his comments on Paul's most carefully constructed piece of writing, the letter to the Romans, Cajetan repeatedly notes how Paul carefully balances praise and blame towards the Jews and the Gentiles, to maximise the impact of his preaching.[61] Paul abandons all such artifice when speaking to the simple, but even this is acknowledged as the tactic of an expert, knowing how to accommodate his speech to his audience (especially when his enemies, the false-apostles, did the opposite).[62] Cajetan remarks with amazement at the display of oratory in the shortest and most personal of Paul's epistles, the letter to Philemon.[63] Just as Moses was

---

55 On Mt 26.15, IV, 117b.
56 For example, on 1 Cor 3.1, V, 158b.
57 On 1 Cor 11.22, V, 124b-125a.
58 On 1 Cor 11.16, V, 123b.
59 On 1 Cor 11.2, V, 121b. Likewise the Romans, on Rom 12.19, V, 72a.
60 On 2 Cor 9.2, V, 184b.
61 On Rom 2.14, V, 11b; on Rom 2.17, V, 12b; on Rom 9.1, V, 54a.
62 On 2 Cor 11.6, V, 191b.
63 On Philem 1.21, V, 328a.

seen to use an artful narrative style for the benefit of his reader, so Paul is seen to make effective use of the art of persuasion. This estimation of Paul contrasts with that of Erasmus, for whom Paul was basically a 'rustic' capable of only occasional rhetorical flair.[64] The implication for preachers is clear: they are not to shy away from the use of 'techniques' in order to engage their listeners and communicate their message; striving to know their listeners, they must craft their words in order to achieve the most effective impact.

7. The Rhetoric of the Historical Psalms

A final example from Cajetan's commentaries on the psalms gathers together a number of the threads under consideration in this paper. In an important note on Psalm 3, the first of the historical psalms, Cajetan explains how the literal historical sense of the psalms can serve the faith of Christians.

Cajetan reminds readers of a practice found amongst legislators whereby a law is promulgated not in a prescriptive form ('this category of action must be done'), but by means of a narrative, not unlike law of precedent ('this is what so-and-so did, and it is to be commended'); the deed described embodies the disposition required by the new law being promulgated. Likewise, the Holy Spirit has arranged the psalms so that the deeds of the holy men and women of the Old Testament are narrated in the form of divine praise. In this way, those who recite them learn both how the Spirit guided the saints of old and how the same Spirit will guide them today, forming in them the same mind and heart.[65] Using a comparison drawn from the public proclamation of law in civil life, Cajetan expresses the effect of praying the psalms in overtly rhetorical terms: moved by the words of the sacred text, the intellect and the emotions are persuaded to take on new thoughts and feelings, and to act in a new way, inspired by the deeds of others. For Cajetan there is nothing irrelevant in the history and religious experience of the people of the old covenant, nor in the human experience of the inspired poet.

8. Conclusions

Although at first sight Cajetan's avowed approach to exegesis seems minimalist (commenting according to the literal sense alone), the resulting commentary is wide-ranging and diverse. Perhaps it would be better to characterise his method as the pursuit of the 'literary sense': in the process of commenting on scripture, Cajetan has had much to say about authors (or story-tellers, or orators) and much to say about readers (or listeners). He has also revealed an understanding of the role of the commentator as a bridge between the two.

---

64   See Rummel, *Erasmus' Annotations on the New Testament. From Philologist to Theologian* (Toronto: University of Toronto Press, 1986), 99–100, 140–41.

65   On Ps 3.1, III, 13b–14a.

Cajetan gives full attention to the inspired human author, allowing to that author all the creativity of a secular poet, orator or chronicler. The human author is not a passive instrument; the fact that the sacred authors were inspired by God in no sense means that they wrote without character and individuality. Words, which themselves are contingent and particular, coming out of a distinct history, language and culture, are placed with consequence in a given sentence, paragraph or book. The human author is responsible for the words of the sacred text.

Cajetan also characterises the reader as active and responsible: entering imaginatively into the mood and details of the scriptural text, with understanding and feeling. In effect, a performer. This involvement might be fairly direct or it might involve the reconstruction of a context through more deliberate research and the wider play of the imagination. This is not usually a solitary task. The reader is initiated by an intermediary: the experienced reader who becomes the commentator, both translating and explaining to others the ancient text.

The commentator must be skilled in a variety of disciplines: language, history, geography, natural science, as well as philosophy and theology. To this extent, Cajetan's is a 'historical-critical' method. The commentator must also have a lively imagination, a sense of narrative and a feel for character and motive. Cajetan may have encountered these qualities in some measure in the exegesis of Aquinas; but they were cultivated before his eyes (and ears) in renaissance art, rhetoric, and pageant. This adds to his method an element of 'rhetorical-criticism', as the commentator seeks out the intention of the author through an understanding of the literary genres and rhetorical devices used.

As a consequence of this, the commentator is interested in the reader's response. The sacred authors wrote in order to elicit a response of faith and action; the commentator has tried to make that purpose transparent. The commentator is in effect taking the role of preacher, one step removed from the pulpit. This brings us to the heart of Cajetan's purpose: himself a preacher, he sought to equip preachers for their task of opening the pages of scripture for others, and of leading them to an ever more faithful response to the Word of God.

Chapter 7

Seeing Through the Drama: Reframing Violent News

Jolyon Mitchell

1. Introduction

Violent images from the supposedly holy land have taken on a sickening familiarity. The debris from a shattered bus lies strewn across the road. A stretcher carries another bloodied victim to an ambulance with open doors. Shocked bystanders sob out their stories. A semblance of order is restored by the reporter's voice-over. She offers a five-line interpretation of over fifty years of war. Then we are shown a suited politician, flanked by thickset bodyguards, who promises 'further immediate retaliation'. Cut, the next night, to an image of the night sky illuminated by traces of white light and flashes of orange explosions. Rarely do we see the full result of these deadly firework displays. There are occasional images of rescue workers among the remains of houses, covering their noses because of the stench of decaying bodies, or masked gunmen shooting at tanks trundling through rubble. There are claims and counter-claims, but one thing is made clear by news: the spiral of vengeance continues. Such images and stories of violence from the West Bank to Kabul and from Baghdad to Bali are the staple diet of many news programmes and newspapers.

In this chapter I wish to investigate how specific news media representations of violence are framed. I concentrate, though not exclusively, on television news. Following an introductory discussion, I continue by demonstrating that the framing of violent news provokes a wide range of responses from viewers: from emotional fatigue to responsive violence. I explore the idea that images and stories of violence can exacerbate violent situations, contributing to conflict. I then develop a case for reframing violent news in such a way that can help audiences to see conflicts and the effects of violence in a new way. Reframing facilitates seeing differently, which in turn can lead to acting differently. I suggest that there are many precedents found in the New Testament and in later artistic representations for reframing violent news. I conclude by showing that participating in Christian narratives, communities, images and practices, provides not only resources for constructive interaction and criticism of news, but also for reframing mediated reality. In other words the practice and performance of theological ethics can help audiences to see through and reframe violent news, thereby bringing a new vision for living in a violent world.[1]

In a well-known café-bar in Edinburgh there is a large ornate frame on one wall. Somewhat idiosyncratically it has no picture within its borders. It simply frames the bright paint behind it. The result of this abstract framing is that you look more carefully at the whole wall, though primarily at what is within the framed part of the wall. Framing directs attention to a specific region of space.[2] Where the frame is placed determines what is included in the picture, and what is excluded. Likewise news, whether on television or in print, provides a frame for looking at an event or a story. Giltin, in his study of the interactions between the student new-left movement and the news media, defines framing as: 'persistent emphasis, selection, and exclusion'. He suggests that using frames helps journalists 'to process large amounts of information quickly and routinely', and then 'package the information for efficient relay to their audiences'.[3] Thus framing is a useful, some would argue a necessary, tool for journalists.

How precisely does journalistic framing operate? Entman's widely quoted description of the characteristics of framing provides the beginning of an answer to this question: 'Framing essentially involves *selection* and *salience*. To frame is to *select some aspects of a perceived reality and make them more salient in a communicating text, in such a way as to promote a particular problem definition, causal interpretation, moral evaluation, and/or treatment recommendation*'.[4] In a similar way we can claim that news frames select, highlight and thus have the potential to direct attention to specific elements of an event, making them more salient. In this context salience 'means making a piece of information more noticeable, meaningful, or memorable to audiences'.[5] This process does not, however, ensure that audiences will necessarily appropriate the frames that they are provided with by the news media.

How a news story, whether it is a bombing in Basra or Madrid, is framed may determine what is seen and what is not seen, but it does not entirely account for the viewers' interpretation of what is seen. Part of the objective of this chapter is to make a case for 'cultivating frame-consciousness' and exploring how audiences can see beyond the frame that they are offered. As Chris Arthur suggests it is 'imperative that we learn to see the frames that the mass media construct and to appreciate the quite

---

1   Some elements of the argument of this chapter appear in an adapted form in my discussion of news in *Media and Christian Ethics* (Cambridge University Press, forthcoming). I am grateful both to the Henry Scott Holland trust and the Institute for Theology, Imagination and the Arts in St Andrews for the encouragement and opportunity to explore this theme.

2   I am grateful to Dr Judith Buchanan for drawing my attention to this example and aspect of framing.

3   T. Giltin, *The whole world is watching: Mass media in the making and unmaking of the new left* (Berkeley, CA: University of California Press, 1980), 7.

4   Robert M. Entman, 'Framing: Toward Clarification of a Fractured Paradigm', *Journal of Communication* 43:4 (Autumn 1993), 52; emphasis in original.

5   Ibid., 53.

different stories that are told outside them'.⁶ The viewer also has a central role in this process. 'In Perth, the ancient capital of Scotland, there's a red sandstone sculpture on a small rise of land overlooking the river Tay ... The sculpture features two large L-shaped pieces of stone. The uprights of each are about six feet high ... The overall effect is of a giant incomplete picture frame, through which the city may be viewed.'⁷ Depending on where you stand your framed view changes. So here the position and perspective of the viewer transforms the vision of reality.⁸

At this point it is important to make clear the distinction between frames employed by news producers or journalists to make an event more salient, and the frames of reference, or as they are sometimes described 'schemata', that an audience uses to interpret the news and the world of their experience. One way of thinking about an audience's frames of reference can be drawn from Erving Goffman's book on *Frame Analysis*. He claims that people 'actively project their frames of reference into the world immediately around them'.⁹ The result is that everybody uses frames of reference to make sense of events, interpret their experiences and organise their everyday lives, as well as defining their involvements. Goffman is particularly concerned about the moments of vulnerability where these frames of reference are transformed, even broken. At first sight, the vast majority of images or stories of violence appear to have little obvious effect. Though, as we will see, occasionally one image can rupture a viewer's imaginative frame of reference, especially if there is a point of personal contact or identification. The viewer's original frames of reference will no longer hold. Reframing occurs in order to accommodate the new information or experience.

Goffman, Giltin, Entman and Arthur are but four contributors to an extensive literature that, over the last twenty-five years, has evolved around frames and framing effects.¹⁰ There is no single definition or theory of framing, though scholars working in the social sciences, including cognitive psychology and the humanities, continue to employ the metaphor of framing. Through content or discourse analysis some have concentrated on the frames that news creates.¹¹ Several studies have identified a small number of recurring news frames, such as conflict, human interest, economic

---

6 Chris Arthur, 'Seeing (beyond) the frame', in *Media Development* 2000/4, p 4.

7 Ibid., 3. The sculpture, by Timothy Shutter, entitled 'Millais' Viewpoint', was made in 1997.

8 Arthur celebrates the incompleteness of this frame, resisting those who seek to 'advance some particular ideal framing, whether religious or political', and instead affirming awareness of the 'many different framings and the limitations of each'. Ibid., 5.

9 Erving Goffman, *Frame Analysis* (London: Harper and Row, 1974), 39.

10 See Holli A. Semetko and Patti M. Valkenburg, 'Framing European Politics: A Content Analysis of Press and Television News', *Journal of Communication* 50:2 (Spring 2000), 93–109.

11 See, for example, Zhongdong Pang and Gerald Kosicki, 'Framing Analysis An Approach to News Discourse', *Political Communication* 10 (1993), 55–75.

consequences, morality and responsibility frames.[12] On the basis of extensive content analysis of television, magazines and newspaper coverage of five major news stories in the late 1980s Russell Neuman, Marion R. Just and Ann N. Crigler produced evidence that suggested conflict was one of the dominant news frames in the United States.[13] Subsequent research from other cultural contexts provides further evidence of how conflictual framing has in certain situations become *one* of journalism's dominant paradigms. For example, Semetko and Valkenburg's work on Dutch newspaper and television coverage of a Heads of Government meeting in 1997 provides detailed evidence of how politics is also frequently covered through a conflict frame.[14]

Unlike journalists who often draw upon conflict frames for making sense of the news stories, Neuman et al. also found that audiences put greater emphasis upon human interest and morality frames.[15] The discrepancy between news providers and audiences over how an event is framed is significant as it raises questions regarding journalistic attachment to conflict. This is partly explained by a professional ethic that perpetuates a divisive construction of reality and believes that conflict increases interest in the story. Following on from these studies, others have employed a range of qualitative research methods to examine the effects of such conflictual frames on audiences. For instance, Joseph Cappella and Kathleen Jamieson's in depth work with 276 participants from across the USA led them to claim that the news media's concentration on conflict leads in many cases to public cynicism about political leaders and the democratic process.[16] The cumulative result of such research is a more developed critical awareness of the significance of framing conflict for both the producer and the consumer of the news.

A number of points emerge from this introductory reflection on framing, pertinent to the discussion of violent news. First, framing by journalists can concentrate our attention on one aspect of life, thereby contributing to, limiting and even distorting our understanding of reality. It is important to remember, however, that framing not only includes, but also excludes. There is a body of research that suggests that some journalists resort to a conflict frame as one of their stock approaches to covering a story. Second, the place that we choose to stand to look through the frame also influences our perception of news' events. This observation serves as a valuable reminder that research into the impact of framing, or as it is more usually described 'framing effects', recognises the vital role played by the audience in creating and recreating frames for themselves. Third, for some writers reframing is in itself a controversial project since if it is used restrictively it implies replacing the original

---

12   See, for example, Semetko and Valkenburg, 'Framing European Politics', 95–96; and W. Russell Neuman, Marion R. Just and Ann N. Crigler, *Common Knowledge: News and the Construction of Political Meaning* (Chicago: University of Chicago Press, 1992), 60–77.
13   Neuman et al., *Common Knowledge*, 75.
14   Semetko and Valkenburg, 'Framing European Politics', 95–96.
15   Neuman et al., *Common Knowledge*, 75.
16   Joseph N. Cappella and Kathleen Hall Jamieson, *Spiral of Cynicism: The Press and the Public Good* (Oxford University Press, 1997).

confinement with another. In contrast to such a belief, this chapter seeks to show how the reframing of violent news need not necessarily lead to an ideal, confined or impoverished view of the world, and can instead provide a hopeful, compassionate and realistic account of violent news.

2. Responding to Violent News

In 'peaceful' countries, what are the common responses to the kaleidoscopic range of violent images? Typically, many viewers switch off or switch over, such is the regularity of these violent narratives. Changing channels comes in many forms, from turning the page to crossing over to the other side with the help of the remote control. 'In a world that moves steadily from massacres to genocide, from images of chaos, destruction, death and madness, from the gassing of Kurds ... to the streets and fields of slaughter of Rwandans, the public', according to Susan Moeller, 'resorts to compassion fatigue as defence mechanism against the knowledge of horror.'[17] Compassion fatigue may be a journalistic cliché to some scholars, but for others it is a reality that finds its roots in the apparently never-ending repetition of images of suffering and violence. If it is not Iraq then it may be violent demonstrations against cartoons mocking the Prophet Mohammed in Beirut or Kabul, or stories of a small boy murdered on a housing estate. The Papal pastoral instruction, *Communio et Progressio* (23 May 1971), in a discussion about the reporting of violence worries specifically that if 'bloody events are too realistically described or too frequently dwelt upon, there is a danger of perverting the image of human life' (43). This may be detrimental to audiences' perception of the world and 'may leave violence and savagery as the accepted way of resolving conflict' (43). These claims are not tested out and are hard to prove conclusively, but nevertheless are almost as common a refrain as the criticism of violent films.

According to the Broadcasting Standards Commission's report on the *Depiction of Violence on Terrestrial Television*, in the UK there was 'a substantial increase in the number of violent incidents portrayed in 1999–2001 compared to 1997 and 1998, largely due to coverage in news and related programmes of violence in Bosnia and following September 11.'[18] The report's conclusions were based on the monitoring of violence across two weeks of prime time programming. The high incidence of violence in British television news also reflected more violence caused by terrorism

---

17   Susan D. Moeller, *Compassion Fatigue: How the Media Sell Disease, Famine, War and Death* (New York and London: Routledge, 1999). Some of her criticisms are now dated following 9/11 and the resulting increased interest and investment in covering foreign news.

18   Broadcasting Standards Commission, *Briefing Update: Depiction of Violence on Terrestrial Television.* No 10, April 2002, 3. The sample was collected over two composite weeks, 30 March–5 May 2001 and 8 September–26 October 2001 and ran from 17:30 hrs to 00:00hrs. Since 2001 the content analyses have been undertaken in conjunction with the British Broadcasting Corporation (BBC) and the Independent Television Commission (ITC).

and motivated by ideals, beliefs or religion.[19] This content analysis excluded the countless other acts of daily violence that never make it into the frames of most Western national news channels: for example, the strafing by helicopters of villagers in central Sudan to clear the way for oil exploration, or the rampages of the so-called 'Lord's Army' in Northern Uganda.[20] The war in Congo is estimated to have claimed over three million lives in the last decade, but receives limited coverage in the majority of the Western media. For many viewers, the violent news reports that do make it onto the news bulletins or into the papers evoke a sense of powerlessness that leaves little room for action.

Another root of what I will call violence fatigue is boredom with the same old story. 'Oh it's just another suicide bomber' or 'I don't want to see yet another starving war baby with flies about her mouth' are not uncommon refrains. After a hard day who wants to be confronted by the harsh glare of violent reality, especially when reruns of *Sex in the City*, *ER* or *CSI* call? The journalist DiGiovanni once noticed a man picking up an issue of *Time* magazine with the picture of a Rwandan mother and child on the front cover. Superimposed over the image were the words: 'THERE ARE NO DEVILS LEFT IN HELL ... THEY ARE ALL IN RWANDA'. DiGiovanni observed that 'it appeared to make no impact. The man's eyes registered, and there was entirely believable boredom. He put the magazine down and bought a copy of *Vanity Fair* with Cindy Crawford on the cover in a bikini rising out of a seashell like Aphrodite. Given the choice of a glorious Cindy Crawford or a starving child [from a war torn country], can you, in a sense, blame him?'[21] It is hardly surprising that we are so easily distracted from the results of conflict, given our constant exposure to ever more violent images. Through these mediated distractions the vision of becoming a peacemaker can be dimmed, to be replaced by frames of reference defined by scepticism, even resentment.

Resentment is a dangerous seed. It often grows into the desire to meet violence with violence. How far might news coverage contribute to, even exacerbate, violence? Johann Galtung, a Norwegian Professor of Peace Studies, believes news often contributes to violent situations, with journalists too often misframing violence. They do this in a number of ways. Some reports decontextualise violence, by focusing on apparently irrational acts and ignoring the structural causes, like poverty, government neglect and military or police repression. This is by no means a new criticism. John Birt and Peter Jay famously set out their 'mission to explain' in the 1970s, arguing that too often news reports had a 'bias against understanding', merely covering the dramatic event, without adequately explaining the causes.[22]

---

19   Broadcasting Standards Commission, *Briefing Update*, 8.

20   Sarah Stewart and Charlotte Sankey (eds), *The Scorched Earth: oil and war in Sudan* (London: Christian Aid, 2001) and see: www.christian-aid.org.uk.

21   Moeller, *Compassion Fatigue*, 236–37, citing Janine DiGovanni, 'Tired Moving of the Pictures', *The Sunday Times*, 14 August 1994, Feature Section.

22   See the introduction of John Eldridge (ed.), *Getting the Message: News, Truth and Power* (London: Routledge, 1993).

Their comments led to changes in some news coverage in various broadcasting organisations. But has it changed enough? Galtung, along with many other scholars, is not convinced. Galtung believes that many reports reduce the number of parties in a conflict to two, when in fact more are involved, and furthermore they ignore the goals of outside interventionists or larger nations. For example, the conflict through the nineties in the former Yugoslavia was sometimes oversimplified to the Serbs versus the Muslims or the Serbs versus the Croats. Invariably there were more than two parties involved. Such dualism can easily lead to what Galtung describes as Manichaeism, portraying one side as good and demonizing the other as 'evil'.[23] This may simplify a complicated story, but it fails to do justice to the complexity of many conflicts. Clearly it is hard to treat as equally newsworthy the suffering, fears and grievances of all sides. In fact it is much easier to create 'villains' and 'victims', suggesting that punishing the villains represents a solution. If a Jewish viewer in Tel-Aviv draws many of her frames of reference for the conflict from pro-Israeli news reporting that shows in graphic detail the results of a suicide bomber, whilst a viewer in Ramallah hears only pro-Palestinian stories from an Arabic news source, then both may be accepting a frame that demands a violent response.

A related weakness, according to Galtung, is the failure to explore the causes of escalation, the lasting ramifications of bereavement and the impact of media coverage itself. Violence is presented as inevitable, 'Armageddon-like'. Alternatives are ignored or under-reported. Galtung recently argued that Middle-Eastern peace initiatives and proposals are rarely explored in detail in the Western press. For Galtung 'when news about attempts to resolve conflicts are absent, fatalism is reinforced. That can engender even more violence, when people have no images or information about possible peaceful outcomes and the promise of healing.' He notes that some news stories confuse cease-fires and negotiations with actual peace.[24] This problem may be compounded if the media not only have a 'perverse fascination with war and violence; [but] they also neglect the peace forces at work'.[25] Images of peaceful outcomes are too often left outside the news frame. This assertion finds support from Entman, who claims that the news frames offered in the run up to the Gulf War, ensured that those proposing or envisaging a negotiated settlement between Iraq and Kuwait were marginalized in North American coverage.[26] Galtung's project is striking in terms of setting out a critical hermeneutic towards news violence. It is important to note, however, that the fact that violence is sometimes misframed does not prove that such framing necessarily leads to further conflict. Galtung's

---

23 Manichaeism has its origins with a man titled Mani (216–277) who grafted aspects of Zoroastrianism, Buddhism, Babylonian Folklore, ideas taken from Marcion and other early writers onto his own sectarian dualist form of Christianity.

24 For more details see: http://www.mediachannel.org/views/dissector/covering violence.shtml.

25 Johan Galtung, in Colleen Roach (ed.) *Communication and Culture in War and Peace* (Sage, London, 1993), xi.

26 Robert M. Entman, 'Framing : Toward Clarification of a Fractured Paradigm', *Journal of Communication*, 43 (1993), 51–58.

critical descriptive work is valuable in terms of understanding the weaknesses in how news violence is framed, but is less persuasive in conclusively proving a direct link between news coverage and audience response.

Nevertheless, an audience that is intent on understanding how news can misframe violence does not need to be persuaded of this causal link to recognise how often news excludes visions or practices of peace. One of the reasons for this is that television news, as suggested earlier, thrives on conflict. Given that television often sets the agenda of all the news media, print, radio and even internet news are also pushed towards leading with the spectacular and dramatically violent events which television relishes. This is doubly problematic, as Ignacio Ramonet suggests: 'events which produce strong pictures ... consequently go to the top of the news hierarchy ... even if, in the absolute, their importance is secondary. The emotional shock that these pictures produce ... is altogether on a different scale from that which the other media can bring about ...'[27] The visually striking one-off event invariably takes precedence over the chronic famine, or other form of humanitarian or environmental disaster, slowly unfolding away from cameras hungry for a memorable image. The perceived editorial imperative of finding yet another dramatic clip or picture contributes to the tendency for television news to be structured episodically. This ensures that viewers are presented with a series of unconnected stories. If audiences choose to sit through the television news, they can be taken from a huge suicide bombing in Baghdad via the burning of an Embassy in Beirut to killings in Darfur. One result of this episodic news process, as opposed to a more thematic approach, according to Shanto Iyengar, 'is the trivialization of public discourse' and the lack of sustained evidence to help audiences to make properly informed moral choices in response to violence.[28] How many people now receive news is rapidly changing with the increased use of the Internet, which provides both alternative sources to view and the opportunity to select individual video and written reports rather than sit through an entire programme. Nonetheless, Internet news providers work under other constraints, including the necessity of framing stories in such a way as to fit onto their site.

Many journalists are only too aware of the limitations of the tools of their trade. Such feelings of inadequacy are heightened in the face of almost indescribable acts of violence such as the genocide in Rwanda. Fergal Keane writes:

> Each of us had experienced war and killing before, but in Rwanda we had stepped into a place in which all previous experience of death and conflict paled into insignificance. Here the journalism of objective assessment and rational comparisons meant nothing. To this day I am at a loss to describe what it was really like. That smell. On your clothes, on your skin. For weeks afterwards, lifting a glass to your lips or sitting down to eat, it could come flashing back. This was not something I could convey with words or photographs

---

27   Ignacio Ramonet, 'The Power of Television Pictures', a web article cited by William E. Biernatzki, 'Terrorism and Mass Media', *Communication Research Trends* 21:1 (2002), 5.

28   Shanto Iyengar, *Is Anyone Responsible? How Television frames Political Issues* (Chicago: University of Chicago Press, 1991), 143.

or film. Set against the vastness of the evil of genocide, journalism was at best a limited vehicle of expression, at worst a crude and inadequate tool ... The experience still leaves me struggling for adequate words ... I have tried to tell the story in film and print but I have begun to accept that the ordinary language of journalism has failed me ... Our trade may be full of imperfections and ambiguities but if we ignore evil we become authors of a guilty silence. [29]

Reframing violent news cannot become an excuse for ignoring the reality of evil, nor the effects on journalists. Pictures often capture both the spectacle and the visible effects of violence, leaving no doubt about the concreteness of evil. This raises a range of theological issues, which are unsurprisingly rarely touched upon by television news hungry for emotionally shocking and spectacular images, rather than sustained arguments about theodicy or the origins of evil.[30] Journalists who step into the heart of darkness to cover a story need not only critical feedback on their work, but also support and compassion. Foreign correspondents who sometimes risk their lives to cover a story, perform a vital function: reminding viewers, who live in comfortable environments, of the hardships experienced beyond the horizon.

In this section I have proposed that news can misframe violence, in such a way that it may reinforce violence fatigue. I have implied that Galtung's claim that violent news provokes more conflict requires further testing. On the basis of the evidence cited in the introductory section on framing effects, however, it appears reasonable to support those who posit a degree of influence. News may only provide selected framings, but it still serves an important role in confronting us with glimpses of our violent world. In order to develop the discussion further I now want to engage in a detailed analysis of one image and how it is framed.

3. Case Study: From Photograph to Icon

Charles Porter IV, a bank clerk, thought 'that demolition crews were tearing down a building when he first heard the explosion'.[31] It was 9.02 a.m., 19 April 1995. He left his work, grabbed his camera from the boot (trunk) of his car, and went in search of a few pictures of the demolition. He was shocked to see through the smoke and dust the collapsed ruins of what had been the front of the Alfred Murray Federal Building in Oklahoma City. As an enthusiastic amateur photographer more used to taking photographs at the local Rodeo this was a different more bewildering world. Nevertheless, he took numerous pictures of the chaotic scene.[32] Some hours later he had the film developed at Wal Mart. He glanced at the photos to check

---

29 Fergal Keane, *Letter to Daniel - Despatches from the Heart* (London: BBC Books and Penguin, 1996), 157–63, written in Nairobi, October 1995, first published in the *Guardian*.
30 See Gordon Graham, *Evil and Christian Ethics* (Cambridge: Cambridge University Press, 2001)
31 See *New York Times*, Friday 21 April 1995, A23.
32 Almost identical photos were also taken by Lester LaRue, and used by *Newsweek*.

the focus was correct, but it was not until some older women cried when they saw the images that he looked at them more carefully. He took his pictures to AP who appeared uninterested, but still scanned them into their computer. They offered him a one-time payment. Within hours newspapers from all over the globe bought the photo. The next day it was on many front pages around the world,[33] becoming an icon of suffering from the Oklahoma bombing. It is not surprising that this was the first amateur photograph to win *both* a Pulitzer prize (for spot photography) and the British picture editors' award. As an image from the news it is a hard to forget Porter's picture of a fireman cradling a limp and bloodied baby.[34]

On Thursday, 20 April 1995, newspapers framed this image through different headlines. *The Daily Mirror*, for example, devoted the entire front page to the picture, apart from a small box insert which included a picture of the shattered building. In small letters at the bottom of the page it read: 'SURVIVOR: A Fireman cradles a miracle baby who came out alive from the Oklahoma City car bomb horror yesterday.' The *Daily Express* ran the image with the headline, 'Slaughter of the Children'. The *Daily Star* was more biblical in their framing: 'Slaughter of the Innocent', echoing the *Los Angeles Times* who described it as 'The Slaughter of the Innocents'.[35]

Most controversially, *Today*, in both English and Scottish editions, next to the photo ran the headline: 'In the Name of Islam'. The vast majority of the British and American papers, both tabloid and broadsheet, whilst not always so unequivocal, agreed with the assessment: this bomb was probably the work of Islamic terrorists. Several news outlets did note that this was the second anniversary of the end of the Waco siege (19 April 1993), suggesting that this was an alternative motive for the attack. The *Daily Express* even linked them together stating that 'Moslems and Waco maniacs suspected'. In the USA, however, numerous radio and television reports also strongly supported the Islamic terrorist theory. This inaccurate framing of both the image and the whole event led to many mosques in America being 'vandalised' or receiving bomb threats, and Muslims being physically assaulted and called 'sand niggers'. 'Shouting "it's a bomb," someone threw a bag into a playground

---

33   See, for example, front pages of the *Independent*, *Daily Telegraph*, *Today*, *Daily Express*, *Daily Mirror*. The *Guardian* ran the picture on page 2. It did not appear in early editions of the *Daily Mail*, which ran a picture of rescuers gazing up at the devastated building. (*Daily Star*, Friday, 21 April 1995).

34   I am particularly indebted to Edward T. Linenthal for his public lecture (at the University of Colorado in Boulder, November 2001) and his excellent book on the same topic of *The Unfinished Bombing: Oklahoma City in American Memory* (Oxford: Oxford University Press, 2001). See especially his 'An American Icon: The Fireman and the Baby', 145–64, which provided many useful additional details to my own research on the uses of this photo.

35   See the *Sun*, 20 April 1995. The Oklahoma bombing received only a one-inch column on the front page. They did not run the picture, and instead led with 'Even Heaven Needs Good Coppers', next to it was a large picture of PC Philip Walters, who was shot dead the day before. The *Sun*, however, resisted the temptation to blame Islamic fundamentalists, simply stating: '75 feared killed in Waco revenge bombing.'

at a Muslim day care center in Dallas, Texas.'³⁶ The arrest and charging of former American soldiers Timothy McVeigh and Terry Nichols ensured that most of the accusations and violence against Muslims halted. By Sunday the story had moved on in the papers and news programmes to explore the roots of this 'home-grown terrorism'. In the rush to offer an immediate explanation, the image and the story were initially wildly misframed. Playing into the cultural reservoir of racism and xenophobia, the result of this misframing was further violence.

It took several hours before the fireman in the picture, Captain Chris Fields, was named, and it was made clear that one-year-old Baylee Almon had not survived. According to one *LA Times* staff writer, 'the hopes and prayers of the millions who saw the photo were all in vain'.³⁷ The picture led to numerous follow-up pieces, concentrating on three figures. First, the fireman Chris Fields, who has a two-year-old son: 'I go hot and cold thinking this victim could have been my child.'³⁸ Second, the policeman, John Avera, who took Baylee from the rubble and handed her on to Fields, both the *Washington Post* and *New York Times* (on 20 April) used a picture of this moment instead of the fireman cradling shot. Third, Baylee's mother Aren Almon-Kok, who had celebrated her daughter's first birthday the day before. When she first saw the picture on the front page the next morning she knew it was her daughter. 'Grief-stricken by her child's death, she was nonetheless relieved and touched by the gentle demeanor of the fireman who handled her child so carefully.'³⁹ By concentrating the frame around three unintentional protagonists the news industry helped to turn a policeman, a fireman and a mother into 'celebrities' surrounding the bloodied body of a one year old. The wider public also played their part, sending hundreds of letters of condolence to Almon-Kok, as well as to Fields and Avera. Many shared stories of the loss of their children. It is clear from these responses, that in a fashion similar to public response to Princess Diana's tragic death, many people turned this event into a shared symbol of suffering. They invested their own meanings into this visual summary of the effects of violence.

The image was soon commodified into statues, key rings, belt buckles and a memorial phone-card for relief efforts. The original photo was toned down in many cases, with much of the blood being removed. The phone card had Baylee's one-year-old birthday photo added to the corner of the card.⁴⁰ Aren wishes the public to remember Baylee alive, not just as a lifeless corpse. This news image, emblematic of so much violence, was rapidly commercialised and understandably softened.

---

36   18. He also cites a 'Rush to Judgment', a 1995 publication of the council on American–Islamic Relations (CAIR), which provides a lengthy list of anti-Muslim activities.

37   'Grief Supplants Hope as Rescued Baby in Photo Dies.' Los Angeles Times (Washington Edition), Friday 21 April 1995, A2.

38   See, for example, newspapers on Friday 21 April 1995: 'Anguish of hero fireman who carried a dead baby', *Daily Express*, 5; and 'Baby Died in My Arms', *Daily Mirror*, p 1 and 3; 'Come on Little Fellow, Breathe, Breathe', *Daily Star*, 4 and 5.

39   See Hal Buel (ed.), *Moments: The Pulitzer Prize Photographs – A Visual Chronicle of Our Time* (Cologne: Könemann, 2000), 232–3.

40   Linenthal, *The Unfinished Bombing*, 150–51.

For many who saw this image whether in the newspapers or on television news, the picture of Fields holding baby Baylee acted like a 'punctum', a pin-prick or an awakener to the compassion of viewers. Part of the power of the image is Fields' concentrated gaze and that he has removed his gloves to hold Baylee. It still has the power to evoke sympathy, but with its constant recycling and familiarity it takes on new meanings for different viewers. Walter Benjamin suggests that the mass production of religious images ensures that what he describes as their 'aura' is diminished.[41] For some viewers the aura of this picture was undermined by its recycling and commercialisation, which led to devaluing the suffering of Baylee and the other 167 people who lost their lives. For others they became material reminders of the tragic events of 19 April 1995. Given that over a third of the population of Oklahoma, 'approximately 387,000 people, knew someone killed or injured', it is not entirely surprising that many invested their own aura onto the picture and associated items, wishing to create, to touch and to own a physical memorial of the event.[42]

Edward Linethal's thought-provoking book on *The Unfinished Bombing* describes three narratives that emerged after the attack on Oklahoma. The first was the **progressive narrative**, which suggested that this act of violent terrorism would be the making of the city and people of Oklahoma, locating the bombing in the 'pioneer and survivor traditions'.[43] The second was the **redemptive narrative**, which I will return to in a moment. The third was the **toxic narrative**, which demonstrates how this is indeed an unfinished bombing, resulting in increased instances of suicides, depression and family break-ups in the following years. In one far from peaceful picture, a mother is painted as screaming as an angel takes her baby away.[44]

As part of the toxic narrative Linenthal suggests that 'children who were glued to the television for days after April 19 also suffered'. Research from a child psychiatry group at the University of Oklahoma identified a 'strong correlation between the emotional distress of children and the amount of television coverage of the bombing they watched'. Unfortunately, 'the blown up building was often shown during the cartoon hours, and as many children watch television alone, without adults to comfort them and assure them of their safety or to correct their fantasies and misunderstandings.' Some 'preschoolers thought that each time they saw the ruins of the Murrah Building a new building had been destroyed, and "some still kick the walls of the buildings they go into just to make sure they will not fall down."'[45] The

---

41 See Walter Benjamin, 'The Work of Art in the Age of Mechanical Reproduction', in *Illuminations*, trans. Harry Zohn, edited and with Introduction by Hannah Arendt (New York: Schocken Books, 1968).

42 Linenthal, *The Unfinished Bombing*, 71. See David Morgan, *Protestants and Pictures: Religion, Visual Culture and the Age of Mass Production* (Oxford: Oxford University Press, 1999).

43 Linenthal, *The Unfinished Bombing*, 52.

44 Ibid., 63.

45 Ibid., 75. Linethal also cites James R. Allen and Barbara A. Allen, 'Transactional Analysis from Oklahoma City: After the Bombing', *Transactional Analysis Journal*, July 1998, 206.

lack of parental involvement in viewing routines, ensures that there is inadequate reframing of violent news.

A *Newsweek* report a few weeks after bombing was highly critical of over-swift redemptive moves, and graphic in its description of the ongoing toxicity of the bombing:

> 'Let the healing begin', said evangelist Billy Graham ... at the memorial service televised throughout the nation. His call was wildly premature. Throughout the city, the aftershocks of the homemade bomb that took 168 lives and wounded more than 400 others are still being felt. One family that lost a child continues to set an extra place at the dinner table. A rescue worker keeps splashing his face with cologne yet still can't rid himself of the stench of rotting bodies. A woman who lost all her children in the blast asks, numbly: 'Am I still a mother?'[46]

This graphic report illustrates how journalistically it is much easier to focus on dramatic trauma, than to express sensitively a hope for healing and regeneration.

Returning to the **redemptive narrative**, this was expressed vividly through both sermons and many local painters reinterpreting Porter's photograph artistically. For example, 'some artists found consolation in their vision of Baylee Almon moving from the arms of Chris Fields to the arms of Jesus Christ, accompanied by angels'. 'Dick Locher's editorial cartoon in the *Chicago Tribune* depicts Chris Fields handing Baylee into God's waiting hands.'[47] Through skilful use of comments by local pastors Linenthal implicitly questions those who claimed that the bombing was part of God's plan. He is clearly uneasy about some of the religious attempts at reframing the event. 'At times, however, I felt overwhelmed by the torrent of immediate religious interpretation of the bombing, as if so many words would somehow make some sense of the event. There seemed little room for silence, a kind of awe-filled, deeply silent sadness in the face of the power of such loss.'[48] This is a powerful observation, and a useful highlighting of the value of silence in the face of such evil and heartbreak. The tragic events of September 11th also raise similar issues about how or indeed whether to speak in the aftermath of violent aggression and human loss. In *Writing in the Dust* Rowan Williams underlines some of the dangers of using suffering as a device for making theological points.[49] Both Linenthal's and Williams' comments serve as a valuable reminder of the dangers inherent in manipulating violent news and the real suffering behind it simply to make a theological point.

---

46   See *Newsweek*, 22 May 1995, 49. (Report by Kenneth L. Woodward with Karen Springen.)
47   Linenthal, *The Unfinished Bombing*, 156.
48   Ibid., 80.
49   Rowan Williams, *Writing in the Dust* (London: Hodder and Stoughton, 2001).

4. Reframing Violent News in the New Testament

In the weeks that followed the Oklahoma bombing, local clergy wrestled with a range of passages from scripture when speaking to their congregations. These included the sufferings of Job, the lamentations of the psalms, the passion narratives and the story of doubting Thomas.[50] A similar process took place after September 11th.[51] It is not surprising that many turned to the scriptures, and especially to the death and resurrection of Christ, as a source for the redemptive reframing of the bombing. The framing and reframing of violence is by no means a new move. This is a recurring process in the New Testament, and merits careful attention especially for those concerned with reframing violent news theologically.

In order to do this I now consider how several New Testament writers attempted in different ways to reframe the news of Jesus' violent death. While some scholars claim that these authors provide the original frames, it appears likely that these writers took the eyewitness accounts and oral traditions that they received and reframed them. There is not space here to discuss the nature or extent of how the tradition evolved. My central contention, however, is that the initial framing of Jesus' death as a tragic meaningless failure, was shattered by the resurrection event. In other words, experiences of the risen Christ, oral and eyewitness accounts and subsequent reflections on the resurrection, provided a powerful impetus for the reframing of Jesus' death carried out by many of the New Testament authors. Paul provides some of the earliest accounts of the resurrection. Nonetheless, countless theologians writing about Paul put considerable emphasis upon his theology of the cross, or even theology from the cross. Ellen Charry, for example, in her book on *The Pastoral Function of Christian Doctrine* (1997) suggests that Paul's way of 'reframing' the significance of Jesus:

> perhaps derives from his own experience of suddenly realizing that God had done something decisive and nothing was as it had been before. His theology takes its point of departure not from a belief but from an event: the event of Christ crucified.[52]

I would want to expand the event described by Charry to 'the event of Christ crucified and Christ risen.' There is a danger of driving a wedge between the crucifixion and resurrection when interpreting Paul's radical reading of Jesus' suffering and death. Morna Hooker claims that some Christians have distorted Paul's teaching by linking his understanding of atonement and reconciliation with Christ's death

---

50 See Marsha Brock Bishop and David Polk (eds), *And The Angels Wept: From the Pulpits of Oklahoma City after the Bombing* (St Louis, MO: Chalice Press, 1995); and Linenthal, *The Unfinished Bombing*, 56.

51 See, for example, David Polk (ed.) *Shaken Foundations: Sermons from America's Pulpits after the Terrorist Attacks* (St Louis, MO: Chalice Press, 2002). See also Jolyon Mitchell, *Media and Christian Ethics* (Cambridge University Press, forthcoming).

52 Ellen Charry, *By the Renewal of Your Minds: The Pastoral Function of Christian Doctrine* (Oxford: Oxford University Press, 1997), 226.

alone, ignoring the resurrection.[53] Paul made shocking and scandalous statements, including that *the* Christ was crucified (1 Cor.1: 23), was cursed by the fact of being hung on a tree (Galatians 3: 13 – see Deuteronomy 21: 23) and was made sin (2 Cor. 5: 21) These are extraordinary claims given Paul's background as a teacher of the law. They reflect a radical interpretative *volte-face*. It is clear from the sustained argument of 1 Corinthians 15 that Paul's reframing of the death of the messiah and his vision for a church community was firmly rooted in both an experience of and a belief in the resurrection. Paul writes of the tradition that he has 'received and passed on',[54] claiming that Christ died, was buried, was raised to life on the third day, and then appeared to Cephas, to the Twelve, to five hundred 'of our brothers', to James, to all the Apostles and last of all to Paul himself (1 Cor.15: 3–7). In this context he admits that he 'had persecuted the church of God' (15: 8). In the terms of my discussion he replaced his original framing of Jesus' life and death, based around fervent opposition to Jesus' earlier followers, with a radically new frame. Is it possible that Paul was driven or compelled to become involved in this process of reframing Jesus' violent death because of his own experience of the risen Christ and the accounts that he received and then passed on?

Mark's gospel provides an example of a different kind of reframing. It has been described as an extended passion narrative, in which Jesus' death casts a shadow over the entire story. This may not be an entirely accurate description, but it hard to read the gospel without becoming aware of the forces conspiring to lead to Jesus' death. On one level the machinations of religious authorities, the loss of popular support, the denial by a northern fisherman, the betrayal by an economic advisor, the political expediency of the local autocrat, and the state sponsored violence of the military combine to explain through a narrative frame why Jesus died.

On another level, a sophisticated reframing of Jesus' death is taking place. For the author of Mark this death is not the tragic demise of a brilliant rabbi, healer and exorcist, nor another example of the triumph of Roman state terrorism; it is an inevitable denouement. In three consecutive chapters readers are presented with a series of predictions that the 'Son of Man must suffer', 'must be killed' and 'will rise again' (Mark 8:31). Or as some suggest a legal term is employed 'will be delivered into the hands of men' (Mark 9:31 RSV) and they will 'mock', 'spit', 'scourge', and 'kill him' (Mark 10:32 RSV). In Mark, the inevitability of Jesus' death is not the result of human forces, nor a 'crushing by the wheel of history' but can partly

---

53 See Morna Hooker's introduction in her *Not Ashamed of the Gospel: New Testament Interpretations of the Death of Christ* (Carlisle: Paternoster, 1994). She is not alone in making this claim, see also: D. M. Stanley, 'Christ's Resurrection in Pauline Soteriology', *Analecta Biblica* 13 (Rome, Biblical Institute Press, 1961); B. McNeil, 'Raised for our Justification', *ITQ* 42 (1975), 97–105; and K. Grayston, *Dying we live* (London: Darton Longman & Todd, 1990.)

54 For a discussion of the significance of this phrase as evidence for the careful passing on of oral tradition see the writings of Birger Gerhardsson, such as *Memory and Manuscript: Oral Tradition and Written Transmission in Rabbinic Judaism and Early Christianity*, trans. Eric Sharpe (Grand Rapids, Michigan: William Eerdmans, 1997).

be explained by the protagonist's tortured volition, 'not what I will, but what thou wilt' (Mark 14:36 KJV and RSV). The vision of his own calling reminds the reader of the divine author behind the story who interrupts the closed world of the narrative at the moments of baptism (Mark 1:11), the transfiguration (Mark 9:7), and with the tearing of the curtain in the temple (Mark 15:38). There is an inherent tension in the Markan narrative between the Jesus who sees that he must die in accordance with God's will and the Jesus who is 'deeply distressed and troubled' in Gethsemane. The account suggests that Jesus had to die, but this does little to soften the piercing cry: 'Why hast thou forsaken me?'

In many ways Jesus' death is presented as a more controlled affair in the Lukan account. Unlike in Mark and Matthew, the author of Luke leaves out of the frame the cry of dereliction. It is not clear whether this omission is a reframing to make the scene less bleak or to give greater weight to what we hear instead: 'Father, forgive them, for they know not what they do' (Luke 23:34 RSV), 'Truly, I say to you, today you will be with me in Paradise' (Luke 23:43 RSV), and finally in a loud voice: 'Father, into thy hands I commit my spirit!' (Luke 23:46 RSV). Many commentators interpret Luke's reframing by omission as an act of editorial softening. The inevitability of Jesus' death is also an important element in the framing of Jesus' death in Luke. Even from before the pivotal moment where he sets his face to Jerusalem (Luke 9:51), the reader is made aware that 'the Son of Man must suffer many things', 'be rejected', 'be killed', ' be raised' (Luke 9:22). Later in the same chapter following the healing of an epileptic boy, Jesus' response to the astonishment of the crowds is enigmatic realism, 'the Son of Man will be delivered into the hands of men' (Luke 9:44). The necessity of the Messiah's suffering is again made clear on the road to Emmaus (Luke 24:26). To an even greater extent than in Mark, with its somewhat abrupt ending, the resurrection account in Luke reframes the entire preceding passion narrative.

On the basis of this brief discussion I have set out a case for at least three kinds of reframing taking place in the New Testament. The first is a reframing that is rooted in a radically changed perception of the nature and meaning of Jesus' death. This is most clearly seen in the Pauline corpus, but can be discerned in other texts, such as the Epistle to the Hebrews. The second kind of reframing is subtler and found in individual specific texts. The Gospel of Mark provides a narrative frame around Jesus' death, which is also reframed by explicit suggestions that this death has meaning. The third type of reframing is inter-textual within the New Testament itself. Whilst not having the time to be drawn into the Synoptic problem and the controversial search for 'Q', textual evidence suggests that the original frames around Jesus' death found in the earliest sources such as Mark are themselves reframed by later New Testament authors to make theological points pertinent to their own situation and community.

5. Approaches to Reframing Violent News

Up to this point in the discussion I have employed the metaphor of framing to describe how violent news is covered. I have suggested that the violent death of Jesus is described, interpreted and reframed in different ways in the New Testament. I now wish to extend the metaphor to include the activity of the audience and suggest that Christians can be involved in a process of reframing violent news. This reframing of the visions of violent reality takes place in the light of Jesus' death and resurrection. There is a danger, however, of moving too swiftly from the experience of grief in the face of violent news to unrealistic hope. Alan E. Lewis' posthumously-published work entitled *Between Cross and Resurrection* provides a valuable counterpoint to this tendency to make over hasty moves away from suffering brought by violence. It also offers an implicit qualification to Hooker's concern not to drive a wedge between crucifixion and resurrection.

Lewis' subtitle, *A Theology of Holy Saturday,* is at the heart of his project. He argues that for many people the second day, is only 'a brief and slender, unnoticed and insignificant feature in the original story'.[55] For Lewis it is pivotal in the Christian story. It is not simply a day of waiting for the resurrection, but according to the logic of the narrative, it is the day after the violent tragedy of the crucifixion. A day characterised by mourning, grief and brokenness; a moment to be lived through and experienced by Christians. This interpretation is given further theological weight by Lewis' own personal struggle with cancer, which he describes as twelve months of Easter Saturdays:

> Lying in a radiation center, as virulent, malignant cells in one's own body and machines which harness other of nature's lethal energies do fiery battle in the struggle between life and death, it is perhaps easier than in happier locations to recognize one's membership in a broken universe. Though pain and suffering can sometimes turn us inward, in self-pitying absorption with our own imagined hardships, they can also newly orient us outward, intensifying the awareness of our connectedness to other things and beings which suffer along with us. In the personal instance of the writer, the lowest weeks of chemotherapy, with respect to its emotional and mental toll, were those which coincided with war in the Persian Gulf, whose images of savage, senseless slaughter, beamed to a bedside of private combat, seemed to seal one's tiny place within a diseased, disordered cosmos, convulsed in an orgy of destruction.[56]

Lewis' personal experience led him to reframe not only his own suffering, but also the world's violence portrayed on television and his own understanding of the Christian story. A theology grounded in Easter Saturday will ensure that reframing does not take on an air of unreality or overconfidence. In several traditions, Easter Saturday, is the day to recall Christ's descent into Hades. Lewis writes: 'Resurrection hope is not for easy, kind release, that happy, beautiful transition to "a better place" so

---

55   Alan E. Lewis, *Between Cross and Resurrection: A Theology of Holy Saturday* (Grand Rapids, Michigan: William B. Eerdmans, 2001), 34.

56   Ibid., 422–23.

often triumphalistically and misleadingly proclaimed in some church quarters, even in circumstances of horrible, catastrophic, or untimely death.'[57] Robust approaches to reframing are characterised by a clear understanding of the reality of evil and the ways in which this process was carried out by the earliest Christian communities, who themselves were often afflicted by violent persecution.

The reframing of Christianity's central violent event is to be found not only in the primary sources, but throughout the Christian tradition. There are precedents in the earliest Christian documents for the reframing of violent news, but there is neither a homogeneous method nor a developed cartography for this process. I am not proposing something that is comparable to what the Comte d'Augivillier, Louis XVI's superintendent of paintings, did. He commissioned the frame-maker Buteaux to design a uniform frame for the king's paintings, thereby replacing many of the original frames.[58] The result was a set of frames that often did not do justice to the pictures that they contained. As I have suggested, there is ample reframing diversity in the New Testament to challenge those who wish to apply an identical mass-produced frame around specific items of violent news. Contrast the Johannine reframing of the 'hour' or kairos of Jesus death with the author of Hebrews' reframing of the sacrificial system where the high priest himself becomes the victim to make a new and living way.[59] Evidently, there are evocative resonances and connections, as Raymond Brown makes clear, but they are distinct redescriptions initially serving different audiences. The desire to make an identical Christian frame for every image of violence that we are presented with has the potential, like Buteaux's frames, of failing to do justice to the anguish of the original event, of ignoring the diversity of reframing in the New Testament and of being insensitive to the needs of the local Christian community.

How then can violent news be reframed in such a way that celebrates the diversity in the New Testament and yet recognises the common narrative at the heart of Christianity? One oblique way of answering that question is by considering a late medieval picture of Jesus on the cross from the fourteenth century, taken from the Abingdon missal. Set in the frame of the painting lie tiny paintings of a bull, a lion, a man and an eagle, one in each corner. These symbols, representing the four gospels, surround the crucifixion. This is a valuable visual reminder of how each gospel emerged from a distinct point-of-view, offering a different perspective on what one commentator describes as 'the grief of God'.[60] Nevertheless, in the New Testament, as in the Abingdon missal, they surround a common historical event: the crucifixion of Jesus. Second, in this picture a man and a woman grieve together at the foot of the cross. Mary and John offer no eye contact to each other or to

---

57   Ibid., 428.
58   See Piers and Caroline Feetham, *The Art of Framing* (London: Ryland, Peters and Small, 1997).
59   See, for example, John 16:32 and Hebrews 10:19–21.
60   See Ellen M. Ross, *The Grief of God: Images of the Suffering Jesus in Late Medieval England* (New York and Oxford: Oxford University Press, 1997).

the viewer, they simply stare at the wounds of Jesus. There are clearly common materials or narratives for Christian communities to reframe news violence, but it is helpful to recognise it as a communal activity. Third, this is a graphic depiction of the suffering of Jesus. Gone is the all-powerful imperial Christ, with eyes open staring down at the viewer, instead here is another example of the man of sorrows who not only sympathises with, but also participates in our suffering. His eyes are shut. His body is smattered in blood. There is no softening of the results of violence. Fourth, his suffering is further framed in the Trinity. The Father looks down, open handed, both offering Jesus to the world and receiving Jesus back to himself. The Spirit, represented symbolically as a dove perches on the cross. Here is a deeply symbolic image rooted in medieval piety, which in the words of Paul Fiddes, shows 'a God who suffers and yet still remains God'.[61]

This image is taken from a prayer book that invites more than imitation of the suffering of Christ, but also participation in the violent narrative. Participation is a vital word for understanding the process of reframing violent news. At least three modes of participation emerge from this image: participation in a Trinitarian God as discussed above, participation in the body of Christ and participation in the biblical narrative. My proposal is that participation in the narratives, in the context of Christian communities, provides a strong base from which to reframe violent news.

Communal reframing may not always provide immediate consolation. A narrative that offers little comfort is the Matthean description of the slaughter of the innocents. In Matthew it is interpreted as a fulfilment of Jeremiah's description of a 'voice heard in Rama, sobbing in bitter grief; it was Rachel weeping for her children and refusing to be comforted' (Mt 2:18 and Jeremiah 31:15 R.E.B.). One recent creative interpretation of the slaughter of the Innocents is to be found in the South African staged version of *The Mysteries,* directed by Dornford-May.[62] On stage, brightly dressed mothers delight in their tiny babies. Laughter turns to tears as the darkly uniformed soldiers kill each child. One of the most pathos filled moments of the whole play was the attempt by Mary, holding the Christ child, to comfort one of the weeping mothers, desolate after the death of her child. It was not clear whether the comfort was accepted. The pain on the Mother's face remained. The Matthean text is equally ambiguous as to whether the grief is healed and the 'bitter weeping' is quenched. Some commentators claim that as the Rachel weeping image is followed in Jeremiah (31:16ff) by a more hopeful call: 'Cease your weeping, shed no more tears', then the author of Matthew is using this citation to demonstrate how Mary's child will bring joy and an end to weeping. This appears to be a tenuous interpretative move as Matthew stops short of quoting the more hopeful phrase of Jeremiah. The

---

61 See Paul S. Fiddes, *The Creative Suffering of God* (Oxford: Clarendon Press, 1988).

62 Opened 26 February and closed 18 May 2002, at the Queen's Theatre, London. A multi-racial cast of 40 used English, Afrikaans, Xhosa and Zulu combined in imaginative physical theatre to reinterpret this narrative.

result of this editing is that the force of the sentence is focused on Rachel weeping as her children are no more.

This tragic scene has resonated with readers in many a contrasting cultural context. For example, the Flemish painter Pieter Brueghel's 1565 version of *The Massacre of the Innocents* illustrates how this story has been translated into a new historical situation. Brueghel reframed the biblical story by setting the infanticide in snow-covered Brabant villages.[63] Many interpreters believe that this haunting picture was inspired by the bloody campaigns that Philip II commanded in order to repress Calvinism and Anabaptism in the Netherlands. The Matthean story also continues to exert a powerful imaginative hold over certain readers today. Read such passages with Christians from war-torn Sudan, Congo or Rwanda, in the early twenty first century, and it is clear that these stories of grief resonate with their all too recent experiences. As they identify directly with such grief filled narratives, these stories provide some of the resources necessary for reframing the violent news that all too often impinges on their own lives.[64] But for those who are far distanced from or fatigued by such media stories, hearing alternative sources of news from the often forgotten parts of the body of Christ provides invaluable glimpses of what is happening beyond the standard news frame. By participating in the narratives together, communities of interpretation gather new materials for reframing violent news.

The desolation of grief is sometimes articulated most vividly not through words, but through artistic representation. Consider Michaelangelo's *Pieta*. Some critics interpret this work as one that reflects the questioning uncertainty of Michaelangelo's final years. Others believe it expresses the grief of his own personal losses. Written in marble it expresses our apparent powerlessness in the face of death. Taken out of its narrative context this is indeed a tragic lonely image: a mother cradling her dead grown-up son. Once, however, this image is placed in a larger narrative context then whilst the image of grief remains to haunt, the hope of resurrection may slowly seep in. This statue stands in St Peter's, Rome. All around its marble form, every day, people break bread, share wine, and make affirmations such as 'Christ is risen, he is risen indeed'. Thus a further approach to reframing violence is to be found in the sustaining and transformative practice of worship.

There is clearly a considerable risk in taking the *Pieta* and putting it alongside a modern photographic Pieta. Flesh, blood, stone and pixels would mingle. This is a dangerous juxtaposition, which demands extreme pastoral sensitivity. Nevertheless, I am suggesting that prayerful reflection on an artistic representation of a moment of

---

63   This is one of at least four versions by Brueghel, another of which, held in the Royal Collections, has had the 'innocents' painted over to look like poultry or other small animals. For a discussion of a wide range of artistic representations of the massacre see: Nigel Spivey, *Enduring Creation: Art, Pain and Fortitude* (Berkeley: University of California Press, 2001), 136–53.

64   This observation is based upon information from C.M.S. regional associate for Sudan, Revd Pauline Walker, informal interview May 2002.

tragedy, located in its narrative context, and celebrated in community, provides a rich resource for reframing violent news. This communal visual hermeneutic recognises the power of images themselves to facilitate the reframing process. In a context where a plethora of static and moving images combined with verbal interpretation can overwhelm a moment of tragedy, a well-chosen single image interpreted in community might well help audiences to reframe a violent event.

The communal nature of this process is well expressed by Giotto's fourteenth-century picture, *Lamentation* (1305–06), found amongst his stunning cycle of frescoes in the Arena Chapel, Padua, Italy. Giotto elaborates on the stark story of the gospels, which describe how Joseph from Arimathea takes the body down, wraps it into a linen shroud, and lays Jesus in a rock-hewn tomb (Matthew 27:57–60, Mark 15:42–46, Luke 23:50–53 and John 19:38–42). For Giotto this is no solitary event, as he shows a community of mourning. All human eyes are directed towards the grieving Mary and the dead Christ. He visually improvises with the narrative, adding new dimensions of space both through his skilful use of perspective and with the inclusion of the lamenting heavenly host. It is one of, if not the most auditory of frescoes in the chapel, with the wailing angels and sobbing bystanders. The scene is depicted outside, with no cross in sight, simply a tree springing to life at the top of the hill.

The claim of this chapter is that reframing can bring about new visions of life, even when confronted by bleakest of news stories. The practice of replacing the original news frame is far from being only a cerebral hermeneutical process. Seeing violent news differently has more than purely perceptual repercussions. Reframing is only part of the process of moving beyond powerless despair in the face of news of an explosion in Bali or yet another bomb in Jerusalem. One of the challenges for Christians is to develop communicative practices that clearly articulate peace, and point to the possibility of breaking cycles of violence. Reframing, therefore, has significant implications for embodied peaceful practice and developing alternative non-violent ways of interacting. One powerful expressive alternative is the practice of forgiveness. 'The alternative to embodying forgiveness is not less death, but more horrifying death and destruction, more frightening terror. Further, embodying forgiveness is the way that offers new life and a hopeful future to those who suffer and those who inflict suffering.'[65] In short the practice of forgiveness has the potential to halt the cycle of violence regularly portrayed in the news. As the Croatian theologian Miroslav Volf suggests: 'forgiveness breaks the power of the remembered past and transcends the claims of the affirmed justice and so makes the spiral of vengeance grind to a halt.'[66] Once again this practice of reframing violence is best located communally, and on the basis of participating in God's forgiveness. 'Only a people who have learned to ask forgiveness – that is, a people who know

---

65 L. Gregory Jones, *Embodying Forgiveness* (Grand Rapids, MI: Eerdmans, 1995), 98.

66 Miroslav Volf, *Exclusion and Embrace* (Nashville, TN: Abingdon Press, 1998), 121

the hard task is not to forgive but to be forgiven – are capable of being the kind of community that can support one another in the demanding task of forgiving the enemy.'[67] The suggestion here is that the craft of forgiveness is a life-long learning practice, developed primarily not simply through reframing violent news, but in the context of a worshipping community.

In the best tradition of framing I have offered four sides in this discussion on approaches to reframing violent news. The implication of this is that by participating in narratives, communities, images and practices, a viewer's frames of reference may be transformed, and violent news can be seen differently.

6. Conclusion

Developing our news literacy skills will enable us to use particular news stories as windows onto a world of suffering. News may rarely command such large audiences as soap operas, but sadly a 'good war' or a particularly tele-visual act of violence usually boosts ratings. As we have been reminded in this essay, a news picture, such as a father and son crouching by a wall on the West Bank, or a video of a supposed 'smart bomb' is a carefully selected and framed image. Even a hostage video or images of soldiers abusing prisoners are edited for consumption on the news. As truth is frequently the first casualty in conflict, then it is important to remember that the news offers a highly selective and limited frame of reality. If news is, as journalist Jonathan Dimbleby once described it, 'a window on the world', it has a narrow frame with a limited horizon. In spite of claims to be objective, neutral and unbiased, news is a social construct that is framed by internal influences and external pressures. As the work of the *Glasgow Media Group* has persuasively shown there are frequently unconscious, sometimes even conscious, biases in journalistic practices. In the words of one of its founding members John Eldridge, 'however natural, actual, immediate it all looks, television news is a massive feat of social construction... Apart from the constraints of time, budget and resources there is, necessarily, selection, compression and simplification in the construction of news stories.'[68] This observation applies not only to television news, but also to newspapers and radio news. An editor, in each of these contexts, may radically reframe the journalist's original framing of a story.

However much a live-news broadcast might give the appearance of spontaneity, it is normally the carefully choreographed product of a stopwatch culture and high-tech production suite, where reality is put together.[69] I am not entirely persuaded by Noam Chomsky and Edward Herman's thesis that television news is part of a giant

---

67 Stanley Hauerwas, 'The Sermon on the Mount, Just War and the Quest for Peace', *Concilium* (1988), 39.

68 John Eldridge 'News, Truth and Power', in idem. (ed.), *Getting the Message – News, Truth and Power* (London: Routledge, 1994), 4,

69 See Philip Schlesinger, *Putting 'Reality' Together* (London: Methuen, 1987).

instrument of propaganda 'manufacturing consent' from its viewers.[70] Nevertheless, as Chomsky and Herman assert, 'the raw material of news' invariably passes through successive filters before being presented to the public. This filtering process merits careful analysis as it influences the ways in which stories are framed. It is important to emphasise that reframing violent news is more than simply the analysis of how a particular war or conflict is framed, it is also about developing an awareness of why particular news stories are there. In other words, the journalist's background, the organisation's routines and the political economy of individual news companies, all deserve judicious consideration, as each play their part in framing a story.

But how does my argument go further than merely providing a post-modern hermeneutic of suspicion for deconstructing violent news? How can the reframing of Christianity's central violent event, found throughout the New Testament and in the later tradition, help us to reframe violent news today? My argument is that this recurring tradition of reframing violence rooted in the resurrection provides resources for resisting the myth of redemptive violence. This myth critiqued by Walter Wink suggests that violence is the only legitimate and effective way of bringing order to chaos.[71] Sadly news coverage often reinforces this insidious belief that the use of force is inevitable and necessary.

In whatever form it comes, the news will never bring lasting peace, nor real reconciliation in the Middle East, the Balkans, Sudan or the latest flashpoint of violence. Covering conflicts creates its own particular set of temptations, for example, the BBC's World Affairs Editor John Simpson is particularly scathing of 'look at me journalism', where the journalist wears a flak-jacket or gas-mask to add unnecessarily to the sense of their own danger.[72] Here reporters become like Baroque or Rococo framers in the 18th century who created ornate frame designs to attract the viewer's attention to their craft, thereby often distracting from, even obscuring, the picture itself. As framers of stories journalists have the potential to perpetuate violence, peace or simply misunderstanding. Unlike Jesus' non-violent action or teaching on forgiveness, news rarely challenges us to change our practices. It may, however, provide starting points and questioning points for those searching for ways of peace, a starting point in terms of how we respond to the other, the violent act, and a questioning point in terms of enquiring about God's presence in and vision for a peace-full world. Seen in this light news may even become an indirect source of peace making. On this basis, I would suggest that it is vital for Christians to reframe violent news.

A theologically-informed news literacy does not stop with the limited perspective of seeing news simply like a framed window, it investigates how news stories can be

---

70 Edward S. Herman and Noam Chomsky, *Manufacturing Consent: The Political Economy of the Mass Media* (London: Vintage, 1994).

71 Walter Wink, *The Powers that Be: Theology for a New Millennium* (New York: Augsburg Fortress, 1998).

72 John Simpson, *A Mad World, My Masters: Tales from a Traveller's Life* (Basingstoke: Macmillan Audio Books, 2000).

reframed. This merits asking even more foundational questions. Feeling powerless in the face of a violent news story may itself be a useful lesson. It highlights the fact that Christians stand not alone cradling their own grief, but in a community which puts reality together in a different fashion, through a distinctive set of narratives, which have at their heart a Galilean preacher who embodied news about living peaceably. This figure provides the focal point for reframing communities, 'in which people learn how to embody the story of Jesus Christ.'[73] One way of achieving this is to ensure that the day is framed not by the rhythm of news but by morning and evening prayer for a world often fractured by violence. This practice at its best will be informed but not defined by news from many different sources. The regular liturgical act of breaking bread and sharing wine reframes the 'dangerous memory' of Jesus' death, and points to a shared hope of reconciliation. At its best television news can inform, educate, remind and even 'speak truth to power'. The daily digital world of violent news may ultimately encourage us to yearn for narratives, communities, and images; habits, prayers and practices which allow us to reframe and redescribe the news, and so to see through violent news and then act differently in our bruised world.

---

73 Gerard Loughlin, *Telling God's Story: Bible, Church and Narrative Theology* (Cambridge: Cambridge University Press, 1996), 86.

Chapter 8

Improvisation in the Theatre as a Model for Christian Ethics

Samuel Wells

There are three broad strands in contemporary writing on Christian ethics. One, which we might call 'universal', works with the conventional deontological and consequential categories and seeks to find common ground with non-religious approaches for the treatment and resolution of issues of public concern. It is generally guided by the modern need to make Christianity reasonable and useful, as a discipline that seeks understanding that suits all people in all situations. A second, which we might call 'subversive', draws attention to the way the 'mainstream' account suppresses alternative voices, excluded for reasons of gender, race, or other social or environmental location, and seeks to make those voices heard, thereby questioning the apparent consensus. It often appeals to a new quasi-church of marginalized values. A third, which we might call 'ecclesial', seeks to articulate a distinctive theological ethic based on the traditions and practices of the Church and the character and acts of God. The first kind does not do justice to the particularity of the Christian tradition. The second kind is stronger on particularity, but has an anthropology that still tends to be wedded to individual autonomy or self-expression. This study pursues the third approach.

1. Faithfulness without a Script

Many theologians have explored the Christian life as the performance of the Christian story.[1] But the notion of performing a script has drawbacks. The script does not provide all the answers. Life throws up circumstances that the gospel seems not to cover. The script is unfinished. There is more to the Christian story than the pages of the Bible disclose. The notion of script can militate against genuine engagement with the world. The idea of a script can suggest the recreation of a golden era – emphasising the replication of past acts, rather than the discovery of new wonders.

---

1   Among many authors, see Nicholas Lash, 'Performing the Scriptures', in *Theology on the Way to Emmaus* (London: SCM, 1986), 37–46; Frances Young, *The Art of Performance* (London: Darton, Longman and Todd, 1990); Walter Brueggemann, *The Bible and the Postmodern Imagination: Texts Under Negotiation* (London: SCM, 1993), 64–70; Stephen Barton, 'New Testament Interpretation as Performance', *Scottish Journal of Theology* 52:2, 179–208.

These drawbacks can encourage the Church to follow predictable courses. Sometimes it lives in the past, aspiring to a world of scriptural purity. Sometimes it dismisses the script, as the fruit of a bygone era, or a curtailment of freedom. Sometimes it seeks to translate the script into contemporary motifs. The confluence of these approaches can lead to considerable bewilderment. The Church feels alone on a rough sea, with no anchor and no stars to steer by.

What is required is a way of being faithful without the reassurance of a script. This is the purpose of improvisation.[2] When improvisers are trained to work in the theatre, they are schooled in a tradition so thoroughly that they learn to act from instinct in ways appropriate to the circumstance. To recognise the significance of improvisation, a number of positive and negative assertions must be appreciated. Improvisation is inevitable: it is the only way to cherish a tradition without being locked in the past. Improvisation is scriptural – it is true to the earliest traditions of the Church: when the disciples met at the Council of Jerusalem, they had to find a way of maintaining the particularity of God's call to Israel in the new context of the Gentile mission.[3] Improvisation is ecclesial – it incorporates key practices of the Church: it is a form of hermeneutics, it is concerned with discernment, it is corporate, it is concerned with engaging with the world. On the negative side, several misapprehensions should be dispelled. Improvisation is not about being original, but about learning and daring to be obvious when all are paralysed. Improvisation is not about being clever or witty, but about allowing oneself to relax, the important work having already been done. Improvisation is not about being demonic, but about trusting the unconscious and conforming it to the service of God.

My understanding of theatrical improvisation is drawn from the tradition of practitioners such as Keith Johnstone, Viola Spolin, Anthony Frost and Ralph Yarrow.[4] Others have written on the tradition of musical improvisation, and this is a

---

2   Gerard Loughlin explains concisely what this means: 'When a person enters the scriptural story he or she does so by entering the Church's performance of that story: he or she is baptised into a biblical and ecclesial drama. It is not so much being written into a book as taking part in a play, a play that has to be improvised on the spot. As Rowan Williams puts it, people are 'invited to "create" themselves in finding a place within this drama – an improvisation in the theatre workshop, but one that purports to be about a comprehensive truth affecting one's identity and future.' *Telling God's Story: Bible, Church and Narrative Theology*, (Cambridge: Cambridge University Press, 1996), 20, quoting Rowan Williams, 'Postmodern Theology and the Judgement of the World', in Frederic B. Burnham (ed.), *Postmodern Theology: Christian Faith in a Pluralist World* (New York: HarperCollins, 1989), 97.

3   Jeremy Begbie in *Theology, Music and Time* (Cambridge: Cambridge University Press, 2000), describes the whole of the *Acts of the Apostles* as 'a stream of new, unpredictable, improvisations' (222–23).

4   Keith Johnstone, *Impro: Improvisation in the Theatre* (London: Methuen, 1981) and *Impro for Storytellers* (London: Faber, 1999); Ronald James and Peter Williams, *A Guide to Improvisation: A Handbook for Teachers* (Kemble Press: Banbury, 1980); Viola Spolin, *Improvisation for the Theatre: A Handbook of Teaching and Directing Techniques* (London:

highly promising line of enquiry, but it is not my concern here.⁵ It is not necessary to be too precise about defining the stage, players, and audience. Both the tradition of improvisation and the Christian story are as interested in disrupting any static notions of this kind as they are in upholding them. For example God, Church and world may respectively each be seen as any of the three (stage, players, and audience), or all, at different times. My treatment will, however, remain true to three features characteristic of most theatrical improvisation: the use of games, the prevalence of humour, and the sense of an implicit but always surprising narrative. My proposal comes in six parts. But I begin with a story.

2. A Story

The story of Harry was related to me by a friend called Robin.⁶ While studying for the Lutheran ministry, Robin was placed in a parish in Akron, Ohio. Harry was a member of Robin's placement parish. The pastoral staff of the parish went to see him at home once a week. They generally brought a tape of the Sunday service, a pew slip, and the sacrament. It tended to be the last role handed out at the staff meeting. The time came for Robin to take her turn on the visiting rota, and discover why.

When Robin first called on Harry, she got a shock. Harry lived in a run-down white clapboard house. He was a big person, sitting in an over-stuffed armchair with an oxygen tank beside it. His legs were virtually useless. The house was pervaded by a smell of must, urine, and dirt. It was repulsive. Nonetheless, Robin went a second time, and gradually Harry came to trust that she would return regularly. As he realised he was not going to be rejected by her, he began to talk more about himself and the way he saw things. Yet he seldom said much about his debilitating physical condition, or the squalor in which he was living.

One day Harry said to Robin, 'It's time for you to have a look in the cellar.' Reluctantly, and somewhat uneasily, Robin walked to the cellar door. She carefully opened it, and looked into the darkness. 'Go down the steps!' Harry insisted, realising her hesitancy. To Robin's astonishment, she saw a large and imposing weaver's loom set up in the basement. There were piles of old clothes and torn strips of cloth. Robin stared in amazement. After trying for some time without success to relate the creativity of what she saw to the dirt and smell of the man she knew, she came back up the stairs, totally bemused.

Harry instructed Robin to bring him a pile of rugs from the kitchen. He took them from her and put them down in front of him, and began to tell the story of his life. He explained that he took in any old clothes that nobody wanted, and scraps of

---

Pitman, 1973); Anthony Frost and Ralph Yarrow, *Improvisation in Drama* (Basingstoke: Macmillan, 1990).

5   Especially Jeremy Begbie, *Theology, Music and Time*, 179–270; and Frances Young, *The Art of Performance*.

6   I have previously related this story in 'Harry's Story: A Story of God's Power and Ours', *Christian*, 99, 3 (Autumn 1999), 10.

cloth from the rubbish heap. He then wove them into something new. The something new was the pile of rag rugs she had found stacked in his kitchen. He then gave what he had made to people who needed a rug. Why did he do it? Because, he said, he felt he was like the old clothes and the waste cloth. He was on the rubbish heap of life – alienated from his friends and his family, unable to work, unable even to breathe properly. He gave Robin his finest rug. Some weeks later, she conducted his funeral.

The time came for her to return to her seminary and complete her studies. At one tutorial she shared Harry's story with a group of her colleagues. After the session, a fellow student touched Robin's arm, took her to one side, and said 'Harry was my uncle.' The student was in tears, for she realised that she had lost her chance of reconciliation with him. She had thought of Harry as a pariah but she could now see he was a saint. Robin retrieved her precious rug, which Harry had given her and gave it to her fellow student. Even after his death, Harry's ministry was transforming the lives of people whom he touched. As Robin told me the story she added, finally, 'I am still moved by his witness.'

I shall now explore improvisation in six stages.

3. Forming Habits

'The battle of Waterloo was won on the playing fields of Eton.' The Duke of Wellington's famous reflection on the climax of the Napoleonic wars was not a statement of personal modesty. It was a recognition that success in battle depends on the character of one's soldiers. It was an observation that Britain had institutions that formed people with the kind of virtues that could survive and even thrive in the demanding circumstances of war. The Duke's claim is that one cannot understand Waterloo without understanding Eton. In fact, what went on in places like Eton was more important than what went on at Waterloo. At Eton, people were trained to shoulder the kind of responsibility they were later to encounter at Waterloo. The real decisions that took place at Waterloo, decisions that shaped the future of European history, had been taken many years earlier. The Duke is saying that ethics is about people, not about actions. The heart of ethics lies in the formation of character. Once out in the 'battlefield', it is too late.

The Duke's claim sits well with the revival in contemporary moral theology of an ethic of virtue. An ethic of virtue says morality is not just about doing the right thing in a crisis, but being a good person all the time. It is therefore not about isolated actions but about agents. It is not about moments of decision but about formation. It is not about universal quandaries but about personal qualities. It is not about what it is right for all to do, but about what it is good for some to be. It is about character.

The Duke's words incline us to focus on the significance of training in moral habit. This is what the Duke called 'Eton'. Training requires commitment, discipline, faithfulness, study, apprenticeship, practice, cooperation, observation, reflection.[7] The point of this formation is to form skills and habits – habits that mean people take the right things for granted and skills that give them ability to do the things they take for granted. When Waterloo comes, it separates those whose character has been appropriately formed from those whose has not. Just as children cannot become adults in an instant, so in every moral 'situation', the real decisions are ones that have been taken some time before. This is what the foolish bridesmaids discovered when their lamp oil ran out in the parable of judgement in Matthew 25. To live well requires both effort and habit. There is a place for both. But great ingenuity or effort at the moment of decision will seldom make up for effort neglected in the time of formation.

The practice of theatrical improvisation is perceived to be about spontaneity, the moment – but it, too, is in fact about years of experiments. Like Wellington's Eton it is also about long preparation before following instinct. Likewise it is about being ready to face the unknown. This state of readiness, the alertness that comes from years of disciplined preparation, is the condition to which improvisers aspire. Jacques Lecoq, one of the leading practitioners in using improvisation as a way of preparing a script for performance, uses the term *la disponibilité*.[8] *La disponibilité* is a condition of relaxed awareness. In this state of awareness the actor senses no need to impose an order on the outside world or on the imagination; there is openness to both receiving and giving. The actor is at one with the whole context: self, other actors, audience, theatre space. It is like the condition of athletes at the height of their form and fitness: but added to that is an awareness of others and an openness to the unknown. The improviser in this state of readiness has to hand all the skills of the trade that I shall explore. There is trust and respect for oneself and the other actors. There is alertness and attention. There is fitness and engagement. There is an understanding of narrative – of what is an end and what is a beginning of a scene or story. There is an ability to keep the narrative going and to explore a situation. There is a willingness to reintroduce discarded material. There is an aptitude for altering and playing with status roles, for relating to others, remembering, sustaining and developing character, and sensing the shape of a story.

A person with skills of this kind has gained them through years of training. Such a player will not strive too hard to be original. The prison of originality arises from a misunderstanding of the nature of spontaneity, rather as the prison of quandary ethics arises from a misconception of the moral life. The great French improviser Jacques Copeau noted that 'Improvisation is an art that has to be learned. ... The art of improvising is not just a gift. It is acquired and perfected by study.'[9]

---

7   On formation see Alasdair MacIntyre, *Three Rival Versions of Moral Enquiry: Encyclopaedia, Genealogy, Tradition* (London: Duckworth, 1990), 58–68; and Stanley Hauerwas, *After Christendom: How the Church is to Behave if Freedom, Justice and a Christian Nation are Bad Ideas* (Nashville: Abingdon, 1991), 93–111.
8   Frost and Yarrow, *Improvisation in Drama*, 151–55.
9   Quoted in Frost and Yarrow, *Improvisation in Drama*, 25.

Perhaps the most widely respected writer on theatrical improvisation, Keith Johnstone, speaks of spontaneity in words that are equally relevant to ethics: 'The improviser has to realise that the more obvious he is, the more original he appears. ... People trying to be original always arrive at the same boring old answers. Ask people to give you an original idea and see the chaos it throws them into. If they said the first thing that came into their head, there'd be no problem. An artist who is inspired is being *obvious*. He's not making any decisions; he's not weighing up one idea against another. ... How else could Dostoyevsky have dictated one novel in the morning and one in the afternoon for three weeks in order to fulfil his contracts?'[10]

Experienced improvisers know that if they have attained a state of relaxed awareness, they can trust themselves to be obvious. It is not too difficult to draw an analogy between this state of relaxed awareness and the Christian experience of contemplative prayer. In the popular imagination, prayer is something one resorts to in a time of crisis. To the Christian disciple, by contrast, prayer can either be moral training in the disciplines of listening to God, or it can be an experience of the grace of 'being obvious' in God's presence. The former is the prayer of effort, the latter the prayer of habit. The aim of the former is to make the latter a matter of instinct – an unselfconscious activity that becomes 'second nature'. The practices and disciplines of Christian discipleship aim to give Christians this state of relaxed awareness, so that they have the freedom – indeed, the skill – to 'be obvious' in what might otherwise seem an anxious crisis.

Wellington's aristocracy prepared for Waterloo on the playing fields. Likewise improvisers train by playing games. Games are a very helpful form of training. A game lasts for a short time. It is understood to be a suspension of conventional rules. It is a project, rather than a life's endeavour. It is thus relatively safe. Because it is safe, one has the freedom to experiment, make mistakes, and discover hidden gifts and talents. By playing a game over and over again one may develop habits and establish skills. One may also perceive analogies with situations in conventional life to which those skills and talents may be transferred and applied. One may quickly see that games are a well-attested method of training for all kinds of practices, and that worship is a game, that trains us for heaven.

Theatrical improvisation is all about games.[11] Games are both training and performance – both preparation and 'situation'. Improvisation thus inspires us to see the whole of life as a game and – far from that being trivial – to imagine the whole of life as worship. Worship, in this sense, is a game that intensifies everyday life, and trains Christians in virtue. Training for worship, training for discipleship is vital – in many ways it *is* worship, it *is* discipleship. Training in improvisation is an analogy for worship and discipleship – an analogy at times so close it becomes the

---

10   Johnstone, *Impro*, 87–88. Virtuous people, such as Thomas More in Robert Bolt's *A Man for All Seasons*, seldom consider themselves to have had a choice.

11   For an extensive list of games and a thorough examination of their political implications, see Augusto Boal, *Games for Actors and Non-Actors*, translated by Adrian Jackson (London: Routledge, 1992).

real thing. Improvisation games are best played by actors with *la disponibilité* – by people of alertness, ready to play. In just the same way, worship is best enjoyed by a community of character – by disciples of holiness, ready to pray.

4. Assessing Status

The great cry of liberation theology is a cry for theology to take seriously its context. This turn towards context is a significant step in uniting ethics and theology. But the insight that comes from theatrical improvisation takes us a step further. It points out that context is an issue not just when there is a notable difference in wealth, education, class, privilege, working pattern or living conditions. Context is an issue in any and every interaction between two or more people. And this is not a static context of environmental situation or conventional social role. It is not something that people accept because they *are*. It is something that people choose in the way they *do* – the way they relate to a given other. Do they act and speak in a way that assumes superiority or inferiority, dominance or submission? This is the choice that improvisers call status. Status informs every single interaction between people – no casual movement or gesture is without significance. There are no innocent remarks or meaningless pauses.[12] Part of the force of the story of Harry and Robin is the slippery status of Robin, a trainee who does the job her seniors avoid, becomes the student of the remarkable outcast Harry, and then a teacher of his niece.

Compare three teachers. One was well liked, but could not keep control of the class. She frequently touched her face, often blinked, tended to twitch and laugh nervously. She invariably arrived breathless and late for class and apologised for doing so, and regularly started sentences with a short 'er' as if she was interrupting the pupils' concentration. A second teacher was widely disliked, but had no trouble keeping discipline, and had no need to resort to punishments or threats. He sat nervelessly still. He paused before each reply or pronouncement, and sometimes interjected a long 'err' before he spoke. His head remained still while he spoke, and he never touched his face. He often used pupils' names when he spoke to them. A third teacher was genuinely loved. She seldom punished, but still kept the attention and interest of the class. She smiled easily, walked tall, but was always relaxed. The atmosphere in the class could be lively and humorous – but then suddenly calm and thoughtful. The first teacher was a low-status player. The second, a compulsive high-status player. The third was a status expert who could raise and lower her own status at will.

At first acquaintance, it is common to assume that high status is much more powerful than low status. But this is far from the case. A crucial breakthrough comes when actors realise that high and low status are simply alternative methods for getting one's way. The next stage is to introduce a conventional relationship, and to witness the difference between the status people are and the status they play. This is

---

12   I owe my understanding of status to Keith Johnstone, *Impro*, 33–74, and *Impro for Storytellers*, 219–31 and 352–53.

the most fascinating dynamic in status interactions. It is generally known as Master-Servant. A common experience of this kind of status transaction is that of customer-shop assistant. The expectation is that the customer calls the tune and the assistant plays it. But the servant often knows best. I once joined a friend who was going into a superior high street outfitter. 'Do you sell those little pieces of plastic you insert into a shirt to stiffen the collar?' my friend asked. The assistant proffered a handful, and said, 'We don't sell them, sir, we give them away.' The servile language masks a high-status response, and prevents it from seeming aggressive. These details provide the fascination in such interplays. The most famous master-servant relations are ones where the servant has all the power, but will lose it the very moment that either party acknowledges it is so – thus Sir Humphrey and Prime Minister James Hacker, Jeeves and Wooster, or perhaps Tony Blair and George W. Bush. The see-sawing and constant reversals of status provide the dynamism.

The first stage in understanding status is to recognise that status transactions are inherent in every relationship. The second is to see that people make choices in their use of language and gesture about whether to play high or low status. The third is to appreciate that 'high' and 'low' are not moral designations, or even measurements of relative power: they are simply alternative strategies for getting one's way. The fourth is to begin to enjoy the dynamics of status interactions displayed in the affirmation and subversion of a conventional relationship. The fifth and last dimension to perceive is the significance of the use of space. These five dimensions of status each have significant implications for the Church and its understanding of its ethical task and its relationship with wider society.

The politics of local church life is, like the life of any organisation, filled with status interactions. Consider the moment at which a date for a future meeting is arranged. One person gets out a tiny diary. Another gets out an enormous diary. Another gets out an electronic diary, which takes some while to warm up. A fourth does not carry a diary, but makes all arrangements through a personal secretary at the office. A fifth does not have a diary, because they consider that they can remember such special events as would break their routine. A sixth has left their diary at home, forgetful as ever. Then dates are suggested. One person explains their unavailability in terms of all their upcoming dental appointments and driving lessons. Another is out of the country for the next month. A third says they will need to consult their partner. A fourth says they could make the suggested time, so long as people understand that means they would be an hour late. A fifth says they could make any time, they are completely flexible. A sixth says they must be getting away, but not to worry, just go ahead and they will try to fit in and let the others know. And then the moment comes when a date is set. Whose absence is insignificant, and whose is decisive?

Status interactions are ubiquitous in the relationship of the local church corporately to the community it serves. How do the size, age, and design of the church building compare to other buildings in the community? Are the doors open, closed or locked? Is the faith and activity of the church broadcast by noticeboard or kept a secret? What is the principal way in which the church encounters local people – through knocking on doors or written leaflets (the salesperson or mail-order company), prearranged meetings between representatives of organisations with common interests (the business person), or the availability of a designated representative at advertised hours for particular services (the professional person)? Does the local church believe it speaks for 'all people of good will' in the community, or does it assume that its voice will probably be a minority view on most issues? Does it expect to lead, join or follow? Does it call its leader pastor, minister or priest, and what social standing does it expect its leader to have in the community? These are all questions of status.

Similar questions arise when the corporate context changes from local to national. Does the Church consider itself to speak for Truth, which needs no defence, or for a group of beleaguered believers, whose interests need upholding? Does the Church consider itself part of Government, concerned with the balance of power and the benefit of all? Or does it presume that it will always be with the marginalized and oppressed, and therefore never at the castle, always at the gate? Where does the Church locate its national centre of operations, and in what kind of premises? How does it institute and regard its leaders? How does it hope or assume non-Christians will regard these leaders? Will that esteem be earned, and if so, how – or can it be taken for granted? These are all questions of status.

5. Accepting and Blocking

'There are people who prefer to say "Yes", and there are people who prefer to say "No". Those who say "Yes" are rewarded by the adventures they have, and those who say "No" are rewarded by the safety they attain.'[13] Improvisation begins when a community of people resolve to find ways of 'saying "Yes"'. Communities generally find several reasons why they prefer instead to 'say "No"'. They tend to see 'saying "Yes"' as impossible, improper, or dangerous.

A simple game, called 'Word at a Time', illustrates what is at stake in saying 'Yes'. The game begins with the actors sitting in a circle. One actor says a single word. This becomes the first word of a story. The actor next in the circle follows immediately with a second word, the next actor says a third, and so on, as quickly as possible, until the story is considered complete. Adverbs are disallowed in order to keep up the pace and avoid delaying tactics. Inexperienced actors invariably try to control the story. But this only succeeds in ruining it. Every person who adds a word has an incipient story in mind, and thus an idea of what word might follow. But each time they must instantly wipe that idea out of their mind – or else they will be paralysed. If the players relax, cease to worry about being 'obvious', remain highly attentive, and simply say whatever comes to mind, they will find the story seems to take on a life of its own, guided by some outside force.[14]

The reason improvisation seems impossible to inexperienced players is that instinctively they spend most of their time trying to avoid being dangerous. The story constantly threatens to become obscene, psychotic, or unoriginal. These all

---

13   Johnstone, *Impro*, 92.
14   Ibid., 131.

represent danger. Thus there is a constant, irresistible, temptation to 'kill' the story. This can be done passively by saying 'Stop' or remaining silent; or actively by trying to control its future, insisting on being clever or original, or closing it without regard to its foregoing content whenever its direction threatens danger.

The breakthrough in improvisation training comes when actors realise that their performance is not a linear method of getting as efficiently as possible from point A to point B. On the contrary, detours are most of the fun. This changes the whole notion of what constitutes a mistake. As one experienced director puts it, 'Mistakes are re-evaluated as possibilities of new directions. ... Rightness is more a question of *attitude*, not of what you do but of how you do it, whether you are prepared to play with what comes along.'[15] Rather like the comedian Ronnie Corbett telling a story, the experienced improviser knows that the simplest narrative interlaced with teasing detours often makes the best drama. This is illustrated by a game called Lantern Lecture.[16] Actor 1 is an explorer showing slides to select friends. Actor 2 is the slides. Actor 1 describes the first slide – 'This is me climbing the Andes'. Actor 2 mimes the slide, then changes position and mimes a second slide. Actor 1 must describe the slide the Actor 2 has adopted – 'This is me being lifted up by a South American condor' – whereupon Actor 1 then continues by describing the next slide, and so on.

Three technical terms may assist in exploring what it means to 'say "Yes"'. The first is the term 'offer'. Anything an actor does may be regarded as an offer. An offer may be a speech, a facial expression or gesture, or an action – even an attempt to remain silent or still. Any of these things may be treated as an invitation to respond, and thus be treated as an offer. Thus in the game 'Word at a Time', each word is both a response to an offer and immediately an offer in itself. Offers are not to be regarded as good or bad in themselves: the key is, what you do with them.

The second term is 'accept'. An actor accepts an offer by any response that maintains the premise of the action that constituted that offer. Imagine a child in the playground puts two fingers together and points them towards another child, and then clicks another finger and says 'Bang! You're dead'. This is an offer. The second child then has the opportunity to respond to that offer. If the child is prepared to accept the offer, they will conventionally do so by yelping a strangled cry and falling over in a crumpled heap, for this maintains the premise of the first child's offer. To do this requires the same skills of the second child that are required to play the game 'Word at a Time'. The second child must be willing and able to wipe from their mind any thoughts they themselves had of actively controlling the outcome of the narrative, and resist the inclination to a passive refusal, such as 'I'm not playing any more.'

The third term is 'block'. Imagine once again that the first child acts a shot and says 'Bang! You're dead.' If the second child were actively to refuse to accept the offer and fall down, but were instead to remain standing and say 'Bang! *You're* dead,

---

15 Frost and Yarrow, *Improvisation in Drama*, 59.
16 See James and Williams, *A Guide to Improvisation*, 49.

not me' then this would be a 'block'. Blocking prevents the action from developing. It undermines one's partner's premise. It may be amusing to watch, but it kills the story. It turns a partnership into a confrontation. It happens when one actor is overwhelmed by the danger or difficulty of keeping the story going. Accepting sees the future as an opportunity – blocking sees the future as a problem. All sorts of possibilities are ruled out by blocking. Imagine once again that the first child shoots and says 'Bang! You're dead.' This time the second child accepts the offer. Now the second child may begin to explore the after-life of the dead soldier, and perhaps reappear to the first soldier as a ghost or angel. But this only becomes possible if the original death, the first offer, is accepted. Now the story can really develop, as the first child may be introduced to other angels, fall in love with one of them, have to choose whether to die in order to be united with their beloved, and so on.

One author lists 17 ways in which inexperienced improvisers can kill a story.[17] Besides blocking, there is wimping (in Word at a Time this would mean postponing the noun with endless adjectives), gossiping (avoiding interaction by discussing things that are happening elsewhere), joining (having the same reaction as your partner), being original (a form of sidetracking that in fact avoids interaction with disturbing material), and gagging (getting a laugh by resisting the story). The director overcomes these destructive tactics through intervening immediately when an actor begins to block, however subtle the block may be.[18]

What would it be like to be committed never to block, always to accept? What would it be like to be surrounded by people who are committed to the practice of accepting all offers? The interactions in such a community seem telepathic. It looks like everything has already been arranged. There is no such thing as an accident or an interruption. Everything becomes an offer that can be accepted. 'The actor who will accept anything that happens seems supernatural; it's the most marvellous thing about improvisation: you are suddenly in contact with people who are unbounded, whose imagination seems to function without limit. ... People with dull lives often think that their lives are dull by chance. In reality everyone chooses more or less what kind of events will happen to them by their conscious patterns of blocking and yielding.'[19] One author goes even further on this point: 'Improvisation is not exchange of information between players: it is communion.'[20]

Blocking appears to some as faithful resilience. But in that it buries its talent in the hillside it may anticipate the punishment handed out to the third slave; and in that it sets its stall against the inevitable tide of time, it may anticipate the heritage of King Canute. I argue that for the Church to block is not desirable, necessary or possible.

---

17   Johnstone, *Impro for Storytellers*, 101–29.
18   Ibid., 145–48. In a game called 'Help him Boris', an interrogator inflicts immediate and merciless punishment (usually with a balloon) if the victim blocks unacceptably.
19   Johnstone, *Impro*, 99–100.
20   Spolin, *Improvisation for the Theatre*, 45.

But is accepting the only alternative? It is certainly essential to learn how to accept, and to learn why and how to avoid blocking. But accepting is not the only alternative. I suggest an approach that requires the skills learned through accepting, but does not stop there. Just because the Church does not take up arms against evil, it does not mean that it simply capitulates to it. The Church does not simply accept the story of evil. It has a story of its own. The Church's story begins before evil began and ends after evil has ended. This story does not accept evil – it over-accepts it.

6. Questioning Givens

Christian ethics is often treated as the negotiation of the rival claims of competing 'givens'. There is, for example, the limitation of time, and the given of death. There is the limitation of knowledge and the human mind, and thus the given of ignorance. There is the limitation of space and the human body, and thus of freedom. And there is the limitation of goodness and the given of sin and evil. The sum of these givens is sometimes understood as Natural Law. Tragedy is generally the story of those who have tried hubristically to ignore such givens, and have consequently met their fate.

It is helpful at this point to make a distinction between 'givens' and 'gifts'.[21] It is the task of the imagination to change or challenge the presumed 'necessities' of the world, to resist the implication that what the Christian community receives are 'givens' rather than 'gifts'. In this sense, 'givens' are things that are simply there and the community must simply adapt to, if it is to remain in the 'real' world, whereas 'gifts' are largely what we make of them. For 'Christian realists', the task of Christian ethics is to adapt to such 'givens' as prevail in the contemporary world - the objective material causes of life. Ethics becomes a process of adjudicating between competing 'givens'.[22] Since the emphasis of givenness is on the giver, ethics is primarily seen from the point of view of those who are in the best position to control the majority of the giving – that is, the powerful. It is thus supposed that if Christians put themselves in positions of power they will influence the 'givens' in a positive way.

For the nonviolent Christian community, by contrast, the only 'given' is the Church's narrative: all else is potentially 'gift'. It is not therefore a question of

---

21   From the considerable literature on the notion of gift, see especially Jacques Derrida, *Given Time I: Counterfeit Money*, translated by Peggy Kamuf (Chicago and London: University of Chicago Press, 1992); Marcel Mauss, *The Gift: The Form and Reason for Exchange in Archaic Societies*, translated by W. D. Halls (London: Routledge, 1990); Jean-Luc Marion, *God Without Being: Hors Texte*, translated by Thomas A. Carlson with a Foreword by David Tracy (Chicago: University of Chicago Press, 1990); John Milbank, 'Can a Gift Be Given? Prolegomena to a Future Trinitarian Metaphysic', *Modern Theology* 11, 1995, 119–61; Loughlin, *Telling God's Story*, 223–45; Begbie, *Theology, Music and Time*, 246–70.

22   'We are not to accept the world with its hates and resentments as a given, but to recognise that we live in a new age which makes possible a new way of life.' Stanley Hauerwas, *The Peaceable Kingdom*, 85.

putting oneself in a position of power. Ethics is not principally about how to do the giving. God is the only true giver. His story of how he deals with his people is the definitive 'given'. Ethics is done by people who are on the *receiving* end, working out how to accept things that present themselves as 'givens' but cannot be since there is only one 'given' – the narrative of scripture and the Church's tradition. Moreover discernment concerns the reception of God's abundant gifts, rather than the distribution of the world's limited givens.[23] Harry's niece had only ever seen her uncle as a given. Through Robin's tutorial, she came for the first time to see him, his condition and his faith as a gift. The process of transforming fate into destiny can be seen as a threefold process: first recognising that much of what seems 'given' is in fact 'gift'; second realising that the key to a 'gift' is not its intrinsic nature or purpose but in how we respond and accept it; and third, receiving the gift in such a way that it becomes part of the continuing story of the way God deals with his people. Thus is fate (a 'given') transformed into destiny (a 'gift'). The key to receiving is to place the apparent 'given' within a larger story and thus render it a 'gift'. That process, as I shall now describe, is called overaccepting.

7. Incorporating Gifts

This brings us to a simple, but immensely significant, game, which demonstrates the suggestive power of improvisation for Christian ethics. The game is called Presents.[24] It is played in pairs. A thinks of a present they would like to give to B, and then mimes giving it to them. B has to guess what it is, and use it accordingly. The players then swap roles, and B passes a mimed present to person A, and so on.

The trouble with this game is, of course, that it can be difficult to identify what the gift is; the players can get frustrated with each other, as each mimes more and more outlandish gifts, leaving the other more and more bewildered. Each actor seems in competition, and feels it. How can this change? The secret to making the game a success is, not to think of interesting things to give, but to concentrate on making the thing one is *given* as interesting as possible. If A simply holds out two hands, as if proffering something in a box, B may be delighted to receive an array of possible gifts: 'Everything you are given delights you. Maybe you wind it up and let it walk about the floor, or you sit it on your arm and let it fly off after a small bird, or maybe you put it on and turn into a gorilla.'[25] If the game is played this way, the stifling sense of competition disappears, and great joy and energy are released.

The change to the game might be simple, but the change in thinking is enormous. All offers are now potential gifts. When the burden of the game lies with the giver, the giver requires the kind of imagination that determines the future. Great frustration

---

23   For more on the distinction between scarcity and abundance, see John Milbank, *The Word Made Strange: Theology, Language, Culture* (Oxford and Cambridge, Massachusetts: Blackwell), especially 219–32.
24   Keith Johnstone, *Impro*, 100–101.
25   Ibid., 101.

arises if the gift is misinterpreted. When, by contrast, the emphasis lies with the receiver, the imagination co-operates, adapts, and develops.

I want to suggest that what the gift game pictures is a revolution in thinking about Christian ethics. Ethics as it is generally described is invariably perceived as a matter of choosing when to say yes and when to say no. But the 'Presents' game shows that in fact Person B has three options when offered a present by person A. B can say, first, no, I am not going to receive this gift. Saying no appears, in the short term, to maintain one's own security. This is the approach associated with the Essene sect of first-century Palestine.[26] Throughout Christian history there have always been groups that said no to some or all 'gifts' that came their way from wider society. The Strict Brethren might be said to represent this position today. It is the position H.R. Niebuhr described as 'Christ against Culture'.[27] There are many things to which it is often said the wider church should say no. The lists sometimes include slavery and murder, often nuclear weapons and embryo research, perhaps abortion and euthanasia, sometimes betting slips, tobacco, and alcohol. Most churches have recognised that one cannot say no to one's culture wholesale. To do so is to deny the goodness of God's creation, and to declare war on society.

So, what else can B do? B can say, second, what *is* this gift? What is it *for*? What am I *supposed* to do with it? This is the way the game is usually played, as I have described above. It is also the way the game is usually played in Christian ethics. B accepts the gift, but does not know what the gift is. The dilemma of B as to the nature of the gift corresponds to the moment of decision that is the focus of quandary ethics. For just as the present is given by A in the game, so are circumstances 'given' at moments of decision, and the decision-maker must adjudicate between them. And just as the game is frustrating when played this way, so is decision-making, and ethics that concentrates on decisions, often immensely trying. The assumption is often made that there *is* a right thing to do in each circumstance. Such reasoning is often based on natural law. Natural law arguments tend to assume that everything was created for a purpose, and that when it is employed about its correct purpose all is well. This is the position of B: desperately wondering what this gift is *for*.

There is a third option. Person B can say, third, how do I want to *receive* this gift? This is the transition that I have described in the way the gift game is played above. It is not a question of what the gift is *supposed* to be: it is a question of what the gift *can* be. One does not say 'What is this gift *for*?' – and even less 'Is this a good gift?'; one says 'How can this gift be understood or used in a faithful way?', 'What does the way we accept this gift say about the kind of people we are and want to be?', 'What can (or has) this gift become in the kingdom of God?' The ethical issues are less about the gift itself than about where it is perceived to fit into the story of the way God deals with his people and how that fitting-in takes place.

---

26 For an interesting application of this kind of thinking to the context of first-century Palestine, see John Howard Yoder, *The Politics of Jesus: Behold the Man! Our Victorious Lamb* (Second Edition, Grand Rapids: Eerdmans, 1994), 96–97.

27 H.R. Niebuhr, *Christ and Culture* (New York: Harper and Row, 1951), 45–82.

This is called 'overaccepting'.[28] Overaccepting is accepting in the light of a larger story. The fear about accepting is that one will be determined by the gift, and thus lose one's integrity and identity. The fear about blocking is that one will seal oneself off from the world, and thus lose one's relevance and humanity. Overaccepting is an active way of receiving that enables one to retain both identity and relevance. It is a way of accepting without losing the initiative. This often involves a change of status. Diana, Princess of Wales was asked in a television interview whether she thought she would ever be Queen. She famously replied 'I will be Queen of people's hearts', thus not blocking the awkwardness of her predicament, but overaccepting the sadness of losing her throne, and placing herself in what she saw as a far more significant narrative. The steel workers of the film *The Full Monty* had been stripped of their dignity by the experience of unemployment. They overaccepted their condition by developing a thriving male-stripper routine. Robin's friend Harry did not block the squalor of his ill health and living conditions, but overaccepted them by converting rubbish into items of usefulness and beauty.

Overaccepting imitates the manner of God's reign. For God does not block his creation: he does not toss away his original material. Since Noah, he has refused to destroy what he has made. But neither does he accept creation on its own terms. Instead, he 'overaccepts' his creation. He sees what it can be, and by the way he incorporates it into his kingdom, through election, incarnation, passion, resurrection, and the sending of the Spirit, he demonstrates his character, the kind of God he is. Christians imitate the character of God to the extent that they overaccept the gifts of creation and culture in the same way God does.[29]

It may be helpful to illustrate the tactic of overaccepting from human experience. The story is told of a concert pianist who was on the point of beginning a performance when there was a scream from the audience. A child had left her seat beside her parent and was running around the auditorium. The concert pianist stepped away from his instrument in order to maintain concentration. The child ran up the steps onto the stage, sat herself down on the stool and began to play discordant notes at random as she pleased. The hushed audience gasped in horror and embarrassment. The pianist walked towards the child and stood behind her as she played. The pianist leant over her and, without disturbing her, placed right and left hands outside her two small hands on the keyboard. The pianist then began to play, in response to her notes, weaving their discordant sounds into an improvised melody. To have thrown the child out would have been to block: to have let her play on would have been to accept; to weave a wonderful melody around her was to receive her as a gift, to overaccept. A similar practice is common among instrumental performers when they

---

28 Johnstone, *Impro*, 102.
29 The best studies of the political dimensions of this claim in New Testament perspective are David Toole, *Waiting for Godot in Sarajevo: Theological Reflections on Nihilism, Tragedy and Apocalypse* (Boulder: Westview, 1997 and London: SCM, 2001), 232–48; and James C. Scott, *Domination and the Art of Resistance: Hidden Transcripts* (New Haven: Yale University Press, 1990).

make mistakes in their play, incorporating what they call passing notes into their performance rather than calling a halt.

8. Reincorporating the Lost

Two questions persistently present themselves. The first question is, on what resources does the Church draw in order to overaccept? In other words, how does the sense of being part of a greater story translate into overaccepting in Christian practice? The second question is, how does the Church address evil, both in the contemporary world and in the Church's own history? In other words, how does the Church accept particularly sinister offers, and how does it accept the fact that in the past it has often blocked that which was good, and accepted that which was evil?

My answer to these questions begins with the building of a road. Imagine Church history as a road, stretching from the past into the future. It is in the character of roads to dig and cleave and thrust their way through the countryside, leaving considerable quantities of debris to either side. This is in some ways an ugly process, as environmental campaigners have insisted in recent years. To take another, less linear analogy, one may compare Church history to a sculpture, at which the sculptor continually chips away, and in so doing creates a great mound of discarded plaster or marble. What has happened in the liberation movement both outside and inside the Church in recent generations has been the cry of the discarded marble, the searing pain of the displaced earth. For the Church has come to realise that history is written by the winners, whereas the faith of Mary's Magnificat proclaims the God who is on the side of the losers. And the losers in Church history have tended to be the same people who have been the losers in society as a whole.

The revelation brought by the liberation movement in the Church in the last thirty years is that the earth cast aside in making the road is at least as much a part of the story as the road itself; that the marble discarded by the sculptor is at least as much a part of the display as the sculpture. It is now much easier to see, for poor and rich alike, that the losers, whose voice has not been heard, are at least as much a part of Church history as those winners who have written it. The Church has got to get used to the face of the poor, because it will see them on thrones in the final act of the drama. That final act is when the promises of Hannah's song and Mary's Magnificat are realised, when the sorrow of this world is turned to dancing. If the Church wants to be a part of that final act, it has to be shaped and formed by its chief characters as they appear in the current act. By working with and being with and in some circumstances being the poor, the excluded, the Church faithfully follows its Lord and anticipates his coming again. The closer the Church is to the poor in this act of the drama, the more prepared it will be to come face to face with God in the final act.

Those who have told stories to children will have experienced that vacant, wandering expression that children sometimes have, which masks a razor-sharp allegiance to the conventions of story telling. Should one try to miss out chunks of the plot, or finish before the end of the story, one suffers the accusing wrath of the deeply wronged. This is the case even if one is making up the story as one is going along. How do children know whether one has or has not reached the end of the story? The key to improvising children's stories is not in thinking up clever or original characters or contexts, but in remembering what has been discarded and reintroducing it at the appropriate moment. Likewise the key to improvising on the Christian story is not in being clever or original, but in being so steeped in the discarded elements of the story that one can draw on them when the vital moment comes.

This brings us to the final practice within the discipline of theatrical improvisation: the practice known as 'reincorporation'. A story is not simply a series of events happening one after another. Such sequences have no reason for stopping in any one place rather than any other. It is not simply a matter of free association: a story requires 'reincorporation'.[30] Reincorporation is what marks the end of the story. When elements found earlier in the story begin to be reincorporated, then some pattern emerges and a sense of completion is possible. Christian ethics seen from an eschatological perspective is always profoundly aware of the end of the story, and of the way this end reincorporates earlier (perhaps all earlier) parts of the narrative. It is reincorporation that distinguishes the end from just another event in the narrative. Reincorporation brings together notions of the end of the story as *telos* or purpose and the end of the story as conclusion.

The key factor in reincorporation is memory. Memory is much more significant than originality. The improviser does not set out to create the future, but responds to the past, reincorporating to form a story. This can be illustrated by a game in which actor A provides free-associated disconnected material, while actor B somehow tries to connect it:

> A: It was a cold winter's night. The wolves howled in the trees. The concert pianist adjusted his sleeves and began to play. An old lady was shovelling snow from her door...
> B: ... When she heard the piano the little old lady began shovelling at a fantastic speed. When she reached the concert hall she cried, 'That pianist is my son!' Wolves appeared at all the windows, and the pianist sprang onto the piano, thick fur growing visibly from under his clothes.[31]

The Christian community is in a position much more similar to actor B than to actor A. The community is not able to determine the 'gifts' it is given: it is obliged to use the skill of its convictions to transform the 'fate' (or givenness) of the disconnected gifts into the destiny of a story consonant with the one given story. It does not do this by changing the subject, or by refusing to continue; both of these would do violence to the emerging narrative. This perspective sees all events in creation as offering possibilities for narrative, needing skills nurtured by the gospel to be reincorporated. The key to successful improvisation is not originality but memory. The more

---

30   Ibid., 112.
31   Ibid., 116–17.

easily forgotten an element is, the more satisfying its reincorporation. Likewise, the deeper the exclusion of a person from the Church's story, the more significant their reincorporation in the story. As was pointed out to Simon the Pharisee, the repentance of the woman who washed Jesus' feet with her hair was more significant than Simon's own repentance.

In a highly suggestive phrase one author on theatrical improvisation emphasises that the skills required for improvisation are not primarily those that come in moments of inspiration (or decision). Instead, the future is formed out of the past. 'The improviser has to be *like a man walking backwards*. He sees where he has been, but he pays no attention to the future. His story can take him anywhere, but he must still "balance" it, and give it shape, by remembering incidents that have been shelved and reincorporating them.'[32] Likewise Robin's friend Harry reincorporated that which others had discarded in his rag rugs. By so doing, he reincorporated broken relationships and over-accepted blocked fellowship, thus embodying the kingdom.

It is time to return the two questions raised at the outset of this section. The first question concerned the resources for improvisation in the Church. The answer is that the Church has ample resources for every eventuality it faces and it finds those resources among the discarded elements of earlier parts of its story. Church history is theology teaching by examples – good examples like St Laurence and St Francis, bad examples like the Inquisition, the Crusades and the Holocaust. In order to gain access to these resources, the Church needs to maintain a lively memory, in which it recalls tales of the good and the bad, and especially of those who have not written their own history – the losers. The greatest improvisers, such as Laurence, did nothing more than reincorporate discarded elements of the story. To do this, one has to be part of a community that knows and lives the story. Remembering the sins of the past is as significant as remembering the saints.

The second question concerned evil. For the Church to think it can simply block evil is contrary to the example of Christ, has no guarantee of success, bypasses the imagination, and tends to ally the Church with powerful forces it may have no place beside. The challenge of evil may be the threat of a rival story, or it may be the denial that there is any story at all. For example Hitler talked of a thousand-year Reich (a rival story), while less exalted Nazis tormented Jews by arguing that if any survivor tried to recall the atrocities of the period, no one would ever believe them (the denial of story). The Church's response to both kinds of unpalatable offer is to tell a much larger story, and to stretch its imagination to the full dimensions and cosmic scope of the Christian story.

9. A Story

My final story happened nine years ago and concerns Bill. Bill left school in a town where one went down the mine, constructed aircraft turbines, or learned to build

---

32   Ibid., 116; my italics.

warships. So he did an apprenticeship in the shipyard, and looked forward to a lifetime of employment. He progressed well, moving upstairs to the office, where he ordered parts for future ships. He married, had two children, got a car and a mortgage. All was well. Then one day, along with almost everyone else at the company, he lost his job. His wife worked part-time at the Post Office, and was a highly capable person. She took on a full-time post, and Bill set to cooking and cleaning. It wasn't enough. They realised they would have to sell the house. Bill set about decorating the house to make it attractive to a buyer. His efforts were lamentable. He lived in fear of his highly competent wife, and her withering criticism, sharpened by her exhaustion. The two daughters of the house witnessed daily-increasing tension. Determined to maintain their Easter observance, the family faithfully shared in the witness of Holy Week, its commemoration of the Passion being borne out in their thinly veiled torture.

Finally, on Holy Saturday, the explosion came. Bill's wife returned after work, desperate to grab some tea and get out to the Easter Vigil, but was stopped in her tracks by the smell of paint. Bill was on the stairs, his ladder through an involuntary hole in the ceiling, and the contents of an upset paint-pot trickling down the stair carpet. She shrieked: 'What's the use of you? You can't get a job, you can't cook, can't keep the house tidy – and put a paintbrush in your hand and you wreck the whole house! You're useless, pointless, hopeless.' The silence was louder than the shouting that preceded it, as Bill accepted each word. But his daughter, a precocious eleven-year-old, intervened. She looked up the stairs at her father, and back down to her mother. 'He's a good dad,' she said, simply. In five words she had taken the right things for granted, recognised as a child it was not her responsibility to make everything come out right, blocked nothing of what her mother had said, questioned the givens her mother had been assuming, over-accepted her mother's words, and reincorporated the forgotten part of the story, the part that genuinely belonged in the final act of God's drama. All six stages of improvisation in five words. Her simple words brought her mother to humble repentance. The mother tearfully related the story to me later the same day.

Chapter 9

The Sense of an Ending: Finitude and the Authentic Performance of Life

Trevor A. Hart

> I hold the world but as the world, Gratiano –
> A stage where every man must play a part,
> And mine a sad one.[1]
>
> All-seeing heaven, what a world is this?[2]

1. The World Stage

Perhaps it is inevitable that playwrights and actors should come, sooner or later, to reflect on the curious relationship that holds between drama and life. If dramatic art is in some sense always a version of – or at least 'based on' – life as we know it, so, in its turn, life as we know it can and has often been figured according to models duly provided by the theatre. As an actor, Shakespeare could hardly help noticing the interstices. The 'microcosmic correspondence' between the two realities was driven home each time he stepped out to perform yet another role on the boards of the Globe theatre, a venue which in construction as well as in name held the two worlds closely together.[3] As playwright, too, the metaphor clearly intrigued him, and is already introduced into his work before the Globe's construction in 1599.[4] The

---

1   *The Merchant of Venice*, 1.1. See George Brandes (ed.), *The Garrick Shakespeare*, Volume 3 (London: William Heinemann, 1905), 6.

2   *Richard III*, 2.1. See George Brandes, *The Garrick Shakespeare*, Volume 6 (London: Heinemann, 1905), 408.

3   See the article 'Globe Theatre' by Gabriel Egan in Michael Dobson and Stanley Wells (eds), *The Oxford Companion to Shakespeare* (Oxford: Oxford University Press, 2001), 165–66.

4   *The Merchant of Venice* is dated 1596–97 by Margreta de Grazia and Stanley Wells (eds), *The Cambridge Companion to Shakespeare* (Cambridge: Cambridge University Press, 2001), xix. The Globe was constructed in 1599 for use by the Chamberlain's Men, a company founded in 1594 and to which Shakespeare seemingly belonged from its inception. See John H. Astington, 'Playhouses, players and playgoers in Shakespeare's time', in De Grazia and

world is a stage and life a drama in which each of us has a particular part to play, and perhaps many different parts. Once deployed, this image provokes questions thick and fast about the 'drama' of all that lies beyond the theatre's limits; questions about the script, about characterisation, about how much freedom a player may have in determining his part and how it is played, about the quality of a performance, and so on. What are literary-critical and dramaturgical questions in the one world are, of course, religious and theological ones in the other. In order to ask and to answer them, we cannot help positing a reality which transcends the drama itself – a playwright, a director, an audience; something which was before and will be after the drama itself is played out, and which in some sense accounts for its existence at all. And if Shakespeare does not often explicitly push such theological questions into the foreground of his plays, one cannot live long with his imagery before some of the more uncomfortable ones begin to impinge. Sometimes, of course, he cannot resist giving us a helpful shove in the right direction:

> As flies to wanton boys are we to th' gods;
> They kill us for their sport.5

It's not precisely the same metaphor, obviously; but it's equally clearly in the same poetic (and theological) ball park. For here we have the gods as those in whose presence (and for whose amusement) our life is played out, with a degree of malicious inter-activity thrown in for good measure. The theatrical image lurking in the background (behind the more immediate and universal improvised entertainment of the 'wanton boys') is that of the ancient 'spectacle' rather than the theatre as Shakespeare himself knew it, but the theological issues lying close to hand are some of the same ones. While he arguably furnishes us with some of the most familiar and elegant examples, though, Shakespeare was certainly not the first to play with such images. They had already occurred to the ancients themselves.

The use of the world-stage image by the Roman philosopher Epictetus (c. 55–135 AD) is among the first significant instances.

> Remember that you are an actor in a play, and the Playwright chooses the manner of it: if he wants it short, it is short; if long, it is long. If he wants you to act a poor man you must act the part with all your powers; and so if your part be a cripple or a magistrate or a plain

---

Wells, *The Cambridge Companion to Shakespeare*, 99–113. Interestingly, Shakespeare's most developed use of the world-stage metaphor is the familiar passage in *As You Like It* (2.7: 'All the world's a stage, and all the men and women merely players ...' and so forth) a play that seems to date from the very period during which the Globe was being built, or immediately thereafter. Other uses of the image occur in *2 Henry IV* (1.1; 1597–98) and *Henry V* (Prologue, 3; 1598–99), immediately prior to the Globe's construction.

5   *King Lear*, 4.1. See George Brandes (ed.), *The Garrick Shakespeare*, Volume 9 (London: Heinemann, 1905), 301.

man. For your business is to act the character that is given you and act it well; the choice of the cast is Another's.⁶

It is Stoic philosophy which provides Epictetus with the specific theological context for his use of the dramatic metaphor; namely, a strong overarching doctrine of divine Providence fused with an equally strong account of the rational-soul's jurisdiction within a circumscribed but definite sphere of concern. Life, he insists, is lived on a stage, against a backdrop and props, and amidst a script and a cast not of our own choosing. And yet not *all* in a human life is determined. There is a sphere within which the exercise of human freedom makes all the difference to the quality of what occurs on stage.⁷ Called to perform a certain 'part' or to play a character over which we have no control whatever, we are nonetheless in a position to perform that part well or badly, and here 'character' in the other sense is of the utmost importance. The highest calling is to face whatever life (the divine Playwright or his script) may send our way, and to respond to it well. Accordingly, we must learn not to desire (or to 'live for') the things which please us, nor, on the other hand, to complain when our part in life is to endure unpleasant and even painful events.⁸ Nothing, Epictetus urges, is evil in itself; it only becomes such when we permit it to *affect* our soul in certain ways, and that is something entirely within our control.⁹ 'Ask not that events should happen as you will, but let your will be that events should happen as they do, and you shall have peace.'¹⁰ And no human circumstances are truly 'tragic'. Tragedy is a theatrical genre, and ought properly to be confined to the world of the stage alone. Tragedies are 'a portrayal in ... metrical form of the sufferings of men who have set their admiration on outward things',¹¹ rather than mastering the appropriate detachment from them. Accordingly, in real life tragedy is what occurs only when fools are compelled to face everyday events, and cannot

---

6   Epictetus, *The Discourses and Manual*, translated with Introduction and Notes in two volumes by P. E. Matheson (Oxford: Clarendon Press, 1916), Vol. II, 219. Catharine Edwards refers us to a tradition according to which, already in the fifth century BC, Democritus observed the same trope: 'The world is a stage, life is a performance; you come, you see, you go away.' See Catharine Edwards, 'Acting and self-actualisation in imperial Rome: some death scenes', in Pat Easterling and Edith Hall (eds), *Greek and Roman Actors: Aspects of an Ancient Profession* (Cambridge: Cambridge University Press, 2002), 377. The work of Epictetus offers a sustained development of the image, and locates it within a clear religious and theological context.

7   'In our power are will and all operations of the will, and beyond our power are the body, the parts of the body, possessions, parents, brothers, children, country, in a word – those whose society we share' (*Discourses*, I.22). See Epictetus, *The Discourses and Manual*, Vol. 1, 110.

8   'The will to get and the will to avoid.' See, for example, *Discourses* I.4; III.2, in Epictetus, *The Discourses and Manual*, Vol. 1, 55; Vol. II, 10–11.

9   See, for example, *Discourses* I.29, in Epictetus, *The Discourses and Manual*, Vol. 1, 131.

10 *Manual* 8, in Epictetus, *The Discourses and Manual*, Vol. 2, 216.

11 *Discourses* I.4, in Epictetus, *The Discourses and Manual*, Vol. 1, 56.

respond as they ought.[12] It is a state of turmoil in the heart, mind and will, and at odds with that 'true nature of things' to which each soul ought voluntarily to adapt itself.[13] 'Blows are not by nature intolerable', Epictetus writes.[14] And if they are, it is *we* who make them so. So yes, life is indeed lived under the gaze of One who is Playwright, Director and Audience. The gods are watching.[15] But they are not toying with us for the sake of their own gratification, wantonly removing legs or wings, or capriciously dispatching us with a down-turned thumb. That's not an appropriate characterization of the human situation at all. Rather, we are offered a part in life's great play, a private performance for the gods no less, and with it the opportunity to become a great actor capable of taking whatever part may be offered to us and rendering it with a noble artistry worthy of that which first created it. So, if we find ourselves given a short rather than a long part, or if we must bear much suffering and disadvantage rather than honour and privilege, there is no room for complaint; rather, we must strive to play even the most ignominious part well, and thereby make our personal contribution to the success of the drama as a whole. Even death itself, Epictetus reassures us, is no evil to be feared; it is simply the divinely ordained end of our allotted time on stage, and, being able to do nothing about it, we should not fear it, but should simply accept it and 'die well', as it were, rather than badly.[16]

Karl Barth was certainly no Stoic, but his theology does manifest an analogous concern to affirm both a high view of Providence and the freedom and ethical

---

12 *Discourses* II.16, in Epictetus, *The Discourses and Manual*, Vol. 1, 198.

13 'Have courage to look up to God and say, 'Deal with me hereafter as Thou wilt, I am as one with Thee, I am Thine. I flinch from nothing so long as Thou thinkest it good. Lead me where Thou wilt, put on me what raiment Thou wilt. Wouldst Thou have me hold office, or eschew it, stay or fly, be poor or rich? For all this I will defend Thee before men. I will shew each thing in its true nature, as it is' (*Discourses* II.16, Epictetus, *The Discourses and Manual*, Vol. 1, 199–200).

14 *Discourses* I.1, in Epictetus, *The Discourses and Manual*, Vol. 1, 47.

15 Edwards reminds us that for the Stoics human actions are meaningful 'insofar as they are witnessed', and alludes to the essentially social and public situation of such performance before a human audience. 'Acting is a success or a failure insofar as it communicates the part to those watching. The audience has expectations'. As such, Stoicism, she suggests, has an inherently 'theatrical' aspect because it is 'intrinsically social'. (Edwards, 'Acting and self-actualisation in imperial Rome: some death scenes', 382–83.) While Epictetus certainly affords due weight to the social location of human action and its implications, the 'audience' he has in mind in his appeal to the metaphor of the world-stage is generally divine rather than human.

16 See, for example, *Discourses* II.1; III.24. Epictetus, *The Discourses and Manual*, Vol. 1, 144–45; Vol. 2, 98–99. It goes without saying that the deaths of others 'close' to us (parents, wives, sons, daughters etc.) are to be treated with the same dispassionate acceptance rather than becoming the occasion for (essentially indulgent) grief. Their parts in the play are over, and Epictetus indicates that we should be moved by them as little as any actor is by the stage 'death' of one of his fellow players. See, for example, *Manual* 11, in Epictetus, *The Discourses and Manual*, Vol. 2, 217.

responsibility of the creature. And it is interesting, therefore, to note that the metaphor of the world-stage commends itself to him:

> In so far as I am caught up in this movement from my beginning to my end, my life becomes my history – we might almost say my drama – in which I am neither the author nor the producer, but the principal actor. I did not place myself in this movement, nor do I maintain myself in it. But I myself am this movement. Between my birth and my death the freedom is given to me to be myself in this movement, in this ascent and descent. To be in this freedom is to live.17

In what follows I propose to explore further the fruitfulness of this image of drama, performance and some of its natural correlates for understanding two particular aspects of human existence: (1) The possession of what psychiatrist Victor Frankl calls the 'will to meaning'[18] due to which narrative patterns of one sort or another suggest themselves naturally as the form of the human hypostatic trace in time ('I myself *am* this movement' in the drama). (2) The way in which our living of life, and more precisely our embracing of discipleship, is *related to* the patterns of meaningfulness which we trace and project; as we perform the part we have been given in the drama. So, this is an exercise in what Frank Kermode calls 'making sense of the ways we make sense of the world'.[19] And, since death is the one thing we can be sure of in life, I shall do so with a particular view to our finitude as human creatures, and the significance of our death for the patterning of life. Is it part of the performance, or the final curtain which indicates that the horizontally challenged lady has now sung, and everyone else can safely leave the theatre? And, as we act out our part, what impact does its inexorable approach have upon our performance?

2. 'Bit-part' or Top of the Bill? Finitude and Fulfilment

Let us suppose that my life is indeed a drama in which I am the principal actor; a drama, then, played out on the stage of the world, and bounded at each end by my birth and my death. *This* is who I am. This is who *I* am. The answer to the question of my 'hypostasis' is answered in this performance, and not in abstraction from it (as though in some eternal programme note).

Some literary allusions (borrowed from novels rather than the theatre) may help further to draw out and sharpen the force of the metaphor and the problems involved in fitting it to the shape of life. First, from the final chapter of George Eliot's novel *Middlemarch*, where we find the following reflection: 'Every limit is a beginning as well as an ending. Who can quit young lives after being so long with them, and not

---

17   Karl Barth, *Church Dogmatics*, III/3 (Edinburgh: T & T Clark Ltd., 1960), 231.

18   Victor Frankl, *Man's Search for Meaning* (New York: Washington Square Press, 1985), 121.

19   Frank Kermode, *The Sense of an Ending* (London: Oxford University Press, 1967), 31.

desire to know what befell them in their after-years?'[20] In the book, this paragraph prefaces, and serves to justify, several pages of narrative closure in which first one minor character and then another is tied neatly, like so many loose ends, into the tapestry of the novel's world. The same narrative contrivance, disparagingly referred to by Henry James as 'a distribution at the last of prizes, pensions, husbands, wives, babies, millions, appended paragraphs and cheerful remarks',[21] is to be found in many classics of the genre (Dostoyevsky's *The Idiot* is another example), and prompts us to ask why. No doubt it would have been *possible* to leave these stories within a story incomplete, fragmentary, unresolved. That the novelist felt the device *needful*, though, tells us something about life as well as fiction; namely, that when it comes to story, we crave some sense of an ending, a resolution, a pattern completed rather than left open and unresolved. We wonder how things turned out, what happened to whom, where they ended up. In life, where we resort habitually to narrative in order to give some account of ourselves, who we are, how we came to be where we now are, it is as if the very meaningfulness of individual lives (our own, or those of others) is at stake in this quest for unified form. Literature, at least, might be judged aesthetically deficient to the extent that it fails to bring its *principal* characters to some satisfying narrative closure. Can we say the same of human lives, of personhood?

Frank Kermode has famously suggested that narrative *imposes* form on what is in reality a chaotic world, and thereby deceives in order to console us. We are beings who crave form and meaning. This is why we find stories so compelling: they provide form where, in reality, there is none to be had. 'It seems', he writes, 'that in 'making sense' of the world we ... feel a need ... to experience that concordance of beginning, middle and end',[22] the overall unity of form which characterizes literary fictions. And in particular, he suggests, it is in the sense of an *ending* which narrative provides that we find the most satisfaction; for it is in the narrative resolution of character that the meaningfulness of the plot as a whole really becomes apparent. Of course we know that life and literature are not the same thing, but the powerful aesthetic satisfaction provided by the contrivances of fictional emplotment may at least reveal a deep down sense that life, too, *ought to be* possessed of shape or pattern, brought to some satisfying closure, its form shown to be meaningful rather than meaningless.

The same sense that *ending* is definitive with respect to the meaningfulness of a life lived is echoed in Heidegger's claim that an authentic personal existence is to be had precisely by facing the inevitability of our own death (the 'end' towards which our existence inexorably moves), accepting it, and 'living toward' it rather than repressing all thought of it. Thereby, he suggests, death becomes the unifying factor in our existence, that to which everything is related, and we are enabled to seize the concrete opportunities and possibilities proper to our particular existences,

---

20 George Eliot, *Middlemarch* (London: Penguin, 1965), 890.
21 Cited in Kermode, *The Sense of an Ending*, 22.
22 Kermode, *The Sense of an Ending*, 35.

being responsible in the face of them, rather than missing or ignoring them.[23] Because he knows that every moment is unrepeatable, and his life itself, which must some day end, is the boundary beyond which there are no motion replays or second chances, 'At any moment, man must decide, for better or for worse, what will be the monument of his existence.'[24]

Jean-Paul Sartre, though, demurred from this view, insisting that the meaningfulness of a particular life could only be discerned from the *specific* ending which it had (rather than 'ending' or 'death' as an abstraction, however inevitable it may be), and – since the particularity of death is almost always unexpected – it cannot be lived towards as something clearly anticipated. Hence, he argues, mortality does not bestow meaning upon our living or reveal its meaning, but in fact robs it of the only sort of meaning we might have found in it. We are *never* the ones to see the whole of our life from the perspective of this ending, and during our living, therefore, we are by definition in no position to discern the meaning of our actions or experiences. 'If we must die', he concludes, 'then our life has no meaning because its problems receive no solution, and because the very meaning of the problems remains undetermined.'[25] Again, we *crave meaning* for our lives, our 'selves', but our finitude, rather than bestowing such meaning finally denies us the opportunity of tracing any.

But this is not all. More must be said. And my other literary allusion is to Ian McEwan's novel *Atonement*. Here, in a coda to the main story, the narrator (whose account is based on events in her own early life) confesses to having falsified her ending in order to render it more bearable and satisfying. The two lovers whose frustrated passion and separation is finally resolved and consummated in the novel, in fact never saw one another again, one having died on the battlefield and the other in a bombing raid in the London blitz. But, the narrator asks, 'How could that constitute an ending? What sense of hope or satisfaction could a reader draw from such an account? ... Who would want to believe that, except in the service of the bleakest realism? I couldn't do it to them. I'm too old, too frightened, too much in love with the shred of life I have remaining.'[26] It is not simply a sense of *an ending as such* that we seem to crave, but a certain sort or quality of ending. A novel which brings all its characters to clear narrative closure may still not provide the sort of aesthetic satisfaction we are hoping for, because it leaves so many half-completed projects, relationships, hopes and aspirations. Some postmodern art deliberately plays on such interruptive endings (Quentin Tarrantino's film *Pulp Fiction* for example), and in some respects it is the stock in trade of those dark literary tragedies where all finally comes to nothing. But the sort of aesthetic satisfaction we derive from such depictions is of a very peculiar sort, and might even be thought to lie in the sense of

---

23 See John Macquarrie, *An Existentialist Theology* (London: SCM Press Ltd., 1955), 116–31.
24 Frankl, *Man's Search for Meaning*, 143.
25 Jean Paul Sartre, *Being and Nothingness* (London: Methuen, 1957), 539–40.
26 Ian McEwan, *Atonement* (London: Jonathan Cape, 2001), 371.

protest which it stirs in us against the fragmentary, broken and unfulfilled potential which they lay before us. What we desire, for the characters on screen or page, and for ourselves and the others with whom we live, is a different sort of ending, an ending in which the opportunity for fulfilment and realization of self is offered and seized, rather than wrenched from human grasp. We crave not just an ending, but a *good* ending in which all shall be well, and all manner of things shall be well.

Here though, it is even more apparent that life cheats us. Even in our own affluent, healthy and ageing modern societies, relatively few people approach the prospect of their death with a sense of being 'sated with years', or of having fulfilled their lives' human potential. We only have to cast our gaze more widely to see a circumstance far more troubling. In the words of one report, due to endemic poverty 'the actual life of most (humans) has been cramped with back-breaking labour, exposed to deadly or debilitating disease, prey to wars and famines, haunted by the loss of children, filled with fear and the ignorance that breeds more fear.'[27] Jürgen Moltmann drives the nail home with characteristic force: 'Think of the life of those who were not permitted to live, and were unable to live: the beloved child, dying at birth; the little boy run over by a car when he was four; the disabled brother who never lived consciously, and never knew his parents; the friend torn to pieces by a bomb at your side when he was sixteen; the throngs of children who die prematurely of hunger in Africa; the countless numbers of the raped and murdered and killed.'[28] What are we to make of the alleged meaningfulness of these lives? Their particular 'endings' are clear enough, but they are not the endings to, do not bestow the meaningfulness upon the lives which we might naturally crave for them. Despite the temporal ending which death inevitably constitutes to our living, few if any human lives appear to constitute anything other than incomplete and unsatisfactory stories, and many present themselves as tragic. Because they are life rather than literature, this sickens rather than satisfies us, and leaves us with the sense that it should all be otherwise. If we could rewrite the endings to their stories, we should do so. But in real life, unlike fiction, we are unable to do so.

In his essay 'Art, religion, and the hermeneutics of authenticity', philosopher Nicholas Davey focuses on the notion of 'the withheld' in art, and relates it to the nature and pattern of certain sorts of religious experience.[29] Aesthetic experience, he notes, especially in the case of art performed, is intensely temporal, and sees meaning brought into form through time. He cites Gadamer: 'Every performance is an event, but not one in any way separate from the work – the work itself is what "takes place".'[30] As meaning unfolds, so what was withheld is disclosed to performer

---

27 Barbara Ward and René Dubos, *Only One Earth* (New York: Penguin, 1972), 35. Cited in John Hick, *Death and Eternal Life* (London: Collins, 1976), 153.

28 Jürgen Moltmann, *The Coming of God* (London: SCM Press Ltd, 1996), 117.

29 In Salim Kemal and Ivan Gaskell (eds), *Performance and authenticity in the arts* (Cambridge: Cambridge University Press, 1999), 66–93.

30 *Truth and Method*, 147, cited in Kemal and Gaskell, *Performance and authenticity in the arts*, 77.

and audience alike. In a statement sounding remarkably consonant with Heidegger's perspective Davey writes: 'As a dwelling between past and future possibilities, authenticity involves a being open to the call of the withheld, not a prising open of the withheld, but a remaining open to and a holding with that which is still withheld from us.'[31] In the case of religious experience, he suggests, we have to do with the anticipation of a meaning as yet to be revealed in the living of a particular life. Such anticipation 'projects a horizon of meaning whereby the incoherent and presently fragmented aspects of a work [or life?] might achieve an envisaged but as-yet-to-be-attained coherence'.[32] Aesthetic experience, in which precisely this comes to pass, Davey notes, lends substance to religious hope and its manifestations in existence. Religious performance, we might say, involves a responsiveness to a call to venture out in faith in a meaning for our lives as yet to be disclosed.

There is, of course, at least one vital difference between performance in art and in life, one shuddering 'it is not' which qualifies the poetic 'it is'. In drama, the performer is confronted with openness and the freedom for realization of a meaning as yet still withheld; yet he also generally has a script, indicating in broad outline at least the shape which his movement towards dramatic closure will take. So too in musical performance. If a rendering of a sonata is of aesthetic value it will disclose new depths of meaning in the work; yet for it to be a performance of *this* sonata, and not some other, it must have an identifiable relationship to a score indicating the limits within which freedom may be exercised. (I am not suggesting that there are not exceptions to this – of course there are. But *most* artistic performance is like this.) But in life it is hardly ever like this. Mostly, as 'actors', we face a future which is open, unknown in its openness, and often threatening in its unknowability. Even our best projections and most reasonable expectations can be and frequently are defied or rudely interrupted by the unexpected development, by 'events' which are no respecter of the neat patterns of our planning. Apart from the singular certainty that we shall one day die, all else is, in the strictest sense, contingent and vulnerable in this way. As we have already seen, the Stoic ideal was one of acceptance and readiness to face whatever might come next, determined not to allow events and emotions to get us down, thereby turning life's drama into a tragedy. But is stoicism (in the technical or the more extended sense) really enough if we are to live well? Do we not need, we might well ask, something *more* to be disclosed, something akin to the actor's score or the musician's script, some indication of the relevant limits within which our own freedom may and must be exercised, so that we know just what it is that we are supposed to be performing?

Perhaps in this respect the performance of life is indeed rather more like a certain sort of improvised drama than the playing of a carefully scripted role. There is something about it, too, which resembles the literary device of *peripeteia*, in which readerly expectations are deliberately thwarted by the omnipotent author generating 'events' to throw in the protagonist's path. If the device is successful, then the

---

31 Davey in Kemal and Gaskell, *Performance and authenticity in the arts*, 89.
32 Davey in Kemal and Gaskell, *Performance and authenticity in the arts*, 69.

expected end is eventually reached, but via anything but the expected routes. And it is this, of course, that keeps us reading, always eager to know what will happen next. Shifting perspective again from the standpoint of 'reader' to that of 'actor', we might say that it is this same structural pattern in which starting points and promised ends are given, but the route between them as yet unclear or 'withheld', that keeps us living, striving, moving forward in our own personal or communal dramas. In other words, while we may not have access to a script, we need, and are offered, some imaginative vision of an end, a closure, a *telos* to our living which bestows meaning and worth upon it, and which grants a sense of direction. To use categories introduced to us already in this volume, we need to be able to relate our here and now to some larger pattern which enables us to overaccept the contingencies and accept them as gift. And we may hope that hitherto undisclosed meanings will be revealed along the way; but we know that the meaningfulness cannot finally be had in the here and now at all. This consideration is one to which we shall return in our final section.

The novelist Gustave Flaubert observed that 'Real life is always misrepresented by those who wish to make it lead up to a conclusion. God alone may do that.'[33] Perhaps our human bid for form, our 'will to meaning', is rooted here in an implicit eschatological sense that, despite the experienced gap between literature/drama and life, our existence and that of others may *yet* be revealed as meaningful through the closure provided by the one in whose hands the drama, the plot, the performance finally lies. Sartre's point remains to be addressed. Can an authentic performance of life, let alone discipleship, be approximated to without some sense, however provisional and partial, of the broad pattern of that meaning which remains to be disclosed? In theological terms, do we not need some sort of eschatological vision to fuel our existence? And if so, what sort?

3. Two Theological Approaches to Meaningfulness and Finitude

I want in this section briefly to consider the ways in which two theologians have handled questions pertaining to the pattern of human existence, especially in relation to the issue of death and what it says about the meaning of human lives considered in eschatological perspective. The two theologians concerned are John Hick and Karl Barth.

In his book *Death and Eternal Life* Hick picks up on some of the problems we have already mentioned. Thus Hick notes that most of the world's population has lived in 'a condition of life so degrading as to insult human dignity'.[34] We see daily the sort of potential that human lives contain, and yet everywhere we see such potential unfulfilled, cut short, and in many cases blighted by terrible suffering while it lasts. If, then, we are to suppose that human life has meaning, that there is fulfilment to be looked for, a pattern to be traced, it is apparent that the span of this

---

33 Cited in P. T. Forsyth, *The Justification of God* (London: Duckworth, 1916), 223.
34 Hick, *Death and Eternal Life,* 154.

life as such is not where we shall find it. The time between birth and death, even in the case of those longest lived, is insufficient for its realization. Furthermore, the traditional Christian focus on the span of this earthly life as the environment within which human salvation is realized (or not) is, Hick insists, 'unrealistic both as regards what is to happen before death and as regards what is to happen after death. If salvation in its fullness involves the actual transformation of human character, it is an observable fact that this does not usually take place in the course of our present earthly life.'[35] Therefore, he concludes, we must suppose that the pattern of a human life continues beyond what we see of it, that its development towards fulfilment is extended temporally, that it is 'given more time' to grow and advance towards that spiritual perfection which alone (however we think of its nature) secures the person's story as a comic, rather than a tragic one.

This, then, is the fundamental claim that Hick makes. Death must not be the point at which the pattern of any particular human life is finally concluded and determined. It can at most be the conclusion of a key stage along the way toward the completion of this pattern. In some sense, when we die, 'the persisting self-conscious ego will continue to exist'. But the model of personal identity which Hick entertains is not at all abstract, but is rooted in particularities of space and time, the contingencies of culture and circumstance. All this, he holds, is necessary to the idea of the self as an entity capable of moral and spiritual development, and hence salvation (rather than mere escape from the exigencies of historical existence). 'For', he writes, 'we have been formed as empirical egos within a particular culture and a particular epoch of history. The language in which we think and speak, the structure of society through which we are related to our neighbours, the traditions and mores which we inherit, the state of public knowledge, the unconscious framework of presuppositions through which we perceive the world, the contingencies of political history ... have all helped to make us what we are.'[36] 'Strip all these culturally conditioned characteristics away', he continues, 'and I should be someone else – or perhaps no one'.[37] We have our identity, in other words, are who we are as embodied selves in more than a merely physical sense. Our being is enfleshed in the realities of a socio-political, cultural and historical context, and the very particular opportunities, challenges and possibilities with which it presents us.

Thus Hick arrives at his preferred account of the patterning of human existence, an account which draws consciously upon, but is quite distinct from, certain Eastern models of reincarnation. The self, he suggests, is extended in time after death through 'a series of lives, each bounded by something analogous to birth and death, lived in other worlds in spaces other than that in which we now are'. This enables him to take seriously both the idea of more time being granted *and* the finite particularity which seems to provide the backdrop, props and cast list needful for the performance which I am called to give (since all these together are constitutive of the I who is

---

35   Hick, *Death and Eternal Life*, 455.
36   Hick, *Death and Eternal Life*, 411.
37   Hick, *Death and Eternal Life*, 412.

called to give it). Each life in the series is finite in itself, each represents, as it were, another act in my personal drama, and each provides opportunity for an advance of the self from the stage of development it had reached at the end of the previous Act. Furthermore, the action of each is directly related to that which is needful for particular stages of the self's development, and has its meaning therein. Here Hick's concern with theodicy dominates the shape of his eschatology. For now we can, indeed must, say that the suffering of this life is revealed at the last to be meaningful, since through participation in our particular portion of it we become the persons we are, and are fitted to progress to the next Act. Hick does not indicate just how many such lives each of us may have to enjoy or endure, though he seems to suppose it may indeed *be* many, depending upon the rate of our progress.

What is notable in Hick's account of salvation and survival of the self through death is the relative absence of reference to God as the one through whose agency and direction all this occurs. The drama – to return to our core metaphor – is played out as a lengthy series of related Acts, but it appears to be largely an improvised performance, with nothing resembling a script, a playwright, or a Director in whose hands the movement to the final scene rests securely. Nothing, of course, could be further from the truth in Barth's theology to which we now turn.

To be human, Barth notes, is to be temporal, to have our existence in time.[38] This is part of our proper creaturely contingency and, as such, distinguishes us from our Creator. Specifically, it is not that we are temporal which differentiates us from God, but the form of temporality in which our existence is played out. God's eternity is not timeless, but rather 'authentic temporality' from which our creaturely temporality derives. In God (for eternity is a perfection of God himself, proper to the form which God's existence takes, and not a field within which God exists and to which he is in any sense subject) 'present, past and future, yesterday, to-day and tomorrow, are not successive, but simultaneous'.[39] As creatures, on the other hand, we live transient lives, existing on the uncomfortable present cusp of a pastness in which all that we value decays and disappears ('is' no more) and a future which threatens possible horrors and terrors, and holds out at best uncertain hopes. Furthermore, our temporality, our 'own time', the span which God has granted us, is precisely that - a limited span, bounded at each end by the events of birth before which we did not exist, and death after which we shall not exist.

Barth recognises that, in our fallenness and guilt, this finitude is experienced by us as a problem, even a threat. But he is not sympathetic to Hick's bid for the extension of our personal drama beyond death. The idea that the granting of further time – even infinite time – would somehow redress the problem of personal fulfilment or salvation, is one that he rejects as a dangerous illusion. 'This could only mean in fact that we should be able to sin infinitely and even quantitatively multiply our guilt

---

38 Karl Barth, *Church Dogmatics,* III/2 (Edinburgh: T & T Clark Ltd, 1960), 437. See also 526.

39 Barth, *Church Dogmatics,* III/2, 437.

on an infinite scale.'[40] Far from treating it as a curse, therefore, Barth suggests, we should view our finitude as a good thing. Death comes as a blessed release from a life in which the forces of chaos and sin reign supreme and torture us. Far from the curve of our pattern of personhood being a gradual climb towards perfection, viewed in itself it is plunging ever further down beneath the point where the graph stops. Could there', Barth asks, 'be any better picture of life in hell than enduring life in enduring time?'[41] Finitude, on the other hand, puts us out of our misery, sets us free from a life of addiction to sin, grants us peace. It is a form of euthanasia.

In positive terms, finitude is a blessing because it bestows particularity, form and thereby meaningfulness upon our personal existence before God. Like Hick, Barth recognizes that human life and identity is rooted and played out in relation to the contingencies of time, place and culture. It is this that gives the creature its specific and genuine reality. 'Only the void is undefined and therefore unlimited.'[42] 'The creature must not exist like the unhappy centre of a circle which has no periphery. It must exist in a genuine circle, its individual environment. It must not exist everywhere, but in a specific place. It must not exist endlessly, but in its own time. It must not comprehend or understand or be capable of or accomplish everything. It has freedom to experience and accomplish that which is proper to it, to do that which it can do, and to be satisfied.'[43] In other words, the limitations of our finitude, culminating finally in the horizon that is our death, provide a shape, a set of horizons, within which our life may and must be lived. It limits the opportunities presented to us, and thereby the demands placed upon us. It furnishes a matrix of relationships, capacities, and possibilities that are ours alone, the hypostatic fingerprint which differentiates us from all others and seals our personal uniqueness before God. We may be playing on the same stage, but the character *we* are called to perform and to *be* is unlike any other in the drama. God's specific limitation of an individual life is thus his granting of overall form *to* that life, a pattern which we are called to develop and to improvise upon in our free performance of life, but which defines the thresholds, the limits within which such freedom may actually be exercised. This pattern, this role, this character within the drama is our particular place within, our personal portion of the whole creation, and we should value it as such.[44] That it comes to an end is indicative of God's affirmation of a particular life, since 'I am and can be only what I am in this one time, in the few years of this single lifetime', and those who resist such limitation 'necessarily resist themselves, for they themselves are none other than those who are limited in this way'.[45] The span of time which God grants us, our allotted portion of time *is* the duration of our 'part' within the wider

---

40   Barth, *Church Dogmatics*, III/2, 631.
41   Barth, *Church Dogmatics*, III/2, 562.
42   Barth, *Church Dogmatics,* III/4 (Edinburgh: T & T Clark Ltd., 1961), 567.
43   Barth, *Church Dogmatics*, III/3, 85.
44   Barth, *Church Dogmatics,* III/4, 569, 573.
45   Barth, *Church Dogmatics,* III/4, 571, 570.

drama of human history. The form is completed. The pattern is what it is, and we are who we are within its limits.

The further and final reason why God's limitation of our time, his granting of particularity to our personhood through finitude, is something to be welcomed rather than eschewed is simply that it is in *this* time, *our* time, *our* particularity, that God makes us the subject of his promise, and calls us to a response of faith and obedience. Our time is our unique opportunity for response, and it is to me (who I am in all my finite limitedness) that God calls, and from whom he looks for a particular personal response. 'The promises must be claimed' by each, Barth writes, 'Otherwise what is objectively true in [Christ] is not true for him. Otherwise he himself is not within the truth of his creatureliness but somewhere outside'.[46] And here it is precisely the form provided by our finitude, the inevitability and unexpectedness of our own death, which grants significance to our living, since it charges the divine summons with an urgency it would not otherwise possess. Now is the day of grace. The opportunity to fulfil our particular creatureliness, to seek the correspondence of the pattern of our personhood with that of Christ's (in all *its* particularity) is one which presents itself to us as who we are and through what we do and become in this limited life, and not otherwise. This, though, if it is indeed a blessing, may seem to us to be a mixed one, a daunting prospect. Our character is cast for us, the stage is set, and all the props in place. But there is no rehearsal, and only a single performance before the reviews are written. Thus a burning question presents itself to us. Is this all there is? And, if not, if the absence of any further time is not the end for us personally, how are we to think of what lies beyond and its relationship to the person we have been granted the freedom to be and become between the limits of our birth and our death?

Here, Barth insists, we must remain largely agnostic. Hence , 'We do not know what and how we shall be when we are no more and have no more time for being in virtue of our death. ... We can only cling to the fact ... that even in our death and as its Lord (God) will be our gracious God, the God who is for us, and that this is the ineffable sum of all goodness, so that everything that happens to us in death will in some way necessarily work together for good'.[47] So, in the strictest sense, 'our consolation, assurance and hope in death are restricted to the existence of God'.[48] The question we must ask is whether such apophatic 'clinging' is really sufficient as an imaginative basis for living hopefully towards death. In fact, of course, Barth does give us something to work with. He cannot help invoking some positive imagined content with respect to this hereafter, even as he adopts a deliberately agnostic approach. Hence death will *not* mean our return to the sort of non-being out of which we were originally called in creation.[49] God will 'be there for us', and will hold us in some form of continued existence with himself.[50] But 'whatever existence

---

46   Barth, *Church Dogmatics*, III/4, 580.
47   Barth, *Church Dogmatics*, III/2, 610.
48   Barth, *Church Dogmatics*, III/2, 616.
49   Barth, *Church Dogmatics*, III/2, 611.
50   Barth, *Church Dogmatics*, III/2, 611.

in death may mean, it cannot consist in a continuation of life in time'.[51] We shall have had our allotted time, and more of it would only be bad rather than good news. Instead, we must imagine some distinct mode of creaturely correspondence to God's own 'authentic temporality' in which past, present and future are no longer strung our in a series of consecutive moments, but coexist in perichoretic simultaneity.[52] Even as one 'who has been', I shall somehow share in God's own eternal life.[53] But here a further problem arises. Who, we must ask, is this 'I' who thus enjoys eternal fellowship with God? What is the relevant content indicated by the pronoun? Again, perhaps a certain level of agnosticism is in order; but in as much as Barth addresses the question directly, he points to an identification of the particular person with who he or she 'has been' in the time allotted to them by God. Thus, 'man is, only as he is in his time. Even in eternal life he will still be in his time'.[54] The 'whole time' given us by God is his gift to us of our distinctive existence, and is thus the subject of our redemptive participation in God's own life. Man 'looks and moves', Barth writes, 'towards the fact that this being of his in time, and therewith its beginning and end ... will be revealed in all its unmerited shame but also its unmerited glory, and may thus *be* eternal life from and in God'.[55] In itself, this seems to exacerbate the problem rather than to resolve it. The pattern of who I shall have been in my life (as brought to closure by death) is, as Barth rightly sees, precisely what needs to be redeemed. Yet the things he is willing to venture (positively or negatively) about the possible shape of this 'eternal future' end up sounding more like a *rescue from* the particulars of our embodied and historical existence than the *redemption of* them.

The issue which divides Hick's view from Barth's from the outset and fundamentally is the claim that the granting of 'more time' to a person's existence might somehow address the theodicy issue. Both begin with a frank recognition of the problem – human lives as actually lived are, by the time death brings them to an end, identifiably incomplete and imperfect, and sometimes woefully so. Hick appeals precisely to this solution (a whole series of temporal extensions to our allotted time), and Barth rejects it outright. This rejection is needful in order to underwrite his conviction that – human beings being what they are – no amount of extra time (time, that is, of the sort and under the conditions we currently know and experience) could ever suffice to address the problem of sin and suffering, but only the radical intervention of God's grace. 'Only God can do that.' In fact, though, Barth takes a further significant step, drawing a sharp contrast between the nature of historical time (essentially linear, sequential and consecutive) and the simultaneous shape of 'eternity'. He also suggests that the pattern of personal identity (who 'I' am in the

---

51   Barth, *Church Dogmatics*, III/2, 589.
52   Barth, *Church Dogmatics*, III/2, 526.
53   Barth, *Church Dogmatics*, III/2, 632–33.
54   Barth, *Church Dogmatics*, III/2, 521. Cf 523: '... whatever I am, I am in my temporal reality, in the totality of what I was and am and will be'. Also 554: 'Man is ... in this span, and not before or after it.'
55   Barth, *Church Dogmatics*, III/2, 633. My italics.

final analysis) will be closed by death, and thus within our allotted span of historical time. Such suggestions do not arise in the form of imaginative 'takes' on how things *might* be in the Eschaton, but are effectively limit statements. They are meant to exclude the feasibility of supposing that anything analogous to the sequential nature of historical time could pertain beyond the bounds of history (or those of a particular life). This, it has to be said, is hardly a necessary insistence on biblical grounds or any other, and sits ill with Barth's professed minimalist agnosticism with regard to the shape of post-mortem existence. Were we to treat it just as one imaginative scenario to set alongside others, though, it remains one with some highly problematic entailments for the way in which we might suppose this life (and our identity as particular persons in it) to be related to the next.

In short, Barth's account leaves no 'time' available for us to imagine anything further taking place in. Put differently, it leaves no 'time' for God to do anything further with us. (And we are capable, surely, of imagining some alternative mode of temporality unlike that we know in all sorts of ways, but in which things might nonetheless still be imagined meaningfully as 'happening'?) In Barth's account, eternity consists, in effect, of the simultaneity of our past, present and future, a pattern played out, as it were, in the presence of God, and now bathed somehow in the glory characterizing the penumbra of that presence. But there is no more time for any further modification of the pattern of a life itself. What will be simultaneously present to us and to God, therefore, we must suppose, is the 'whole time' of a particular life bounded by birth and death, and lived in the world. Yet this seems to leave us trapped eternally with what, by the time of our death, we 'shall have been', an inference that hardly addresses the theodicy issue satisfactorily. Arguably, it exacerbates it. Of course, in meeting this concern, Barth insists that we shall nonetheless by then be in the presence of God, and none of this will blight our eternal joy. But this seems to meet the problem only by effectively disentangling the substance of a particular personal identity (the 'me' who will be there with God to witness and enjoy all this) from the content of a particular life as lived and suffered. Eschewing the imagination of post-mortem temporality altogether, Barth is driven to a very high level of imaginative abstraction (the concrete is inexorably embedded in time); and this leads in turn to a vision in which, rather than the content of our life being *redeemed* in any identifiable sense, we are effectively rescued *from* it (even though 'it' is in some sense still 'ours'). Barth may be at one with one important element in the theological tradition here, placing emphasis upon death as a decisive cut-off point where much about the creature's form and eternal destiny is already decided; but he is equally clearly at odds with the wider rich and fertile imagining of the redeemed state in Scripture (for instance, in the prophets) as a transformation and renewal of what this life amounts to, a raising of it to new life in which it both remains the creature that it has been, and yet is transfigured into a joyful and glorious version of itself which we can, as yet, *only* imagine. The pattern of history, and of individual lives lived within it, need to be reconfigured, healed, cleansed, completed and brought to fulfillment. But this, we must suppose, 'takes time', time beyond the limits of historical existence itself. To the extent that we refuse at least to *imagine* any such time, we risk positing an arbitrary disjunction between this life and the next, tracing no meaningful connection between the two stages. Far from justifying God's decision to create (which is what Barth intends), this in turn calls into question the status of our embodied, historical existence as the unequivocal object of God's redemptive purpose and activity, and thereby devalues it.

4. Hope, Improvised Performance and Eschatological Imagination

What, Jürgen Moltmann asks, should we make of the Pauline claim that '"this mortal life will put on immortality" (1 Cor. 15:54)? ... Will this life be "immortalized", as obituary notices sometimes say? If that meant that this life from birth to death is recorded as if on a video, and stored up in the heaven of eternity, that would be anything but a joyful prospect: immortalized with all the terrible experiences, faults, failings and sicknesses? How would we imagine the immortalizing of a severely disabled human life, or the immortalizing of a child who died young?'[56] It is this question, answered in the light of convictions about God's justice, that leads Moltmann finally to demur from Barth and to affirm a version of the doctrine of the intermediate state in which further 'time' is granted by God for the task of completing his creation and fitting us individually for eternity. 'I shall again come back to my life', Moltmann writes, 'and in the light of God's grace and in the power of his mercy put right what has gone awry, finish what was begun, pick up what was neglected, forgive the trespasses, heal the hurts, and be permitted to gather up the moments of happiness and to transform mourning into joy'.[57] This is certainly no mere extension of our creaturely time, or 'another chance' to get it right this time. It is a qualitatively distinct form of temporality in the presence of Christ, spanning the time between our death and the general resurrection of the dead, and furnishing space for us to become the persons God intended and intends us to be. Like Barth, Moltmann sees the content of eternity as a transformed version of temporality. Indeed, his own account of the 'aeonic' time of God's new creation is similar in many respects to Barth's proposed eternity of 'simultaneity'.[58] Like Barth, too, he insists that the content of this aeonic reality will be directly related to the particular lives we live in the here and now. Unlike Barth, though, he understands death not as that which closes and completes the pattern of a life, but as a penultimate scene leaving 'time' yet for the necessary healing, sanctification and fulfilment of a life in God's hands. The Gestalt of an individual life, therefore, is not apparent from the perspective afforded by its point of death, but only eschatologically, in the transformation of its form by the Spirit.

---

56 Moltmann, *The Coming of God*, 70.
57 Moltmann, *The Coming of God*, 117.
58 See, for example, Moltmann, *The Way of Jesus Christ* (London: SCM Press Ltd., 1990), 330. For a critical account of Moltmann see Richard Bauckham, 'Time and Eternity' in Bauckham (ed.), *God Will Be All in All: The Eschatology of Jürgen Moltmann* (Edinburgh: T & T Clark, 1999), 155–226.

Let's attempt, then, to cash out these eschatologies in relation to our dramatic metaphor. Hick presents our personal existence as a series of largely unrelated performances, hardly even 'acts' in a unified story, except insofar as they are all linked by their relationship to a common human 'actor' or subject. From another angle we might think of them as 'rehearsals', designed specifically to fit this actor for an existence in eternity (the 'command performance' for which such thorough preparation is necessary). And this, we should note, places a particular value on the pattern of personal development: Salvation pertains to, is constituted by, the *final stage* in the drama. All else is preparatory, and thus of merely transient significance. In truth, though, the performative metaphor breaks down badly at this point, and is really much better replaced by a more timeless, contemplative model of aesthetic experience. Like Barth, although Hick tries hard to hold on to personal particularity, he finally loses touch with it in his own way, spreading identity much too thinly over a whole series of particular lives lived consecutively, and affirming its eventual absorption into the atemporal pattern of 'atman' or the 'universal self'.[59] Barth, meanwhile, places his initial emphasis entirely differently. Life itself – and we only get one allocated span of time between our birth and our death – *is* the drama. There is no further 'final act' to be played out. What remains beyond death is a 'redemptive' eternalising of the various acts in the drama of our lives. It is those same acts revisited, viewed now in the light of the denouement and bathed in the light of another story, Christ's, which has been played out in juxtaposition to it. And the relevant action in question is God's, not ours. Our life, in its entirety, is in this sense both the singular time and the sole object of redemption. There is no rehearsal, and no post-production party. But, for reasons which we have addressed above, Barth's emphatic eschewal of post-mortem time undercuts some of what he intends. Specifically, it leads him, too, in the direction of an abstraction of personhood from the particulars of a life as lived, makes it difficult to imagine in concrete terms how this life may actually *be* the object of God's redemptive activity, and thus raises questions about the meaningfulness and value of the lives we live. Moltmann, too, wants to insist that the whole pattern of our living, and not just its most developed stage, is the object of God's redemptive action. But the 'whole pattern' of our living, he insists, is more than it amounts to at the point of our dying. In order to address the problems raised by Barth's account, Moltmann, as it were, introduces another intermediate series of dramatic 'scenes', a performative transform which shifts us decisively from the pattern of what we 'shall have been' by the time of our death, and prepares that pattern for its eternalization in the presence of God. What perdures in the new creation (Moltmann's favourite biblical image for the final act), therefore, is not the drama of a particular life *as lived*, but that same life redeemed, transfigured, its evil purged and its lacks made good.

I noted earlier that life is *unlike* drama in as much as no precise script for the remaining sections of the Act exists[60] (or, if it does exist, its larger shape is known

---

59 See Hick, *Death and Eternal Life*, 450f.
60 See Sam Wells' essay, above.

only to the Playwright and Director, and not yet to the actors). Perhaps, I suggested, life is indeed in this respect (viz., from the standpoint of the actor) rather more like improvisation than the performance of a script. I want now in closing to suggest that it may be well-likened to a particular form of improvisation; namely, the musical cadenza. Here, within a space left precisely for the purpose, the musician improvises in a manner which fits both what has gone before and (crucially) what lies still in the future. It is this view to what is yet to come which differentiates the patterning of Christian performance in certain respects from some forms of improvisation. Our performance is rooted and nurtured necessarily in a tradition, a pattern assimilated, a set of habits acquired and skills gained. And it demands the skilful (though I don't want to allow the virtuosity of the cadenza much space in the appropriation of the metaphor) and imaginative application of these to new and unexpected circumstances. There is a vital Christological component to this performance which time does not permit us to deal with here. Let me simply refer the reader to the sensitive and helpful treatment provided by David Brown in *Discipleship and Imagination*. 'Discipleship', Brown writes, 'is ... both a matter of locating ourselves within Jesus' story *and* acknowledging the way in which our own situation differs significantly from his.'[61] Nonetheless the pattern of his performance is a vital nourishing source for ours, not just as we reflect on it in the narrative, but as the Spirit unites us to him, takes our imagination captive and makes our performance part of the same drama, the same piece. In this sense the action of our lives is an improvised development of themes drawn from an earlier act.

At the same time, though, the performance has a vital eschatological dimension and energy. In our Christian 'will to meaning', we do not just look backwards, but perform hopefully towards a promised and imagined end. It is same promise and its imaginative apprehension which releases energy for our living the life of discipleship.[62] To return for a moment to Davey, we recall his insistence that 'As a dwelling between past and future possibilities, authenticity involves a being open to the call of the withheld, ... remaining open to and a holding with that which is still withheld from us.'[63] In the case of Christian performance, there is precisely this sense of an existence 'between the times'. That which is withheld from us, though, is also granted us to grasp, at least in the form of hints and clues. There is imaginative apprehension of our end together with God, even though comprehension is (perhaps will forever be) beyond our intellectual reach. The biblical symbols of 'bodily resurrection' and 'new creation' seem to me both to fit into this category, and both point clearly in the direction of a redemptive renewal of current states of affairs, and one which clearly does not occur prior to our death. While Moltmann's imaginative

---

61   David Brown, *Discipleship and Imagination: Christian Tradition and Truth* (Oxford: Oxford University Press, 2000), 8.

62   See further on this Richard Bauckham and Trevor Hart, *Hope Against Hope: Christian Eschatology at the Turn of the Millennium* (Grand Rapids: Eerdmans, 1999), esp. 44–71.

63   Davey in Kemal and Gaskell, *Performance and authenticity in the arts*, 89.

proposal of an 'intermediate state' may well raise its own theological questions and concerns, so far as the inculcation of an ecology of 'hopeful performance' is concerned, it stands identifiably in this same tradition, affording a way of imagining in concrete and sufficiently coherent terms (ones we can 'make sense of') how it might be that, in our post-mortem existence with God, the broken, distorted and incomplete patterns of particular lives may yet, in God's hands, come to satisfying closure and be rendered fit for our eternal enjoyment, and God's.

PART 3
Artistry as Christian Practice

According to philosopher Nicholas Wolterstorff, "works of art are objects and instruments of action. They are all inextricably embedded in the fabric of human intention. They are objects and instruments of action whereby we carry out our intentions with respect to the world, our fellows, ourselves, and our gods".[1] Returning to a theological engagement with the arts as such, therefore, the third part of our book explores different ways in which art forms (including some technically non-performative ones – literature, poetry, painting) may also constitute a set of Christian practices in which the tradition is, as it were, authentically 'performed', producing works which break open and instantiate its meaning faithfully in profound new ways for a constantly shifting context. Patrick Sherry considers how artists of various sorts – painters, writers, filmmakers, musicians – may evoke or 'show' the world in all its fallenness, rubbing our noses in it in order finally to depict possibilities of liberation and re-creation. Such 'showing' can take different forms. Most significantly, some instances of the 'arts of redemption', he suggests, have meaning chiefly in so far as they serve effectively to *illustrate* something else which is already familiar, whereas others constitute 'primary expressions' of religious ideas, having their meaning within themselves, and deepening theological and religious understanding as we engage with them on their own terms. Malcolm Guite explores wider aspects of "the truth that comes through feigning", offering a sharp rejoinder to modernism's empiricist bifurcation of the imaginative and the literal or 'real', and attending in particular to the capacity of dramatic performance to discover "*the true* through *the seeming*". Despite its inescapable association with iconoclasm, the Reformation did not leave Protestantism entirely bereft of art; on the contrary, 'images' of one sort or another were central to the ways in which reformed Christians made sense of their faith in day to day life. In his contribution to this volume, William Dyrness traces the distinctive 'visual culture' which emerged very early out of the Reformers' eschewal of many medieval practices, finding expression in such forms as architecture and garden design, as well as more familiar prints, etchings and woodcuts, and all indicating the development of an identifiable 'Protestant imagination', and distinctively Protestant forms of visual piety. The final two essays each reflect on ways in which (to borrow terms from Richard Viladesau[2]) art may provide not just 'texts for' but also 'texts of' theology, works, that is to say, which in their own distinctive and irreplaceable way interpret and deepen our understanding of realities and ideas lying at the heart

---

1   Wolterstorff, *Art in Action*, 3.
2   See Richard Viladesau, *Theology and the Arts: Encountering God through Music, Art and Rhetoric* (New York: Paulist Press, 2000), 123ff.

of Christian faith and tradition. Rosemary Muir Wright traces some examples of depictions of the transfiguration of Jesus in western painting, concentrating on the subtle relationships pertaining between word and image which characterize the visual response to and encoding of theological truth in art, and which are vital to our understanding of the peculiar religious power of the image as such. David Brown's essay examines ways in which the doctrine of the bodily ascension of Christ has been appropriated through Christian history, looking not at conventional doctrinal treatments of it, but at attempts to render its meaning in art, a form of 'theological' interpretation in which "attempts to engage an audience are more directly in play". Taking examples from painting, literature, sculpture and music, Brown pursues the thesis that theologizing of this less conventional sort is more satisfactory in its "emphasis on the potential relevance of the doctrine to the viewer, listener or reader", having "as much concern with the impact on us as on Christ. This means there is a desire to speak of a body transfigured that opens up the possibility of our own transfiguration." It is through such artistic appropriations and explorations of meaning, as well as other more familiar sorts, that the Christian tradition has been, is and no doubt will continue to be performed faithfully and authentically, and handed on to coming generations of those who live in the faith of Christ.

Chapter 10

The Arts of Redemption

Patrick Sherry

We are familiar with the idea that one function of an artist or a writer is to celebrate the beauty of creation, seeing it as reflecting God's glory. But artists and writers may also depict a fallen world: sometimes they may just do this and, as it were, rub our noses in it. More often, they do so as a prelude to depicting possibilities of liberation or re-creation. My purpose in this paper is to look at examples of such art and literature, and to ask what light they shed on the Christian doctrine of Redemption. I shall call them 'the arts of redemption', borrowing a phrase from John W. Dixon's book *Nature and Grace in Art*. I shall first say a little about such arts, and then ask how they may contribute to our religious understanding.

1. The Arts of Redemption

Dixon introduced this phrase as part of a general argument, that the different types of Christian art correspond to the principal events in the Christian drama. Thus he differentiates, for example, 'the arts of creation', which celebrate God's creation, 'the arts of image', which explore the structure of creation and seek to understand its parts and order, 'the arts of the fall', which investigate the tragic consequences of the fall and penetrate the nature of our fallen existence, and 'the arts of redemption', in which 'the artist is occupied with the redemptive act itself or the kind of world that results from the transfiguration of creation in redemption'.[1] Of the last of these Dixon says,

> The art of redemption is art immediately under the grace of God. This art is not informed by the innocence of delight that characterizes the art of creation but by a glory transfigured out of pain. Tragedy here has been redeemed and transformed, not obliterated or forgotten, but caught up in a new meaning and a new life; the city of God is not given but is arrived at on a pilgrimage.[2]

---

1   John W. Dixon, *Nature and Grace in Art* (Chapel Hill, NC, 1963), 72. Further possible categories might be 'the arts of Paradise' (which could include both those looking back to a past Golden Age and those anticipating one to come), and 'the arts of damnation'.
2   Ibid., 78.

As examples of this kind of art, Dixon instances Donatello's pulpits, Michelangelo's and Titian's *Pietas*, and Piero della Francesca's *Resurrection*.³ These examples indicate, I take it, that such art need not actually portray suffering, ugliness, or disorder, though it may do so. What is essential for Dixon is transformation: '... the transfiguration of earth, the search for the grace beyond hope ... the holiness of Christ penetrating the material and bringing into being the new earth.'⁴

Dixon's few examples are of painting and sculpture. But one should also include examples from other *genres*. There are poems like George Herbert's *Redemption* or T. S. Eliot's *Four Quartets*, and plays too: the theme of the passion and death of Christ was of course the subject of many medieval Mystery Plays, but 'Plays of Redemption' would also include other ones that deal with themes like guilt, repentance, atonement, and forgiveness (for example, Shakespeare's *Measure for Measure* and *King Lear*). The ancient Greek tragedians too dealt with the great themes of guilt, expiation, and forgiveness, especially Aeschylus in the *Oresteia* trilogy, and also with that of dying for others. The figure of Alcestis, who offered up her life to save her husband Admetus from death, and who was the subject of a play by Euripides, was regarded by some early Christian writers as prefiguring Christ, both in her self-giving and in her being raised from the dead by Hercules' overcoming Death. (And Hercules, in turn, was also regarded as a precursor of Christ, in his harrowing of Hell.)⁵

More recently, there is the *genre* of the novel to consider: both Dostoevsky and Tolstoy, for example, were concerned in their different ways with guilt and redemption, especially in *Crime and Punishment* and *Resurrection*. A particular theme worth picking out is that of vicarious suffering, conveyed, for example in Francois Mauriac's novels *The Knot of Vipers* and *A Woman of the Pharisees*, in which characters offer up their suffering for others. It is also found, I think, in Georges Bernanos' *The Diary of a Country Priest*, in which the unnamed priest is represented as a sacrificial victim dying for his village, and in his scenario *Dialogues of the Carmelites* (used by Francois Poulenc as the basis of an opera).

Films are an interesting and difficult case. As 'moving images' they have some of the virtues of both narratives and visual arts, though their relative brevity imposes limitations (a film might give some sense of Jesus' personality, but could it convey his saving work?). Tarkovsky's *Sacrifice* confronts us with the idea of renunciation on behalf of others; Tim Robbins' *Dead Man Walking* with the issue of salvation. Whereas the prison chaplain in Robbins' film seems to think that the only important thing is that the condemned murderer, Matthew Poncelet, should receive the sacraments before he dies, Sister Helen Prejean believes that his salvation will

---

3   Ibid., 155.
4   Ibid., 199.
5   Martin Hengel, *The Atonement: The Origins of the Doctrine in the New Testament*, trans. John Bowden (London, 1980), 9, 20. Hamish Swanson discusses Handel's use of such stories in his operas, in his *Handel* (London, 1990), 49–52.

depend in the first instance on honesty and taking responsibility for what he has done.[6]

Many films that do not set out to be overtly religious often draw on religious themes: *ET* reflects the story of the Incarnation, and *One Flew Over the Cuckoo's Nest* embodies the model of the Suffering Servant. They may also convey hopes of liberation, for example, from physical slavery, emotional bondage, or lack of opportunity. They may show a hero who carries out a redemptive task by defeating evil powers that threaten a community; or a more ordinary person who sacrifices himself or herself for others; or an averagely sinful person changed by events, as is Thornhill (played by Cary Grant) in Alfred Hitchcock's *North by Northwest*.[7]

A more central, and perhaps also more difficult, case is that of music. Beethoven's *Fidelio* might be described as an opera of liberation, and Wagner's *Parsifal* one of redemption. Bach's *Passions* are based on Gospel narratives; similarly, Handel's *Messiah* draws on Biblical texts. It is tempting to say, of the religious examples, that their redemptive significance depends, as with hymns, on the texts. But this is to ignore the effect that music itself may have, regardless of a libretto or text. Felix Mendelssohn wrote to Robert Schumann of Bach's chorale prelude '*Schmucke dich, O liebe Seele*' that 'if life were to deprive you of hope and faith, this one chorale would bring it all back again to you'.[8] This suggests that we need to look at such effects. We also need to ask: if music can express feelings, can it express ones as specific as repentance, or a wish to forgive or to be forgiven? Does the aria 'And He shall feed His Flock' in Handel's *Messiah* convey something of what Paul Evdokimov[9] calls the tenderness of God even to someone who does not hear or understand the words? There is also the problem of the extent to which someone from a non-Western culture can understand Western music, and vice versa.

These are just a few examples to flesh out Dixon's phrase 'arts of redemption'. There is also, of course, what might be called 'anti-redemptive' art. One thinks of Thomas Hardy's *Tess of the D'Urbervilles* and *Jude the Obscure*. There is art which brushes aside the issue. In Albert Camus' *The Plague* Fr Paneloux says to Dr Rieux after they have both attended a dying child, 'you, too, are working for man's

---

6   See Simon J. Taylor, '"A Searching Experience': Salvation in the film *Dead Man Walking* and R.C. Moberly', *Theology*, ci (1998), 104–11. More generally, see, out of a growing literature, Clive Marsh and Gaye Ortiz (eds), *Explorations in Theology and Film: Movies and Meaning* (Oxford, 1997).

7   See Christopher Deacy, 'an application of the religious concept of redemption in film noir', in *Scottish Journal of Religious Studies*, vol. xviii (1997), 197–212; idem, 'Screen Christologies: An Evaluation of the Role of Christ-Figures in Film', *Journal of Contemporary Religion* xiv (1999), 325–37; and John R. May (ed.), *Image and Likeness: Religious Visions in American Film Classics* (New York, 1992).

8   Albert Schweitzer, *J. S. Bach*, vol. I, trans. E. Newman (London, 1923), 245.

9   Paul Evdokimov, *La Femme et le salut du monde* (Paris, 1978), 167. He is echoing, for example, Isaiah 66:13.

salvation'. The doctor replies, 'salvation's much too big a word for me. I don't aim so high. I'm concerned with man's health, and for me his health comes first.'[10]

The question that these few examples raise is that of whether they add to our understanding of soteriology. Already, I think, it is apparent that many different models of redemption are implicit in the examples: atonement through suffering (both for oneself and on behalf of others), seen in the case of Mauriac's novels with their suffering servants; reconciliation; and transfiguration through the risen Christ – in the case of Eastern icons, transfiguration of the whole cosmos; as well as more general ideas like repentance and forgiveness. It is also apparent that different arts have their own strengths and weaknesses, fitting different aspects or phases of redemption. If redemption is a process which is worked out over a period of time, then narrative arts like novels and biographies will be particularly appropriate, and to some extent plays and films. But, again, do these examples lead to an increase in our religious understanding?

Understanding, of course, is a difficult and multi-faceted concept, and one that is hard to discuss in general terms. Seeing the point of what someone says may take more than intellectual ability; and missing it, especially in personal relations, may sometimes be more of a moral than an intellectual fault. Often helping people to see the point requires us to *show* them something. So the answer to my question about religious understanding may be that the arts of redemption increase our religious understanding in so far as they *show* us things or express them. As Wittgenstein said on occasion, 'don't think, but look!'[11] – or, we might add, 'listen', or 'touch'.

2. Illustrations and Primary Expressions

Someone who explicitly appealed to the idea of 'showing' here was the American novelist and short story writer Flannery O'Connor. 'Fiction writing', she suggests, 'is very seldom a matter of saying things: it is a matter of showing things.'[12] But there are different ways of showing people things; and in works of literature the ways may be subtle and complex, involving dramatization, allegory, and various other means of indirect communication. And what of music? Here the term 'express' seems more appropriate than 'show'. Moreover, some showings are dependent on something else for being understood, whilst others are not so dependent and so are primary. So we need to look more closely at the idea of showing.

The basic distinction that I want to make now is between illustrations (of many different kinds) and primary expressions; that is, between things that are more dependent on something else to convey their meaning, and things not so dependent.

---

10   Albert Camus, *The* Plague, Part IV, Ch. 3, trans. S.Gilbert (Harmondsworth, 1999), 209. Incidentally, it is not possible to make this contrast easily in all languages.

11   See, for example, Ludwig Wittgenstein, *Philosophical Investigations*, The German Text, with a Revised English Translation, 3rd edition, translated by G. E. M. Anscombe (Oxford: Blackwell, 2001), §66, 27e.

12   Flannery O'Connor, *Mystery and Manners* (London, 1972), 93.

Some such distinction is needed if we consider certain questions that are suggested by some works of art and literature. Do works like Grünewald's Isenheim altarpiece or Bach's *St Matthew Passion* increase our understanding of redemption and sacrifice, or support particular soteriological theories? Or are they simply works which, although they may be moving, vivid, and imaginative, are dependent on other modes of expression, especially theology? In Canto vii of the *Paradiso* Dante gives a conventional Anselmian version of the doctrine of the Atonement, but does he increase the understanding of this approach for anyone who has read St Anselm? Does he show us anything new, or is it just 'versified Anselm'? Similarly, does Milton, in *Paradise Lost*, Book xii, add anything to what St Ambrose and others have said about the *felix culpa* of Adam's sin? Or do Racine and Mauriac, who were influenced by Jansenism, increase our understanding of it, or make it seem more attractive and plausible?

Sometimes, it seems, artistic and literary examples, whatever their merits, do not add anything to our religious or theological understanding. Indeed, on occasion, we need theology in order to understand art and literature, for example in the case of Spenser's *Amoretti* no.68 (a poem about the Cross), or many mediaeval illuminations, or even some well known works like the van Eyck Brothers' Ghent Altarpiece. Often signs and symbols lose their immediate power, and have to be explained.

On the other hand, some artists and writers, especially in a secular culture, have seen their task as being to foster religious understanding by producing primary expressions of religious ideas. Flannery O'Connor, for example, believed that redemption through Christ was a decisive event, but realized that she was writing for people who might well know no theology and who might find the very ideas of sin, grace, and redemption unfamiliar or absurd. Since, however, as we have seen, she thought that fiction can show us things, it might well turn out to be the best way of expressing such ideas to many people today.

Thus we have a distinction between illustrations and primary expressions of religious ideas. In the former case the artist or writer often acknowledges a dependence on something else (for instance Botticelli's illustrations of Dante's *Divine Comedy*) or else points to a general moral, as in the case of Aesop's *Fables*. Of course both illustrations and primary expressions often shed light on something more general. In the former case, though, the connection is usually made explicit, often because the more general has been discovered already, and the illustration is used to clarify it; whereas, by contrast, primary expressions are usually derived from people's own life experience and feelings. Even when they convey important general truths, this is rarely made explicit. Thus writers like Sophocles and Dostoevsky have been praised for implicitly expressing and thereby anticipating the insights of a Freud or a Girard. So, writing of Dostoevsky's use of Christian symbolism, René Girard himself says, '...the truths painfully extracted from the psychological underground call for this symbolism.... The novelist does not attempt to 'illustrate' the principles of Christian faith, but he obeys the internal dynamics of his own creation'[13].

In a similar spirit, Martha Nussbaum cautions against regarding tragic dramas as just sources of philosophical examples; and more generally, advocates a conception of ethical understanding that gives priority to the perception of particular people and situations rather than abstract rules.[14] Putting both these points together, art and literature are for her especially appropriate methods of representation here, for they deal with moral particularities. Moreover, at their best they touch on what is most profound in human life, with certain actions fraught with great significance, and with deep human responses. These are things which need to be shown before they are explained (if they can be explained).

Nussbaum has a lot to say about narratives, particularly novels, at this point. For her they are especially suitable for capturing the time-bound character of human existence, and for showing the ways in which our beliefs, decisions, and policies are worked out over our lives. Her discussion is highly relevant to what might be called 'novels of redemption', in which evil is shown as overcome in the narrative of a life, as in Dostoevsky's *Crime and Punishment* or Graham Greene's *The Power and the Glory*. Indeed, Nussbaum's proposal has wider relevance for any narrative that attempts to show how redemption is worked out through particular events (not to speak of narratives depicting unredeemed evil, for example, William Styron's *Sophie's Choice*).

Unfortunately, however, Nussbaum does not discuss religious art and literature in the works mentioned, so we need rather to go on to say a little more about religious 'showings' and other primary expressions, including narratives. We have here a variety of things to consider. The chorale 'O Sacred Head so Wounded' in Bach's *St Matthew Passion* is primarily an expression of pity, devotion, and love of Christ, rather than a statement of some doctrine. Similarly, the '*Agnus Dei*' in Beethoven's *Missa Solemnis* is a heartfelt prayer for mercy and peace: the composer called the '*dona nobis pacem*' a 'prayer for inner and outer peace'[15]. A picture of the Resurrection or a poem about the Cross is, however, trying to capture the religious meaning of events or actions, and perhaps also of their consequences. They may also, of course, convey deep feelings about them. The aria 'I know that my Redeemer liveth' in Handel's *Messiah* both expresses Handel's faith in Christ and, I think, feelings of joy, peace, and reconciliation. Similarly, '*non confundar in aeternum*' in Berlioz's *Te Deum* is both an expression of faith and a cry of hope. And images like those of Christ the Healer, the Good Shepherd, and the risen one both depict something and at the same

---

13   René Girard, *Feodor Dostoevski: Resurrection from the Underground*, trans. J. G. Williams (New York, 1997), 100.

14   Martha C. Nussbaum, *Love's Knowledge: Essays on Philosophy and Literature* (New York, 1998), ix, 256–57; idem, *The Fragility of Goodness: Luck and Ethics in Greek Tragedy* (Cambridge, 1986), 12–17.

15   Wilfrid Mellers, *Beethoven and the Voice of God* (London, 1983), 305.

time express people's deepest feelings and needs, for example, to be healed, to be freed of their burdens, and to be given new hope.

In religious cases the distinction between primary expressions or showings and illustrations would be between works which convey their message immediately to anyone familiar with the relevant artistic and literary idioms, and those requiring a lot of background knowledge and explanation as well as a familiarity with the fundamental beliefs and practices of a religion. But often it is a matter of degree. The '*Agnus Dei*' of Beethoven's *Missa Solemnis* expresses Beethoven's prayers for mercy and peace, but a full understanding would require some knowledge of the Mass and of the background behind the phrase 'Lamb of God'. Similarly Grünewald's *Crucifixion* in his Isenheim altarpiece conveys the horrors of Christ's death more powerfully than most paintings of the subject. But there are varying degrees of understanding possible here also, not just of the Gospel background, but of, for example, the lamb and the chalice at the foot of the Cross in the painting.

Often, too, the showing or primary expression presents something that is in a sense familiar to us, but in a new way. To take a different type of example, that of the novel, Colin McGinn claims, 'an effective work of fiction is precisely a refashioning of the obvious in such a way that we are enabled to experience it afresh'. For example, he says, Mary Shelley in *Frankenstein* 'found a way of stating the obvious while appearing to tell us of extraordinary events.... Thus the extraordinariness of the ordinary is brought home to us.'[16] McGinn thinks that Shelley uses the situation of Frankenstein's monster to show the nature of the human condition, especially our feelings of physical imperfection, of being 'thrown' into the world and isolated at times, or of being rejected or downtrodden.

In the case of religious art and literature what McGinn calls the 'obvious' might be the human condition, as in his example, or else the fundamental beliefs and practices of a religion. Thus the primary purpose of a painter depicting the Nativity or the Crucifixion might well be to encourage devotion among the beholders of the picture. Likewise with a hymn-writer. One of the problems of our time and culture, however, is that we can no longer assume any familiarity with religious beliefs and practices. And when paintings, illuminated manuscripts, and so on are iconographically very sophisticated or complex, the problem is exacerbated. Even when people are religiously well informed, explanations may yet be required in a different age or context, for example, for some representations of the Cross, or of the Blessed Virgin Mary as the Second Eve. This is especially so when particular theologies are implicit in the works (for example, concerning the connection between the death of Christ on the Cross and the Eucharist). This point also applies to literature: it requires considerable theological sophistication to understand the 'conceits' of seventeenth-century poets like Donne and Herbert.[17]

When a work of art or literature needs a lot of background information or explanation in order to be understood, it tends to be treated as an illustration rather

---

16   Colin McGinn, *Evil, Ethics, and Fiction* (Oxford, 1997), 169–70.
17   See J. A. W. Bennett, *The Poetry of the Passion* (Oxford, 1982), 154ff.

than a primary expression. I should add that I do not regard the term 'illustration' as a derogatory one. It covers a wide variety of things: even the narrow category of book illustrations includes, for example, envisaged scenes in children's story books, engineers' drawings, diagrams in manuals on ball-room dancing, and miniatures in illuminated Books of Hours. Classical paintings are sometimes used as illustrations in modern Bibles and catechisms; and although, for instance, Botticelli's illustrations to the *Divine Comedy* are dependent on the text for being fully understood, they have an artistic importance that most illustrations to books do not have. Moreover, etymologically, an illustration is something that makes things clear by shedding light on them. A further consideration is that a mainly illustrative work of art or literature may incorporate powerful symbols which draw on subconscious responses and thereby have a healing effect. For symbols may move people without their quite knowing why or how.

The last point is highly relevant to liturgy, too; and reformers who ignore it risk producing new liturgies that are too verbalized, intellectualized, and didactic, thus failing to appreciate the importance of fostering people's understanding by expressing and showing things, often indirectly, as well as by explicit teaching. And what I have said about healing indicates that art, whether illustrations or primary expressions, may, like liturgy, be a channel of grace, and thereby have a redemptive impact (I put it this way in order to avoid saying that art can redeem us – something that smacks of idolatry).

To sum up this section: I have suggested two general ways in which art and literature can foster religious understanding by showing or expressing things:

(i) they may provide illustrations of religious ideas and beliefs – at their best, imaginative and illuminating ones;
(ii) they may be primary expressions or showings of these ideas and beliefs.

3. Showing Redemption

I now need to revert specifically to the arts of redemption. The examples I have already given seem to suggest a number of ways in which such arts can be primary expressions or showings.

First, much art and literature expresses profound human reactions like repentance, forgiveness, hope, the desire to atone for wrongdoing, and awareness of the need for purification. These particular reactions are found expressed in works like Rembrandt's painting *The Return of the Prodigal Son*, Shakespeare's *Measure for Measure*, and Newman's *The Dream of Gerontius*. Such examples provide something like what Wittgenstein called a 'perspicuous representation',[18] and thereby further our understanding of such basic reactions.

Second, going a step further, art and literature can attempt to show forth the true nature of human actions and transactions, and their consequences. Thus in *Crime*

---

18   See Wittgenstein, *Philosophical Investigations*, §122, 42e.

and Punishment Dostoevsky depicts Raskolnikov as justifying to himself the murder of the old moneylender because she was no better than a louse or a beetle – indeed she was worse, because she actually harmed people; but the author seeks to persuade us otherwise. He described himself as 'a realist in the higher sense'.[19] Similarly, Mauriac described himself as a 'metaphysician working in the concrete'. He writes, 'the sinner about whom the theologian gives us an abstract idea, I make incarnate'; the art of the imaginative writer is to make 'visible, tangible, odiferous a world full of wicked pleasures – and of sanctity, too'.[20]

Third, the artist or writer (the latter especially) may try to show forth the workings of grace, in the redemption of a sinner, or in the character of a saint, or, most strikingly, in a sinner turned saint (for instance, St Mary Magdalen in popular tradition). Thus in *The Knot of Vipers* Mauriac depicts the redemption of the evil Louis; and, as we have seen, in many of his novels there is a saintly character who suffers on behalf of others. In *God and Mammon* he writes:

> What we call a beautiful character has become beautiful at the cost of a struggle against itself, and this struggle should not stop until the bitter end. The evil which the beautiful character has to overcome in itself and from which it has to sever itself, is a reality which the novelist must account for. If there is a reason for the existence of the novelist on earth it is this: to show the element which holds out against God in the highest and noblest characters – the innermost evils and dissimulations: and also to light up the secret source of purity in creatures who seem to us fallen.[21]

Similarly, Dostoevsky depicts the saintly Fr Zossima in *The Brothers Karamazov*. We learn of the monk's earlier history as a man of the world, and of his influence on other characters in the novel, especially Alyosha; and we are shown, in turn, the effect of the latter on others.

Sometimes, too, the most effective way in which a writer can illustrate the effects of grace is by depicting its seeming absence. Mauriac does this in many of his novels (for example, again, the earlier part of *The Knot of Vipers*) as does Flannery O'Connor in her novels and short stories. The latter sought also to convey the costing nature of grace, and our resistance to it.

Novelists and dramatists, of course, have a restricted canvas: the human heart and what stems from it, especially human relationships. But perhaps this is as good a place as any to start from, if one is trying to discern possibilities of redemption.

---

19   Quoted from the Russian collected edition of Dostoevsky's work in Robert Lee Jackson, *Dialogues with Dostoevsky: The Overwhelming Questions* (Stanford, 1993), 14. See also David A. Lowe (ed.), Fyodor Dostoevski, *Complete Letters*, vol. III (Ann Arbor, 1991), 137, for a further elucidation of this point, in a letter to Nikolai Strakhov in 1869.

20   Francois Mauriac, *Journal* II and *Journal* III, in *Oeuvres Completes*, vol. xi (Paris, 1963), 154, 262.

21   Idem, *God and Mammon* (London, 1936), 78–9.

4. Conclusion

In this paper I have sought to flesh out Dixon's suggestive phrase 'the arts of redemption', then to argue that we must distinguish between primary expressions or showings and illustrations, and finally to sketch out a few ways in which there can be primary expressions of ideas of redemption. It is worth making two final comments. First, some artists and writers, such as Hardy, reject or ignore all such talk. Sceptics may attack not only the ethics, eschatology, or metaphysics of a religion, but also its analysis of the human condition and the remedies it offers. Thus there is non-redemptive, and even anti-redemptive art, as I have said. The reader, viewer, or listener may, therefore, have to decide for himself or herself which is the more convincing. Who depicts the world as it really is, Dostoevsky or Hardy? Rembrandt or Francis Bacon? Who has seen life in all its fullness, reflected on it with profundity, and conveyed his or her vision most convincingly? Who has discerned our deepest needs, and depicted possibilities of fulfilling them?

Secondly, and related to this, in appealing to the notions of primary showings or expressions I am not saying that such things are not subject to criticism at the religious level, even within the faith-community. I may show you something which you find perverted, heretical, shallow, and so on. Elsewhere[22] I have argued that there can be religious or theological criticisms of showings. An example is Ulrich Simon's and others' criticism of the ending of Goethe's *Faust*; Goethe, unlike Marlowe, has Faust carried away to heaven by angels singing 'He who strives ever onward, him we can redeem.' Conversely, a work of art may question a theology. In Ibsen's *Brand* the playwright exposes the hardness at the core of a country clergyman's faith and conduct. Moreover, it seems to follow, the relationship between art and theology may be reciprocal, a claim explored by Simon Taylor in an article exploring the dialectical relationship between the film *Dead Man Walking* and R.C. Moberly's classic treatise, *Atonement and Personality*.[23]

The three possibilities that I have just sketched out show, I think, that the relations between the arts and literature of redemption, on the one hand, and religion and theology, on the other are complex. There is a reciprocity here, and both sides are often faced with a lack of understanding in those whom they are addressing. Thus perhaps we should see the relationship between them as analogous to a conversation, in which two partners comment on or criticize each other's contributions, in an attempt to reach a common understanding and to communicate with a third party.

---

22   'Saying and Showing: Art, Literature, and Religious Understanding', in *Modern Theology*, 18/1 (January 2002), 37–48.

23   See Simon J. Taylor, '"A Searching Experience": Salvation in the film *Dead Man Walking* and R.C. Moberly', *Theology* ci (1998), 104–11.

Chapter 11

Our Truest Poetry is the Most Feigning ... Poetry, Playfulness and Truth

Malcolm Guite

1. Modernism's Loss of Playfulness

How are we to come at the truth? Is she waiting passively to be arrived at, her permanent address the end of the final syllogism in our science or philosophy? Or is she both more active and more elusive? Does she slip quietly up beside us, to join in our games and our rituals, making herself suddenly and abundantly available in the midst of our playfulness, responding more to the invitations of our imagination than to the imperatives of our reason? Since the Enlightenment our culture has been assuming that truth waits passively to be arrived at, but it is the purpose of this chapter to suggest that she is easier to find in the midst of our playfulness and that the most playful of our poets and playwrights have been telling us that all along.

The case against playfulness, against the truth that comes through feigning, had its triumph, at least in British culture, in the second half of the seventeenth century. Here is one of its classic exponents:

> It is our task 'to separate the knowledge of *Nature*, from the colours of *Rhetoric*, the devices of *Fancy* or the delightful deceit of *Fables.*'[1]

These are the words of Thomas Sprat, writing what amounted to the manifesto of the modern age, in his History of the Royal Society published in 1667. He wrote at the beginning of the Enlightenment, assisting at the birth of modernism. We read him at the end of the Enlightenment project, wondering whether modernism's successor will draw from pre-modern wisdom, or descend into a post-modern, or perhaps even hyper-modern nihilism and folly. Sprat's words certainly stand in sharp contrast to the wisdom of the previous age which was rooted in the idea that fables, stories and myths were the medium most completely embodying the deepest truths we need to know, so that most of the wisdom of the ancient world as well as the Judaeo-Christian

---

[1] *A History of the Royal Society of London for the Improving of Natural Knowledge*, first edition 1667, taken from the facsimile edited by Cope and Jones. this and subsequent extracts from Sprat's influential work can be found on http://newarkwww.rutgers.edu/~jlynch/Texts/sprat.html accessed on 7 February 2007.

tradition was in fact embodied in myth story and song. The classic exponent of that earlier view, writing only a couple of generations before Sprat, was Shakespeare, for whom the notion of telling a fable in order to get at a truth went very deep indeed, emerging, for example, even in the light-hearted exchange between Audrey and Touchstone the fool in *As You Like It*:

> AUD. I do not know what *poetical* is: is it honest in deed and word? is it a true thing?
> TOUCH. No, truly; for the truest poetry is the most feigning...[2]

The modern attack was not only on story but also on the poetry of image and metaphor. Sprat goes on to demand 'a close, naked, natural way of speaking, positive expressions, clear senses, a native easiness, bringing all things as near the mathematical-plainness as they can, and preferring the language of the artisans, countrymen and merchants before that of wits and scholars'.[3]

For laudable purposes of their own, the founders of modernism were attempting to create a complete separation between 'Reason' and 'Imagination' *as they understood these terms.* What they created was a kind of cultural apartheid. The entire realm of 'objective' truth was to be the exclusive terrain of *reason* at its narrowest and the faculties of *imagination* and *intuition* were only relevant to a purely private and 'subjective' truth. If it can't be weighed and measured, these men were saying, it's not really there.

It was not just poetry that was marginalised. This new arrangement affected everything, even the Faith, which was forced to choose, either to be relegated to something subjective or to become a pseudo-science, reducing the great mysteries, embedded in the ancient story-telling of scripture, to quantifiable facts, patient only of a literal interpretation. Theology became divided between increasingly vague and amorphous liberalism, happy to keep re-inventing the faith as a subjective comfort, and an increasingly strident fundamentalism which tried to treat the vast subtle poem of scripture as a single objective scientific treatise whose every word was literally and *only literally* true.

We live, however, in the midst of another wave of change. That old Enlightenment apartheid is crumbling as surely as political apartheid. The gap is being closed. We are seeking to know and understand in new ways. One of the most encouraging developments of our time is in the history and philosophy of science. It was necessary for Seventeenth century scientists and scientific philosophers to distance themselves from imagination as they perceived it in order to find a new language in which to put a series of new questions to nature. But scientists can now see that the great achievements of 'Scientific reason' are also exercises of imagination. The big breakthroughs involve a leap of imagination, and a playful creation or extension of model and metaphor. Reason itself works on terms, and with tools provided by

---

    2   *As You Like It* Act III scene 3. See George Brandes (ed.), *The Garrick Shakespeare*, Volume 3 (London: William Heinemann, 1905), 164.
    3   Ibid.. See above note 1.

imagination. Philosophers of knowledge like Michael Polanyi[4] and scientists such as John Polkinghorne[5] are calling for a new understanding, which integrates and sees the intimate links between ways of knowing which were once sealed off from one another. For this reason we can at last call the poets back to our aid. They have kept and told the stories that bound us to life and brought our attention back again, to those realities the Enlightenment found it necessary to ignore. They have chronicled the first Enlightenment 'divorce' between Reason and Imagination, but have also suggested, and indeed modelled in their method, the possibility of a renewed and even more fruitful reunion. But how do poets change the way we see, and what kind of new vision is it they offer?

In one sense all poets enjoy the freedom and possibilities of fiction, the stories they tell need not be outwardly true, nor need the voice and tone in which their poem speaks be their own. On the other hand if they are to succeed in moving us, everything in their poetry must be full of truth, it must, as we shall see, grow '*to something of great constancy*'[6]. We are so used to the conventions of fiction, so used to engaging in what Coleridge beautifully called the willing suspension of disbelief, that we miss the paradox beneath our noses, that truth arises not from the labouring *reason* of the poet, but from his or her playfulness, and freedom to invent. A poet who is also a playwright obviously enjoys this freedom to an even greater degree and is perhaps even more conscious both of the deliberate feigning and of the real truth to be found in his art.

Given the concern in this volume with, among others, the themes of performance and responsibility I thought it might be interesting to look at how the performance of a drama enables us to find *the true* through *the seeming*. I shall focus in on two specific moments in the works of Shakespeare where we can see some of these themes most clearly. Since we are considering the role of performance and the *play* itself I have chosen two plays in which Shakespeare plays with the idea of a play within a play. We will look at these themes first in the comedy of *A Midsummer Night's Dream*, and then see how Shakespeare returns to and develops them, after all the experience of the histories and tragedies, in the romance of *The Tempest*, so that we see the ideas transposed between two distinct genres of play.

2. Playfulness and Truth in *A Midsummer Night's Dream*

We shall begin with the *playfulness* in every sense of *A Midsummer Night's Dream* and allow Theseus and Hippolyta's famous dialogue about truth and imagination to set some of our themes. Before we engage with this dialogue it's worth remembering the context in which it takes place. It functions as both an epilogue to the main

---

4   See Begbie, *Voicing Creation's Praise* (London: T&T Clarke, 1991), 201–2 for an account of Polanyi's notion of personal knowledge.

5   See below p. 208 and note 8.

6   *A Midsummer Night's Dream* Act V scene 1. See Brandes (ed.), *The Garrick Shakespeare*, Volume 2, 283.

action of the play, and as a prologue to the play within the play. The four lovers, it will be remembered, leave the day-lit rationalism of Theseus' court to encounter the moonlight transformations of Puck, and find themselves caught up in the elemental quarrel of Oberon and Titania. They leave the court mis-matched and miserable, caught in a chain of frustration and betrayal; they return rightly matched and joyful, ready to enter into the fruitfulness of love, of which the play's closing nuptials are a sign. Puck has so cast a spell on the lovers who are now at last, through the play of magic, rightly linked again to one another, so that on waking they imagine that their transformations have only been a dream. They tell their story to Theseus and Hippolyta, not knowing whether they will be believed or whether to believe themselves:

> HIP. 'Tis strange my Theseus, that these lovers speak of.
> THE. More strange than true: I never may believe
> These antique fables, nor these fairy toys.
> Lovers and madmen have such seething brains,
> Such shaping fantasies, that apprehend
> More than cool reason ever comprehends.
> The lunatic, the lover and the poet
> Are of imagination all compact:
> One sees more devils than vast hell can hold,
> That is, the madman: the lover, all as frantic,
> Sees Helen's beauty in a brow of Egypt:
> The poet's eye, in fine frenzy rolling,
> Doth glance from heaven to earth, from earth to heaven;
> And as imagination bodies forth
> The forms of things unknown, the poet's pen
> Turns them to shapes and gives to airy nothing
> A local habitation and a name.
> Such tricks hath strong imagination,
> That, if it would but apprehend some joy,
> It comprehends some bringer of that joy;
> Or in the night, imagining some fear,
> How easy is a bush supposed a bear!
> HIP. But all the story of the night told over,
> And all their minds transfigured so together,
> More witnesseth than fancy's images
> And grows to something of great constancy;
> But, howsoever, strange and admirable.[7]

Like the quarrel between Oberon and Titania, the quarrel between Theseus and Hippolyta is not simply a matter of individuals disagreeing. These characters embody great truths and principles, which are, in all of us also, quarrelling and also, perhaps through our imaginative participation in this play, on their way to being reconciled. So it is at this moment of the play that in and through the meeting and the words of

---

7   Act V, scene 1. See Brandes, *The Garrick Shakespeare*, Vol. 2, 282–3.

Theseus and Hippolyta we have a meeting in our minds of *reason* and *imagination*. Let us first look at what Theseus has to say on *reason's* behalf against, or *apparently* against, *imagination*:

Literal Meaning

On the surface and most straightforward level he is simply saying: I don't believe it! I deny that these events, which the lovers have narrated, actually took place. I think they have been deceived by their over-wrought imaginations, and their imaginations were over-wrought because they were in love.

But Theseus goes on to describe the way imagination itself works, and in so doing concedes almost everything his reason hopes to deny. He generalises from this particular denial to a denial of all 'antique fables' and fairy toys and in so doing, cuts off, with delicious dramatic irony, both the branch on which he is sitting and the stage on which he is standing. For here is *Theseus*, whose entire existence to us and to our minds and imaginations rests on the fact that he has come down to us from antiquity through the medium of *antique fables*, saying 'well of course you can't believe these antique fables, I don't believe them myself.' Here is Theseus re-made in the imagination of Shakespeare, and engendered or embodied in us by the power of Shakespeare's poetry, telling us, in the very medium of that poetry, 'well of course you all know there's nothing in poetry.'

Dialectic between Apprehend and Comprehend

In the course of this speech Theseus twice makes a distinction between comprehension and apprehension, and in many ways these are key terms not only for the play, but for theology, and especially perhaps for theology in the present age. Theseus is choosing now to confine reality to that which he can *comprehend* and to deny reality to that which he can only *apprehend*, but his distinction, though not his opposition, between these two modes of knowing is potentially helpful and worth examining more closely.

In some ways Theseus' speech, with its distrust of antique fable and shaping fantasies, and its emphasis on cool reason and comprehension might be seen as an anticipation of the coming view of the new or modern world, exemplified by Sprat;

> Lovers and madmen have such seething brains,
> Such shaping fantasies, that *apprehend*
> More than cool reason ever *comprehends*.

The most striking thing about his attack on imagination is not a failure of *imagination*, which in fact animates the whole speech, but a failure of *reason*. There is a serious logical flaw in his speech. He begins with a proper and useful distinction between *apprehension* and *comprehension* as modes of knowing: we have 'shaping fantasies' which *apprehend* more than cool reason ever *comprehends*. But he then goes on to *imply*, without ever *proving*, that what we *apprehend* is not real. And he implies that it is not real first by a sleight of hand and than by a suggestion of motive. The sleight of hand is in the elision from *things unknown* to *airy nothing*:

> As imagination bodies forth
> the form of things *unknown,* the poet's pen
> Turns them to shapes and gives to airy *nothing*
> A local habitation and a name.

Just because a thing is *unknown,* or unknown to reason, it does not follow that it is simply *nothing*. The very fact that imagination is able to discern a form which it bodies forth and names, may suggest that it not only has its own mode of existence but that its existence is able to impinge on, and to have effects, to operate as a cause within, the realm of things which reason can in fact comprehend. We require the strong imagination to be active in bodying forth the form of things unknown precisely because, far from being airy nothing, these things however incomprehensible, may have a huge influence on things we do comprehend. Contemporary theories of knowledge now emphasise that it is just this prior intuition and shaping imagination, this imaginative playing with the possible arrangement and re-arrangement of available data which makes science possible. The purpose of imagination, in its playfulness and poetry in particular, is to be a bridge between reason and intuitive apprehension, to find for apprehension just those shapes, those local habitations and names which make for comprehension. Indeed you could argue that all great poetry operates out of a creative holding in tension of these two ways of knowing. It is generated between the apprehension of the hitherto unknowable, which gives it its depth, resonance and meaning, and the comprehension of the shapes and images in which its bodies forth its apprehensions which is what allows it to communicate at all. We can see poems failing when they capitulate to either one of these poles: when they are so comprehensible as to lead us nowhere, give us nothing, and remain on a trite surface, or when they are so full of unclothed or un-embodied apprehension that they offer us no common bridge in language or picture to the poet's truth and so remain obscure and opaque. But we can equally see, when a poem succeeds, when its knowable images, the glassy surface of its mirror of imitation, is suddenly a window that lets us pass through into the new world the poet has apprehended.

Hippolyta's Reply

So Theseus on the literal level denies the lovers' story and makes the case against imagination and for cool reason. How does Hippolyta reply?

> But all the story of the night told over,
> And all their minds transfigured so together,
> More witnesseth than fancy's images
> And grows to something of great constancy...

Just as at a literal level, and in terms of the plot of the play, Theseus' speech attacks the veracity of the lovers' story, so at the same level, Hippolyta defends it. At a literal level she is simply saying: 'when we look at these stories over again, and especially when we put them together, they cohere, they make sense, and all the lovers seem to be referring to the same thing. Their minds are transfigured so together, and their separate stories ' grow to something of great constancy,' so they can't have been making it up. But there is more: her defence of 'the story of the night told over' amounts to a defence of imagination and of the poet's art, as well as spelling out the criteria by which its success might be judged. Consider again what Hippolyta says:

> *And all their minds transfigured so together*

The achievement of art is, the *transfiguring* of our minds by means of imagination so that we see both what the poet sees and what he *sees through what he sees*. In the case of the playwright's art it is the *transfiguring* of our minds *together*. There is a *corporate* transfiguration, a corporate entering into the world of the poet's imagination and a corporate seeing through it, of the truth he intends. This is in fact happening at the very moment that Hippolyta speaks of it and through the very means of her speech. When this speech is spoken by an actress, what is happening is that we the audience have voluntarily succumbed to the enchantment of the play-wright, whose art, like Puck's love potion, has so worked on our eyes that our vision is altered. In one sense we know perfectly well that we are sitting in a theatre watching a well-known actress, but at another level we have ourselves been in the fairy wood and lived its moonlight scenes. The two characters whom we are watching combine in their persons antique fable and fairy toy, and represent in their characters reason and imagination, working as forces both within the plot of the play, and in our own lives and minds. Our minds are indeed transfigured, for through the costumes and the lights and the greasepaint and the outer sounds of the familiar speeches we are seeing into the heart of language itself, into the very forge and generative place of poetry, as Shakespeare celebrates the mystery of his art.

Inner Coherence and Growth in a Work of Art

Hippolyta goes on to say that there must be some truth in the lovers' tale because when we return to it, when it is *told over* it *grows to something of great constancy*. And this is true not just of an episode in this play, but of all great works of art. Once it has been finished a work of art develops a life of its own which is in some sense independent of its author. A good work of art has an independent inner coherence which does indeed 'grow to something of great constancy' the more often we 'tell it over', that is, enter into its world, allow it to transfigure our minds. How does this work? How is it that a single play, like this one, a finite collection of words composed by a finite mind, can take on such a life of its own, can seem to gather to itself and embody so much, and to do so consistently and with such inner cohesion and integrity? The best hint as to how this happens is to be taken from Shakespeare/Hippolyta's choice of the word *grows*. The work grows in our minds because its structure and unity are *organic*. The principles of its inner organisation, the way all its parts are related to its whole is like the organisation and accommodation of a living thing. The sense that a work of imagination might grow and develop according to its own inner laws in just the same way that in the outer world life itself grows and develops is hinted at in Shakespeare's choice of the word *bodies*. Imagination *bodies forth the form of things unknown.*

There is more to be said here and a whole theology of the incarnation might well be developed from reflection on Shakespeare's juxtaposition of those two words *imagination* and *bodies*, and especially from the felicitous use of the word *bodies* not as a plural noun but as a verb in the present tense. Meditation on the paradoxes of this speech would certainly be fruitful for a renewed theology of imagination and the arts.

Relation between Art and Nature Leading to the Conjunction of Opposites

Part of the way in which the parts and elements of this play are all organically related to the whole can be seen in the way the structure of the plot develops the meaning of the poetry. Theseus and Hippolyta each make a speech defending a particular way of knowing, reason on the one hand and imagination on the other, but the context in which they set out their different viewpoints is a preparation for marriage, the entire play is a kind of preface to their marriage and it concludes with a blessing of their marriage bed. Indeed it could be argued that the play, which ends with three marriages in the realm of the visible, and a reconciliation in the invisible realm, is about marriage in every sense. It is about the fruitful conjunction of opposites at every level, the bringing together of contraries that seem to quarrel, but in whose conjunction is not only harmony but a kind of overspill of creative energy into fruitfulness and blessing.

So the marriage of Theseus and Hippolyta represents the necessary and fruitful union of reason and imagination. It is saying that the divorce between reason and imagination which Sprat was to propose will only injure us, and prevent us really knowing and being blessed by truth. Rather we must find a way of knowing which involves *both* the way reason *comprehends and* the way imagination *apprehends*. Indeed, we can go further. Just as in marriage the two 'become one flesh', so reason and imagination can be understood as different aspects or modes of a single human capacity to respond creatively to God's world, a capacity which is part of the *Imago Dei* in us. This applies just as much to our understanding of the mysteries of life and growth in the outer world of nature as it does in the inner world of art. Allowing poetry to transfigure our vision heals the false fragmentation our culture has endured since the enlightenment. To find a way of making a marriage, a fruitful union of the apparent opposition of reason and imagination is perhaps the most urgent task of our own time.

Performance and the Play within the Play

The exchange between Theseus and Hippolyta forms an interlude, between the magical transfigurations of the moonlit wood, and *the play within the play*, the ludicrous enactments of Bottom and his friends, the 'rude mechanicals'. In a way the contrast could not better illustrate the difference between the true work of art, with its imaginative invitation to a willing suspension of disbelief, and a mere outward imitation which, failing to engage the imagination, fails equally to please the reason. The success of Shakespeare's play depends on a kind of invited feigning, on a mutual consent that our minds should be transfigured together. In some sense we have to agree to be deceived in order to reach a truth. But the authors and actors of the play within the play cannot grasp this. They are afraid it would be wrong to deceive the gentry with the appearances of their play in case they frighten them. But all their special efforts *not to feign*, or rather to *undeceive* with each of the players solemnly informing their audience, in the middle of the action, as to who they *really* are, actually prevent them from telling their story at all, and at no point is anybody's mind transfigured. Their concern with accuracy about the bodily surface of reality prevents them from embodying anything real at all. So, for example they introduce the moon as a physical character in the play. There is a wonderful irony here, for *moonlight* is perhaps the central and most beautifully embodied and imagined thing in the whole of Shakespeare's play. *Midsummer Night's Dream* is flooded with a most unearthly and magical moonlight from its very opening lines, *but oh methinks how slow this old moon wanes* through to the *glimmering light* in which Oberon and Titania give the house its final blessing. So it is a moment of rich comedy when into the midst of this imaginatively moon-enchanted play Shakespeare introduces another play in which a man stands physically in front of people carrying a lantern they can all see with their outer eyes and announcing solemnly that he is the moon, and thinks that this will be a better embodiment of moonlight than any mere words can be.

The 'mechanicals'' attempt to keep reminding everybody who they 'really' are, thus destroying their own art, serves conveniently as a parable for the whole poverty of some approaches to knowledge since the Enlightenment - the poverty of reductionism. The reductionist looks at the mystery of the world, its moonlight and sunlight, its rains and rivers, dissects it all and says: 'it's not *really* this, it's not the sublime mystery it seems to be hinting at, it's *really* only x or y' or some other such formula. It's as though someone at the performance of a great piece of music were to take along an oscilloscope and insist that nothing had happened there but the movement of wavy lines on his instrument. But the realism of the 'rude mechanicals', the realism of a reductionist, is not only shallow, it is also false, as this very play shows. The reality is that we live not in a dead world of mere surfaces, but in the midst of a mystery which, if we will let it transfigure our minds,

grows to something of great constancy
but howsoever strange and admirable.

This very point is now made as often by scientists as by poets, since the more deeply scientists delve into the very nature of matter, the less able they feel to give a simply reductionist account of it. This development is very succinctly summarised in John Polkinghorne's popular book *One World*, in his chapter on 'levels of description'.[8]

3. Such Stuff as Dreams are Made on: Appearance and Reality in *The Tempest*

It is instructive to turn now from the early enchantments of the *Dream*, standing as it does near the threshold of Shakespeare's major work, to *The Tempest*, that other magical play concerned also with the relation of inner and outer, of reality and appearance, which comes at the end of his career and whose epilogue is believed by many to be Shakespeare's own farewell to the stage. Like the *Dream*, the *Tempest* uses magical or imaginary characters to embody aspects of our inner nature and also hidden aspects of the outer nature which surrounds us. Just as Oberon and Titania are in some sense the hidden forms, the 'parents and originals', of much in both the outer and inner worlds of the *Dream*, so Prospero's two servants Ariel and Caliban are the local habitations and names given by Shakespeare to profound aspects of our own human nature. They embody our greed and resentment on the one hand, and our yearning for flight and freedom on the other. We are certain to recognise Ariel within ourselves, but equally bound, under the searching light of Shakespeare's poetry, to say of Caliban, as Prospero does, 'This thing of darkness I acknowledge mine'[9].

Just as we found themes which are woven throughout the *Dream* focused in the exchange between Hippolyta and Theseus, so we can find many of the themes of the *Tempest* focused in a single speech of Prospero's which happens, as with the Dream, just after the play within the play. But first *The Tempest* itself, and then Prospero's speech need to be set into context.

The Place of The Tempest *in Shakespeare's Works*

The *Dream* is a comedy, and for all its extraordinary profundity in the matter of imagination and poetry, there is in its lightness of touch, an absence of engagement with the deepest issues of suffering, sin and mortality, especially with the great issues of Judgement and Mercy. Whilst in the late romances, of which the *Tempest* is the last, Shakespeare can in some sense be seen to return to some of the themes of his earliest plays, it is not a naive return. Between *Midsummer Night's Dream* and *The Tempest* lie the Histories and Tragedies. By the time he writes *The Tempest* he

---

8   John Polkinghorne, *One World; the interaction of theology and science* (London: SPCK, 1986), 86–96.

9   *The Tempest* Act V scene 1. See George Brandes (ed.), *The Garrick Shakespeare*, Volume 1 (London: William Heinemann, 1905), 84.

has faced and outfaced the self-doubts and searching of *Hamlet*, *Othello*'s terrible twisting of the energy of love, *Macbeth*'s uncanny mapping of the degradation of the soul, and *Lear*'s encounter, in himself and others, with humankind's 'monsters of the deep'. The power of *The Tempest* comes from the fact that it is not a fantasy of escape, but one in which the darkest themes explored in the tragedies can find their resolution. The final affirmations, explicit and implicit, at the end of *The Tempest* have a special value. 'We can say of them what Karl Barth says of the enormous *Yes* at the centre of Mozart's music, that it has weight and significance because it overpowers and contains a *No*.'[10]

Theme and Counter-Theme

Indeed *The Tempest* both begins and builds as though it were a revenge tragedy. It has all the classic elements; Prospero, the wronged Duke, manages by his magic art to summon together all those who have wronged him. Their guilt is proved many times in the course of the play, both by their own confession and by the subsequent scenes Prospero has himself contrived to test their characters. Prospero does not reveal his hand until the very last act, but by the beginning of the fourth act we have a strong sense of the coming denouement and a Jacobean audience might reasonably have expected a last-judgement-type scene in which Prospero is justly avenged on the guilty, and rewards the faithful. But running throughout the play is a counter-theme of *mercy*, of unexpected graces and salvations, of being given up for lost only to be saved at the last minute from the wreck. This is true of the original story of Prospero and Miranda's survival in the drifting boat, it is true of the opening tempest and the apparent wreck of the ship and loss of its crew, when they are in fact all restored and recovered, it is true of the love between Ferdinand and Miranda with Prospero's apparent opposition giving way to the reality of his loving purpose and good will to them both. This theme of the sudden revelation of mercy and restoration in the midst of apparent catastrophe, is seamlessly woven together with the other two pairs of apparent opposites, Control and Release, and Truth and Illusion, whose tension and interplay does so much to generate the play's energy and meaning.

By the beginning of Act IV theme and counter-theme are hung finely in the balance, we do not know, and perhaps Prospero himself does not know, whether when he reveals the truth to his brother and the other conspirators he will find it in himself to forgive them or not. When the tension is at its height it is relieved by a sudden *jeu d'esprit* on Prospero's part, when he suddenly kindles his own and our imaginations to 'Bestow upon the eyes of this young couple / Some vanity of my art.'[11] That 'vanity' takes the form of a play or masque in which the goddesses

---

10   Seamus Heaney alludes to this passage in Barth in praising one of Yeats' last poems in his book of essays *The Redress of Poetry* (London: Faber & Faber, 1995), 163; but I think his insight applies as much, if not more, to Shakespeare's last plays

11   *The Tempest* Act IV scene 1. See Brandes (ed), *The Garrick Shakespeare*, Vol. 1, 63-4.

Iris, Ceres and Juno appear to bless the proposed marriage between Ferdinand and Miranda, and fill the stage suddenly with music and images of union and fruitfulness, as though the curtain of the world had for a moment been drawn aside to give us a glimpse of a heaven in which there is at last a resolution of all the tensions with which the play is charged, and we wonder whether it was as much for his own benefit as for Ferdinand and Miranda's that Prospero summoned the vision, but it vanishes in noise and confusion as suddenly as it had come, and then Prospero speaks these words:

> PROS. *You do look, my son, in a moved sort,*
> *As if you were dismay'd: be cheerful, sir.*
> *Our revels now are ended. These our actors,*
> *As I foretold you, were all spirits and*
> *Are melted into air, into thin air:*
> *And, like the baseless fabric of this vision,*
> *The cloud-capp'd towers, the gorgeous palaces,*
> *The solemn temples, the great globe itself,*
> *Yea, all which it inherit, shall dissolve*
> *And, like this insubstantial pageant faded,*
> *Leave not a rack behind. We are such stuff*
> *As dreams are made on, and our little life*
> *Is rounded with a sleep. Sir, I am vex'd;*
> *Bear with my weakness; my, brain is troubled:*
> *Be not disturb'd with my infirmity:*
> *If you be pleased, retire into my cell*
> *And there repose: a turn or two I'll walk*
> *To still my beating mind.*[12]

Literal Meaning

Like the exchange between Theseus and Hippolyta in the *Dream*, this speech works simultaneously at a number of different levels, and the *revels*, the *insubstantial pageant*, to which it refers may be understood, in this context, in at least five different ways. Firstly *our revels now are ended* refers to the *insubstantial pageant* or masque which they, (the characters) and we (the audience) have just been watching. These 'actors' were, as Prospero had forewarned, invisible spirits of the air summoned by his art, and they, and the magical glimpses of heaven which were their scenery, have faded back into the air whence they were woven.

The End of Prospero's Game-Playing

However to hear Prospero, at this point in the play, saying that the revels are ended, the dream-playing is over, is bound to carry a reference to the way in which Prospero

---

12   Act IV, scene 1. See Brandes (ed.), *The Garrick Shakespeare*, Vol. 1, 68.

has in fact been orchestrating the plot of what happens in the play so far. He has been the playwright within the play. He has brought the characters together, he has set the scenes in which they have encountered one another, he has led them through these scenes with each other and with the illusions of his art, till at last they come to a moment of real encounter with him, whom most of them have not seen yet. This encounter is to come in the final act when Prospero lays asides his robes and appears to his brother and the other conspirators plainly as the person he is. The revels are ended, there is a reality of personal encounter, with its perils and its possibilities of redemption for all of them to face. The insubstantial pageant is broken by the arrival of that moment for encounter.

The End of the Play?

But there is a third level of reference, for here we have an actor in a play, one who has been presenting appearances of reality to us through the medium of his performance, and his words carry beyond the fellow characters to whom they are directed, out to the audience itself, and we cannot help hearing this reference to vanishing actors and beautiful scenery that suddenly fades away, as a reference to the very play that we are watching. For a while Shakespeare has filled our minds with cloud-capped towers, with gorgeous palaces and solemn temples, now he is reminding us that this beautiful vision will fade from us and return us to those other encounters and confrontations for which the fading vision may perhaps have been preparing us.

The End of Shakespeare's Career and of the Globe Theatre

For the original audience, sensing the widening ripples which the flung stone of this speech cast in their minds, there must have been a particular frisson on the outward movement from *towers* through *palaces* to *temples* and finally *the globe*, which led them to a fourth and particular level of understanding:

> The cloud-capp'd towers, the gorgeous palaces,
> The solemn temples, the great globe itself,
> Yea, all which it inherit, shall dissolve
> And, like this insubstantial pageant faded,
> Leave not a rack behind.

If the tradition that Shakespeare intended this play as his farewell to the theatre, and that he himself played the part of Prospero, is right, then his contemporaries would have felt the reference to the *great globe itself*. The Globe Theatre had been the scene of so many extraordinary visions, and here the artist who had conjured those visions for them, was resigning from his art, dissolving the pageant before their eyes and strangely implying that they themselves will be dissolved with it.

The Eschaton, the End of All Things

And this sense of a wider dissolution brings us to the fifth and deepest reference of these lines. They refer to the end, or the apparent end, not simply of this episode, this play, or even Shakespeare's art and theatre, but to the end of all things, the end of our lives and the end of the world.

And After the End?

What does Shakespeare intend us to understand by the two key metaphors he uses here for the relation between our present experience and what might lie behind or beyond them, the metaphor of a play and its ending, and of dream and awakening?

In one sense Prospero is alluding to and developing the idea which Shakespeare had used in many other plays that 'all the world's a stage', an idea which had been given very forceful expression in Raleigh's brilliant little poem 'What is our life?' which gives a good sense for the sort of feel the life/stage metaphor had for Shakespeare's contemporaries.[13] In his poem, Raleigh picks up on the brevity and comedy, the illusions and delusions, of our lives. Human life is 'a play of passion' a 'short comedy' played out under heaven's judicious gaze; our mothers' wombs are dressing rooms where we are costumed for our part, and death the falling of the curtain which ends the play. But although the potential bleakness of his juxtaposed womb/tomb imagery has been developed by some moderns,[14] Raleigh's poem is not bleak in the modern sense, because for all the 'judicious sharpness' of its gaze, *heaven* is nevertheless the spectator of the play of our lives, and there is at least implicit in the notion of dying *in earnest* some sense that beyond the illusions and tragicomedies of our lives, we may encounter a heaven so real that in comparison with it all that seemed real before was no more than *a play of passion*. The notion of our present life as a *play* is fundamentally ambiguous; it can be used to suggest falsehood and futility, something that doesn't ultimately matter, or to suggest the reverse. Just as a play is a beautifully wrought work of art which allows us to engage with a feigned truth in such a way as to enable us for a deeper truth (our truest poetry is our most feigning), so the world and all our experiences in it, may be a great work of art and imagination, beyond which is a reality for which the play of the world has been preparing us.

---

13 See *Silver Poets of the Sixteenth Century*, ed. Gerard Bullett (London: Dent (Everyman Edition), 1960), 296.

14 Most notably by Beckett whose 'they give birth astride of a grave, the light gleams an instant then all is night once more' probably owes something to this poem. See *Waiting for Godot* (London: Faber & Faber, 1956) Act II, 89.

The End as Futility

Shakespeare had explored the bleakest side of the metaphor in many of his plays, most notably in *Macbeth*. There Macbeth's soul has been so brutalised and alienated by the course of violence on which he set himself that he greets the news of his wife's suicide not with grief, but with indifference and futility, expressed through the metaphor of life as a play:

> MACB. She should have died hereafter;
> There would have been a time for such a word.
> Tomorrow, and tomorrow, and tomorrow,
> Creeps in this petty pace from day to day
> To the last syllable of recorded time
> And all our yesterdays have lighted fools
> The way to dusty death. Out, out, brief candle
> Life's but a walking shadow, a poor player
> That struts and frets his hour upon the stage,
> And then is heard no more: it is a tale
> Told by an idiot, full of sound and fury,
> Signifying nothing.[15] (Act V scene5 lines 12–28)

Macbeth's speech here expresses the alienation from life which is the consequence of the dehumanising choices he has made, choices which demand that 'blood will have blood', that from a bloody course once chosen there is no going back. 'I am in blood / Stepp'd in so far that, should I wade no more, / Returning were as tedious as go o'er'.[16] By contrast Prospero is on the threshold of choosing mercy, and for him the ending of our revels and the dissolution of this insubstantial pageant, is itself a prelude to something more, something to which, as the epilogue of *The Tempest* makes clear, mercy is the only key. Whereas for Macbeth the actors in the play of life are walking *shadows*, Prospero's choice of word is *spirits*, *these our actors as I foretold you are spirits*, they are the natural inhabitants of a realm beyond the one in which they have been playing. Although they melt into thin air, and like the baseless fabric of this vision leave not a rack behind, there is a strong sense that they, and the cloud-capped canopies, melt from us into something else, or in their melting reveal something else. The placing of Prospero's speech in the play carries this sense. These lines occur at the beginning of act *four* not the end of act *five*. We witness the dissolution of the pageant but it leaves not a blank stage or a falling curtain, but a stage set for a moment of encounter, judgement and reconciliation in which Prospero confronts and forgives his brother. But if, on our fifth and final level of reference, the *insubstantial pageant* is not only the play within the play but the whole world and all of us in it then the strong implication is that when

---

15 See Brandes (ed.), *The Garrick Shakespeare*, Vol. 4 , 285.
16 Act III scene 4. See Brandes (ed.), *The Garrick Shakespeare*, Vol. 4, 251–2.

> The cloud-capp'd towers, the gorgeous palaces,
> The solemn temples, the great globe itself,
> Yea all which it inherit, shall dissolve
> And, like this insubstantial pageant faded,
> Leave not a rack behind.[17]

We ourselves will step from the seemings of this world, from the theatre of the great globe, not into the nothingness of Macbeth's alienation, but into an encounter as potentially fraught, but also potentially fruitful, as that which occupies act five of *The Tempest*.

The End as Judgement and Renewal

This motif of the re-surfacing of the lost, is there in Shakespeare's choice of the ambiguous *rack* in *leave not a **rack** behind*. This play opens with the apparent wreck of a ship and all its crew, who re-surface marvellously and for their own redemption in the rest of the play. Likewise the device of the play within the play itself directs the energy of the life/play metaphor Prospero is using. The play is over he is saying, and yet by virtue of his continued presence on the stage we know that the play goes on. We might of course object that when the whole play itself is over then indeed there will be no surviving of the characters beyond it, then indeed they will *leave not a wrack behind*. But Shakespeare has something further to add. He ends his last play and his whole work in drama, and his life in London with what must have been, when it was first performed, a stunning *coup de theatre*. All the characters are gathered on stage at the end of act five, Prospero gives his peace and blessing to Alonso and co. for their voyage home, and in the beautiful last lines, at last sets Ariel free. The reconciled company prepare to follow Prospero into his cell to hear his full story before they sail to Italy, with Prospero's last words 'please you draw near' the play is over, the curtain falls. And then, as the audience are preparing to leave, the curtain moves and Prospero appears again and speaks this epilogue:

---

17   *The Tempest*, Act IV scene 1. See Brandes (ed.), *The Garrick Shakespeare*, Vol. 1, 68.

> Now my charms are all o'erthrown,
> And what strength I have's mine own,
> Which is most faint: now, 'tis true,
> I must be here confined by you,
> Or sent to Naples. Let me not,
> Since I have my dukedom got
> And pardon'd the deceiver, dwell
> In this bare island by your spell;
> But release me from my bands
> With the help of your good hands:
> Gentle breath of yours my sails
> Must fill, or else my project fails,
> Which was to please. Now I want
> Spirits to enforce, art to enchant,
> And my ending is despair,
> Unless I be relieved by prayer,
> Which pierces so that it assaults
> Mercy itself and frees all faults.
> As you from crimes would pardon'd be,
> Let your indulgence set me free.[18]

At one level this is simply the actor/playwright graciously asking for applause, pretending to be confined to the island of the stage unless released by the applause of the audience:

> But release me from my bands
> With the help of your good hands

But, in the context of all that has gone before, it is far more than that. For a second time the revels have ended and still Prospero, who has forgiven and delivered his enemies, survives the dissolution and stands in need of deliverance himself. He steps as it were from the Great Globe, from the whole theatre of life, to find that he is still himself and still has an audience. (*Heaven the judicious sharp spectator is*, they would all remember from Raleigh) And so he appeals to his audience for mercy on the grounds of mercy, both the mercy he has shown and the mercy his auditors might themselves hope for; *let me not, since I have.. pardoned the deceiver dwell in this bare Island by your spell* and, in the final and telling couplet:

> As you from crimes would pardon'd be,
> Let your indulgence set me free

Something astonishing is happening here. If we accept the sense we have given to the play/life metaphor in Prospero's earlier speech, then by emerging from the curtain *after the play is over* to sue for prayer and mercy in the epilogue the character Prospero has, as it were, died from the world of the play and emerged into the other

---

18   Epilogue. See Brandes (ed.), *The Garrick Shakespeare*, Vol. 1, 86.

transcendent world of the audience, to appeal for mercy and to be released to freedom by them, as surely as he has himself just released Ariel. His dying out of the world of the play into another world must of course set the audience in mind of the ending of the play of this life and their dying out of that to face what? what audience? to ask for what release? The play/life metaphor hovers again between its potentials as an alternate expression of despair or of hope and Prospero/Shakespeare, who had after all given those famously despairing lines to Macbeth, picks up the ambiguity in a direct appeal to the audience:

> And my ending is despair,
> Unless I be relieved by prayer,
> Which pierces so that it assaults
> Mercy itself and frees all faults.

If my prayer, says Prospero, pierces and assaults your mercy as I encounter you beyond the world of the play, how much more might our prayers pierce and assault a Mercy which undergirds and is beyond the play of this world, the baseless fabric of this vision. For as surely as this play has ended and I have had to leave it, so surely shall both you and I find one day this great globe dissolve around us, as we leave it. Then we ourselves will have an encounter! Then we will look for pardon! How he brings that home with the flourish of the final couplet before he leaves the stage:

> As you from crimes would pardon'd be,
> Let your indulgence set me free.

Throughout this play, as throughout all his works, Shakespeare has been playing with ideas about truth and feigning, appearance and reality, the relation between the nature to which his art holds a mirror and that other nature, beyond or behind the nature reason measures, from which so much light shines through the window of his art. In this final epilogue he throws out a bridge from the reality of the play, through the reality of the actor/playwright, to the reality of the audience's own lives, and the keystone of that whole bridge, binding all these realities together and allowing them to communicate with one another, is the over-arching Presence and Mercy of One who is present to every level of reality and who is to be engaged and pierced by prayer.

4. Conclusion

Where has all this poetry and playfulness got us in relation to truth? We have seen how a distinction was made between Reason and Imagination which led to a false opposition between them. We have also seen the need to reunite them, to find in them, as the *Dream* puts it. the 'parents and originals' that work together and mutually sustain one another. We have seen in *The Tempest* how a playful imagination can tease out severe and testing questions about truth itself, and about specifically theological truth, as for example the *Tempest*'s imaginative exploration of what would now be called eschatology.

Both our *comprehension* and our *apprehension* of the world are mediated by a series of images and stories which imagination transfigures into metaphor and emblem. These metaphors and emblems in their turn allow us to come at truth, and truth to come at us, in ways which would not otherwise have been possible. Theseus and Hippolyta mend their quarrel. Science comes to recognise imagination as the medium, not the enemy, of its reasoning. So theology in its turn needs both to befriend and to analyse the imagination as part of its quest for truth. The theologian will do well to make both poetry and playfulness companions on that quest.

Chapter 12

Seeing the Word
Aspects of the Visual Culture of the Reformation

William Dyrness

Changes in the visual culture that resulted from the Reformation are often thought to have been sudden and dramatic – characterized both by the radical preaching of the Reformers and the crowds dismantling images and altarpieces in their churches. But such a picture is misleading. Alteration of attitudes toward images and ritual took place slowly and was often contested and contravened. In this chapter we will seek to show that the continued presence of images was accompanied by a gradual change in the way the world was shaped imaginatively. These changes both reflected and influenced theological understandings of the way God's presence was manifest in the world.[1]

The influence of the Reformation in England was carried by those most influenced by Calvin, who later became known as Puritans.[2] These shared with Protestants generally in England an antipathy to the Pope and the sense that England was a chosen nation. But they wanted to take the Reformation further and deeper. They shared Calvin's sense of the corruption of human nature and the need for a radical conversion and a continuing dependence of God's grace. They worshiped in plainly decorated churches and looked to the Bible as their primary authority, spending much of their time reading and memorizing it.[3] What kind of impact did these believers have on the development of English culture?

---

1   This chapter is an earlier and somewhat revised version of sections of my 'England and the visual culture of the Reformation', published in *Reformed Theology and Visual Culture: The Protestant Imagination from Calvin to Edwards* (Cambridge: Cambridge University Press, 2004).

2   What initially were called 'radical' Protestants later came to be called 'Puritans', which was initially a term of reproach. On the development and use of this term see Christopher Hill, *Society and Puritanism in Pre-Revolutionary England* (London: Secker and Warburg, 1964). See Also Christopher Dursten and Jacqueline Eales (eds), *The Culture of English Puritanism, 1560–1700* (New York: St Martins, 1996).

3   These characteristics constitute, Dursten and Eales argue, a kind of 'mentalité' (ibid., 9).

For most believers the most obvious effect of the Reformation was the disappearance of images from their own churches and the new worship patterns that were introduced.[4] The changes in belief and practice that characterize the Reformation, it must be remembered, were carried out almost exclusively at the parish level. Moreover these changes were not being proposed exclusively by the clergy, the people concurred, and even help construct the emerging visual world. And, while they played a different role than they had done previously, images by no means disappeared from their every day lives. There is a growing amount of evidence for the continuing role that images – and other art forms – played in the culture, even among those closest to the Reformation.[5]

1. Cheap Prints and Woodcuts

The issue for the Reformers was not a complete rejection of the visual, so much as the new theological orientation and the corresponding change which resulted in the way culture was formed. The visual element, as cultural practices generally, may appear in places one does not expect to find it, or in forms that have less prestige – at least from our modern perspective. Printing, for example, made possible the production of inexpensive prints which, often, were put with a text and distributed in broadsheets. From evidence that has survived, such prints were cheap enough so that even the poorest could buy them to decorate their homes. Robert Scribner has argued that, in Germany, these popular images were used as propaganda to promote the Reformation cause.[6] Their imagery created, he argues, a kind of symbolic universe in which the truth of the Reformers' preaching was often contrasted with the lies (and immorality) of the monks and priests.[7]

---

4   'The Reformation for most believers meant the Reformation of their parish church.' M. Aston, *England's Iconoclasts*, Vol. 1, (Oxford: Oxford University Press, 1988), p. 16.

5   The more traditional view represented, for example, by John Bossy *Christianity in the West 1400–1700*(Oxford: Oxford University Press, 1985) has been corrected by scholars who have paid more attention to the reception of the Reformation by the people. See, for example, Robert W. Scribner, *For the Sake of the Simple Folk: Popular Propaganda in the German Reformation* (Cambridge: Cambridge University Press, 1981) and Tessa Watt, *Cheap Print and Popular Piety: 1550–1640* (Cambridge: Cambridge University Press, 1991). See further Anthony Wells-Cole, *Art and Decoration in Elizabethan and Jacobean England: The Influence of Continental Prints, 1558–1625* (New Haven: Yale University Press, 1997). Such studies suggest that popular culture both responded to and altered the teaching of the Reformers.

6   Scribner, *For the Sake of the Simple Folk*, 249. He sees these as allied to the preaching mission of the Reformation.

7   Ibid., 8–10. Craig Harbison quotes an Italian in Padua who commented that Lutherans there refused to look at any image 'except those printed on paper'. 'Introduction', ed. Harbison *Symbols in Transformation: Iconographic Themes at the Time of the Reformation: An exhibition of Erwin Panofsky* (Princeton: The Art Museum of Princeton University), p. 15.

Something similar appeared in the ballads and broadsides distributed in England by travelling minstrels – then called then vagrants – at fairs, alehouses and town squares.[8] This phenomenon underlines the interconnection of print and image and the close connection between oral and print culture. Often the broad seller would use his vocal performance of the ballad to sell the printed text of his song, which may or may not have been decorated with images.[9] Alehouses and private homes would certainly have been decorated with these and the painted cloths that were popular in England, reinforcing in imagery the beliefs and ideas of the developing Reformation. Because of their popularity and the composition of the materials, very few of the popular prints survive.[10] A large percentage of these ballads, up into the 1570s at least, conveyed a moral, or religious lesson. All of this spoke of the widespread impact of Reformation ideas,[11] as well as the continuing tolerance for visual imagery.

A more significant example of the role of visual imagery was the use of woodcuts and, later, etchings in printed books. This was common both on the continent and in England. In some cases prints of very high caliber appeared in works of Protestant scholars and publishers.[12] Luther's catechism appeared adorned with prints illustrating many of the commandments and doctrines – even with images of God and the trinity.

Even Calvin's works frequently had images on the title page[13]. Typical is the title page of the 1554 edition of the *Institutes*, which appears more than once, of an axe at the base of a tree, with the Latin inscription around: 'Now the axe is laid at the root of the tree, every tree that does not bear good fruit, is cut down and thrown into the fire' (Matt. 3:10). Another on the *Commentary on the Gospels* (1561) pictures an angel (with a scythe, representing the final judgment) pulling someone from a cave. Around this is written in French, 'From deep places and full of obscurity, God in time extracts truth.' Or the image on both the English translation of the *Form of Prayers* (1556) and the *Catechism* (1556), of a man pointing his walking stick, with a banner over him saying (in Latin) 'Enter by the difficult way' and around him (in English) 'the way to life is straight, and few find it' (Mt. 7:14). The close connection of text (usually of Scripture) and image underlines the fact that the image served to

---

8   See Watt, *Cheap Prints*, 11ff.

9   Ibid., 23.

10   Wells-Cole, *Art and Decoration*, 5.

11   Though these ideas were often modified, Tessa Watt notes, 'by the more conservative outlook of the larger public'. *Cheap Prints*, 4.

12   John N. King, *English Reformation Literature: The Tudor Origins of the Protestant Tradition* (Princeton: Princeton University Press, 1982), 462–64.

13   We know that these images were chosen by Calvin's publisher Robert Estienne and probably not by Calvin himself, though he certainly must have agreed with their use. See Elizabeth Armstrong, *Robert Estienne, Royal Printer: An Historical Study of the Elder Stephanus*. Revised edition. Courtenay Studies in Reformation Theology 6 (Appleford: The Sutton Courtenay Press, 1986).

support the verbal message.[14] In general more images appear in the vernacular texts, than those in Latin, and the numbers decline until images in books are outlawed in 1580.

In England Thomas Cranmer's catechism had prints, at least one of which was by Hans Holbein. Consider the simple print illustrating the Seventh petition of the Lord's Prayer – 'Deliver us from Evil'.[15] Here Jesus delivers a demoniac of a spirit which is actually pictured emerging from the mouth of the man, as amazed and skeptical leaders look on. But Cranmer cautions in the 'sermon' on the second commandment against bowing down to any creature. 'For what can be more contrarie to the dignitie of man, than he, whom God hath made Lorde over all creatures to kneel or do reverence to the image of a creature.'[16] For we are made to stand and look up to God not to kneel before a creature. As to images of Christ and the saints, he admits their bodily nature and allows images of them, 'I will not utterly deny but they may be had. Still for charity sakes they should be kept out of the church. For the goodness that may come from them is not comparable to the evil of idolatry. Why not lift your eyes and your hands to heaven where God is?'

Of more significance was the fact that the two most influential books of the English Reformation – the Bible and John Foxe's *Acts and Monuments* – were illustrated with a large number of prints, some of which were of a high quality.[17] In an important sense these books came to stand in place of the teeming medieval images that populated the imaginative world of the medieval believer. By mid-century in England most images and crucifixes had been removed from the churches. 'Their place in the Church,' writes Ernest Gilman, 'would now be filled by scriptural verses painted on the walls and altar cloths, and by the literary monuments of the Reformation, the English Bible and Foxe's Book of Martyrs.'[18] Most famous of these prints was the title page of the Coverdale Bible, printed in 1535 (probably in Cologne), and by Hans Holbein.[19]

Dominating the images at the top where in medieval iconography God would preside, stands the Hebrew word for God: Jahweh – who could not be 'pictured'. On one side Adam and Eve, on the right a victorious risen Christ – banners read: 'In what day so ever thou eatest thereof thou shalt die', and 'This is my deare sonne in

---

14   See Patrick Collinson, *The Birthpangs of Protestant England: Religious and Cultural Change in the Sixteenth and Seventeenth Centuries* (London: MacMillan, 1988), 117.

15   For illustration, see Dyrness, *Reformed Theology and Visual Culture*, 97.

16   *Catechismus* (London: 1548). Pagination is inconsistent and, in this section, missing.

17   See James Strachan, *Early Bible Illustrations: A Short Study based on some Fifteenth and early Sixteenth Century Printed Texts* (Cambridge: Cambridge University Press, 1957). He notes that before the Reformation most Bibles printed in Europe contained illustrations.

18   Ernest B. Gilman. Iconoclasm and Poetry in the English Reformation (Chicago: University of Chicago, 1986), p. 7.

19   Although this is not certain. For illustration, see Dyrness, *Reformed Theology and Visual Culture*, 99.

whom I delight, heare him'. Down the left side Moses appears receiving and Ezra(?) reading the law, on the other side Christ sends out the disciples to 'preach the Gospel' and an image of Acts 2 shows the disciples receiving the Holy Spirit. Below clerics receive the scriptures from the king. Banners there reiterate: 'O how swete are thy words unto my throte, yeh more than hony' (Ps. 119: 103) and 'I am not ashamed of the Gospell of Christ, for it is the power of God' (Rom 1:16). Additionally in this 1535 Bible there are prints of God creating Eve out of Adam's side; Cain killing Abel; even Bathsheba at her bath!

In the Great Bible of 1541 the frontispiece reverses the Coverdale image and features the king receiving the Bible from the translator, along with lively images of Pharaoh's dream, the burning bush (in which other events from the life of Moses are also portrayed), and David slaying Goliath. The famous Geneva Bible (appearing in 1560)[20] is less lavishly illustrated though there are images of Israel following the cloud through the Red Sea as the Frontispiece, under which is written 'The Lord will fight for you, therefore holde you your peace' (Ex. 14:14). Included among the others are the Ark during the flood and encampment of Israel with the tabernacle. Images in this Bible are particularly significant as this became the most widely read edition up to (and even for a while after) the famous King James Version in 1611.[21]

Equally prominent in the shaping of Protestant life and imagination was the enormous *Actes and Monuments of Matters most Memorable*, by John Foxe (1516-1587), which first appeared in 1563 in a single folio volume.[22] Here the history of the church is interpreted in terms of the persecutions visited upon the true followers of Christ. Foxe's purpose was to extol the martyrs of the reign of Queen Mary, but he put this in the context of a history of the church in which Satan has regularly attacked God's servants.

The graphic and detailed descriptions of the martyrs' deaths were accompanied by the equally graphic prints, images and words reinforcing one another. The great influence of Foxe's work was enhanced by its being approved and recognized by the Bishops of the Church of England, who in 1571 placed chained copies in every church. It probably did more than any other book to develop the notion of England and its people as having been especially chosen by God.[23]

Protestants then during the first generation of the Reformation would have been confronted with graphic images of the stories they heard read in Church and of the testimonies of those who suffered during the reign of Mary. In the images in

---

20   So-called for its having been printed in Geneva by Rowland Hall.

21   Wells-Cole contends the 1560 edition is the Bible 'people would have read at home and it remained so until well after the publication in 1611 of the Authorized Version' (*Art and Decoration*, xii). Strachan notes, however, that the woodcuts dropped out of later editions of the Geneva Bible. Indeed by the time the AV appeared 'the fashion for small woodcut illustrations had died out'. *Early Bible Illustrations*, 86.

22   Printed in London by John Day. An expanded (and larger) version appeared in two large volumes in 1583, which was later updated and reprinted into the seventeenth century.

23   W. Haller, *The Elect Nation: The Meaning and Relevance of Foxe's* Book of Martyrs (New York: Harper & Row, 1963). And see King, *English Reformation Literature*, p. 428.

catechisms, the Bible and Foxe's 'Book of Martyrs' one might describe the beginning of a Protestant iconography. On the one hand these images primarily reinforce the centrality of Scriptural texts and events. These events, or their contemporary equivalents, are clearly and simply pictured, in ways that would be accessible to anyone, often with accompanying words. On the other hand, in Foxe's *Acts and Monuments*, the so-called 'Book of Martyrs', the saints of the church featured in medieval iconography are replaced by martyrs and 'heroes of the faith' who suffered for their faith. In many ways Foxe develops a Protestant hagiography. Pictures often appear with accompanying legends to underline the significance of the person.

In all instances, the images were not meant to stand alone as 'works of art' – even if some would qualify as fine prints. For they were not made to be seen as ends in themselves. Here words and images interact so that the one reinforces the other, making the impact of the event clear – especially for children and lay readers. As John King puts it, the 'illustrations serve to break down whatever barrier may exist between reader and text'.[24] Lying behind this of course are the theological convictions that the transcendent God is mediated only by a faithful (and internal) appropriation of Scripture. It is through the word, read, preached and heard, that the saving truth of God's love is brought home to the hearts of the hearer by the ministry of the Holy Spirit. Art, when it is allowed, is subordinated to this much more important work. Reformation art, like medieval philosophy, functions *ancilla domini* – a means to a higher end.

Histories of art regularly pass over the Reformation quickly as insignificant for subsequent art history. The art historians are right in one sense: no particular tradition of visual art is begun by the use of images such as those we have described. Nor does the use of imagery flower as the sixteenth century goes on – quite the opposite. In 1580 all biblical images were banned in Geneva, even in printed books; in England a clear reaction to imagery takes hold after that date.[25] In spite of this growing reaction against imagery it is surely a mistake to ignore the cultural significance of what might be called the theological imagination that was developing. While the influence might be subtle it is surely not absent in subsequent art history.

2. Protestant Architecture and Gardens

Visual culture appears not only in the specific images that might be placed in books or hung on walls of house or church, but above all in the structuring of the spaces in which believers were to live. It has been known for some time that some of the most important architects in seventeenth century France were Huguenots, but nothing much was made of this fact until recently. In fact when the Calvinist

---

24 King, *English Reformation Literature*, 129.
25 S. Michalski, *The Reformation and the Visual Arts*, 72. On the situation in England see Patrick Collinson, *The Birthpangs of Protestant England: Religious and Cultural change in the Sixteenth and Seventeenth Centuries* (London: MacMillan, 1988), 99ff. Also see the qualifications suggested in Tessa Watt, *Cheap Prints*, 135.

Bernard Palissy's works were edited and published in 1888 the editors expressed their amusement at his attempts to mix his Protestantism with 'ancient truth'. His placing of biblical passages on the four fountains of the garden, they note, may come from his piety, but they are also odd.[26] But recently Catherine Randall has argued that these architects worked out of a particularly Calvinist conception both of space and the natural world. For them Calvin's *Institutes* provided a kind of blueprint that served as a (usually hidden) agenda for their work for the Catholic Court of France. Randall notes: 'Scripturally modeled structures and spaces provide the theatre for the enactment of salvation in the text of these Calvinist architects.'[27]

The most famous of these was Bernard Palissy (1510–90). He was born in Saint-Pons in the south of France, where he became a part of the newly formed Reformed congregation, though he spent much of his life working for the French Court in Paris. Perhaps his most famous work was in planning the Tuileries palaces and Gardens for Catherine de Medici.[28] In 'La Recept Veritable' published in 1563 he lays out his views (what he calls his philosophy) of architecture and agriculture.[29] Here he expresses what must be called modern ideas of working with nature, and respecting the dignity of creation – he has harsh words for those ignorant people who destroy the forests and by this their own future (101–103). But the central notion of the work is the elaborate plan for his 'delectable garden'. In a description that recalls Augustine's conversion experience, he recalls his hearing psalm 104 beautifully sung, and contemplates the sense of this psalm. In what must be an early use of 'imagination' in the modern sense, on the basis of this psalm, he 'pictures' to himself a garden where exiles from persecution can come and find rest. Interestingly he says that he contemplated drawing the landscapes of the psalm in some pictures. But seeing that paintings do not last long, he decided to find a convenient place to construct a garden, that matched the design and beauty of the psalm. Having already drawn this garden in my mind, he says, I considered how I might be able to erect such a palace or amphitheatre (24).

Palissy's plans are based on the fact that God has made the earth to replenish itself, an activity that goes on all the time (46). His garden is built as a square with arboreal arches at each side, intersected with pathways that meet at a pyramid in the center (71–95). There are four fountains inscribed with biblical phrases such as 'the fountain of wisdom is the word of the Lord' and 'the fear of the Lord is the beginning of wisdom' (85, 86).

Though never explicitly stated it is clear that the garden is an image of salvation. For he notes it is a 'refuge' (24) from those who would destroy him, and a retreat

---

26   Bernard Palissy, *Les Oeuvres de Bernard Palissy*, edited by P. Fillon (Niort: Clouzot Librairie, 1888), Vol. 1, li.
27   Catherine Randall Coates 'Structuring Protestant Scriptural Space in Sixteenth Century Catholic France', *SCJ* 25:2 (1994), 341–53 (349); also *Building Codes: The Aesthetics of Calvinism in Early Modern Europe* (Philadelphia: University of Pennsylvania, 1999).
28   Palissy, *Oeuvres*, Vol. I, lix, lx.
29   Ibid., 1–129. Page numbers in the text are to this work. Translations are mine.

from these 'perilous and evil times' (95). Sometimes when I'm asleep, he says, I seem to be already in my garden enjoying its fruit. When he 'comes to consider the marvelous actions that the Lord has asked his creation to perform ... I am completely amazed by the providence of God' (97, 98). Even when he leaves the garden he is able to see wisdom everywhere: All is clothed with wisdom (99). After lamenting those ignorant and foolish people who despise those who work with their hands and spend their time seeking benefices to purchase, he concludes there will always be those who persecute the righteous. 'Take your refuge then in your chief, protector and captain, our Lord Jesus Christ, who, in his time and place, will know how to avenge the wrongs done to him, and to us' (114).

The object then of his work in planning, planting and building, is to make his work an image of his 'delectable garden', that is an image of redemption. For when one has found his or her refuge one can see the world in terms of the wisdom that God has placed in it. But this vista can be missed! One can only 'see' this natural symbolism if one's eyes are purified, that is if one sees through the eyes of faith. As if to give flesh and blood to his 'image of salvation', at the end of his work he tells the story of his own Reformed Church at Saint-Pons beginning in 1546. Little by little it prospered and became widely admired in spite of suffering and much persecution, like Daniel in the Lion's Den, he notes (118). But on Sunday these folk, 'take walks in the meadow, woods, or some other pleasant place, and in such places they love to sing all kinds of holy songs' (125). For, despite their enemies, having found their peace in Christ, they are able to go out and enjoy the peace that God has placed in the world.

Catherine Randall points out how closely Palissy follows the structure implied in Calvin's *Institutes*. Indeed his imaginary garden, Randall argues, is an 'entexted structure' that reflects the transformation that Christ has made possible. Though fallen, through artifice the world can be restructured, in the same way that the invisible church for Calvin may be super-imposed on the visible. 'Palissy's garden renders literal Calvin's conception of believers as a new "garden of Eden".'[30]

A further example is French architect Salomon de Caus, a French Huguenot who came to England in 1611 to redesign the gardens of Richmond Palace in the 'new manner'. De Caus's views on his work are laid out in his work on perspective published in London in 1612.[31] Interestingly, like Palissy, Caus makes no explicit reference to Calvin, but, also like that architect, he seems at times to be repeating sections of the *Institutes*. All that is built should be, asserts de Caus in his notice to the reader, for utility and pleasure. This is true for all the work of architects, engineers and painters. Especially the latter, he says. 'The art of painting consists in representing a natural thing and making it appear natural when it is seen. This cannot be well done without using appropriate reasons which are unique to this science and

---

30   *Building Codes*, 45–55 (55).

31   Salomon de Caus, *La Perspective avec La Raison des ombres et miroirs* (London: Norbon, 1612), n.p.. See the discussion of his work in England in Roy C. Strong, *The English Icon: Elizabethan and Jacobean Portraiture* (London: Pantheon, 1969)..

which serve to put all lines and traces in their place.' Nothing gives pleasure when it is seen like perspective, he notes, both in writing and drawing. But it is not easy to sense by writing alone when dealing with natural objects, these must be 'pictured' and built. In his only reference to God he says simply at the close of the introduction: 'May God guard you.' Then follows a discourse, amply illustrated with drawings, on properly drawing and building in perspective and in the proper relation to light and shadow. All centers on the eye, lines represent the surface of the earth or right angles to that surface, light and shade come from the rays of the sun or fire. Palissy interestingly had similarly noted that all structure in architecture comes from the tree and the human body.

Much of this of course is not original and could have been said by anyone trained in the classic sources rediscovered in the Renaissance, especially, in this case, Vitrivius. But that is just the point. This is not an art that intends to call attention to itself. Catherine Randall notes that these architects coded a hidden agenda in their work, which was intended to leave no trace. They mean their efforts to be a 'process which will enact the Reformation of the created order (and then will be no longer necessary)'.[32] Art here serves religion, but not at all in the medieval sense. It now serves what is to these architects the higher calling of religion, that program of making right a distorted created order. Walking in a 'delectable garden', strolling in a well ordered space, one does not necessarily think of God. But these are spaces that can, to these builders, 'picture' God nevertheless.

Notice further the role of the creative capabilities of the mind. If anything the human imagination is challenged to play a greater role in making and building than it did in making devotional images. For it was only after Palissy had already pictured this garden in his mind, on the basis of the 'sense' of Scripture, that he was able to begin the actual design of projects. The irony of the Protestant imagination may be said to lie precisely here: While denying the right to picture anything that might be mistaken for God, and by forcing faith inward, into the deepest recesses of the human spirit, religion was creating a space for the mind to operate differently. From picturing what was absent, imagination is redirected here to picture things which have never yet existed; and this new world having been imagined, is precisely what subsequent generations of Reformed Protestants set about constructing.[33]

3. A New (Protestant) Culture

Modern art historians who spend their time in museums and galleries may be forgiven for not finding much of interest in the Reformation period. For the Reformers of this period had a larger project in mind: the structuring of a new order of society that better reflected their (newly appropriated) understanding of Scripture. To their minds

---

32   Randall, 'Structuring Protestant Scriptural Space', 346.
33   See Huston Diehl's parallel suggestion concerning attitudes toward the labyrinth in 'Into the Maze of self: the Protestant Transformation of the image of the Labyrinth', *Journal of Medieval and Renaissance Studies* 16: 2 (1986), 281–301.

of course, the art which survived from the Middle Ages, not only did little to promote this project, it often stood in the way. Nevertheless, for a while they tolerated a great deal of imagery, as we have seen, as long as it was purged of older associations.

The concern of the Reformers for the larger issues of society grew from their reading and exposition of Scripture. The culture that resulted, was, through and through, a Scripture culture. But, as Patrick Collinson remarks, the Bible was for them not a straightjacket, but a 'rich and infinitely varied source of imagination and formal inspiration'.[34] We have seen already that it stimulated what imagery was allowed, and it may have been a stimulus for architectural design, even drama. The source of this influence was not, in the first instance, though, the direct application of biblical truth to life, but the reading, hearing, singing, and memorizing of Scripture which formed the center and focus of Protestant worship, indeed of all of life. This focus developed its own set of cultural practices. The culture which resulted distanced itself from certain kinds of images, but at the same time encouraged other forms of visual culture.

The most public contact with Scripture for most people would have been the regular preaching of the word in worship. Peter Burke notes that 'Protestant culture was a sermon culture. Sermons might last for hours and they might be a great emotional experience involving audience participation, with members of the congregation exclaiming, sighing or weeping.'[35] As the century wore on the performance of the sermon took on more and more importance, until it became for many people their primary cultural experience, even their main source of political information and ideas.[36] Since the ear was more to be trusted than the eye, late sixteenth century preachers could pull out all the stops and use any dramatic technique available to catch the attention of the congregation.[37] The modern attention given to the Elizabethan theatre may serve to obscure the contemporary significance of preaching as a cultural event. Paul Seaver argues that 'even in sophisticated London the popular preachers attracted larger audiences week after week than Shakespeare or Jonson did in their prime.'[38]

Scripture reading, preaching and memorization not only occupied the Sabbath times of believer's lives but also created a unique form of popular culture.[39] This culture centered of course on the preaching of sermons, which in many ways had

---

34 Ibid., 95.

35 Burke, *Popular Culture*, 226.

36 Hill, *Society and Puritanism*, 32. See also Phyllis Mack Crew, *Calvinist Preaching and Iconoclasm in the Netherlands 1544–1569* (Cambridge: Cambridge University Press, 1978).

37 Bryan Crockett, '"Holy Cozenage" and the Renaissance Cult of the Ear' in *Sixteenth Century Journal*, 24.1 (1993), 47–65..

38 Paul Seaver, *The Puritan Lectureship: the Politics of Religious Dissent* (Palo Alto: Stanford University Press, 1970), 5.

39 See Patrick Collinson, 'Elizabethan and Jacobean Puritanism as forms of popular culture', in Durston, Christopher and Eales, Jacequline (eds), *The Culture of English Puritanism, 1560–1700* (New York: St. Martin's, 1996).

become dramatic performances. So important was this that people would travel long distances in the company of 'friends in the Lord' to hear an unusually good preacher. On the way they would share and receive hospitality, and sing the Psalms which they had grown to love at their services. As the dignified and majestic singing of Psalms became their hallmark, Calvinists were, in fact, often called 'Psalm singers'. They sang everywhere, at home, at work, in prison, even on the way to their death.40 Even their enemies called their haunting tunes, melodious and delectable, and many were attracted to their services because of it.

In many ways the center of this popular culture was to be found in the special fasts which the Puritans held. These were not the regular fasts of the Church calendar (nor were they sanctioned by the Bishop) but specially organized fasts for some particular purpose. They often amounted to a kind of religious rally, where special preachers would be invited, offerings would be received for special causes, and a general time of religious awakening – sometimes including ecstatic experiences and exorcisms. Often people would travel great distances to these fasts, in a kind of Protestant version of the pilgrimage. Indeed Collinson points out that in many respects these were a kind of Protestant version of the old, now forbidden, festival days.[41]

4. A New Imaginative Structure

In terms of cultural production Protestants did not so much deny culture, as is sometimes argued, as transfer their cultural energies into new forms. Traditional recreations were out, though there remained a residue of these – they did allow horse-racing, foot races, bonfires, gala dinners and, above all, sermons.[42] Traditional forms of graphic art and painting were not emphasized, but, as Tessa Watt shows, they 'transferred their efforts to other forms of print, to be used in very different contexts'.[43] Prayer books, Psalters, books of sermons, handbooks of devotion, religious treatises of various kinds proliferated. These are not without their own literary value, nor without influence on the development of literature, as we have hinted. Still we need to acknowledge that by 1580 a certain tightening had taken place. By this time all religious drama was banished. Already in the 1560s all pictures were being eliminated in 'almanacs' published in Geneva and Lyon, by 1580 all images were banned from books published in Geneva. After this time in Calvinist influenced areas Bibles and other books were no longer illustrated (and

---

40   W. Stanford Reid. 'The Battle Hymns of the Lord: Calvinist Psalmody of the 16th century', *Sixteenth Century Essays and Studies*, Vol. II (1971), 44.

41   Collinson, 'Elizabethan and Jacobean Puritanism', 50ff. See also Leigh Schmidt, *Holy Fairs: Scottish Communions and American Revivals in the Early Modern* Period (Princeton: Princeton University Press, 1989).

42   Collinson, 'Elizabethan and Jacobean Puritanism', 44.

43   Watt, *Cheap Prints*, 69.

those that were, continued to use prints previously produced). What was happening around 1580 to cause this retreat from traditional imagery?

Collinson has argued that this date marks the beginning of a period that he calls, after Karl-Josef Höltigen, iconophobic. This momentous change he describes as a change from the visual to 'the invisible, abstract and didactic word.'[44] Tessa Watt, while acknowledging that a tightening takes place in mid Elizabethan Protestant culture, thinks this thesis misleading. She argues that 'Collinson has overstated the extent to which people were cut off from traditional Christian imagery.'[45] For one thing the thesis overlooks the way that the visual and the oral are interrelated in culture. While Reformers tried to cut the ancient link between worship and the visual (and even the dramatic), this did not keep the people from responding to visual and dramatic elements in the worship. Moreover, in the prints, wall hangings, even in the published books a – sometimes rich – visual culture survived amidst the strictures of the Reformers' teaching.

Still something was changing toward the end of the century. Perhaps, up to this point, the question that the Reformers had faced from the beginning had not been finally answered: Having given up the complex iconography of the Middle Ages, how is one to embody and communicate the truth to the faithful? Preaching the Word was central of course, but what visible shape would this take? Calvin provided an important part of the answer to that in proposing the shape of the creed, as embodied in the *Institutes*, as a kind of 'icon' by which the truth of God and the world may be accessed. We have suggested that certain architects and dramatists may have, perhaps unconsciously, developed the implications of this new understanding of God's 'invisible' presence in creation and human affairs. But beyond these isolated (and unsystematic) instances, all attempts at using imagery, drama, even cultural festivities, in the service of the communication of Christian truth appeared to be given up by around 1580.

We might think of the change in terms of two influences that came together during this time. These developments would gradually begin to influence the larger culture in respect to the visible shape that Christian truth should now take.

On the one hand the continuing polemic against what the Reformers saw as decadent forms of popular culture, effectively closed down creativity in these areas. Only the purely Christian subcultural practices which we have described were now encouraged. On the other hand a new way of 'imagining' the world was emerging that would take the place of previous ways of thinking about truth and, eventually, about culture.

---

44 Collinson, *Birthpangs of Protestant England*, 99, 117. Collinson echoes the thesis of Walter Ong in *Orality and Literacy: The Technologizing of the Word* (London: Methuen, 1982).
45 Watt, *Cheap Prints*, 135, 136.

First it is clear that polemics against a decadent culture were not new, they appear in Calvin, and, in England in William Tyndale, among others.[46] But around 1580 such attacks seemed suddenly to proliferate. In 1581, for example, Thomas Lovell published 'A Dialogue Between Custom and Veritie concerning the use and abuse of Dauncing and Minstlery'.[47] In his Epistle to the Reader, Lovell notes significantly that the benefits which God bestowed upon us are so great that our weak wits are not able to comprehend them. For this reason our best and wisest course is to follow the law (in Scripture) which is given to us 'pure and whole' and not at any time seek to 'please ourselves.' He goes on to elaborate this point: pleasing ourselves means to speak our own words and go after our own imagination, and seek our own will. All of this 'going our own way', focusing as it does on 'imagination' (used in an entirely negative sense) which might be said to accompany (a certain kind of) cultural production, is contrasted simply with the encouragement that we 'do good'. He concludes: 'For when we do more practice our vain pleasures, then do we more after our own wicked imagination.' He focuses in particular on the Sabbath, he notes, because it is a 'figure' of our endless life with God which he grants us in his mercy. By contrast to common practices of popular culture, the Sabbath is decidedly not consecrated to the abominable idol of fleshly pleasure.

In the following dialogue between custom and veritie, Lovell proceeds (in rhymed verse!) to describe the contrast between these forms of culture. Dancing comes in for particular attack. David danced before the Lord, but, alas, 'in these days in this dance few delight.' Dancing should be avoided because it arouses passion, and, besides, there are far better ways of finding a wife. Even if the rare person can partake of such activities safely, many others would fall. He concludes: Not against right use, but the abuse

> Of things has been my fight.
> God grant his spirit may quicken us
> > Good fruit our trees may bring.
> We may not fall in firey lake
> > Where doth no mercy spring.

As is typical of Puritan polemics, Lovell insists the activity itself is not wrong. But no guidance or encouragement is offered as to what shape such 'right use' might take. Indeed any mental activity which might be used to think about this in a wholesome way is forbidden as vain imagination. Whatever young readers might have thought about such a treatise (the 'poetic' form Lovell uses surely is meant to attract their

---

46 See Tyndale's famous exchange with Sir Thomas More, 'The Dialogue concerning Tyndale', in More's *English Works* (1557), edited by W. E. Campbell (London: Eyre and Spottiswoode, 1927).

47 London: John Allde. Not paginated. In this and the following reference I have modernized the English.

attention to what he has to say), they would find there no help in 'transforming' such cultural practices.[48]

Two years later Phillip Stubbes published his work: 'The Anatomie of Abuses, a briefe summarie of notable vices'.[49] Stubbes addresses here plays, dancing, gaming and 'such like'. Not as though he is opposed to 'any kind of exercise in general', he pleads, 'but only their abuses'. When these are cut away, Stubbes argues, these practices are 'not only of great ancestries, but also very honest and commendable exercises' (1, 2). There follows then a dialogue between Spudeus and Philoponus. The latter has just returned from a long journey to an imaginary land, clearly meant to represent the 'worldly' life of many of his contemporaries, and which he proceeds to describe: It is a blessed land, with a wicked people. But why can't we just let them be, Spudeus asks? We cannot, Philoponus responds, for their sufferings are our sufferings, and we are called to weep with those who weep. Of the abuses listed, pride heads the list, as the beginning of all evil of heart, mouth and apparel (10). The latter, Stubbes argues, offends God worse than other things. Going beyond Calvin, he argues that decency is enough in respect to our dress; we must reject 'novel inventions and new fangled fasions' (14). He complains at length about make-up, ruffles, shoes, socks, earrings, coats, even perfume. All of this which serves to paint our living sepulchre is clearly meant to 'delight the eyes of unchaste beholders' (24). All inventors of such things are clearly guilty of the evil which follows (83) – an indictment that surely must have discouraged any creativity among tailors and jewellers!

Unsurprisingly, all forms of sexual impurity and gluttony are attacked. As to the latter, food is given merely to sustain us. We are 'not to delight and wallow therein continually' (113). As in Lovell, this way of life should replaced by one in which we do good to our neighbor. In contrast to practices which appeal to our lust and vanity, he argues forcefully, we should give liberally to the poor (115). Then he proceeds to attack especially those things which increase the burden of the poor: drunkenness, enclosure of the commons, usury (which he likens to murder) and the abuse of the Sabbath.

Turning to stage plays, Stubbes has particularly strong words for the divines who had (previously) written what he calls sacrilegious plays. Profane plays only nourish vice and feature mostly vagrants and beggars. Of maypole activities he claims, on good authority he says, that of a hundred women who go, only a third return undefiled. Though there could be a dancing before the Lord (189), dancing, in general, is an introduction to whoredom (196). Even music which is a good gift of God has been abused by minstrelsy. Bear baiting is forbidden as the abuse of one of God's creatures, as is cockfighting and hunting (210). God is abused when these

---

48 Though it may not have been Lovell's intent, soon after his attack, godly popular songs were out of fashion. *Birthpangs*, 110.

49 London: Richard Jones, 1983. Pagination added in the copy in the Huntington Library.

creatures are! All of this, Stubbes concludes in a typically millennial vein, suggests that the latter days of which Scripture speak are already at hand.

What is striking to the modern reader is the mixture of relatively radical social views, concerning care for the poor (and the social and economic adjustments that are needed) and the treatment of animals, along with what appears to be a reactionary refusal to allow any rethinking or reworking of the contemporary popular culture. Stubbes' worry is clearly not about the absence of creativity in the cultural sphere, but a more deep-seated anxiety about society itself. Cultural energies were being refocused toward these more pressing needs, and all their creativity was challenged into this larger social and cultural project.

But paralleling, and in many ways shaping, this cultural critique is the development of what is no less than an entire alternative religious imagination with repercussions in every area of culture. This is the project of giving the world a new mental shape. The example of Palissy illustrates the way in which, for many Reformed believers, Calvin's *Institutes* themselves functioned as a kind of verbal 'icon'. A life that is shaped according to this plan, Reformed Christians believed, like creation itself, will mirror the divine presence. This fresh way of 'imaging' truth diminished the prospects in some cultural areas, but it led to other kinds of culture products that are often overlooked.[50] An important stage in this process can be seen in editions of the Institutes that appeared after Calvin's death in 1564. In the 1580 edition, the structuring of the *Institutes* took its final shape. This was accompanied by 'epitomes' which 'summed up' the argument of the work. The 1585 edition includes a long complex structure of the argument in the preface of the work that was to become definitive into the seventeenth century.[51] At about this same time other epitomes of Calvin's works began to appear, some with elaborate charts.

Highly influential in all this was the 'logic' of Peter Ramus, a French Huguenot who died in the St. Barthomew's massacre in 1572.[52] Ramus was a extremely popular and influential professor of rhetoric and logic in Paris, becoming in midcentury first Director, then Regius Professor in the Collège de France, converting to Protestantism in 1561. He believed his logic to be the key to all right knowledge and that it was the natural extension of Calvin's understanding of the world as ordered by God. There were 1100 separate printings of Ramist works between 1550 and 1650, and his Dialectic (1555) alone went through more than 100 editions during that period.[53]

---

50   Watt, Cheap Prints, p. 54.

51   See Richard A. Muller, 'In the Light of Orthodoxy: The "Method and Disposition" of Calvin's *Institutio* from the perspective of Calvin's late-sixteenth century editors' in Sixteenth Century Journal, 28.4 (1997), 1203–1229.

52   See ibid., 1221. On Ramus life and work see Walter J. Ong, *Ramus and the Decay of Dialogue: From the Art of Discourse to the Art of Reason* (Harvard: Harvard University Press, 1958); R. Hooykaas, *Humanisme, science et réforme: Pierre de la Ramée* (Leyden: E. J. Brill, 1958). For the general background of Renaissance logic see Neal W. Gilbert, *Renaissance Concepts of Method* (New York: Columbia University Press, 1960).

53   Hooykaas believes it was one of the three or four most influential works in the sixteenth century. Hooykaas, *Humanisme*, 3; and Ong, *Decay*, 5. Hooykaas notes that his

Two elements of Ramus' work call for special attention, both having to do with the implications for the developing mental habits of Protestants. The first is his emphasis on following what he regarded as the natural order of things as a way of reaching their true essence. By this he meant that a given subject should be laid out, and even diagrammed in a way that reflected its true structure. Those who studied and followed Ramus had a sense of being liberated from the accretions of medieval logic and pedagogy. While traditional scholars read and reread texts in order to write their commentaries, Ramus said that one must learn what is actually practical. In light of the definitions, partitions, digressions and axioms by which medieval reasoning proceeded, it is not hard to imagine that Ramus' ordered structure seemed to be a breath of fresh air. Like the spiritual liberation Reformation believers experienced from the confusing mediations of medieval saints, their teachers must have felt an intellectual release by following Ramus' model of approaching material directly and ordering it clearly.

A particular aesthetic style of course followed necessarily from this direct method. Ramus, writing in 1569, had this to say about the work of poets:

> This is what the poet does as a major part of his tactics, when he sets out to sway the people, the many-headed monster. He deceives in all sorts of ways. He starts at the middle, often proceeding thence to the beginning, and getting on to the end by some equivocal and unexpected dodge.[54]

As a result those poets who would 'delight and move' will not, except indirectly, be able to teach. And clear teaching of course is a driving motive of Ramus' (and other Reformers') thinking. Such thinking did not discourage poetry altogether, but it surely discouraged a certain kind of poetry. Indeed subsequent Protestant poets would boast of their liberation from elaborate metaphoric strictures. See for example the following poem of George Herbert (1593–1633), Jordan I:

---

conversion to Protestantism was really the last step in a gradual evolution, rather than a crisis (99).

54   Quoted in ibid., 253.

Who sayes that fictions onely and false hair
Become a verse? Is there in truth no beautie?
Is all good structure in a winding stair?
May no lines passe except they do their dutie
Not to a true, but painted chair?

Is it no verse, except enchanted groves
And sudden arbours shadow course-spunne lines?
Must purling streams refresh a lover's loves?
Must all be vail'd, while he that reades divines,
Catching the sense at two removes?

Shepherds are honest people; let them sing;
Riddle who list, for me, and pull for Prime.
I envie no man's nightingale or spring;
Nor let them punish with loss of rhyme,
Who plainly say, *My God, my King*.[55]

Is there in truth no beauty? This could be a summary of the developing Puritan aesthetic. There is beauty, the Puritan who read Calvin and now Ramus would say, only in truth. Because this best suits the order of things which God has made.

But the second element that was learned from Ramus, is equally important. There is not only a practical and natural directness to Ramus' dialectic, but also a handy way that this can be put down in a visual form. The truth can be readily 'outlined' – to give it its modern term, so that one can tell at a glance the structure of the material under consideration. While this may seem strange to us living on the far side of the scientific revolution, Ramus and those that followed him, when they put objects or concepts down in this clear and ordered way, felt that they were getting closer to the things as they actually are.

Ramus himself uses a metaphor that helps us understand something of the euphoria he felt over this new approach to truth and reality. All the rules and principles are there, we can learn them but they may still do us no good. Imagine then that you put all of them on small slips of paper and placed these in a giant urn and mix them thoroughly. Now what dialectic can help one order all these properly? The method is simple. Place them all around and discover the universal and general first, then the secondary and special afterward. So pick out of the urn what is most general of all, then that which is a part (or parts) of that, and so on until all has been laid out.[56]

Ramus' influence in England was large, especially among the Puritans. Partly this is due to the way his practical orientation connected with ideas that pre-existed him there.[57] But as his works became more widely known it is possible to note

---

55   George Herbert Palmer (ed.), *The English Works of George Herbert Newly Arranged and Annotated and Considered in Relation to His Life*, Volume 2 (London: Hodder and Stoughton, 1905), 87–9.
56   In Ong, *Decay*, 245, 246.
57   See Hooykaas, *Humanisme*, 115.

specific ways his thinking made its impact. Professors at Cambridge were already reading him during the 1560s, but the first English translation appeared in 1581 as *The Logik of the Most Excellent Philosopher P. Ramus Martyr*.[58] Here his work is condensed into a little under one hundred pages, for a generation of eager readers. Something of the sense of entering a new world is captured in the address to the reader. There the various aspects of Ramus' work are correlated with justice (leaving aside rhetoric including only what is unique to logic), verity (use only the rules and precepts which are necessarily true), and wisdom (treat general matters generally and particulars particularly without mixture).[59] Then follows book one, 'invention' and book two 'judgment' – arguments are ordered so that we can judge rightly. 'And last he shall knit and join together with apt transitions the end of every declaration with the beginning of the next. And so having defined, divided, and knit together the parts of the etymology, he shall make everything more manifest and plain, with most fit and special examples.' Any violation of this through insertion of digressions and irrelevancies 'is preposterous and out of all good fashion and order.'[60]

The influence of Ramist thinking was soon visible in the physical layout of published works in England. The 1983 edition of Foxe's 'Book of Martyrs', now expanded to two large volumes, while continuing to reprint the images from the earlier work, now has Ramist diagrams added at significant points to 'sum up' the argument.[61]

The 1600 and 1603 editions of the Geneva Bible no longer include images but they do include a significant diagram facing the first chapter of Genesis which lays out the structure of the Scripture – the running commentaries of Gilby have been reduced to this 'epitome' of the teaching of Scripture.

Tessa Watt comments of this period: 'All of the author's or publisher's visual creativity has gone into arranging the brackets and exploiting the possibilities of ... different fonts, which organization is somehow meant to render Scriptural precepts more accessible.'[62]

Broadsides which combined this new 'visual order' with the teaching of Scripture became common. Late in the sixteenth century, for example, we find a broadside picturing two gloves which are to be used to teach the young. Each finger, as it is ticked off, recalls one of the ten commandments. To the image is added a godly poem by William Powell (d. 1567). Such broadsides were meant to be devotional aids, not so very different from those medieval preachers might have used. Except that now the image is an ordered structure that will assist one in assessing one's life in relation to God's truth and one's approaching death. The image is meant to be inwardly appropriated, but is believed to 'show' the structure of reality as it really is.

---

58   Translated by M. Poll and M. Hamlini (London: Thomas Vantrolier, 1581).
59   Ibid., 8–10.
60   Ibid., 96, 97.
61   For illustration see Dyrness, *Reformed Theology and Visual Culture*, 134. The chart included in the Geneva Bible in 1600 and 1603 is to be seen in Figure 14 (136).
62   Watt, *Cheap Prints*, 242.

This new appropriation of reality, Frances Yates argued, is really an appropriation of the ancient art of memory.63 Every subject is now to be laid out and arranged in a dialectical order and then memorized in this order. It has become an epitome. But, she notes, the older idea of putting actual images in the places to be memorized has gone. In its place are divided and composed items in their order. Ironically, she notes the actual images in their medieval presentation had been employed to convey moral and religious truth. But they are banished, she claims, by an internal 'iconoclasm', corresponding, and following from the outer one.

Something is clearly lost, and she is right to point it out. But at the same time is there not something that is encouraged? William Perkins writing near the end of the century gives a hint of what this might be. In his famous work A Reformed Catholike: Or, a Declaration shewing how neere we may come to the present church of Rome in sundrie points of religion and wherein we must forever depart64 Perkins writes what would have passed for ecumenical discussion in the late sixteenth century. Responding to the suggestion of some that the Protestant and Catholic churches may be reunited he suggests points in which there is agreement and others where there is none – where the difference is as between light and darkness. As one of the points in which they differ, he proceeds, in the ninth part to address images in particular. He acknowledges the civil use (in buildings and on coins) and even the private use to which images may rightly be put. He reiterates Calvin's point: 'We hold the historical use of images to be good and lawful therefore and that is to represent to the eye the acts of histories, whether they be human or divine: and thus we thinke the histories of the Bible may be painted in private places' (172). The true pattern of virtue however, he insists, comes not by an artist but by the word of God. Here Perkins seems to go beyond Calvin. For this pattern, Perkins claims, is what provides us with the 'real presence of Christ': When the word comes to the ear 'the thing signified comes to the mind; and thus by relation the word and the thing spoken of, are both present together' (185).65 This is no 'iconoclasm of the mind'. To the contrary, the mind is actually allowed, and now absent the surrounding visual cues, given space and opportunity, to 'picture' what is being said.

An important instance of this is the writing of Richard Bernard, a minister in Nottinghamshire, in 1610. His devotional work is pointedly entitled: 'Contemplative Pictures with wholesome Precepts'.66 Following Ramus he contrasts 'disputation' with the kind of practical religion that follows from an inward grasp of God's truth. 'By troublesome disputations men get knowledge to approve the good, but by quiet meditations men grow to more conscience (sic) in their ways, and do increase in grace' (Preface). What now will be the focus of this meditation? One is to meditate

---

63   Which, she argues, has a long tradition behind it going back to Cicero. See Frances Yates, *The Art of Memory* (London: Routledge, Kegan and Paul, 1966), 232–35.

64   Iohn Legat: Printer to the University of Cambridge, 1598. Pages in text.

65   Perkins goes on to say that when we take it the body and blood of Christ are both present 'to our mind'.

66   London: William Hall, 1610. Pages in the text, preface is not paginated.

on the 'pictures' that Bernard proceeds to draw (the book has no images). These inward 'images' are contrasted with the external ones which the Catholic Church approves. As he describes his purpose in the preface:

> Here ... of all these are certain pictures, not popish and sensible for superstition, but mental for divine contemplation; whereto are added wholesome precepts for direction after godly meditation, God's picture, to behold him, that is good; to admire his excellency, to fear his majesty, to praise his bounty.

The first chapter is 'the Picture of God'. This includes a graphic description of God based on biblical language: 'His face is a flame of fire, his voice thunder, his wrath, dread and terrible horror' (5). Then he describes how creation also speaks of this God, concluding: 'Fear this God, believe him to be, know him rightly, behold him invisibly, conceive him without idolatry' (12). Then there is the 'Picture of the Father': 'Did ever a loving father put his darling to death, to prevent from his enemy the force of his wrath? We see it not, stories record it not, nature suffers it not. Yet this father killeth his best son, to kiss his worst creature' (24, 25). There follows 'pictures' of the Devil, and evil ('the creature's deformity'). To the latter is appended the precept: 'Love not (reader) the works of darkness, lest thy eyes cannot behold the light' (84). Upon reflecting on heaven the reader is admonished: 'O mortal man, do thou often meditate of (sic) this happiness. Let it eat up thy heart with desire to enjoy it' (103). Finally the picture of hell as darkness, or a lake burning in a hollow cave striking 'terrour with lamentation' (108).

One can imagine an early seventeenth-century family reading this around the dinner table. Or a believer carrying the small book with them on a journey. This is the contemporary prayer book. Visible imagery is missing, identified as it is with superstition. But the visual dimension of faith is nevertheless present. For the inward appropriation of truth, by faith, does nothing to discourage the imaging of this truth. And the figures encouraged are to be drawn in the most graphic and emotional terms possible. After forming an image of heaven one is to 'let it eat up thy heart'. But for these readers it is not only God's truth, but God himself which is apprehended this way. When the peasant fled home with his indulgence, he bowed down before it as before the very God. There was no sense that images could cultivate a proper awareness of God, as medieval theologians had taught. Rather each believer at the hearing of the truth and by the prompting of the Holy Spirit, draws the image for herself, within. And, somehow, on this assessment, God is there to be drawn and found.

These developments support David Freedberg's argument that the impulse to image the world in figures cannot be suppressed.[67] Reformed believers came to reject some ways of giving shape to the world. But the impact both of the preaching of the Reformers and their own study of Scripture led them to ways of thinking about and shaping the world that were to have a profound cultural influence. One

---

67 David Freedberg, *The Power of Images: Studies in the History and Theory of Response* (Chicago: University of Chicago Press, 1989), 55.

might recast Freedberg's observation by saying that traditions cannot for long be without any influence on the arts that are produced. In the following century music and literature in particular were to be transformed by this tradition, especially by its architectural and documentary character. But this influence would also give the world a characteristic visual shape as well, one that would reflect the inwardness and simplicity of biblical faith.

Chapter 13

Created and Uncreated Light: The Transfiguration in Western Art

Rosemary Muir Wright

> ' Et transfiguratus est ante eos et resplenduit facies eius sicut sol
> (Matt. 17:2) '

1. Learning to See

It is easily assumed that religious art in some way illustrates the words of the Bible and that to recognise what the painting is 'saying' one need only look up the relevant passage in scripture. This tendency to look at art as if it functioned as the visual equivalent of words is wrong footed. Even the title of a particular Biblical subject does not guarantee that any spectator would necessarily recognise that subject in the representation before them. Recognition is dependent on the spectator having previously seen some other representation of this subject, indeed possibly several examples. What makes the image intelligible, in other words, is the instantaneous recognition of something visually familiar.[1] Without this predisposition to recognise the subject, religious art cannot begin to activate the words of the text. There is no doubt that an unavoidable relationship does exist between the religious subject matter of a painting and the Biblical source to which the representation refers. But the relationship is much more subtle than one of visual equivalence. The artist is not concerned with the explanation of words, but with the response to the image conjured up by those words.

From the earliest evidence of the Western Church's pronouncement on images, it is clear that worshippers reacted to the images themselves. Pope Gregory's letters to Bishop Serenus testify to the fact that response to images was a crucial factor in religious experience and one that the Church could ill-afford to ignore. In fact his pastoral concerns for the effects of imagery in churches suggests that the imaginative faculty was easily stimulated, especially by pictures, which were unfamiliar.[2]

---

[1] Brendan Cassidy, 'Iconography in Theory and Practice', *Visual Resources* XI (1995), 323–48.

[2] Celia Chazelle, 'Pictures, books and the illiterate. Pope Gregory I's letters to Serenus of Marseilles', *Word and Image* 6 (1990), 138–53, especially 139.

For a picture is displayed in churches on this account, in order that those who do not know letters may at least read by seeing on the walls what they are unable to read in books. Therefore your fraternity should preserve those things and prohibit the people from adoring them...

As aids to whose who could not read Latin, religious images, especially narrative images, could assist in teaching the laity only if the laity was already familiar with the story. The images could not tell them something that they did not already know. Paintings in churches were not the equivalent of instruction manuals. Gregory's second letter in particular refers to narrative pictures (images of events narrated in Scripture) in churches, especially to wall decoration, where the use of sequential images encouraged the parallel with reading stories. Nonetheless the notion that religious painting could somehow instruct the viewer in the teachings of the Church has somehow persisted. It is manifest not only in the early development of Christian imagery but also in the nineteenth-century religious revivals in both the Catholic and the Protestant confessions, with particular emphasis on the instruction of the young.[3]

What needs much more attention is the question of response to religious imagery. If we were to focus on the visual impact of the painting rather than its biblical source, we might come closer to isolating those factors that give the image its particular power. The creative imagination of the artist has to do with generating an instantaneous match between feeling and idea so that the spectator 'sees' something new. Imagination enables us to see what we have not seen before. This seeing is, of course, not simply a matter of perception even in the literal sense. It is also a matter of emotion. Gregory, like Bernard of Clairvaux and numerous Church authorities thereafter, had recogised the inherent dangers of imaginative response. Something of the energising tension – between the shaping of religious ideas and the affective response of the viewer – would need to be deliberately harnessed to the service of church doctrine to ensure a measure of control. The conviction of 'visual truth' could, it was supposed, be appropriated to theological truth despite the latter's complexity. Just as visual integrity is generated when idea and feeling are at one, so too is theological conviction. Nowhere is this made more explicit than in the tradition of images of the Transfiguration.

2. Establishing the Pattern

In the West, the Gospel accounts (especially that of Luke) provide the basic clues for recognizing the subject: three disciples, the cloud, Moses and Elijah, a radiant Christ. These elements in combination establish the location as Mount Tabor and the theophanic moment as one at which Jesus is identified as Son of God and the Christ of the *Parousia*. The artist must combine narrative considerations with a

---

3   David Morgan, *Visual Piety. A History of Popular Religious Images* (London, 1998); and idem., *Protestants and Pictures* (Oxford, 1999).

theological interpretation in which Christ shares in the Divine Glory (the *Gloria Dei* of the Vulgate, the *Doxa* of the Septuagint). In fact the narrative aspect is almost subsumed in the artist's overriding concern for the theological. Central to the theme is the visualization of light as energy rather than illumination. To see this distinction the viewer must be familiar with the iconography of the Transfiguration by which the power of celestial brightness is revealed. Recognition is encouraged by the narrative aspects of the subject in which the disciples react with fear and confusion to the apparition of white light on the mountaintop. But no artist could create this subject *ex nihilo*. Nor could the textual source, as verbal description, supply the compositional formula on its own. Prior to any visualisation of the theme, therefore, the artist needed to engage with the iconographic tradition. Even the modern painter, Sieger Köder, in depicting the Mount of Transfiguration (see Figure 1) is compelled to draw directly upon this visual tradition in his work to ensure recognition for his subject.[4] Something of the imaginative conviction of a work of art is derived from this way in which it re-ignites an iconographic tradition.

3. The Byzantine Pattern

Although this paper deals with the treatment of the theme in the West, the Eastern or Byzantine model was a powerful influence in shaping the visual formula. There was a strong Byzantine tradition which represented the deity revealed on Mount Tabor by a golden mandorla emitting bars of light; the rays of light implied both the energy of divine splendour and the powerful utterance of God speaking, as it were, through the body of Jesus within the radiance. Like lasers, these bars make contact with the figures of Moses and Elijah and the disciples, fixing them in position by their beam. The earliest example of this use of the light beam is in the sixth-century apse of the Church of St Mary at St Catherine's Monastery, Sinai. This model established the visual components which were subsequently to constitute essential elements for the theme's recognition – the mandorla enclosing a radiant figure of Christ, flanked by the monumental figures of Moses and Elijah, hovering above the kneeling disciples who are clearly terrified. Greek letters identify the characters so that there is no ambiguity.

In the Eastern Church the Transfiguration theme provided a doctrinal justification for icons. The defence was clearly stated in the Refutations of Theodore the Studite: 'the invisible one had an appearance or likeness, the formless one had a form, and the measureless one came encompassed within a measure.' The disclosure to the apostles of the reality of the divine nature through the body of Jesus on Mount Tabor was effectively the disclosure of something that could be revealed to the contemplative.[5]

---

4   I am grateful to the Revd Vanessa Herrick of Ridley Hall, Cambridge for providing me with this image and to David Chalmers, University of St Andrews, for information on the artist.

5   See Jaroslav Pelikan, *Imago Dei. The Byzantine Apologia for Icons* (Princeton, 1990), 92–96, who cites the Homily on the Transfiguration by John of Damascus, as part of

The theme was especially popular for the apse decoration of Byzantine churches like that of the Church of the Dormition, Daphne, Greece, where the late eleventh-century mosaic decoration in the curvature of the apse appears to wrap itself around the spectator standing below. Because the prophet figures of Moses and Elijah are usually turned inwards toward the figure of the transfigured Christ, the curvature of the vault creates the illusion that they turn into the space of the apse, so that the spectator intersects their dialogue across the apsidal space, and is absorbed into the miraculous event. Bodily enclosed in the event the spectator is tuned like the stricken disciples to hear the inaudible words of the voice from the cloud. The glory of the LORD was given symbolic form in the mandorla shape itself, while the golden rays suggest that this glory is something which the human eye may behold.[6] For the Byzantine artists these rays were of light before creation, the symbolic equivalent of divine energy.

The Eastern rite accorded to the Transfiguration equal rank as a feast with those of the Nativity, Epiphany, Ascension and Pentecost. Consequently, the theme appears regularly as the subject of icon painting as well as in liturgical books like the Rabbula Gospels[7] (586) where the Transfiguration appears in the marginal illustration without the accompanying apostles. Doctrinal differences between the Eastern and the Western Churches resulted in a distinctive Eastern reading of the Transfiguration, according to which the light of the Transfigured Christ represented the 'energies' of God rather than his essence.[8] Icons stressed the mystical aspect of the theme by celebrating the cosmic effects of the redemption of Christ. The twelfth-century mosaic icon of the Transfiguration from Constantinople (now in the Louvre), for example, epitomizes this compositional formula when reduced to the scale of a panel. While the disciples still kneel, the aspect of terror has given way to one of wonder. This same iconic formula spread far and wide, exported along the liturgical and economic trade routes to the Latin West.[9]

In fact, the iconographic presentation of the Transfiguration in the West also points clearly to a theological association of this central gospel event with others, notably the crucifixion, resurrection and ascension of Jesus. The town of Ravenna, conquered by the Byzantines in 540, and lying near the centre of the Latin Empire, was always likely to reveal Byzantine schemes appropriated to a Western setting. The sixth-century church of Sant' Apollinare in Classe, for example, evinced the Eastern church's effective absorption of the Crucifixion in the Resurrection by its starkly 'modern' version of the theme in the apse mosaic. Sant' Apollinare was erected by a wealthy private citizen, Julianos Argentarios, whose choice of the apse

---

the defense of icons. See also T. F. Mathews, *The Art of Byzantium* (London, 1998), 112–13.

6   A. M. Ramsey, *The Glory of God and the Transfiguration of Christ* (London, 1944).

7   Florence, Laurentian Library, MS.Plut. 1.56.

8   Pelikan, *Imago Dei*, 95, discusses the doctrine of deification, formulated in terms of this key distinction by Gregory Palamas, a fourteenth-century monk at Mount Athos.

9   Cf. the interior mosaic of the theme created in Norman Sicily in the Palatine Chapel in Palermo and in the Cathedral at Monreale. See John Lowden, *Early Christian and Byzantine Art* (London, 1997), 368, fig. 228.

decoration may have been influenced by the sermons of Leo the Great. Leo's 51st sermon for example had linked the Transfiguration with Christ's victory in the sign of the cross.[10] The apse mosaic took the formal shape of a *crux gemnata* which allowed the designer to express both the concept of the *kabod* (the glory of God) and the physical phenomenon of divine glory in the form of reflected light. The jewelled cross rising into the enclosing curve of the apse not only emphasised the redemptive act of Jesus' death, but also the way in which the figure of Christ had subsequently been transformed into the *splendor* of light through the symbolism of translucent gems and pearls. This has been described as the sole surviving example of a symbolic representation of the Transfiguration.[11]

The link between the appearance on Mount Tabor and the cross had also been established in the Sinai mosaic, which linked the cross with the Paschal Lamb. The apsidal mosaic culminated in a cross-filled medallion, while the angel guardians in the spandrels presented the *clipeus* of the sacrificial lamb. This connection with the *agnus dei* is clearly demonstrated in the earliest manuscript illustration in the West on folio 4 verso of the Ottoboni Gospels produced in the 840s, possibly based on a Byzantine source. The subject was familiar in Ottonian iconography, perhaps encouraged by the circulation of Byzantine ivories especially after the marriage of Otto II to the Byzantine princess Theophanu. The manuscript had only two full-page miniatures on the recto and verso side of a single folio; the glorified Lamb of God surrounded by the four Evangelist symbols on the recto side, with the Transfiguration on the verso. The artist used *tituli* above the heads of Christ and Moses and Elijah to ensure the identification of the prophets in the absence of a heavenly mandorla or light rays. Early Christian images of the Transfiguration had stressed the witness of the disciples.[12] Byzantine models had expressed the devastating effect of this witness by scattering the apostles, effectively separating them. While this aspect is clearly presented in the upturned glance of the cowering Peter, the artist of the Ottoboni Gospels has bonded the figures of the three witnesses into a single volumetric shape formed at the lower angles by the other two disciples, whose covered faces evoke the terror described by the text. Piled together below the vision, the apostles form a compact block.

The novel compositional formula of the Ottoboni Gospels may have been created from memories of related topics depicted in ivory carvings, like the fifth-century ivory plaque of the Ascension and the Maries at the Tomb, now in Munich.[13] These

---

10   Gertrud Schiller, *Ikonographie der christlichen Kunst*, I (Gütersloh, 1990), 147: 'The Incarnation of the Logos effected by the Holy Ghost through Mary and the Transfiguration which took place on Mt. Tabor proclaim that Christ is the Son of God and that he was sent from heaven. They sound for the world redeeming power of his victory won in the sign of the cross.'

11   Ibid., 148.

12   George Henderson, *Vision and Image in Early Christian England* (Cambridge, 1999), 15–16.

13   Lawrence Nees, 'On Carolingian Book Painters: the Ottoboni Gospels and its Transfiguration Master', *Art Bulletin* lxxxiii (2001), 209–39.

iconographic borrowings and blends are not simply a matter of fresh visual inventions. The various elements carry with them into the new creation something of their original meanings, so that the iconography of the new composition is accordingly enriched. The huddled group of the apostles vividly recalls the fearful disciples in the Munich ivory as they react to the Ascension, or more likely the Resurrection, of Christ who strides up the mountain side behind them. This Ascension imagery is probably meant to double for the Resurrection. Lawrence Nees points out that the 21st Sermon of Gregory the Great had made the connection between the theme of Christ breaking the Gates of Hell and Samson taking away the gates of Gaza to the top of the hill. It is this latter scene which is recalled in the ivory, as Christ strides up the mountain in anticipation of the Ascension. While such ivory panels are a likely source of the theme's circulation in the West, it is also possible that the Transfiguration was the subject of small, engraved gems, designed for the decoration of metalwork or jeweled crosses. One such gem appears on folio 9 recto of the Soissons Evangeliary, set, as it were, into the painted metalwork frame of the arch of the second Canon Table.[14] In the Soissons example, two of the disciples lie prostrate under the feet of Christ following Byzantine precedent. The contrast with the Carolingian invention in the Ottoboni Gospels suggests that the ninth-century professional who was responsible for folio 4 verso in the Gospels deliberately encouraged the thematic link with the Resurrection by his adaptation of the single huddled group of disciples covering their faces against the light.

At this formative stage of the iconography it is clear that artists were working from a range of sources, freely adapting motifs at will and absorbing former subjects into new compositions in a manner which must have taken account of the viewers' familiarity with the models. Thus the Transfigured Christ of Mount Tabor was also the Christ of the Resurrection and the Ascension.

4. Beholding the Glory of God in the Body of Jesus

In depicting other instances where the body of Christ appeared in a changed state, like the Resurrection or the Ascension, the artistic focus was on the physical body and its transcendence of fleshly mortality. In the case of the Transfiguration however, artists had to stress the revelation of deity through the humanity of Christ without losing sight of the physical form in which that deity was manifested. How was the medieval artist, trained to represent biblical narrative as history, to deal with the miraculous apparition of the glory of the Godhead? The most effective solution was to exploit the Byzantine formula of rays of light emanating from the almond shaped mandorla, which traditionally had signified the Divine presence in Byzantine models. This is clearly demonstrated on folio 4 recto of the two-volume Floreffe Bible (London, British Library, Add. Ms.17738), written and illuminated for the Premonstratensian canons of Floreffe Abbey in Flanders. The stylistic impact of two main waves of Byzantine

---

14   Götz Denzinger, 'Das Lorscher Evangeliar und seine Ornamentik', in Hermann Shefers (ed.), *Das Lorscher Evangeliar* (Darmstadt, 2000), 99–100 and note 66.

influence from Constantinople during the twelfth century has been documented.[15] In addition to this visual access to Byzantine Greek culture it is clear that Western designers understood the intellectual content of the eastern iconography. Here, the Transfiguration was seen as a sign of the highest form of contemplation, one in which the worshipper moved towards a desired union with God. On the right-hand page, the Transfiguration is combined with a representation of the Last Supper. The scenes are composed in such a way that Christ forms the vertical axis, and the two zones of the upper room and Mount Tabor are set one into the other by the lip of Christ's halo which extends into the inscription below the Transfiguration scene. Although the disciples are separated, forming the socle-like base to the statuesque figures above, it is Peter, rather than John, who is set directly below Christ, thus emphasising, as did the Ottoboni Master, the Petrine foundation of the Western Church. The centrality of Peter in the Bible's programme is underlined by the choice of Peter's account of the Transfiguration (2 Peter 1:17–18) for the banderole inscriptions on either side of Christ, signifying the voice of God.[16] The dramatic unity of the groups – Christ, apostles and prophets – is created by the divine rays which sear from the body of Christ to make contact with each figure. In the West, the Byzantine rays of light-energy had been interpreted as the seven gifts of the Spirit of God, as described in Isaiah 11:1–3. The reward of spiritual gifts derived from the exercise of contemplation, would have been particularly meaningful to a readership of ascetic canons regular. The Eucharistic connection is here made explicit in the lower scene of the Last Supper in which Christ hands Judas the sop. John sleeps on Christ's breast by virtue of his special intimacy with Christ. Just so the Canons of Floreffe, in contemplating this page, were similarly open to intimacy with God through the very act of 'seeing', like Peter, the divinity of Christ.

5. Transfiguration as Mystical and Historical Event

Transferred to panel, the Byzantine type was effectively used in pictorial sequences of the life of Christ. The visionary element of divine light expressed in this formula allowed the theme's insertion in the narrative cycles dealing with the events leading up to the Passion and its aftermath. As a single episode in the Gospel narrative the scene of the Transfiguration could be understood as part of an unfolding drama. This aspect is particularly evident in the narrative cycle on the back of the great double-sided altarpiece for the Cathedral of Siena painted by Duccio and assistants between 1308

---

15   Kurt Weitzmann, *Art in the Medieval West and its Contacts with Byzantium* (London, 1982).

16   Helen C. Evans and William D. Wixom (eds) *The Glory of Byzantium; art and culture of the Middle Byzantine Era AD. 843–1261* (New York, 1997), 478. 'It provides as well an extraordinarily sophisticated example of the reception of Byzantine art in the West, demonstrating that artists and patrons not only were sensitive to the visual beauty of Byzantine models but in at least this case were also aware of the complex theological issues that lay at their heart.'

and 1311.[17] Duccio's decision to adhere to essentially Byzantine pictorial conventions allowed for a creative interplay between the eastern formula and northern Gothic art. This combined a new expressive vitality of form with a smoothness of movement easing the narrative flow from episode to episode. In his panel of the Transfiguration however, Duccio emphasises the hieratic mystical nature of the event, set as it is against a gold background on which the contours of the prophet saints are etched as on a gold plate. The gold leaf effectively prevents the use of gold rays but Duccio has utilised the effect of the golden ambiance to suggest the radiance of divine light which catches the edges of the folds of Christ's garments in patterns of gold striation. Following the Byzantine model, the apostles are set apart from each other but they do not hide their faces in fear nor fall over under the impact of the Divine voice. Instead they gaze in wonder, as must the clergy assembled in their choir behind the high altar.

The challenge to this Byzantine formula can be associated with the new strategies of visual illusion created in the fifteenth century in Italy. How were artists to represent the miraculous apparition of the glory of the Transfiguration in a context of real space and real light? Everything in the composition had now to be subject to the representation of a convincing illusion in which light and atmosphere created a setting for events of tangible immediacy. Given the fundamentally naturalistic approach, the artists had to distinguish between light as natural radiance and light as glory. The eastern tradition had offered the almond-shaped mandorla with its radiant bars to suggest a supernatural light of powerful trajectory, the energy of uncreated light. This issue of transforming light was much more problematic for Western art as a result of the pictorial rediscoveries of three-dimensional space in the Quattrocento. The problem intensified with the introduction in 1457 of the Feast of the Transfiguration on 6 August to the Calendar of the Western Church.[18] Pope Calixtus authorised the Office with the Epistle (2 Peter I: 16–19), the Gospel (Matthew XVII: 1–9) and a Collect to ensure that a full liturgical repertoire was on hand, providing incidentally useful source material for the theme's representation when used in large scale representation.

6. Created and Uncreated Light

Fundamental to representations of the theme was the implicit distinction between the mystical and the episodic treatment of the subject. This distinction had been maintained in the manuscript tradition by the location of the imagery in the context of the surrounding text. A similar distinction is sustained when the theme is the

---

17   John White, *Duccio. Tuscan Art and the Medieval Workshop* (London, 1979). See also D. Norman, *Siena, Florence and Padua. Art, Society and Religion (1280–1400), Case Studies* (New Haven and London, 1995), 61, Plate 70.

18   The Bull of Calixtus III was instigated by the victory against the Turks. Following the Fall of Constantinople the call to the Crusade was preached in Vicenza by John da Capustrano.

subject of a panel. Because the episode on Mount Tabor acted as a watershed in the interpretation of the events of Christ's life, by opening into the story of the Passion, it could be used as a single narrative event within a larger sequence often within a predella panel.[19] When the Transfiguration was the subject of a single panel the focus was on the theological content. Given the naturalistic techniques of the Italian fifteenth century in creating a world verifiable by the norms of experience, the problematic issue does seem to have been the nature of the celestial brightness by which Christ was transformed.

Renaissance artists struggled to represent the actuality of the experience as recorded in the New Testament, taking their cue from the textual description of the event, which associated sight with sound. For the Western Church, God had revealed himself in the transfigured Christ whose dazzling whiteness projected the eye of faith forward in time to the Christ of the *Parousia*. Artists concentrated on the visual assurance of Christ's eschatological role. The lections provided the resource material to present this explosive entry of Divine power into the phenomenal world. The texts provided the essential grounding elements, the three named apostles, Peter, James and John, the bright cloud (the testimony of sight), the voice (the testimony of sound), the figures of Moses and Elijah (the testimony of vision or spiritual seeing). All this was rendered concrete by the mountaintop setting, as if this detail of place, so reminiscent of the 'holy ground' of Mount Sinai, established the actuality of God's intervention. In particular, the artists had to find a way of translating the whiteness/splendour of Christ's transfigured state so that it was both convincing in terms of visual experience and distinguished from the radiance of natural light.

One of the most assured painters of light was Fra Angelico, whose frescoed Transfiguration in cell six in the Florentine Monastery of San Marco literally brought the experience of the Transfiguration into the lives of the community of Dominicans (see Figure 2). Despite the corporate life of the convent, each monk was allowed individual freedom to seek his own path through the exercise of a lifelong habit of prayer.[20] Angelico's composition assumes familiarity with the Byzantine compositional type, but concentrates on the physical experience on Mount Tabor as one which almost penetrates the space of the cell itself, forcing theological reality into the physical reality of the viewer's situation. The outward gesture of Peter directly

---

19 For example the inclusion of the scene as part of a visionary sequence with the Assumption of the Virgin by Lotto, Recanati, or as one of the plaques of a golden book cover from Mount Athos, or one episode in the narrative fresco cycle of Giusto de' Menabuoi, 1375–76 in the Baptistry of Padua Cathedral.

20 William Hood, *Fra Angelico at San Marco*, Yale, 1993. The Dominican prayer treatise of the mid-thirteenth century, *De Modo Orandi*, which is based on a supposed eye-witness account of the manner of St Dominic at prayer. It described nine modes of prayer which were to be distinguished by the appropriate gesture so that the required psychological state would be induced. These gestures of prayer were demonstrable in the cells of the novices, the clerics and the *conversi*. Such gestures are visible in the two respondents pressed into each side of the fresco in Cell 6, who are set as it were outside the action while taking up one of the modes of prayer offered by the treatise.

confronts the cell's inhabitant who is drawn to occupy the shallow space at the base of the mountaintop. This space is carefully designated as co-extensive with that of the viewer, by the upturned sole of John's bare foot, and the pliant drapery of his mantle falling in folds which replicated the actual folds of the cell's kneeling occupant. The gold edges of John's robe threaten to breach the invisible plane of the wall so that in one instant the kneeling figures inhabit the space of the cell, while in another the viewer is drawn across the threshold to enter into the immediate vision of the Transfigured Christ. Moses and Elijah are reduced to spectral heads appearing above wispy clouds. The most astonishing innovation is the brilliant oval of Christ's eggshell mandorla. Angelico has exploited the brilliance of the white intonaco to create a luminosity that comes from within the whiteness itself. On to this, the contours of Christ's white mantle are etched as white on white. Triumphant and monumental, the figure of Christ evokes the T shape of the opening initial to the sacrament of the Mass, the *Te Igitur*. There is no doubt that such an identification would be intentional, encouraging the viewer to see the iconographic overlay of the outstretched arms of Christ crucified.

7. God in the Substance of his Creation?

The new naturalism of the Renaissance is evident in the large Transfiguration now in Naples painted by Giovanni Bellini, 1478–79 for the Fioccardo Chapel in Vicenza Cathedral.[21] Designed for a funerary chapel and protected from the aisle space by an iron gate, the painting offered a privileged perception of God incarnate in the 'flesh' of his own creation. Bellini's Christ is the embodiment of this Godhead, for he is represented as being as much part of the living world of nature as the sunlight itself. Translucent as marble, the monumental figure is the axial pivot between the heavens and the earth. Like the barren and the fruitful tree on either side of the hillock which serves as Mount Tabor, Christ's head is crowned by a band of grayish cloud to be easily distinguished from the icy white puffs of cloud gathering behind the horizon. From the centre of the grey overshadowing band above his head there emerges a pale effulgence, evoking the presence and voice of the God who announces the identity of the Son.[22] In an earlier panel (now in the Museo Civico Correr in Venice, c. 1455–60) Bellini had used rings of cloud to evoke the glory of God, distinguishing them from other cloud formations in the painting by a difference in behaviour and structure. Thus, although interpreted in a naturalistic way, the presence of the Godhead in creation's midst was distinguished clearly enough from empirical phenomena. The prevalence of Byzantine influence in Venice may account for the Eastern formula of the separate placement of the apostles in the Naples painting. They are caught in natural sunlight, their forms casting soft shadows on the surrounding ground. But Bellini's transfigured Christ shares a place with the organic life of the autumnal landscape in which

---

21   See Frederick Hartt, *History of Italian Renaissance Art*, 4th edn. (London: Thames and Hudson, 1994), colourplate 78, 415.

22   Bellini would have been familiar with Netherlandish models in which God the Father appears through an aureole of cloud above the head of the transfigured Christ.

herdsman and traveller make their own paths. Indeed the background structures may recall specific sites, the bell tower of Sant' Apollinare in Classe and the mausoleum of Theoderic in Ravenna. Moses and Elijah materialise out of air, set against the world of nature but not of it. Just as the October light might suggest the passion through the dying of the year, so the figures of the prophets testify to the coming resurrection of the dead. Crisp edged, they seem to lack actual substance despite the bulky folds of their drapery – as if they owed their visibility to the raking light of Christ's garments. Their profound inward gaze contrasts with the open stare of Christ. The tiny rays of his halo are almost invisible compared with the luminosity of his garments crackling into folds with the imperceptible movement of his body. The *orans* gesture gives to the figure something of a sacramental import, which might reflect the likely dedication of the altar itself to San Salvatore.[23]

8. A Statement of Allegiance?

The selection of the Transfiguration for an altarpiece might have been dictated by political motives, as an explicit indication of loyalty to the Pope in a period of shifting allegiances among Italian states. An example may be the commission for a painting of the Transfiguration for the Church of Santa Maria di Castel Nuovo. The painting (now in the Pinacoteca Civica, Recanati) by Lorenzo Lotto was executed for the high altar of the Benedictine Confraternity between 1510 and 1512. In this representation the experience on Mount Tabor is seen from well below the position of the apostles who tumble back in disarray almost into the liminal space of the chapel. These figures display a new psychological tension which extends to the prophets, who in turn fall to their knees before the radiant figure of Christ on the crest of the hill. Lotto has reverted to the older use of golden inscriptions to identify the figures and to signify the Divine voice. The strange spatial disturbance and the sense of emotional energies destabilising the composition imply – in complete contrast to the painting by Bellini – the non-natural character of the event. The drapery of Christ swirls around his feet, implying a draught of supernatural wind from the opening rent in the heavens. In this case the altarpiece had three predella panels, which provided a coherent programme in connection with the main subject. Two of these offered an extended gloss on the main panel (Christ leading the disciples to Mount Tabor and the Ascension), while the Eucharistic theme of the central panel depicting the Agony in the Garden associated the altarpiece with the celebration on the altar table below.[24] Lotto also reinforces the link by which the transfigured Christ of Mount Tabor was seen as prefiguring the Christ of the Resurrection, by his luminous verticality before which the watchers fall to the ground in terror. Lotto's energised version of the subject was popular in Lombardy according to other variants also in the Brera Gallery in Milan.[25]

---

23   Meinolf Dalhoff, *Giovanni Bellini: Die Verklärung Christi* (Münster, 1997), 37.
24   Peter Humfrey, *Lorenzo Lotto* (New Haven and London, 1997), 37.
25   See works by Pordenone and Previtali in Peter Humfrey, *La Pittura Veneta del Rinascimento a Brera* (Florence, 1990).

9. Behold He Cometh on Clouds ...

The problem for the Renaissance artists of reconciling the splendour of the whiteness of the Transfigured Christ with the behaviour and effects of natural light, found a solution, probably perfected by Raphael, in the opening of the heavenly realms to the perception of earthly sight. This aperture allowed a glimpse of the light of the heavens – at once brilliance and energy – to be borne through the cloud-filled air. The vision of Ezekiel had described the glory of God as borne on energy laden clouds enwrapped with light, an image which now directly informed the quest for a naturalistic sign for the glory of God.[26] In the final effect, the clouds are forced open as it were by a Divine energy. But these clouds are dense, composed in their innermost reaches of translucent angel heads, like energy charged spectres suffused with the golden radiance of the inner heavens. Through this light-filled vapour the worshipper catches the briefest glimpse of myriads of souls glinting like the lights of infinite galaxies. In Raphael's last painting, the 'Transfiguration and the Failure to Heal', 1517–20 (see Figure 3), this extraordinary glory lifts Christ from the mountaintop itself.

The painting had a competitive edge from the beginning in being set against a work by Sebastiano del Piombo, for whom Michelangelo had supplied the drawings. Both paintings were intended as gifts to the Cathedral of Narbonne, the titular church of Cardinal Giulio de Medici. It may be that the vision of the Transfiguration did not of itself provide enough drama, and that Raphael felt the need to exploit something latent in the theme to extend the subject to include the episode of the failure to heal.[27] This theme may have been personal to both Raphael and the Cardinal as indicative of the powerless of man in the absence of the salvific power of God through Christ. Raphael's drawings reveal , that, as work progressed, the meaning of the upper part of the painting changed too, so that the link with the Resurrection became more pronounced. An early design shows the three apostles falling on their faces overshadowed by a dark ring of cloud before which Christ stands on the mountain. In the final design he is lifted into the cloud ring, turning slow rotation as he appears in Raphael's drawings for the Resurrection altarpiece. The introduction of a secondary subject in the lower half further changed the dynamics of the upper section of the Transfiguration to create a new relationship between the dramatic action of the Transfiguration itself and the emotional crisis of the figures below, locked in a tragedy of desperate human need. The rigidity of the contours of the body of the demoniac

---

26   John Shearman, 'Raphael's Clouds, and Correggio's', in ed. Micaela Sambucco Hamoud and Maria Letizia Strocchi *Studi su Raffaelo:a atti del Congresso Internazionale di Studi, Urbino-Firenze 6–14 Aprile 1984* (2 volumes, Urbino, 1984), vol 2, pp 657–68. He quotes from Gregory the Great's Commentary on Ezekiel 'in the midst of the great cloud (a brilliance) like a kind of electrum, that is, from the middle of the fire; de medio eius (splendor) quasi species electri, idest, de medio ignis'. This cloud wrapping phenomenon, unlike the static landscape cloud, he equates with the 'Gloria Dei' of the Vulgate.

27   This episode is one in which a demonic boy is brought by his parents to the apostles to be healed. The stories follow each other in the Gospels and although there is no causal ink between them, the sequence may have offered Raphael exactly the dramatic element needed.

dramatises the diagonal connection between the two events. This incident of the possessed boy is set against the bright but overshadowing cloud of divine energy which takes on an eschatological dimension, prefiguring as it does the vision of John of Patmos, 'and behold he cometh on clouds and every eye shall see him' ('*ecce venit cum nubibus*').[28] The energy of glory is dramatically contrasted with the natural lighting of the sunset in order to emphasise the cosmic nature of the divine radiance as uncreated light. The same energy penetrates the scene below in the dramatic reactions of the crowd at the foot of the mountain.

10. A Meditation for a Funeral Chapel?

The energising power of the Transfiguration is accentuated in the painting by Siciolante in the Chapel of the Cross in Santa Maria in Aracoeli in Rome, 1573–75. Following as it did the guidelines offered to the Bishops at Trent for the commissioning of religious paintings, the formula of Siciolante's painting became an Italian standard for the sixteenth and seventeenth centuries alike.[29] The canonical interpretation may have depended on the image of God the Father designed originally for the vault above the painting, to which the upturned eyes of Christ were directed. This image thereby provided the Divine voice and the source of the spectral lighting, the visual equivalent of Gregory's *electrum*. Siciolante retains the strange overshadowing cloud, but sets Christ on the ground, while the disciples lie below on a earthy terrace as if awakening from a deep sleep evocative of death. This visual reference to the sleeping apostles at Gethsemane may have been deliberate as the painting was designed for a mortuary chapel. In this version the prophets are keenly alert. The energy of Christ's radiance thrills along the edges of their garments as they stride with vigour towards him in marked contrast to the supine apostles. Despite the impression that this event takes place outside time and space, the painter is careful to detail the plants and grasses of the earth which share in the radiance of the transfigured Christ.

In marked contrast the huge altarpiece for the high altar of San Pietro Martire in Bologna installed in 1596 forces the moment of the Transfiguration into the time and space of the worshipper. At almost five metres high, the size of the panel drives home the impact of the blinding light for the spectator entering the nave. All that was poised in suspension in Siciolante's painting is here violently disrupted.[30] The painter, Ludovico Carracci, has spun the gentle rotation of Raphael's Christ in the Vatican Transfiguration into a whiplash turn, which threatens to spin out of control. The energy of this bodily turn expresses the dynamism of the Divine *doxa* which rises

---

28 Shearman, 'Raphael's Clouds, and Correggio's', 656, describes the novelty of this kind of transportative cloud as 'the pictorial invention of the Biblical Doxa, that energy-loaded, dynamic Glory of Jehovah with all the meteorologically naturalistic character it has in the Old Testament.'

29 John Hunter, *Girolamo Siciolante, pittore da Sermoneta* (1521–75), Florence, 168–70.

30 Andrea Emiliani, *Ludovico Carracci* (Bologna, 1993), catalogue entry 42, 92–93.

behind him, propelling uncreated energy through the cloud of the inner heavens as if through a conduit so that it erupts into the physical world.

11. The Challenge of the Transfiguration

Perhaps because of the visual complexity involved in depicting an event in which heaven and earth meet, the Transfiguration eventually gave way as a theme for altarpieces to images in which human flesh was transfigured in other ways, usually through scenes of martyrdom. Visions of heaven opening out to suffering saints were more flexible themes for the post-Tridentine Church offering that combination of drama and transcendence which characterized altarpiece design before the period of the Enlightenment. The subject did not lend itself to visual logic and emotional rationality.

The recovery of the Transfiguration theme presents a challenge, perhaps intentional, to those modern artists who have attempted it. Sieger Köder's Transfiguration recalls the Byzantine type, while also alluding to the Western models by which the apostles 'see' Christ's divinity manifest.[31] The painting begs the question as to whether this 'seeing' is with the eye of sense or with the mind's eye, for all three shut their eyes against the glare. And Köder draws a clear visual distinction between the heavenly glory into which both Christ and the prophets are caught up, and the darklands of the lower third of the painting. Köder's Christ is sucked into the maelstom of light as if momentarily drawn back into the inner heavens from which he came, yet his open handed gesture touches the praying hands of both Moses and Elijah. The tiny lasers of light from these hands penetrate the zone of the sub-lunar world to reach the apostles as mere reflection. Nonetheless, the Divine has entered visibly into creation, and the luminosity which touches their upturned eyes and, incidentally, those of the spectator is indeed a reflection of the glory of God.

Bearing in mind the rationale of this volume of essays, this exploration of the developing iconography of the Transfiguration seems to support the notion that 'the tradition is authentically performed' as each work of art opens up fresh layers of meaning appropriate to the context in which it is viewed. And as has been pointed out, this context is constantly shifting. This raises the question of response to images with which the essay began. While our knowledge of the Bible and the history of the theme's representation, shape our assumptions about a painting's meaning, the critical element, as Gregory pointed out, is our response to the image itself.

---

31 Gertrud Widmann, *Bild und Gleichnis, Werke von Sieger Köder* (Ostfildern, 1997).

Figure 1   Sieger Köder: Verklärung
           (© Sieger Köder)

Figure 2   Fra Angelico (1387–1455): Transfiguration (© 1990; Photo SCALA, Florence – courtesy of the Ministero Beni e Att. Culturali; Florence, Museo di San Marco)

Figure 3 Raphael (1483–1520) Transfiguration, (© 1990; Photo SCALA, Florence; Vatican, Pinacoteca)

Figure 4 Fra Angelico (1387–1455): Noli me tangere (© 1990; Photo SCALA, Florence – courtesy of the Ministero Beni e Att. Culturali; Florence, Museo di San Marco)

Chapter 14

The Ascension and Transfigured Bodies

David Brown

In this essay I want to examine the doctrine of the Ascension and the way it has been appropriated through Christian history, particularly through the visual arts but also to a limited degree in some other media, including poetry, music and more literary sermons. My objective in doing so is not to decry more conventional doctrinal treatments but rather to consider what happens when attempts to engage an audience are more directly in play. Inevitably, questions of significance and relevance become more important, as strategies are devised to ensure, on the part of viewer, reader or listener, continuing interest in the doctrine. There may be some interesting lessons for the Church and theology, as perhaps of all the doctrines concerned with Christ's life this is the one that is most often treated as marginal to the whole story. To the typical conservative it appears as merely transitional, a marker for the end of Christ's earthly life and promissory of the gift of the Spirit to come; to the more radically minded resurrection and ascension are in any case to be seen as one, and so Luke's two accounts viewed as merely rather wooden ways of saying that the appearances had now come to an end. Neither group thus accords the notion much weight in its own right.

On the other hand it certainly needs to be conceded that the image of the Ascension that is most familiar these days – with Christ's feet peeking beneath a cloud – scarcely at first sight appears any more promising. Yet what I want to suggest is that a more extensive examination of the range of imagery employed compels a rather different estimate. To see why, I propose considering in turn two major types of focus, first Christ's exchange with Mary Magdalene in the Garden and then the departure as such. The latter in particular will enable us to draw on poetry and music as well as art. The advantage of the former is that it reminds us that the biblical material is in any case far wider than the two familiar references in Luke-Acts.[1] So part of my intention will be to highlight the way in which artists draw on that wider material, as well as note some of the tensions in moving from one medium to another (from the literary to the visual). In both cases I shall contend that precisely because the artistic tradition is concerned to engage, there is much more emphasis on the potential relevance of the doctrine to the viewer, listener or reader, and so as much concern with the impact on us as on Christ. This means there is a desire to speak of a body transfigured that opens up the possibility of our own transfiguration.

---

1   Luke 24.50–3; Acts 1.6–11.

1. Mary Magdalene's Encounter and Transformation

'Touch me not; for I am not yet ascended to my Father' (John 20.17). So common are representations of this theme in art, of Mary Magdalene being repelled by Christ, that it has generated its own specific name (from the Vulgate), *Noli me tangere*. That very familiarity, though, can all too easily hide from us the startling oddness of what is being said. A more easily explicable comment would surely have been for Christ to enjoin just such a touch precisely because it was the last opportunity Mary Magdalene would have had before Christ entered a different sort of reality. Little wonder then that textual emendations are sometimes proposed to ease the strain, with, for example, Mary told instead 'not to fear' because Christ had not yet entered into his more august, supernatural reality.[2] However, on the whole commentators both ancient and modern have preferred to keep with the rebuke, 'do not keep holding on:' Christ's destiny is calling him elsewhere. Both Chrysostom and Augustine postulate insufficient reverence on Mary's part for Christ's new, more august state.[3] Chrysostom adds that Christ tried to express this as gently as possible, and that is why his meaning is not as clear as it might be. Among modern commentators Barrett's view may be taken as representative: she is wrongly 'trying to recapture the past'.[4] Something, though, still seems to be lacking in such explanations, as the grammar surely speaks of promise as well as of threat: the 'for' entails a connection, and so appears to imply touch once more or something greater once Christ's new identity is established. If I may draw a rather trivial parallel, think of a child rebuked, 'don't touch the chocolates; the guests have still to arrive'. Certainly, part of the point is deprivation in the immediate moment, but there is normally also an implicit promise as well: being allowed to share with the guests when they finally arrive.

It is intriguing, therefore, to observe that painters have generally insisted upon just such a promise also for Mary in that rebuke, and so an ascension that impinges on her life no less than on Christ's. Take, for example, Giotto's work from the early fourteenth century at the Scrovegni Chapel in Padua.[5] On the bottom left hand side of the fresco five soldiers lie asleep, while two large angels sit behind on the closed sarcophagus tomb – closed, perhaps to emphasise the supernatural character of Christ's emergence. Behind is barren landscape that slopes down towards the right of the painting, where Christ is walking out of the fresco carrying a banner in his left hand that declares him *Victor Mortis* ('victor over death'). He looks back towards a kneeling Mary, his right hand indicating a stay for her hands already stretching

---

2   The proposal (requiring only a small emendation of the Greek) of J. H. Bernard, *Gospel according to St. John* (Edinburgh: T & T Clark, 1928), II, 669–70.
3   Chrysostom, *Homilies on John*, 86; Augustine, *Tractates on John*, 121.
4   C. K. Barrett, *The Gospel according to St John* (London: SPCK, 2nd edn, 1978), 565.
5   Also sometimes known as the Arena Chapel because it was once the site of a Roman amphitheatre. For illustration, see B. Cole, *Giotto: The Scrovegni Chapel, Padua* (New York: George Braziller, 1993), no. 36; A. M. von der Haegen, *Giotto* (Cologne: Könemann, 1998), no. 95.

towards him. Their eyes, however, meet tenderly, and in between them blossoms the only green shrubbery visible in the entire painting. If the predominant white and gold of Christ and the two angels contrasts markedly with the more substantial colours for the soldiers and for Mary, she shares not only a golden halo with the heavenly figures but also the deep red of her cloak is taken up in both the tomb and the patterning of the angel's wings (only one pair is visible). All this suggests to me a deliberate attempt on the part of Giotto to hint that the stay is temporary and a closer relationship in the offing, one that will blossom into the eternal life that the angels already have. One might contrast that work with Fra Angelico's of the same incident a century later in one of the cells of San Marco in Florence (see Figure 4), where no hints of such a future resolution seem offered.[6] Here the garden setting is taken literally, and a palisade encloses a green lawn richly carpeted with flowers with tall cypresses and palms in the background. On the left is a large rock tomb with a door entrance, the encounter with Mary and Christ being placed centre-stage. Although Christ has a mattock over his shoulder and their eyes do meet, the overall impression is of an encounter between two different orders of reality without resolution, for Mary's head is set against the backdrop of the tomb, while Christ's feet seem scarcely to touch the ground, as though he were virtually already elsewhere.[7]

While Fra Angelico may be more consonant with exegesis of the passage both ancient and modern, it is Giotto who better captures, for whatever reason, the tensions implicit between the two halves of the verse. Yet he does so, not because of meditation on the meaning of the text as such but rather because of the way in which by his time the legend of Mary Magdalene had developed. Ever since Pope Gregory the Great had equated Mary Magdalene with the sinner who had anointed Jesus and with Mary of Bethany, the composite figure had become the most popular saint in western Christendom after the Virgin Mary.[8] This development allowed both men and women to locate themselves within the story of Jesus, and so see themselves as not only sinners like Mary but also, again like her, part of a continuing and deepening relationship with Christ that now offered still greater possibilities of intimacy. Anselm's prayer puts the point well: 'Most blessed lady, I the most wicked of men do not touch once more upon your sins as a taunt or reproach but seek to grasp the boundless mercy by which they were blotted out ... For it is not difficult for you to obtain whatever you wish from so loving and so kind a Lord, who is your friend living and reigning.'[9] Indeed, it is a pattern that has continued up to our own day, as in the familiar song attributed to her by Tim Rice in Andrew Lloyd Webber's musical Jesus Christ Superstar, 'I don't know how to love him.' She has

---

6   For illustration, see C. Lloyd, *Fra Angelico* (London: Phaidon, 1992 ed.), no. 29. The painting dates from 1441, Giotto's from c. 1310.

7   Christ's feet are crossed, with the right foot only just holding back the onward advance of the left.

8   I examine this development, and seek to defend it from its critics (from feminist theologians and from those who believe that historical accuracy must always assume primacy) in my *Discipleship and Imagination* (Oxford: Oxford University Press, 2000), 31–61.

9   Anselm, *Oratio*, 16 (my translation).

'had so many men before' but she is 'really changed' and so does not know how to respond. She toys with a number of opposing options, representative of both the creative and the destructive possibilities of love. If the uncertainties are typically modern, the general strategy is not: a character in the story is being used to negotiate one's own personal attitude to Jesus, and so not only his change of status but also one's own. Bodily sin is thus a metaphor for a much wider issue, a transformation or transfiguration of one's present identity. As we shall see, Giotto is by no means alone in applying his art in this way.

Correggio's version from the 1520s and now in the Prado in Madrid is intriguing for a number of reasons, not least because almost certainly it was commissioned for a private patron rather than for a church.10 This may be one reason why the vegetation behind the encounter is done in such detail (scarcely a garden but luxuriant with various kinds of trees and bushes), for the painting could be better lit than was ever likely to be the case in a church. The absence of a halo or any sign of Christ's wounds should not, however, be confused with secularisation, as though a private patron necessarily brought a lessening of religious focus. Rather, what we have is the typical Renaissance interest in using the human to mediate the divine. The gardener's implements are now cast aside, inconspicuously in the bottom right hand corner, and the primary focus in now in the intensity of the gaze between Mary Magdalene and Christ. Her loose hair and yellow patterned dress suggest the prostitute of the composite figure to which I have already alluded. The kneeling figure stretches her head to gaze longingly and hopefully at the young figure of Christ who returns her gaze but points heavenwards. An oak behind gives an age, solidity and height that his own youthful form lacks, reinforced by the symbolic heavenly blue of the robe he is wearing. It is the sort of painting which, the more one looks at, the more one is drawn by its power into its underlying religious message. Mary's right hand steadying herself at the bottom left in fact creates a strong diagonal that forces one's own eyes through hers into Christ's, and beyond into his upward pointing left hand and the tree rising above. Christ, we are being told, is able to draw Mary despite her sin into his own heavenly direction, a perspective that puts in the past his own wounds (they are not shown) and thus Mary's also.

Roughly contemporary and with similar symbolism for the tree is Titian's version, one of the best-known paintings in the National Gallery in London.11 A youthful work (Titian was to live another sixty years), it is nonetheless highly creative.12 Gone is any reference to the tomb itself, and the scene is set in idyllic rolling countryside with a large farmstead in the background and sheep grazing nearby. Intriguingly, X-rays have revealed that Titian's first thought was to portray Christ in the traditional manner with him walking away from Mary Magdalene and

---

10   For illustration and some commentary, D. Ekserdjian, *Correggio* (New Haven: Yale University Press, 1997), 156–59.

11   For illustration, M. Kaminski, *Titian* (Cologne: Könemann, 1998), 24.

12   Painted about 1514 when Titian was somewhere between 24 and 27; Titian survived till 1576.

wearing a gardener's sun-hat. In the final version, however, Christ turns fully round to face her, and only a subdued reference to her mistaken identity of him survives (a hoe in Christ's left hand). Instead, Mary is allowed (on bended knees) to reach even as far as the white grave-clothes with which Jesus has invested himself. The eyes of the pair are entirely for each other, and there is no contrary gesture from Christ, apart from a gentle pulling of the shroud slightly closer to himself. It is only gradually that viewers discover a deeper dimension to what is being portrayed, as their eyes are drawn along the curve of Mary's bent body and up through the tree between them and so heavenwards. In short, given the composite identification of Mary mentioned above and her popularity in the Venice of the time, all sinners are in effect being told that, like Mary, they too can through their penitence before Christ win through and advance heavenwards.

Other examples with a similar emphasis might be mentioned, but perhaps more interesting, by way of contrast, is Rembrandt's approach a century later. Not only does he choose a different moment in the encounter from the norm but also a quite different focus.13 The impact on Mary as our representative so noticeable in earlier paintings is now replaced by a focus on Christ himself as divine. Although dressed as a gardener, light seems to emanate from him, and in turn prevent shadow from falling on Mary who is looking up towards him. It is a transcendent light which one of the two angels sitting on the tomb also shares. In the latter case the intention may be to underline the supernatural way in which Christ has broken out of the tomb, since, as with Giotto's version, the angels sit firmly on the lid. With Christ, though, the motive is more profound, to transform Mary's look from the alarm suggested in her hands (caught in mid-motion with the anointing cloth still in her grasp) to the reverential awe of recognition now indicated in her face. Unobserving, the other two female visitors to the tomb are already travelling down the path back to Jerusalem, visible in the distance with its cathedral-like temple (identifiable as such, if only because of the two pillars of Jachin and Boaz in front).14 Yet, although it is a powerful picture, one cannot help feeling that nonetheless something has been lost, in omitting the direct engagement of the viewer. Mary's experience is now unique, a divine epiphany, and so no longer comparable to our own.

The work dates from 1638, and so from relatively early in Rembrandt's career (he was thirty-two). A couple of decades earlier, Bishop Lancelot Andrewes preached three powerful Easter Day sermons on the theme of the Ascension.15 Like Rembrandt he too stressed the divinity but in a way that insists on the continuing relevance of Christ's humanity to our own. He is convinced that the Ascension is the more important of the two doctrines: 'better lie still in our graves, better never rise,

---

13 'Christ appearing to Mary Magdalen', now in Buckingham Palace, London. For illustration and some commentary, see C. Brown, J. Kelch and P. van Thiel, *Rembrandt: The Master & his Workshop* (New Haven: Yale University Press, 1991), 204–7.

14 I Kings 7.21; 2 Chron. 3.17.

15 Sermons for 1620, 1621, 1622: available in M. Dorman (ed.), *The Sermons of Lancelot Andrewes* (Edinburgh: Pentland Press, 1993), II, 145–78.

than rise and rising not to ascend'.16 Picking up the theme of Christ as gardener, he speaks of him as the one 'who made such a herb grow out of the ground this day as the like was never seen before, a dead body to shoot forth alive out of the grave ... By virtue of this morning's act, he will garden our bodies too, turn all our graves into garden plots.'17 But for that to happen we must follow the example of Mary and learn the due reverence that can pull us heavenwards. For Andrewes Mary discovered the right kind of reverence subsequently when she caught at his feet, as described in Matthew.18 But, if that supposition differs from the pictorial representations which already show her kneeling in this incident, Andrewes insists on a still greater sense of intimacy after Christ has departed, in his eucharistic presence. Modern commentators tend to dismiss the possibility that this is what was intended (in particular by the 'for'), but on the other side three observations may be made. The first is that the importance of touch is stressed generally in John. Secondly, metaphorical as well as literal uses occur elsewhere in Scripture, and so it is not as though to accept the implication requires a crudely literalistic reading of what is meant by 'touch'.19 Finally, in John 6 Christ as our eucharistic food is actually explicitly linked with the ascension.20 So, however one reads that earlier passage, John 20 could be referring back to the new type of intimacy which it suggests – Christ once more present but in a new way.

If eucharistic presence is not an aspect taken up in modern art, it is nonetheless surprising how strong the other continuities remain. As an initial example, consider a painting from one of the founders of the Nabi movement, Maurice Denis (d. 1943), himself much interested in religious art.21 It shares the decorative emphasis associated with that movement.22 Christ seems almost to dance heavenward. Although he looks back, neither Mary nor another, accompanying woman look at him. Instead, their heads are bowed in prayer, each engrossed in their own flowering plot whose richness echoes the larger formalised garden in the background. In the centre of Mary's plot a tree blossoms. It looks as though, despite the painting's Latin title Noli me tangere (recorded within the picture itself), the artist intended to capture a moment subsequent to Christ's rebuke. Mary now, like us, relies on faith alone. She is at the foot of the steps that take Christ to heaven and knows that with prayerful attention to her own allotted sphere she too can progress that way in due course.

---

16   1622; II, 171.

17   1620; II, 152.

18   1621; II, 159; Matthew 28.9.

19   For the importance of touch in John, note particularly I John 1.1; for metaphorical uses of touch see, for example, I Sam. 10.26; Jer. 1.9; Isaiah, 41.13.

20   John 6.62.

21   The painting, dating from 1896, is illustrated in N. Grubb, *Scènes de la vie du Christ* (Paris: Editions Abbeyville, 1996), 137. The Nabis (who also included Bonnard, Maillol and Vuillard) saw themselves as 'prophets' of a new, anti-naturalist style that stressed the flatness of the canvas and often engaged with symbolist concerns.

22   Édouard Vuillard's work is perhaps best know in this connection. In some of his paintings his mother and sister seem almost to merge with the wallpaper.

Among twentieth century representations in Britain, three in particular seem worth singling out. As one enters Ely Cathedral, the exchange between the two is presented by two skeletal metal figures sculpted by David Wynne, Mary recoiling a little as Jesus points heavenwards with both hands upraised. It offers a simple but effective message, as one enters the church, of Christ's summons to a different order of living and reality. In the Methodist Art Collection is Roy de Maistre's 1958 work.23 Here a massive Christ overwhelms a diminutive Magdalene kneeling at his feet. While any doubt about Christ's divinity is silenced not only by the scale of his person but also by his yellow halo and the light emanating from his person, it is hard to detect any clear impact on Mary, for her face is turned away from us and towards Christ. In a sense that could be an improvement since it allows an unmediated response from us to this august figure, but the disadvantage is that all cues for an appropriate response must now come from the figure of Christ himself. Perhaps that is why de Maistre added the letters for 'love' on Christ's cloak, to help guide our response. In the early 1960s Walter Hussey commissioned from Graham Sutherland a version of the scene for the Magdalen Chapel in Chichester Cathedral. With Sutherland's reputation now greatly eclipsed by that of his erstwhile friend, Francis Bacon, it will be interesting to see whether the various exhibitions associated with 2003, the centenary of Sutherland's birth, do anything to revive his waning reputation.24 Best-known of course for his work in Coventry Cathedral, the two versions that he did for Chichester are nonetheless also impressive.25 In both Mary is portrayed kneeling at the foot of an open metal staircase (apparently borrowed from the garden wall of Sutherland's French home), up which Christ is advancing, his outstretched left arm pointing the way. The cathedral version which has Christ wearing a gardener's hat is to my mind too cluttered, but, whichever version is preferred, the introduction of the staircase was an inspired thought, since it reminds us of John's first use of ascension imagery with Christ himself the staircase upon which angels descend and ascend.26 A strong claim is thus made for the indispensability of his mediatorial role.

Intriguingly, in that last painting it is an assertion addressed once more to Mary in her role as sinner, for her tightly hugging dress is apparently evocative of the type of clothes once to be seen on 1950s prostitutes in London's Bond Street. It looks as though despite the animadversions of biblical scholars the old equation lives on, and not just in art. Twentieth century poets as varied as Boris Pasternak and David Constantine make the same sort of appeal, and one can understand why. Mary is there for sinners like us, to assure us that Christ's upward pointing is not simply a destiny reserved for himself but also applies to our own flawed condition. It is the

---

23   The Collection is now housed at Westminster College, Oxford.

24   A recent, helpful survey of his more secular art is to be found in M. Fréchuret et al., *Sutherland: une retrospective* (Antibes: Musée Picasso, 1998).

25   The other is now in Pallant House, also in Chichester. Pamela Tudor-Craig compared the two in the *Church Times* (2 May 2003, 28), unlike me giving the palm to the version in the cathedral. Where she does seem right is in the better quality of the faces in the latter.

26   John 1.51, based on Jacob's vision at Bethel: Gen. 28.10–17. The Greek implies that the Son of Man is himself the ladder rather than simply at the foot of it.

nature of that transformation that the artistic tradition tries to address, not always very successfully, in the other major type of representation to which I now turn.

2. Conflicting Aims and the Ascent of Humanity

The most familiar depiction of the ascent itself has now become the common butt of jokes, used to parody art at its most naïve and literal. As we shall see, by no means all attempts are of this kind, but before examining the more adventurous it will be worth considering a few of the type under suspicion, to see what exactly has gone wrong. One of the great masterpieces of English Romanesque art is the so-called Cloisters Cross, now owned by the Metropolitan Museum in New York. On the cross's front there is a depiction in ivory of the Ascension with all of Christ's body above the waist already disappeared within the clouds.[27] The Virgin Mary and three disciples look on close by, while the heads of four more are immediately beneath his feet.[28] The strangeness of the literalism lies not so much in itself as in its juxtaposition with the exact opposite: the four heads are just above a tiny, triangular pinnacle of rock used to represent the mountain on which the scene is set. Literalism and symbolism are thus placed in uneasy tension. Apparently, this form of representation was itself an English invention.[29] On the continent Christ was depicted either departing on a cloud or else being pulled by the father's hand into the heavens. English preachers, however, apparently worried about the potential implication that the Son might be thought to need help, and so insisted on him piercing the clouds by his own efforts.

The aim was thus a laudable one, of emphasising Christ's full divinity. The sadness was that it made the incident seem quaint or ridiculous rather than itself awe-inspiring. To restore mystery and majesty, there was a need to move in one or other of two opposing directions: either to depict the scene after the disappearance or else to elaborate and enhance the disappearing feet. The potential of the former is well illustrated by a carving from eleventh century Cologne. The sadness of the Virgin Mary and the disciples as they look heavenwards leave us in no doubt to which event allusion is being made. Even so, there is too much of a sense of absence for the depiction to be entirely satisfactory, whereas an 1170 Psalter illustration points to what can be achieved by turning in the opposite direction. Angels attend to Christ's feet while he himself disappears into no ordinary cloud but a multi-coloured penumbra of concentric circles that suggest the perfection of a divinity that is all embracing in its power.[30] Unfortunately, few artists experimented with those more elaborate forms, and so feet sticking out from a cloud continue to proliferate over the

---

27   For illustrations, see E. C. Parker and C. T. Little, *The Cloister Cross: its Art and its Meaning* (London: Harvey Miller, 1994), VIII and 88.

28   Acts 1.14 was used to deduce the presence of Mary.

29   Argued by M. Shapiro, *Late Antiquity, Early Christian and Medieval Art* (London: Chatto & Windus, 1980), 267–88. He dates its origin to about AD 1000.

30   For illustration from this Psalter, now in Glasgow University Library, see Parker and Little, *The Cloister Cross*, 90.

subsequent centuries. Normally, a crowd of disciples is to be found as onlookers, but occasionally the Virgin Mary is there on her own, contemplating what has happened to her son. The intention is not to exalt Mary but rather to use her as a medium (like Mary Magdalene in the other incident) to negotiate a relation for the believer with her Son.31 Sadly, it was the simple English version that was also eventually to become the norm on the continent, as in a painting by Schongauer (d. 1491), now a sad contrast in its location at Colmar to the brilliance of Grünewald's Isenheim altarpiece located nearby in the same museum.

Schongauer may equally be used to illustrate more pedestrian representations of the resurrection in which Christ stands victorious on his open tomb. The problem is not the truth of the claim but that it seems to say almost too little – a great mystery has become a laboured fact. It was a conclusion to which artists also came in the sixteenth and seventeenth century. In their attempts to rectify the problem and thus give adequate expression to the mystery and majesty of the resurrection, however, any clear division between resurrection and ascension seemed to dissolve. To set the issue in context, we need first to retrace our steps and observe the earlier alternative iconography for the ascension in continental Europe. Giotto's work in the Scrovegni Chapel may be used by way of illustration.[32] Everything is focused on Christ sailing heavenwards on a cloud, his hands upraised. The disciples below are in two groups separated by two angels pointing heavenwards. There are, however, two further groups in the heavens themselves, also with arms upraised. Two centuries later, Perugino, Raphael's teacher, attempted a similar strategy, with angels playing instruments in the heavens as Christ ascends.[33] Nonetheless, Giotto's simpler gesture seems the more successful, not least because he mixes saints and angels and gives the impression of the saints having been carried into the heavens through the adoption of a similar gesture to Christ's: faithful trust pulling them through.

In 1475, however, Giovanni Bellini set Christ's resurrection similarly in the sky amidst clouds, with the soldiers looking on astonished from below.34 Although the idea did not immediately catch on, certainly from the time of the Council of Trent onwards it was to become quite a common form of depiction, and one can see why.35 For the majesty of the event was no longer now in doubt. A century later, El Greco's version (now in the Prado in Madrid) is one of the great triumphs of art.36 Christ is visibly rising in triumph, even pulling most of the semi-naked soldiers with him. One exception leans on his elbow, his flippant indifference accentuated by the

---

31 For a good example, see J. Plummer, *The Hours of Catherine of Cleves* (New York: George Braziller, 1966), no. 94 (part of the Hours of the Virgin).
32 Cole, *Giotto*, no. 37.
33 For illustration, V. Garibaldi, *Perugino* (Florence: Scala, 1997), 45.
34 Black and white illustration in G. Arbore, *Bellini* (London: Abbey, 1978), no. 21.
35 Titian was among the first to adopt the new form. For two examples from the 1520s and 1540s (the former adopted as the front cover for Tom Wright's recent book on the resurrection); see M. Kaminski, Titian (Cologne: Könemann, 1998), 39, 73.
36 Illustrated in L. Bronstein, *El Greco* (London: Thames and Hudson, 1991), no. 23.

helmet he wears, adorned as it is by coloured feathers. The other major exception, however, exercises a quite different role, his whole body thrown back towards us as he rejects Christ and attempts a counter-thrust to the general direction of the picture. The play and counterplay of forces cannot help but involve us in the action, and call from us some sort of response or decision.[37]

Such depictions become especially interesting where direct comparison is possible between how the artist has conceived resurrection and ascension. This is so with Tintoretto's work for the Scuola Grande of San Rocco in Venice, work done in the late 1570s. In his Resurrection Christ has almost become a bird as he flies out the tomb which four large angels have forced open, his pink shroud billowing in the wind like the wings of a great bird.[38] The pink may well be intended to recall the distant pink figure of God the Father in his own magnificent depiction of Jacob's Ladder elsewhere in the room.[39] There, however, the Father is a tiny figure in the infinite distance, whereas here Christ dominates the picture. There is drama in abundance, but the two women on the left have yet to arrive on the scene, while we are deprived sight of the faces of those already there. It is almost as though Tintoretto wants us to focus on the miracle itself, whereas in his Ascension human interplay is undoubtedly part of his aim.[40] Awe is the predominant response as angels accompany Christ rising in the clouds, olive and palm branches in their hands. The great surprise, though, is the reversal of reality. It is now this world that appears insubstantial compared with the reality to which Christ is returning.[41]

Rembrandt also has a Resurrection and Ascension only three years apart (1639 and 1636), both now at the Alte Pinakothek in Munich.[42] The former also has a dramatic, flying figure, but it is an angel rather than Christ, emblazoned in a heavenly shaft of light. Apparently, it was a late decision on Rembrandt's part to include Christ himself. Unfortunately, this was clearly a mistake since he remains a weak figure only just emerging from the tomb and from death. The Ascension by contrast is a marvellous evocation of Christ inviting us into participation in his own exaltation. Little cherubs clutch at his cloud as he ascends in a blaze of light emanating from the dove of the Holy Spirit far above. The disciples, however, are not so much awestruck as caught up in wonder and rapture and the desire to share, eyes and hands alike exhibiting a fervid intensity. It has been suggested that in this work 'Rembrandt went as far as he dared toward Catholic apostasy,' in attempting a likeness of God.[43] But the point is not that Christ has or is becoming divine, but

---

37   The extent of the success can be seen by comparing the work to an earlier attempt in Toledo: illustrated in R. G. Mann, *El Greco and his Patrons* (Cambridge: Cambridge University Press, 1986), no. 5.

38   Illustrated in F. Valcanover, *Jacopo Tintoretto and the Scuola Grande of San Rocco* (Venice: Storti Edizioni, 1983), 66.

39   Valcanover, *Jacopo Tintoretto*, 53.

40   Valcanover, *Jacopo Tintoretto*, 80.

41   Indicated by scale and by the relative strength of the colours for the two realities.

42   Illustrated in S. Schama, *Rembrandt's Eyes* (London: Penguin, 1999), 441, 444.

43   Schama's view, 441.

rather that his humanity is now exalted to a new and heavenly state. Indeed, as if to underline the fact, Rembrandt gives Christ a rather chunky set of legs.

In the twentieth century the range of experimentation has been quite broad. If angels accompanying Christ in heaven continue to be used to try to give a greater sense of majesty to the Ascension,[44] equally resurrection scenes sometimes borrow imagery that would seem to be more appropriate to the Ascension. So, for example, André Kamba Luesa from Zaire adopts a majesty figure of Christ dancing as symbolic of the resurrection, with rocks rent apart and diminutive human figures on either side sharing in his joy.[45] That same image of the dancer is also used by the Indonesian artist, Bagong Kussudiardja, explicitly for the ascension, with a young Christ dancing his way heavenwards as a graceful swan accompanies him in the background.[46] Even where there can be no doubt that the allusion is to the resurrection, dance can still sometimes be implicit. Paul Granlund has a magnificent sculpture that depicts Christ at the moment he splits apart the tomb.[47] But it is not just strength that is depicted, for in the process he seems almost like a bird ready to take elegant flight.

But of all modern Ascensions it is Salvador Dalí's of 1958 that is the most distinctive, the most original.[48] The sea-line of his beloved Port Lligat is just visible at the bottom, but the painting is dominated by an ascending Christ viewed from below as tunnel-like he enters what looks like a great hollow globe or cone stretching ever upwards, at the top of which perches a welcoming dove, its presence accentuated by a larger feminine form above.[49] The yellow cone pierces dramatic, red, fissured clouds in the background, but perhaps the most interesting feature is Christ's feet. For they are in no sense idealised. They have the same dirt and roughness that is to be found in the hands of Christ in Dalí's Glasgow painting of the Christ of St John of the Cross. It looks as though, like Rembrandt, he wanted to stress the continuing corporeality of Christ even in his exalted state.

This complex history does pose a number of difficult questions. The inappropriateness of literal representations, whether of ascension or of resurrection, can almost go without saying. The resultant merging of the two is, however, not without its problems. Biblical scholars, even some of a more conservative mould, often do speak in similar terms, with resurrection experiences sometimes seen

---

44   For two examples from the United States, J. B. Simpson and G. H. Eatman, *A Treasury of Anglican Art* (New York: Rizzoli, 2002), 128–29.

45   The work dates from 1992; illustrated in R. O'Grady, *Christ for All People: Celebrating a World of Christian Art* (Auckland: Pace, 2001), 143.

46   Illustrated in S. A. Blain (ed.), *Imaging the Word* (Cleveland: United Church Press, 1995), Vol. 2, 202.

47   Illustrated in K. T. Lawrence (ed.), *Imagining the Word* (Cleveland: United Church Press, 1994), Vol. 1, 185.

48   Illustrated in D. Ades, *Dalí's Optical Illusions* (New Haven: Yale University Press, 2000), no. 56.

49   Her features are borrowed from those of his wife, Gala.

as what the already ascended Christ offered to his disciples.[50] But, however the chronology is tackled, the experience and content of the two doctrines do seem significantly different. The resurrection speaks of triumph over death as Christ continues to be available to his disciples in an intimate, if not always immediately recognisable, manner; the ascension about his location elsewhere. To make his resurrection already a shooting off elsewhere, however figurative, is surely to allude to something else, and is scarcely endorsed by Scripture, which significantly offers no description of the actual event in any of the gospels. Admittedly, the description of the ascension is itself also minimal. Yet it does speak essentially of glory in a way that the resurrection appearances, at least as we now have them, do not. God the Son is once more with his Father, but so too is his exalted humanity, a humanity that is stressed by the angelic witnesses declaring that he will return in like manner. It is that joint reality that both Rembrandt and Dalí were attempting to express in combining glory and more obvious signs of an earthly humanity. In this they succeeded where many another artist failed. They also thereby underlined how profoundly significant the words of the angels in Luke's account really were: it is the human 'Jesus' who is being taken up into heaven and who will return again.[51]

Poets and composers too have struggled to find adequate imagery to capture that sense of a continuing but transfigured humanity. Easier is the more basic assertion of its continuing relevance to us, as in these lines of John Donne:

Nor doth hee by afcending, fhow alone,
    But firft hee, and hee firft enters the way,
    O ftrong Ramme, which haft batter'd heaven for mee,
    Mild lambe which with thy blood, haft mark'd the path;
Bright torch, which fhin'ft, that I the way may fee.[52]

His near contemporary, Henry Vaughan, has several poems on the theme, but perhaps the most intriguing from a theological perspective is the one which toys with what the Ascension's new human reality might be like. The first and last verses of his *Ascension-Hymn* plays with two types of transformation:

---

50   Raymond Brown comments: 'from the moment that God raises Jesus up, he is in heaven ... if he makes appearances, he appears from heaven'; *The Gospel according to John* (New York: Doubleday, 1970), 1013. F. F. Bruce takes a similar view: 'the resurrection appearances ... were visitations from that eternal order to which his "body of glory" now belonged'; *The Book of the Acts* (Grand Rapids: Eerdmans, 1988), 37.

51   Acts 1.11.

52   From *Ascention* in John Donne, Poems by J. D. with elegies on the author's death (London: printed by M(iles) F(letcher) for Iohn Marriott, 1633), 32.

> Dust and clay
> Man's ancient wear!
> Here you must stay,
>   But I elsewhere;
> Souls sojourn here, but may not rest;
> Who will ascent, must be undrest.

If these lines sound as though Vaughan wishes to speak only of an ascent of the soul, the final verse indicates that here we are dealing with metaphor ('undressed' is 'the old Man'), and that in fact he envisages the whole of what Christ or we are entering this new reality:

> He alone
> And none else can
> Bring bone to bone
> And rebuild man;
> And by His all-subduing might
> Make clay ascend more quick than light.[53]

Modern poets such as John Updike or Denise Levertov often assume a very physical resurrection, but when it comes to the ascension their judgment can be more uncertain.[54] Levertov is a fascinating figure, given her mixed background (she was the daughter of a Welsh mother and of a Russian Jew who eventually became an Anglican priest). Perhaps this is what led her to insist on a rather literal reading of the resurrection. It therefore comes all the more as a surprise that the ascension is presented as a dissolving of all that makes us most material, one might almost say most human. 'Human cells', 'molecules,' even 'the five senses' must now all go. At one level her questions look exactly right. Whatever heaven is like, it is not contiguous with our space and time, and so Christ's human reality there cannot be the same as it was here. But so insistent are such claims that it looks almost as though she is questioning whether that new reality is human at all. Yet, like Vaughan, she too ends on a different note, speaking of the 'last self-enjoined task of Incarnation' being to 'mother' 'his birth'. There is a new human reality mothered into birth, a body hugely different from what he had on earth but nonetheless one that continues his incarnational identity into that new context.

---

53   E. K. Chambers (ed.), *The Poems of Henry Vaughan, Silurist*, Volume 1 (London: Lawrence & Bullen Ltd, 1896), 180–81. For other poems on the Ascension see A. Rudrum (ed.), *Henry Vaughan: The Complete Poems* (Harmondsworth: Penguin, 1983 ed.), 185–86, 243–47.

54   For physical resurrection, cf. John Updike's *Seven Stanzas at Easter* accessed at <www.edow.org/spirituality/updike.html> on 29 November 2006 and Levertov's *On Belief in the Physical Resurrection of Jesus*; the latter is available in her *Sands of the Well* (Newcastle: Bloodaxe, 1998), 115–16. See Levertov's poem *Ascension* in her *A Door in the Hive*; *Evening Train* (Newcastle: Bloodaxe, 1993), 207.

Both art and poetry are thus, with varying degrees of success, struggling to give adequate expression to the doctrine. Christ's divinity has to be asserted, but so too does his transformed humanity, and both pictures and words have difficulty in finding the right images or metaphors for such a transformation. It might be thought that music would fare better, since progression in music inevitably speaks of movement and so of change. Perhaps the most commonly sung ascension anthem these days is Gerald Finzi's God is gone up, his setting of Edward Taylor's poem based on Psalm 47. It is a fine piece of music, but the stress is all on acknowledgement of Christ's divinity. We need, therefore, to go further back in time if a more balanced emphasis is sought. Anonymous 4, a now internationally known group of four female singers based in New York, have recently reconstructed and sung a mass setting for Ascension, as they believe it might have sounded in AD 1000.55 Appropriate tropes have been added to the ordinary throughout.56 The introit takes the form of a dialogue and specifically addresses the question, quem creditis super astra ascendisse? ('whom do you believe to have ascended beyond the heavens?') stressing in response both humanity and divinity, a theme that is repeated at the offertory when Christ is described as 'carrying into heaven the wounds of his life-giving cross as his emblem.' If the Alleluia before the Gospel picks the biblical image of 'captivity led captive,'57 at the troped communion we are told 'the body which we now receive on earth already sits at the right hand of the Father in heaven.' Jumping to the eighteenth century, we can listen to a setting of the events, admired by both Mozart and Beethoven, C. P. E. Bach's Die Auferstehung und Himmelfahrt Jesu.58 If the final chorus, like Finzi, turns to Psalm 47 and is really a celebration of divine power with its elaborate contrapuntal writing, the rest of the piece leaves us in no doubt that it is as a man that Christ has triumphed. It is perhaps Olivier Messiaen, though, in the twentieth century who best captures the two aspects. His 1932 work L'Ascension, originally scored for orchestra but also available for organ, consists of four meditations, three on words from John's Gospel and the fourth on the collect for the day. The last of the four has a melody that ascends gradually,59 and it is this notion that forms the basis for the parallel

---

55   Anonymous 4, *1000: A Mass for the End of Time* (Harmonia Mundi, 2000). The chosen title seems to me unfortunate, but was chosen apparently to capture the apocalyptic fervour around at the time of the new millennium, and the ascension's promise of Christ's return.

56   The 'ordinary' is the fixed element in the mass, 'tropes' additional commentary, usually, but by no means always, biblical quotation.

57   Applied to the Ascension in Ephesians, 4.8 (quoting Ps. 68.18), the verse is being used to speak of Christ as victorious over all the forces of evil ranged against him.

58   First performed in 1774, Mozart actually conducted three performances in Vienna in 1788.

59   *Priere du Christ montant vers son Pere*. There is a fine performance on the organ of Beauvais cathedral by Jennifer Bate, personally endorsed by Messaien (recorded in 1982 and available on the Regis label).

piece in his more famous work, *Quatuor pour la fin du Temps*.[60] Written and first performed while he was imprisoned at Görlitz in 1941, an earlier section uses cello and piano to portray the eternity of the Word, while this final section has violin and piano gradually ascend, finally disappearing into silence.

Sermons, as one might expect, do often focus on the impact of what happened on us as believers. So, for example, if on the one hand Bede in the eighth century is concerned to differentiate this ascension from all others, he also remains in no doubt about its implications for humanity.[61] He writes of the disciples: 'how sweet were the tears which they poured forth when ... they discerned that their God and Lord was now bringing thither part of their own nature.' Indeed, Bede finds not only humanity thus exalted but implicitly all of creation: 'he lifted up this earth on the wings of the wind when he elevated what he had taken from the earth.'[62] Newman's sermons so often exhibit mastery of prose style, with accompanying striking image or phrase, that it is with some disappointment that one reads what he has to say for successive years on this theme. There is plenty on Christ as our heavenly mediator, but only one sermon focuses on the image of ascent itself. It is unsurprising that mountains are drawn into the discussion, but I detected only one occasion when he showed a little of his usual fire, and even then he is somewhat apologetic. For, following the hints in John's Gospel he observes: 'we may even say that, when our Lord was lifted on the cross, then, too, he presented to us the same example of a soul raised heavenwards and hid in God.'[63]

It is therefore something of a relief to turn to Austin Farrer's provocative treatment of the theme.[64] His starting point is the familiar ascension hymn:

Hail the day that sees him rise
Glorious to his native skies

Initially the theology sounds fine, but further reflection, Farrer argues, suggests quite otherwise. Christ's divinity never had a birth; so the skies can scarcely be 'native' to him except in some highly metaphorical sense. But equally the skies – heaven – were not native to humanity prior to this point. As Farrer observes, 'the marvel is not that the celestial Son of God returns where he belongs, but that the earthborn Jesus rises

---

60 The conclusion of the quartet, VIII: Louange à l'immortalité de Jésus. The contrasting earlier section is V: Louange à l'eternité de Jésus.

61 *Homilies on the Gospels*, II, 15. I have used the translation by L. T. Martin and D. Hurst (Kalamazoo: Cistercian Publications, 1991), 135–47, esp. 141, 143. Bede's Latin text seems to have spoken of Elijah being taken up 'as if into heaven': 145 (not the usual Vulgate reading).

62 Cf. Ps. 18.10.

63 J. H. Newman, *Parochial and Plain Sermons* (San Francisco: Ignatius Press, 1987), V, 15, 1306–13, esp. 1308. For a mediatorial example, see II, 18, 356–62.

64 L. Houlden (ed.), *Austin Farrer: The Essential Sermons* (London: SPCK, 1991), 69–71, esp. 70.

into the native heaven of that divine life which had become man in him ... he is the man glorified, which each of us may hope by his grace to become.'[65]

3. Conclusion

In this essay I have been concerned to illustrate the way in which artistic appropriation of Scripture and Christian doctrine does not simply echo what it has learnt from these sources but also tries to develop further some of its unresolved tensions, in ways that are sometimes illuminating and sometimes not. Thus in the encounter of Christ with Mary Magdalene the artistic tradition was clearly unhappy that her story should end on a note of rebuke, and so pursued how the exchange might still in its turn have produced a deepening of the relationship, not only for Mary but also for us in the transfiguration of our own bodily desires. Again, creative work on the ascent itself in art, music and poetry all alike struggled with what it might mean to say that Christ's humanity continued into a quite different, new reality. If no clear answers are given, there is a stronger insistence than is always noticeable in academic theology that it must be a gloried human being that survives the transformation, and not just an exalted deity. Rembrandt's chunky legs and Dalí's dirty feet promise the gradual, ascending rise of Messiaen's music for us also in a way that, for example, Gerard Manley Hopkins' beautified Christ does not. In a sermon of 1879 he had declared: 'for myself I make no secret I look forward to seeing the matchless beauty of Christ's body in the heavenly light.'[66] That image, though, speaks too much of a world utterly different from our own, whereas the encounter with Mary Magdalene and the flawed ascending body alike give us hope, for the absorption of ordinary and troubled humanity into that more wondrous reality.[67]

---

65 Farrer also pursues a similar theme in *A Celebration of Faith* (London: Hodder & Stoughton, 1970), 96–99.
66 Sermon for 23 November 1879; W. H. Gardner (ed.), *Gerard Manley Hopkins: A Selection of his Poetry and Prose* (Harmondsworth: Penguin, 1953), 137–39.
67 I am grateful to Ann Loades for comments on an earlier draft. For some helpful reflections of her own on related themes, see H. Walton and S. Durber (eds), *Silence in Heaven* (London: SCM, 1994), 9–13, 130–34.

Resonances and Challenges: A Response to the Volume

Jeremy Begbie

When a violinist draws a bow across a string, the violin's wooden body will respond to the vibrations of the string transmitted through the bridge; one of its natural frequencies will closely match the frequency of the string and – if the body is carefully variegated and crafted – related frequencies will also be stimulated, resulting in a rich and full sound. The wood resonates with the string. Trevor Hart and Steven Guthrie have gathered these essays out of the belief that the multi-faceted metaphor of artistic performance has the power to generate a range of resonant responses from the infinitely variegated and divinely shaped 'body' of Christian truth. That is to say, the metaphor has the capacity to enable the natural frequencies of the Christian Gospel to 'sound forth' in a rich and full way.

It is, then, around the notion of performance and its natural correlates and entailments that we are invited to find the coherence of these essays. Some of the essays address the matter of performance directly: the first three, for example, deal at length with theatrical drama. In the case of those that do not engage with 'performing' in its ordinary or literal sense, we are asked nonetheless to read them from this perspective. Thus the enactment of Christian identity in and by the Church can be considered as a 'performance' of sorts, and a range of art forms (whether or not 'performative' in the strict sense) can be interpreted as embodiments or enactments of Christian truth and tradition. The collection as a whole, then, does not comprise a linear argument, nor a singular, systematised proposal, still less anything exhaustive or comprehensive, but rather an invitation to explore the multiple theological resonances that can be set in motion by an artistic metaphor.

Here I offer some reflections on this exercise, mainly as an attempt to clarify what is and what is not being offered here. I shall then on to highlight two challenges in particular that I believe emerge for theology.

Resonance Realism[1]

To begin with, the process of 'setting off' theological resonances exemplified here is a process of responsible, disciplined enquiry and discovery. It is not a matter of simply allowing one thought to suggest another at random, with little or no sense of

---

[1] I owe this term to an unpublished paper by John Puddefoot, given at a conference in Cambridge in 1994. I am grateful to Dr Puddefoot for pointing me to the fruitfulness of the model of resonance as applied to theological method.

responsibility to anything other than our own metaphorical thought processes (though there may at times be a proper place in theology for relatively 'free association'). When a violin-maker tests a note on a new instrument, her intention is to hear if the wood is responding; she is, in effect, wanting the integrity of the wood (or at least part of it) to be focused and rendered perceptible in sound. Indeed, eventually she will want every note to be full and rich; she will want the wood of that instrument to 'come to sound' in the fullest way possible. One of the most striking things about these essays is what we might call their 'realist' flavour: that is, while there is no underplaying or denying that all our commerce with the world is mediated through history, language and culture (something brought out very strongly in Michael Partridge's contribution), there appears to be a shared conviction that theology is nonetheless constrained and ordered chiefly by realities other than those constructed by human agents, supremely the reality of the triune God. (This is something one can by no means take for granted in much of the current theology-and-arts dialogue.) If the theological resonances of 'performance' are sought, they are indeed 'theological', their *logos* or configuration will be that of the triune God whose identity is manifest supremely in Jesus Christ. There is an inescapable precedence evident here, the priority of a living God, and, to be sure, it is an *active* precedence – we can only speak *logoi* to and about God because God has first spoken his Word to us. (On this particular point there is an important disanalogy with the resonant violin body: though we do indeed search for metaphors that 'resonate' with God and God's truth, we do so only because this God has already 'sounded forth' to us.)

Of course, there will be the suspicion among many that involvement in the arts threatens this 'realist' concern. It is one that I have often encountered among theologians. There is a strong sense that to undertake any serious theology in the company of artists inevitably compromises our access to truth. (Recall Audrey in *As You Like It*: (Act 3, Scene 3)'I do not know what "poetical" is. Is it honest in deed and word? Is it a true thing?') It is suspected that the intense investment of human subjectivity assumed to be especially characteristic of the arts (both for practitioner and receiver) together with the heavily constructivist quality of the arts (they are, after all, humanly *made*) render them very poor vehicles for accessing the nature of any realities independent of ourselves or what we fashion, let alone the reality of God. Closely linked to this, there is the fear that the arts will of necessity muddy the channels of epistemological rigour, compromising the kind of clarity possible with, say, certain kinds of philosophical discourse. (Malcolm Guite, in his essay, addresses some of the complex streams of thought that have led to these reservations and fears.)

What has guided the editors of this collection, however, and emerges into the open at many points in the essays themselves, is a belief in the 'heuristic' capacity of the arts (and the metaphors which derive from them): their ability to advance discovery, to 'make room' for theological realities to declare themselves. Again, the model of resonance is appropriate: though the wooden body of the violin is met by a dynamic activity – the vibrations of the string transmitted through the bridge – the integrity of the wood is not compromised, but enabled to declare itself in sound. The New Testament scholar Tom Wright brings out something of this in some recent reflections on music. 'If all theology, all sermons, had to be set to music,' he says, 'our teaching and preaching would not only be more mellifluous; it might also approximate more closely to God's truth, the truth revealed in and as the Word made flesh, crucified and risen.'[2]

Implicit here is the conviction that not only do the arts have this heuristic ability, but that they are able to exercise it in quite distinctive and particular ways, ways not always shared by other more traditional modes of theological knowing and enquiry. (This is part of what informs Sherry's distinction between 'illustration' and 'primary expression'.) In the case of the violin, strings will bring about resonances in the violin's wood that, say, a voice cannot bring about. As every love-sick teenager knows, there are times when only a song will do. So we find in many places the authors delving into the very particular powers of art forms to elucidate theological subject-matter (for example, David Brown on specific capacities of visual art, Malcolm Guite on techniques of prose and poetry, Steven Guthrie on the embodied character of musical perception). This speaks to that suspicion of art's lack of clarity that I mentioned earlier. Against the presumption that the arts will inevitably cloud our perception, it has long been recognised that there are dimensions of theological truth that can only properly be heard, or at least allow themselves to be heard with greatest lucidity, through the arts. It is a point made tellingly in Martha Nussbaum's penetrating study *Love's Knowledge*. Her focus is in the inclusion of narrative literature in philosophical enquiry, particularly in the pursuit of ethical wisdom. But her words ring true for theology also. She argues that when a writer chooses one style or form rather than another, the substance of what is said is inevitably affected, and that this applies to philosophical writing as much as anything else (even though some philosophers can be reluctant to admit it). 'Style itself makes its claims, expresses its own sense of what matters. Literary form is not separable from philosophical content but is, itself, part of content – an integral part, then, of the search for and the statement of truth.'[3] More than this, she claims that 'certain truths about human life can *only* be fittingly and accurately stated in the language and forms characteristic of the narrative artist.'[4] In other words – and she demonstrates this at some length – matters of ethics, or at least some fundamental ethical issues and concerns, *compel* the inclusion of narrative literature. She reflects on her early experience of teaching philosophy in an academic context:

> [T]he conventional style of Anglo-American philosophical prose usually prevailed: a style correct, scientific, abstract, hygienically pallid, a style that seemed to be regarded as a kind of all-purpose solvent in which philosophical issues of any kind at all could be efficiently disentangled, and all conclusions neatly disengaged. That there might be *other*

---

2   N. T. Wright, 'Resurrection: From Theology to Music and Back Again', in Jeremy Begbie (ed.), *Sounding the Depths: Theology Through the Arts* (London: SCM, 2002), 210f.
3   Martha Nussbaum, *Love's Knowledge: Essays on Philosophy and Literature* (Oxford: OUP, 1990), 3.
4   Ibid., 5. My emphasis.

ways of being precise, *other* conceptions of lucidity and completeness that might be held to be *more* appropriate for ethical thought – this was, on the whole, neither asserted nor even denied.'[5]

Integrities in Resonance

Clearly, in order for the arts to play their unique part in witnessing to and embodying theological wisdom, due respect needs to be paid to their integrity. This is another notable feature of these essays. If the discussion is marked by a realist orientation, within that orientation there is also a strong concern to do justice to the particularities of artistic practices (in this case, those of performance) and the metaphors that arise from them.

The point is worth underlining, since many will feel decidedly edgy about any attempt to draw on the arts with theological ends in mind. It will be feared that the arts will not be allowed to do their own kind of work in their own kind of way, that their distinctiveness and particularity will be distorted through trying to force them into ready-made doctrinal positions; in short, that their integrity will be stifled. Any notion of 'using' the arts (or an artistic metaphor) in the 'service' of theology would seem to suggest some kind of diminishment, perhaps even a crude exploitation of the arts. (Is this not what happens with propaganda?) The writers, however, show they are more than aware of such dangers. Not only are we given examples of scrupulous artistic analysis, we are also warned about the drawbacks of failing to attend to the way various art forms actually operate: hence the sharp words from two of the authors about using dramatic analogies that ignore features intrinsic to theatrical performance, features that have much to say to theology (Khovacs, Edelman). Again, the model of resonance helps us see what is intended: when we play a string to evoke a sound from another string, the first string is indeed an 'instrument' (in more senses than one), a tool of our endeavours. But this does not in any way threaten its integrity. Similarly, an art form can serve theological interests without necessarily being disfigured or distorted in the process.

Respecting the integrity of this or that art will mean acknowledging that the basic realities of the arts are embodied actions (which may or may not involve 'works' or 'texts'): singing, listening, painting, and so on. The arts, as is so often (over)stressed in postmodern discourse, are not so much 'objects' or 'things' as ways of being in the world, ways we negotiate the world we inhabit – a major reason for the fittingness of the 'performance' metaphor as applied to the arts. It is noteworthy that the authors frequently call the reader 'into' an art form ('consider this painting...', or 'notice this feature of the poem...' or whatever); despite the drawbacks imposed by the academic essay format, they are keen that to some extent we encounter the music, play, or whatever, that we are drawn into art's life. If artistic performance does yield fertile resources for theology, it will do so first of all when it is taken seriously *as*

---

5   Ibid., 19. My emphases.

a practice or cluster of practices. Khovacs writes: 'it is not merely that playwrights have something to say (that plays "mean") but that they want to say it in a certain way – that plays mean through performance.' The consequences for theology done with or through the arts are clear: at some point, one needs to come to terms directly with the art in question, to allow it to pull us into its own dynamic. Any testing of artistic metaphors needs to reckon with this. One cannot test the fruitfulness of, say, a dramatic metaphor for theology without, at least at some stage, experiencing drama. It may be quite proper to 'stand back' and test metaphors in relation to what are acknowledged as theology's normative constraints (God's self-witness in Jesus Christ, attested in Scripture). But since these metaphors have arisen from concrete practices, this cannot be done unless we have allowed the art in question to engage with the dynamic of revelation *as* an art form, and allowed ourselves to be caught up in it. This is another reason why resonance is such an appropriate model, since there is no neutral ground from which we can check the adequacy of resonance: we have to try it out in practice, to play the note and listen for the resonances that are returned to us.

By the same token, respecting integrity means recognising limitations. And here I find myself wanting to underline quite heavily the limitations of the performance metaphor itself, especially as applied to the Christian life, with the presence of a verbal script assumed (analogous to the Bible). For it is not at all clear that this can do justice to the contingent, the unpredictable, indeed, to the damaging circumstances that life so often delivers out of the blue. A number of writers allude to this. Quash would like von Balthasar's theology to be 'more genuinely open to the future';[6] Khovacs (drawing on Craigo-Snell) urges that rehearsal be accorded a proper place in the theological appropriation of dramatic metaphor. Hart reminds us that as 'actors' (those who practise Christian faith),

> we face a future which is open, unknown in its openness, and often threatening in its unknowability. Even our best projections and most reasonable expectations can be and frequently are defied or rudely interrupted by the unexpected development, by 'events' which are no respecter of the neat patterns of our planning.

This prompts him to continue: 'Perhaps in this respect the performance of life is indeed rather more like a certain sort of improvised drama than the playing of a carefully scripted role.'

Specifically, Hart goes on to speak of the Christian life as an improvised cadenza. But it is Samuel Wells who pushes us most strongly towards improvisation. Insofar as it is understood as performing a script, the performance metaphor has major drawbacks when applied to living in faithfulness to the Bible. He writes:

> The script does not provide all the answers. Life throws up circumstances that the gospel seems not to cover. The script is unfinished. There is more to the Christian story than the

---

6   Quash develops these themes much more fully in *Theology and the Drama of History* (Cambridge: Cambridge University Press, 2005).

pages of the Bible disclose. The notion of script can militate against genuine engagement with the world. The idea of a script can suggest the recreation of a golden era – emphasising the replication of past acts, rather than the discovery of new wonders. These drawbacks can encourage the Church to follow predictable courses. Sometimes it lives in the past, aspiring to a world of scriptural purity. Sometimes it dismisses the script, as the fruit of a bygone era, or a curtailment of freedom. Sometimes it seeks to translate the script into contemporary motifs. The confluence of these approaches can lead to considerable bewilderment. The Church feels alone on a rough sea, with no anchor and no stars to steer by.

How can we live and act faithfully as Christians without a script that dictates every move for us? Through improvising, Wells believes. In improvisation, we act as part of a community embedded in a tradition in ways that are faithful to Scripture, yet at the same time, just because we are so embedded we can respond appropriately and flexibly to any number of fresh, unpredictable contexts. (We might add that musical improvisation can introduce us with a singular intensity to this interplay of faithfulness and contingency since most often not dependent on words at all; it is *nothing but* sounds and actions. Hart's recourse to the cadenza metaphor is significant in this respect.)

This is not to recommend a wholesale abandonment of the notion of performance in favour of improvisation; nor is it to suggest that the idea of performance has reached the end of its shelf-life in contemporary theology. It is only to stress that the theological resonances the performance metaphor will 'set off' are limited, and it is part of recognising artistic integrity to know just where those limits are.

Challenges

I have tried to highlight two broad concerns which seem to emerge from these essays when taken as a whole: a concern to be oriented chiefly to the 'realist' claims of Christian orthodoxy, and a concern that the integrities of artistic *modi operandi* are honoured, and honoured not least *in order* to be true to faith's realist commitments. This throws up very sharply what I believe to be an enormous challenge for the future conversation between theology and the arts, and one that has, as far as I can tell, received relatively little attention. It is this: to develop an *appropriate rigour* when working with the arts in theology, one that is unambiguous about where theology's final and ultimate responsibilities lie, and about the criteria which govern such responsibility, while at the same time allowing various art form(s) to show us that there are in fact a variety of ways in which rigour can be exercised and carried through. This is an immensely demanding and complex task, but as the exchanges between artists and theologians gather momentum, it cannot be shirked. On the one hand lie the hazards of some sort of anti-aesthetic rationalism, on the other an undisciplined aestheticism in which fidelity to the self-communicating God of Jesus Christ slips out of sight. It ought to be a major part of the future theology-and-the-arts agenda to demonstrate that these need not be the only two options.

In closing, it is worth registering a further challenge these essays provoke. And I suspect it will be one of the major issues in the ongoing conversation between theology and the arts in the years to come. It turns on what on the face of it is a very bland two-fold observation: that different art forms have different capacities and at the same time frequently interact with each other. Speaking of the different genres to be found in Scripture's 'polyphony', Quash proposes that

> All of these genres are valuable. Each has its own surplus of meaning to contribute to the others. Each genre will have particular strengths at opening up and exploring particular aspects of reality. Each will have a particular range and depth of penetration. Thus the theologian who has the ability to command a wide set of genres will find his or her capacity to conceptualize, to interpret, and to participate in the life of the Christian community and the wider world, enriched in consequence.

If for 'genre' we read 'art form', and think about the way the arts have related to each other in Christian life and thought through the ages, it is obvious that 'polyphony' has not always been the order of the day. The relationships between different art forms have often been strained, even destructive. And they have often been closely tied up with less than helpful views about the relative importance of our five senses. In the history of Christian thought we often find one type of art – and with it, one sense – privileged above others. William Dyrness charts some of these tendencies in Protestantism, but they can be found in many other traditions. They frequently generate dichotomies (word vs. image, ear vs. eye, prose vs. poetry, and so forth) which are often arranged as hierarchies (word over image, hearing over seeing, prose over poetry), hierarchies which have a habit of flipping into their opposites. Of course, to suggest *a priori* that all art forms or sensory modes must be given equal weight and value in theology is disingenuous. Here I simply want to draw attention to what would seem to be a major responsibility of the theologian in this context: to find ways in which, in the service of the Christian Gospel, one can be alert to the *distinctiveness* of different art forms and their associated sensory modes, and at the same time be alert to ways in which they can (and frequently do) *interrelate*. Rosemary Muir Wright is especially sensitive to these matter in her chapter, and in his treatment of the 'visual culture of the Reformation', Dyrness rightly criticises those approaches which overlook

> the way that the visual and the oral are interrelated in culture. While reformers tried to cut the ancient link between worship and the visual (and even the dramatic), this did not keep the people from responding to visual and dramatic elements in the worship. Moreover, in the prints, wall hangings, even in the published books a – sometimes rich – visual culture survived amidst the strictures of the reformers teaching.

In response to the frequent calls we hear for the 'recovery' of the visual in Churches, or of the aural, of painting or music or whatever, we might do well to ask the question: 'In relation to what?' History shows that pendulum swings in theology are not uncommon, and attempts simply to 'recover' things can easily leave the Church as impoverished as before, only now with a new art or sense needlessly degraded or marginalised. So, for example, instead of castigating the postmodern sensibility for its captivity to 'the image' and insisting on a recovery of 'the aural', we could remind ourselves that most of the images which bombard a teenager today already come with sound; the crucial question then becomes not 'how do we recover a sense of hearing as against seeing?', but 'how can the Church encourage deeper ways of seeing, that can interact fruitfully with deeper ways of hearing?' In short, the challenge is not to identify an art form or sense that is superior in every respect for theology, but to be aware of the distinctive strengths and limitations of each, with a view to each making its own particular contribution to the enrichment of Christian life and thought, and often in direct relation to each other – polyphony indeed.

Index

Ades, D. 267
Aeschylus 16, 190
Aesop 193
Allmen, J-J von 98
Andrewes, Lancelot 261, 262
Angelico, Fra 112, 249, 250, 255, 256, 259
Anonymous 4, The 270
Anscombe, G. E. M. 192
Anselm 193, 259
Aquinas, Thomas 100, 109, 111, 112, 114, 115, 116, 117, 121
Arbore, G. 265
Arendt, Hannah 134
Aristotle 14, 15, 100
Aristotelian 53, 62, 111
Armstrong, Elizabeth 221
Artaud, Anton 53, 54
Arthur, Chris 124, 125
Astington, John H. 167
Aston, M. 220
Atlantic Theatre Company 60, 64
Augustine 49, 50, 84, 111, 114, 225, 258
Avera, John 133
Austin, J.L. 4, 55

Bach, C. P. E. 270
Bach, Johann Sebastian 191, 193, 194
Bacon, Francis 198, 263
Bailin, Sharon 42, 46
Bakhtin, Mikhail 14, 23-27, 29-31
Balthasar, Hans Urs von 7, 8, 11, 13, 14, 16-25, 27-31, 33-40, 44-45, 47-50, 277
    Theo-drama 7, 8, 21, 28, 31, 33, 34, 36, 38, 39, 45, 48
Barrett, C.K. 258
Barth, Karl 29, 74, 170-171, 176, 178-184, 209
Barton, Stephen C. 6, 147
Bate, Jennifer 270
Bauckham, Richard 6, 183, 185
Beckett, Samuel 19, 20, 52, 212
Bede, The Venerable 271

Beer, John 16
Beethoven, Ludwig van 191, 194, 195, 270
Begbie, Jeremy 8, 105, 148-9, 158, 201, 273-80
Bell, Catherine 69, 71
Bellini, Giovanni 250, 251, 265
Benedetti, Jean 56, 71
Bennett, J. A. W. 195
Benjamin, Walter 134
Bernanos, Georges 190
Bernard, J. H. 258
Bernard, Richard 237-8
Bernard of Clairvaux, St. 101, 242
Bial, Henry 59, 71
Biernatzki, William E. 130
Bishop, Marsha Brock 136
Blain, S. A. 167
Blake, William 22
Boal, Augusto 43, 54, 152
Boethius 14, 15, 16
Bolt, Robert 152
Borsato, Diane 47
Bossy, John 220
Botticelli 193, 196
Bourdieu, Pierre 69
Bowden, John 190
Bradby, David 49
Brandes, George 167, 168, 200, 201, 202, 208, 209, 210, 213, 214, 215
Brecht, Bertolt 11, 43-44, 59-72
Brissett, Dennis 3
Brock, Sebastian 101
Brook, Peter 42, 52, 53, 66, 67, 71
Bronstein, L. 265
Brown, C. 261
Brown, Colin 98
Brown, David 70, 72, 185, 188, 257-272, 275
Brown, Raymond 140, 268
Brown, Warren S. 93

Bruce, F. F. 268
Brueghel, Pieter 142
Brueggemann, Walter 147
Buchanan, Judith 124
Buel, Hal 133
Burke, Peter 228
Burnham, Frederic B. 148

Cajetan, Cardinal 74, 109-21
Calixtus III, Pope 248
Calvin, John 219, 221, 225, 226, 228, 229, 230, 231, 232, 233, 235, 237
Campbell, W. E. 231
Camus, Albert 191, 192
Cappella, Joseph N. 126
Carlson, Marvin 49
Carracci, Ludovico 253
Carrol Noël 44
Carson, D. A. 97
Cassidy, Brendan 241
Centi, T. 116
Chrysostom, St John 258
Chalmers, David 243
Chambers, E. K. 269
Charlemagne 100
Charry, Ellen 136
Chaucer, Geoffrey 5, 15, 16
Chazelle, Celia 241
Chekhov, Anton 20, 43, 54, 59, 62
Chomsky, Noam 144, 145
Cicero 110, 111, 237
Cole, B. 258, 265
Collier, Jeremy 52, 72
Collinson, Patrick 222, 224, 228, 229, 230
Constantine, David 263
Copeau, Jacques 151
Correggio 252, 253, 260
Cortesi, Paolo 116
Craigo-Snell, Shannon 11, 38-9, 45-9, 277
Cranmer, Thomas 222
Crew, Phyllis Mack 228
Crigler, Ann N. 126
Crockett, Bryan 228
Cunningham, Merce 52

Da Capustrano, John 248
Dalhoff, Meinolf 251
Dalí, Salvador 267, 268, 272
D'Amico, John F. D. 110, 116

Dante Alighieri 14, 27, 193
Da Vinci, Leonardo 117
D'Aubignac, Abbé 40
D'Augivillier, Comte 140
Davey, Nicholas 174, 175, 185
Deacy, Christopher 191
De Caus, Salomon 226
De Grazia, Margreta 167
Della Francesca, Piero 190
Del Piombo, Sebastiano 252
De Maistre, Roy 263
De Medici, Catherine 224
De Medici, Giulio 252
De' Menabuoi, Giusto 249
Democritus 169
Denis, Maurice 262
Denzinger, Götz 246
Derrida, Jacques 158
Diehl, Huston 227
DiGiovanni, Janine 128
Dixon, John W. 46, 189-90, 191, 198
Dobson, Christopher 34
Dobson, Michael 167
Donatello 190
Donne, John 195, 268
Donovan, Vincent 87
Dorman, M. 261
Dornford-May, Mark 141
Dostoevsky, Fyodor 25, 26, 152, 172, 190, 193, 194, 197, 198
Drabble, Margaret 19
Drewery, Benjamin 6
Dryden, John 100
Dubos, René 174
Duccio 247, 248
Durber, S. 272
Dursten, Christopher 219, 228
Dyrness, William 9, 187, 219-239, 279

Eales, Jacqueline 219, 228
Easterling, Pat 169
Eatman, G. H. 267
Eco, Umberto 43
Edelman, Joshua 7, 11, 51-72, 276
Edgley, Charles 3
Edie, James M. 93
Edwards, Catharine 169, 170,
Egan, Robert 33
Ekserdjian, D. 260

Eldridge, John 128, 144
Eliot, George 171, 172
Eliot, T. S. 22, 53, 190
Emerson, Caryl 24, 25, 26, 27, 29, 31
Emiliani, Andrea 253
Entman, Robert M. 124, 125, 129
Epictetus 168-170
Erasmus 109, 110, 120
Estienne, Robert 221
Euripides 16, 190
Evans, Helen C. 247
Evdokimov, Paul 191
Eyck, Hubert van and Jan van 193
Eysenck, Michael W. 92, 93

Farrer, Austin 271-2
Feetham, Caroline 140
Feetham, Piers 140
Fessio, Joseph 21
Fiddes, Paul S. 141
Finzi, Gerald 270
Flaubert, Gustav 176
Fo, Dario 61, 63, 72
Fodor, James 7
Ford, David 18
Forsyth, P. T. 105, 176
Foxe, John 222, 223, 224, 236
Frankl, Victor 171, 173
Fréchuret, M. 263
Freedberg, David 238-9
Freud, Sigmund 193
Frost, Anthony 148, 149, 151, 156

Gadamer, Hans-Georg 174
Galtung, Johann 128, 129, 131
Gardner, L. 14
Gardner, W. H. 272
Garibaldi, V. 265
Gaskell, Ivan 3, 174, 175, 185
Gerhardsson, Birger 137
Gilbert, Neal W. 233
Gilby, Thomas 100, 236
Gilman, Ernest 222
Giltin, T. 124, 125
Giotto (di Bondoni) 143, 258-60, 261, 265
Girard, René 193-4
Goethe, Johann Wolfgang von 198
Goffman, Erving 125
Goodman, Nelson 46

Goswami, Usha 92-3
Graham, Billy 135
Graham, Gordon 131
Granlund, Paul 267
Grayston, K. 137
Greco, El 265, 266
Greene, Graham 194
Gregory the Great, Pope 241-242, 246, 252, 253, 254, 259
Griffiths, Richard 109
Griggs, E. L. 16
Grotowski, Jerzy 52, 54
Grubb, N. 262
Grünewald, Matthias 193, 195, 265
Guite, Malcolm 187, 199-217, 274, 275
Gurdon, Edmund 101
Gurr, Andrew 41
Guthrie, Steven R. 9, 73, 91-107, 273, 275

Haegen, A. M. von der 258
Hall, Edith 169
Hall, Rowland 223
Haller, W. 223
Händel, George Friederich 190, 191, 194
Harbison, Craig 220
Hardy, Thomas 191, 198
Harris, Max 51, 53, 71, 72
Harrop, John 33
Hart, Trevor A. 1-9, 105, 167-85, 273, 277
Hartt, Frederick 250
Hattori, Yoshiaki 97
Hauerwas, Stanley 7, 8, 144, 151, 158
Heaney, Seamus 209
Hegel, G. W. F. 23, 34, 67
Heidegger, Martin 172, 175
Henderson, George 245
Hengel, Martin 190
Herbert, George 190, 195, 234, 235
Herman, Edward 144, 145
Herrick, Vanessa 243
Hick, John 74, 174, 176-179, 181, 184
Higgins, Sydney 33
Hildegard of Bingen 33
Hill, Christopher 219, 228
Hill, Geoffrey 18
Hitchcock, Alfred 191
Holbein, Hans 222
Holquist, Michael 24
Höltigen, Karl-Josef 230

Hood, William 249
Hooker, Morna 136, 137, 139
Hooykaas, R. 233, 235
Hopkins, Gerard Manley 272
Houlden, L. 271
Humfrey, Peter 251
Hunter, John 253
Hussey, Walter 263

Ibsen, Henrik 20, 43, 198
Inhelder, B. 92
Isidore of Seville 14
Iyengar, Shanto 130

Jackson, Robert Lee 197
James, Henry 172
James, Ronald 148, 156
Jameson, Fredrick 4
Jamieson, Kathleen 126
Jelinek, Elfriede 54
John of Damascus 243
Johnson, Mark 3, 93-5
Johnstone, Keith 148, 152, 153, 155, 157, 159, 161
Jones, L. Gregory 143
Just, Marion R. 126

Kamba Luesa, André 267
Kaminski, M. 260, 265
Keane, Mark T. 92, 93
Keane, Fergal 130, 131
Kehl, Medard 22
Kelch, J. 261
Kelly, H. A. 15
Kemal, Salim 3, 174, 175, 185
Kermode, Frank 171, 172
Khovacs, Ivan Patricio 11, 30, 33-50, 276, 277
Kierkegaard, Søren 69
King, John N. 221, 223, 224
Kline, Kevin 30, 42
Knight, Harold 98
Köder, Sieger 9, 243, 254, 255
Kosicki, Gerald 125
Kristeller, Paul Oskar 1, 111
Kussudiardja, Bagong 267

LaRue, Lester 131
Lash, Nicholas 5, 6, 147

Lawrence, K. T. 267
Lehmann, Hans-Theis 54, 72
Leo the Great, Pope 245
Levertov, Denise 269
Lewis, Alan E. 139
Lewis, C. S. 91
Lindbeck 54, 70
Linenthal, Edward T. 132, 133, 134, 135
Little, C. T. 264
Lloyd, C. 259
Lloyd Webber, Andrew 259
Loades, Ann 272
Löser, Werner 22
Lotto, Lorenzo 249, 251
Loughlin, Gerard 146, 148, 158
Lovell, Thomas 231, 232
Lowden, John 244
Lowe, David A. 197
Luther, Martin 221
Lyotard, Jean-Francois 4

McEwan, Ian 173
McGinn, Colin 195
MacIntyre, Alasdair 151
MacKinnon, Donald 14-15, 17-18, 22
McLuhan, Marshall 43
McNeil, B. 137
Macquarrie, John 173
Malony, H. Newton 93
Mamet, David 11, 60, 64-6, 70, 72
Manichaeism 129
Marcion 129
Marion, Jean-Luc 158
Maritain, Jacques 26
Marlowe, Christopher 198
Marowitz, Charles 64, 72
Marsh, Clive 191
Martin, Carol 59, 71
Mathews, T. F. 244
Mauriac, François 190, 192, 193, 197
Mauss, Marcel 158
May, John R. 191
Mellers, Wilfrid 194
Mendelssohn, Felix 191
Merleau-Ponty, Marcel 93
Merlin, Bella 65, 72
Messiaen, Olivier 270, 272
Michalski, S. 224
Michelangelo 110, 142, 190, 252

Micks, Marianne H. 98
Milbank, John 158, 159
Milton, John 193
Mitchell, Jolyon 9, 74, 123-146
Moberly, R. C. 191, 198
Moeller, Susan 127, 128
Moltmann, Jürgen 74, 102, 174, 183-185
Monfasani, John 111
More, Thomas 152, 231
Morgan, David 134, 242
Morson, Gary 24, 25, 27, 29, 31
Moss, D. 14
Mozart, Wolfgang Amadeus 209, 270
Muller, Richard A. 233
Murphy, Francesca 26
Murphy, Nancey 93

Nees, Lawrence 245, 246
Neuman, W.Russell 126
Newman, John Henry 196, 271
Newton, Sir Isaac 16-17
Nichols, Aidan 37, 39
Nichols, Terry 133
Niebuhr, H. R. 160
Norman, D. 248
Nussbaum, Martha 194, 275

O'Connor, Flannery 192, 193, 197
O'Connor, Michael 74, 109-21
O'Grady, R. 267
O'Malley, John W. O. 110, 111
O'Neil, John 93
Oates, John 92
Ong, Walter 230, 233, 235
Ortiz, Gaye 191

Paino, Fiorell 33
Palissy, Bernard 225, 226, 227, 233
Palmer, George Herbert 235
Pang, Zhongdong 125
Parker, E. C. 264
Parmenides 118
Partridge, Michael 73, 75-89, 274
Pasternak, Boris 263
Payne, Ronald 34
Pelikan, Jaroslav 243, 244
Perkins, William 237
Perugino, Pietro 265
Peterson, David 97, 98

Pfeiffer, Heinrich 110
Piaget, Jean 92, 93
Plato, Platonism 100, 106, 110, 111, 118
Plummer, J. 265
Polanyi, Michael 93, 95, 201
Polk, David 136
Polkinghorne, John 201, 208
Pordenone, G. A. 251
Potter, Robert 33
Powell, William 236
Previtali, Andrea 251
Puddefoot, John 273
Pythagoras 111

Quash, Ben 11, 13-32, 34, 36-38, 277, 279

Rabanus Maurus 100
Rabelais, François 25
Racine, Jean 193
Raleigh, Walter 212, 215
Ramonet, Ignacio 130
Ramsey, A. M. 244
Ramus, Peter 233-236, 237
Randall Coates, Catherine 225, 226, 227
Raphael 110, 252, 253, 256, 265
Reid, W. Stanford 229
Rembrandt *see* Rijn, van
Rice, Tim 259
Riches, John 21
Rijn, Rembrandt van 196, 198, 261, 266-267, 268, 272
Rink, John 5
Roach, Colleen 129
Robbins, Tim 190
Ross, Ellen M. 140
Rozik, Eli 72
Rudrum, A. 269
Rummel, Erika 120

Saltz, David 42, 44
Sankey, Charlotte 128
Sartre, Jean-Paul 59, 173, 176
Schama, Simon 266
Schechner, Richard 2, 5, 52, 63, 72
Schiller, Gertrud 245
Schlesinger, Philip 144
Schmidt, Leigh 229
Schongauer 265
Schönweiss, H. 98

Schumann, Robert 191
Schweitzer, Albert 191
Scott, James C. 161
Scribner, Robert W. 220
Scruton, Roger 105
Semetko, Hoyyi A. 125, 126
Seneca 14
Shakespeare, William 15-16, 20, 41, 44, 46,
    49, 167-8, 190, 196, 200, 201-3,
    205-17, 228
  Hamlet 30, 42, 44, 45, 46, 47, 56, 209
Shapiro, M. 264
Shearman, John 252, 253
Sheldon, Sue 92
Shelley, Mary 195
Shepherd, Simon 4
Sherry, Patrick 187, 189-98, 275
Siciolante, Girolamo 253
Simon, Ulrich 198
Simpson, John 145
Simpson, J. B. 267
Sirotta, Victoria 101
Smail, Thomas A. 102
Smalley, Beryl 117
Smith, James K. A. 49, 50
Socrates 118
Sophocles 16, 64, 193
Spenser, Edmund 193
Spivey, Nigel 142
Spolin, Viola 148, 157
Sprat, Thomas 199, 200, 203, 206
Springen, Karen 135
Stackhouse, John G. 7, 39, 51, 72
Stanislavski, Constantin 11, 42, 51, 54-60,
    62-6, 68-72
Stanley, D. M. 137
States, Bert O. 33, 38
Stevenson, Leslie 99
Stewart, Sarah 128
Stinger, Charles 110
Strachan, James 222, 223
Strassberg, Lee 56, 57, 58, 72
Strong, Roy C. 226
Stubbes, Phillip 232, 233
Styron, William 194
Surin, Kenneth 18
Sutherland, Graham 263
Swanson, Hamish 190

Taliaferro, Charles 93
Tarkovsky, Andrei 190
Tarrantino, Quentin 173
Taylor, Edward 270
Taylor, Simon J. 191, 198
Thiel, P. van 261
Theodore the Studite 243
Tintoretto 266
Titian 190, 260, 265
Tolstoy, Leo 190
Toole, David 161
Tracy, David 158
Trinkaus, Charles 110
Tudor-Craig, Pamela 263
Turcan, Marie 49
Twycross, Meg 72
Tyndale, William 231

Underhill, Evelyn 98
Updike, John 269

Valcanover, F. 266
Valkenburg, Patti M. 125, 126
Vanhoozer, Kevin 7, 8, 11, 28, 38-43, 45,
    48, 49, 51-2, 53-5, 58, 64, 66-7, 68,
    70-71, 72
Vaughan, Henry 268, 269
Viladesau, Richard 187
Volf, Miroslav 143
Vuillard, Édouard 262

Wagner, Richard 191
Walker, Revd Pauline 142
Wallis, Mick 4
Walton, H. 272
Ward, Barbara 174
Ward, G. 14
Ward, J. Neville   22-3, 24
Watt, Tessa 220, 221, 224, 229, 230, 233,
    236
Weber, Carl 63, 72
Weitzmann, Kurt 247
Wells, Samuel 8, 74, 147-65, 184, 277-8
Wells, Stanley 167-8
Wells-Cole, Anthony 220, 221, 223
White, Alfred D. 43
White, John 248
Widmann, Gertrud 254
Williams, Anna 23

Williams, David 49
Williams, Peter 148, 156
Williams, Rowan 135, 148
Williams, Tennessee 66
Wink, Walter 145
Wittgenstein, Ludwig 192, 196
Wixom, William D. 247
Wolterstorff, Nicholas 1, 8, 45-6, 47-8, 187
Wood, David 92
Woodward, Kenneth L. 135
Wordsworth, William 16

Wright, N. T. 6, 265, 275
Wright, Rosemary Muir 9, 188, 241-56, 279
Wyclif, John 5
Wynne, David 263

Yarrow, Ralph 148, 149, 151, 156
Yates, Frances 237
Yoder, John Howard 160
Young, Frances 5, 6, 147, 149

Zuckerkandl, Victor 105